DAVID J. SHARP
The University of Western Ontario

CASES IN BUSINESS ETHICS

D0521517

SAGE Publications
Thousand Oaks ■ London ■ New Delhi

CONTENTS

Introduction to the Ivey Casebook Series

As the title of this series suggests, these books all draw from the Ivey Business School's case collection. Ivey has long had the world's second largest collection of decision-oriented, field-based business cases. Well more than a million copies of Ivey cases are studied every year. There are more than 2,000 cases in Ivey's current collection, with more than 6,000 in the total collection. Each year approximately 200 new titles are registered at Ivey Publishing (www.ivey.uwo.ca/cases), and a similar number are retired. Nearly all Ivey cases have teaching notes available to qualified instructors. The cases included in this volume are all from the current collection.

The vision for the series was a result of conversations I had with Sage's Senior Editor, Al Bruckner, starting in September 2002. Over the subsequent months, we were able to shape a model for the books in the series that we felt would meet a market need.

Each volume in the series contains text and cases. "Some" text was deemed essential in order to provide a basic overview of the particular field and to place the selected cases in an appropriate context. We made a conscious decision to not include hundreds of pages of text material in each volume in recognition of the fact that many professors prefer to supplement basic text material with readings or lectures customized to their interests and to those of their students.

The editors of the books in this series are all highly qualified experts in their respective fields. I was delighted when each agreed to prepare a volume. We very much welcome your comments on this casebook.

—Paul W. Beamish
Series Editor

PREFACE

A casual reading of the business press shows that the world of commerce continues to present managers with ethical challenges and that, in many cases, the challenges are more than they are able to resist. Is this situation acceptable to society? Can managers learn ethics? I believe that the answers are no and yes, respectively, and that this book can help.

The purpose of this book is not to provide simple answers to today's many business ethics questions. There are no simple answers. Nor does it try to preach a morality of business—to do so is an ineffective learning process. Rather, it presents a collection of decisions—messy, real-world business decisions—that have to be made by a class who adopt the role of a manager. The cases were not written by experts in business ethics but by experts in various functional disciplines who had an interest in business ethics and were concerned by the business practices that they saw. The purpose of this book is to raise students' awareness of the range of ethical issues faced in business, to begin to develop their ability to argue effectively about ethical dilemmas, to build their decision-making skills, and to enhance the legitimacy of ethical arguments in business decision making.

The cases included in this text offer business students an opportunity to grapple with a wide variety of challenging ethical problems. At a minimum, the cases provide students with familiarity with the enormous range of ethical issues that could confront managers in their day-to-day work. However, with the help of the class discussion leader, they can accomplish much more. First, to the extent that the class discussion demonstrates that a particular "way of thinking" about a moral problem is both useful and acceptable, it legitimizes business ethics in a world where a moral point of view is still far from mainstream managerial thinking. Second, class discussion can, if well guided, provide thoughtful, critical application of ethical theories to business decision making. Finally, even if students are only partially prepared for class (which I do *not* advocate!), the issues raised in the cases permit a lively discussion in which multiple points of view are brought to bear on the decision at hand—in other words, learning while having fun!

Every one of these cases, taken from the Richard Ivey School of Business case catalog, is based on a real-life decision faced by a manager at work. They are business cases, not ethics cases. They do not pretend to be a comprehensive catalog of ethical issues that might arise in a corporation, nor even the most prevalent. However, they do provide a wide array of business decisions that will challenge students to think carefully about the ethics of doing business. In many cases, where former employees provided information, for example, the author may have disguised companies' names and industries, but the description of the issues remains true to the facts. However, where the case data were available from public sources, all facts are presented as accurately as possible. As is normal in case writing, the case may have simplified the decision context for pedagogical reasons and to enable a meaningfully complete class discussion in about an hour and 20 minutes. A few cases describe best practice, or close to it, but many document worst practice. Both offer valuable learning.

The organization of a book of this nature is challenging because business ethics is holistic. I have chosen to use different stakeholders merely as a general focus of each chapter while recognizing that most cases involve the interplay of the interests of two or more stakeholders. In any event, many of the cases can be taught with different pedagogical purposes—for instance, a case that describes a junior manager in a difficult corporate context can be used to explore a senior manager's responsibility to change the corporate context, the junior individual's decision about what to do, given that questionable context, or both. Sadly for the practice of management, but fortunately for writers of business cases with an ethical dimension that was inadequately considered at the time, there is much material to choose from.

The first chapter provides an introduction to business ethics, as well as the case method for learning. The second chapter explores the ethical issues relating to shareholders. One aspect of this is that shareholders do not have unbridled rights to the proceeds of corporate activity—managers must balance the interests of shareholders with those of other stakeholders. The second ethical problem arises from the nature of the agency relationship between shareholders and managers. To protect the legitimate interests of shareholders from the self-interest of its managers, corporations put in place management accounting and control systems. These reward managers in the form of bonuses for achieving performance targets such as stock price increases, meeting budgets, and so on. Unfortunately, control systems are imperfect systems and often create incentives for perverse behavior. To what extent should managers benefit themselves, when they know that it is at the expense of the shareholders? The third chapter addresses ethical problems arising between a firm and its customers. The unequal distribution of power and information, particularly in retail marketing, creates opportunities for firms to mislead their customers with deceptive packaging and advertising. The fourth chapter includes cases that address some aspects of the firm's ethical responsibility to its employees, including issues of privacy, policies for personal relationships, and discrimination. In the fifth chapter, we explore several intriguing dilemmas arising from international operations of business, ranging from the perennial problem of apparently different ethical values and business practices in different countries to the problem of the extraterritorial applicability of national legal systems. In the sixth chapter, the cases address ethical issues in the area of business strategy, including corporate value systems (exemplary and otherwise), the questionable use of the Internet for marketing purposes, and the morality of protecting a monopoly arising from a patent. Chapter 7 expands on the previous two chapters into specific issues of corporate social responsibility, including the environment, the support or otherwise of highly questionable governments, and profiting from very poor customers. In the final chapter, the cases explore personal integrity and moral virtue. The cases provide situations in which an individual can profit from possibly questionable transactions, the morality of cutting administrative and regulatory corners to simplify work, dealing with subordinates who have violated ethical and corporate norms, and whistle-blowing.

ACKNOWLEDGMENTS

I would like to thank my colleagues and former colleagues at the Richard Ivey School of Business, whose concern for a better practice of management and interest in teaching the moral dimension of business caused these cases to be documented for the benefit of the next generation of business leaders.

INTRODUCTION

Business ethics is very complex. There are two important dimensions to this complexity. First, business ethics analysis takes the view that multiple stakeholders have simultaneous legitimate interests in the outcomes of decisions. A typical list of stakeholders would include shareholders, bondholders, employees, customers, suppliers, employees, neighbors, and various levels of government. What those interests are (or should be), however, is subject to debate, and in most cases, they conflict. In contrast, the typical disciplines of business focus on a single stakeholder—organizational behavior has a focus on employees, marketing on customers, and finance on shareholders and bondholders, for example.

Second, business ethics analysis makes use of several ethical theories in an attempt to answer the question, "What is the right thing to do?" These philosophical theories provide a rigorous way of thinking about the nature of claims of various stakeholders. The nature of these claims is often very different from the ownership rights typically encountered in business. For example, a typical amoral business analysis of drug companies that have developed effective drugs for the treatment of AIDS would argue that they have the right to earn profits from their products. Indeed, they are assigned intellectual property rights (patents) under many legal systems by which they are given the legal right to monopoly profits (without which, their argument goes, they would be unable to afford the huge cost and high risk of new drug development). One inevitable consequence is that only the wealthy can afford the drug. Even a casual ethical analysis, however, would identify, among others, the following arguments:

1. There is something "wrong" with the huge disparity in individual wealth around the world—it seems unfair.

2. Poor people with AIDS might have some sort of rights to the drug.

3. Drug companies have some obligation toward the poor, and there is some level of monopoly profitability that most people would find offensive (and even that the offensiveness is worse when the profits are made from people's illnesses).

In the example above, shareholders have the *right* to earn profits on their investment, but that right conflicts with the idea of moral equity or *fairness* to poor people. A fairness argument says that it is morally wrong that some people can be treated for AIDS because they are rich (they had the good fortune to be born in a developed country), but others cannot because they are poor. A theory of *rights* is pitted against a theory of *fairness*—how, if at all, can they be reconciled? Without formal ethics training, most business students (and professors) find it difficult to go beyond this checklist stage. As rational business students, we feel the need to quantify these claims, to evaluate the strongest, but we lack the tools. In many cases, a decision requires the simultaneous application of several theories; each theory uses a different approach or framework, and often the theories present conflicting solutions. No analytical method is available to solve this problem.

THE CASE LEARNING METHOD

The case method of learning therefore ideally suits the complexity of business ethics. A case is a description of a real business decision, presented with most of its complexity (including both relevant and irrelevant information, as would be available to the decision maker). In an ideal case-learning process, students should spend an hour or so on their own, reading the case and attempting to identify the problem, the alternatives available, and the criteria by which the alternatives can be evaluated. If time and facilities permit, students should meet briefly in small learning teams to exchange views but not to try to reach consensus. At this point, students will be fully aware of the issues but will likely not be able to make complete sense of the decision. Finally, in class, the discussion between students, but directed by the teacher, should lead from the specifics of the decision in the case to generalities, that is, the applicable theory. Thus, in contrast to the lecture method, in which students first learn the theory and then apply it in problems, in the case method, they infer the theory from practice. Although the case method may at first appear inefficient because the class discussion often follows ideas that turn out to be flawed and so is an apparent waste of class time, its highly participatory method is highly effective in that the lessons are indelibly learned. I can still vividly recall the issues around a case discussion in my own graduate program a quarter century ago, in which an animated discussion between a classmate and myself eventually convinced me that my point of view was wrong!

Paradoxically, cases allow students to accelerate their learning and to slow down their decision making at the same time. They accelerate learning by providing, in the course of a few weeks, more opportunities to confront, analyze, and decide difficult moral decisions than most managers meet in their careers. They slow decision making by slowing down time—giving students the luxury of taking time to think carefully about criteria, alternative actions available, consequences of those actions for various stakeholders, and how they might implement their decisions. In the real world of business, ethical dilemmas often arrive unannounced, and managers may have only seconds in which to make critical decisions for their companies—decisions that will also send signals to peers and colleagues about the kind of managers they are. If students have already met and thought through a similar dilemma, they will be far better prepared! In that respect, the purpose of this book is to develop what Aristotle called moral ability, which he felt could be achieved only by learning and repetition. Today, we call it virtue.

THE LANGUAGE OF BUSINESS ETHICS

The purpose of this book is not to provide a comprehensive review of ethical theories, but to be able to use the language of ethics, a short and simplified overview of the major frameworks is a necessary prelude to the cases. Ethics has its special vocabulary, theories, and ways of reasoning. The purpose here is not to make the reader an expert (or even a novice) moral philosopher but perhaps an amateur, in the best sense of the word. The following section therefore provides a very simplified summary of some of the more important ethical theories, in the interests of easier communication. For a more thorough introduction to the subject, students should consult a business ethics textbook.

Ethics is not merely some abstract desirable idea. A society is able to function only if its members adopt a code of behavior under which individuals restrict their self-interest for the greater long-term good of the society. Business ethics is the study and application of what is right and wrong; that is, what is appropriate behavior for managers acting on behalf of their companies. The cases in this book provide situations in which the student has to take the role of a manager and decide on the right course of action. What is "right"?

Ethical theory provides several theories (or criteria) by which an action may be evaluated. Three of these are fundamental to business ethics and provide powerful insights into right and wrong. Two others are also included below because, although weaker and more limited in their application, they nevertheless are often (incorrectly) used in business.

The first theory, one that appeals to businesspeople because it uses a cost-benefit concept similar to that used in business and provides the moral foundation of classical economics, is *utilitarianism.* This principle, first espoused by Jeremy Bentham in the late 18th century, argues that an action is ethical if it produces the greatest good (or utility) for society overall. It is criticized because it is usually impossible to measure utility and because it fails to address the problem of unequal distribution of utility. For example, is an action ethical if it significantly increases the utility of the very rich, while leaving a few poor people slightly worse off, in such a way that total wealth is greatly increased?

The ethics of *justice* or *fairness,* best known in the writings of the 20th-century philosopher John Rawls, addresses this inequity. Rawls felt that principles of justice were more important than utilitarianism; therefore, the action described above is unethical according to Rawls, even though a utilitarian might argue otherwise. An important type of justice in business is *distributive justice,* in which society's benefits should be fairly shared. In its simplest form, it means that similar people (i.e., similar in respect to the treatment in question) should be treated equally and dissimilar people unequally. For example, male and female employees should be paid equally for the same work because they are equal as employees, but it is also fair to pay senior or more qualified employees more than less qualified employees, as long as their qualifications are relevant to their work. This theory also has the disadvantage that it is difficult to quantify; how much more should someone with 20 years of experience be paid compared to a novice? It is unlikely that one could find an answer that everyone would agree to. The economic evidence shows that income distributions vary widely around the world.

The third theory concerns *rights,* a theory first developed by Immanuel Kant in the 18th century. A right is someone's entitlement to something, such as a minimum living wage, privacy, and safe working conditions, to which a society agrees. Moral rights are usually considered universal and often labeled *human rights.* Throughout history, humans have attempted to codify and document their rights; the Magna Carta, the American Constitution, and the United Nations Charter are just three of the better known. Most collective agreements document workers' and employers' rights. Kant also proposed what he called a "categorical imperative," which, in its simplest form, means that an action that you take is right if the reason you would do it is the same as the reason you would want everyone else to do it. A similar version is the Golden Rule: "Do unto others as you would have them do unto you." Importantly, rights usually imply reciprocal obligations or duties. If an employee has a right to a safe workplace, then it follows that employers have a duty to provide safe workplaces. A problem for Kantian rights is that they place limits on individuals' freedoms.

The problem with these three theories is that when they are applied in a given decision situation, they often require contradictory solutions, and we have no comprehensive theory by which one theory can be weighed against the others. The benefit of the case method is that it provides students with an opportunity to evaluate carefully all three in a particular business situation and to come to an informed judgment about the "right" or most persuasive course of action.

Two additional theories deserve mention because they are often applicable in business situations, *relativism* and *egoism*. Relativism argues that, at least in some cases, there is no single "right" answer but that it depends on where you are. For example, although we may agree that we have a right to privacy, it is evident that the degree of privacy that people consider adequate varies around the world. Some societies are very communitarian, others more individualist. A relativist argument is often used to justify an unethical action (such as paying bribes) on the grounds that it is customary business practice in some parts of the world. The weakness of this argument is that in most cases, even if it is customary in a country, it is still considered unethical there. Thus, the debate around relativism is around its applicability: Which behaviors (or values) are legitimately different in different cultures, and which are universal? Relativism is also the theory behind the argument that "it is right for me to do this because everyone does it"—an argument that, of course, is false. Egoism is a theory that addresses the legitimacy of self-interest. It is at the core of traditional economics—Adam Smith's "invisible hand" is driven by a self-interest that was assumed to be ethical. The difficulty arises when self-interest dominates the other considerations noted above—rights and fairness, for example. Again, we have no universal theory that can tell us when too much self-interest becomes unethical, but it is quite likely that relativism may provide insights—the legitimacy of self-interest may be culture bound, in that what is seen as excessively selfish in one country would be acceptable in another.

One of the challenges for the practicing manager is that she or he has to *make a decision*—a clear-cut "do something." Yet moral issues are rarely clearly right or wrong—usually it is a matter of degree, which results in the classic but inconclusive "on one hand . . . on the other hand" debate. For managers, the debate must be resolved; they have to use their judgment and must necessarily make moral compromises when taking an action. "Doing the right thing" involves trade-offs. The cases in this book provide plenty of opportunities to identify and articulate the arguments that can be made both for and against a decision, and that is a very valuable lesson in its own right. But unless students are forced to *make a decision* after a full discussion, the *management* learning opportunity will be lost. Students will often disagree on the most appropriate course of action, but by the end of a class discussion, each must individually come to a decision, an implementation plan where appropriate. They must be comfortable with its consequences and the knowledge that after full and thoughtful discussion and exchange of views, they made what was for them the right decision in the circumstances.

To my wife Crystal

1

ETHICS OF THE FIRM'S RELATIONSHIP WITH ITS SHAREHOLDERS

The ethics of the relationship between the firm's owners (shareholders) and those employed to manage the firm's assets on their behalf (managers) involves issues of deontology—written (and unwritten) duties and obligations, rights of shareholders, and the trade-off between the manager's self-interest and that of shareholders.

Most business practitioners and academics would agree that shareholders—the legal owners of a business—are a corporation's most important stakeholders. People invest their scarce capital in the business; they bear the risk and are therefore entitled to a reward for doing so. This assumption, taken for granted in the economics and finance literatures, is at the foundation of most business studies in finance. However, it is only an assumption, and it is questioned in the business ethics literature.

The finance and economics disciplines have developed an enormous body of rigorous theory driven by the assumption that the purpose of business is to maximize profits. Milton Friedman (1970) clearly articulated this point of view in a celebrated and controversial article. In this article, he argued that the sole responsibility of managers is to maximize shareholder returns so long as they stay within the law, and anything less—specifically, an attempt to engage in philanthropic activity—would constitute a breach of their fiduciary duty unless it served the purpose of increasing shareholder profits. This point of view has sparked a lively and unresolved debate around the relative importance of other stakeholders—some arguing that, in essence, Friedman is right, whereas others take the view that a corporation is not merely the property of its shareholders but is a social entity in its own right, with multiple responsibilities to multiple stakeholders. The latter view is criticized on theoretical grounds for its vagueness and lack of rigor, particularly when compared to financial economics theory.

The competing claims of shareholders relative to other stakeholders arise vividly in downsizing decisions, where the interests of shareholders should be weighed against those employees who lose their jobs. A collective agreement may specify the layoff process, including rights of seniority. However, this simply moves the ethical decisions from the time of the layoff to the time of negotiation of the agreement. When production is moved from one plant to another (e.g., in a developing country), the costs borne by the former employees who lose their jobs have to be weighed against not only the shareholders who benefit from lower production costs but also the people employed in the developing country, who may otherwise have no employment.

The Northeastern Mutual Life case illustrates several of these issues. Because of falling profitability, the chief executive officer of this large insurance company has to evaluate the rights of various stakeholders as he plans to reduce staff. He must quantify in dollar terms the moral claims of shareholders and various other stakeholders and apply ethical analysis where legal requirements are unclear. In particular, he must decide how to manage the layoffs and the implications to the company of the payout of pension benefits.

A second ethical problem associated with shareholders arises from the nature of the agency relationship between shareholders and managers. The capitalist system is driven by an implicit assumption that people are driven by their legitimate self-interest. Agency theory, the theoretical foundation of much of academic accounting, assumes that managers are self-interested and are not burdened by ethical considerations; therefore, the central problem for shareholders is to put controls in place to ensure that managers do not expropriate excessively the shareholders' wealth for themselves.

To protect the legitimate interests of shareholders from the self-interest of its managers, who may have different objectives from shareholders (e.g., in their willingness to take risks) and who generally have better information about the business than its shareholders, the owners put in place management accounting, control, and financial reporting systems. These define management objectives in terms of contractually measurable performance criteria, such as an increase in stock price, meeting budgets, and so on. They also reward managers in the form of bonuses for achieving these performance targets. For example, managers are given stock options—as a result, their wealth increases along with that of shareholders when the stock price increases. Incentive compensation schemes are supposed to align the interests of managers with shareholders. Unfortunately, control systems are imperfect and often create incentives for perverse behavior. For example, if meeting budgeted profit targets is a performance criterion, managers can reduce the degree of difficulty of the budget (sandbagging) or can manipulate actual performance, most easily by deferring discretionary expenditure to beyond the end of the budget period. Managers can also manipulate the measurement of performance by stretching the definition of revenues (upwards) and expenses (downwards). WorldCom, for example, eliminated several billion dollars of expenses by reclassifying them as assets.

A particular concern arises when the rewards for aggressive behavior are very high. For example, suppose that a sales manager has to meet a particular level of sales in a year. If she meets this target, she receives a substantial bonus—say, $25,000—but if she misses it, she receives nothing. Suppose also that with 1 week to go to the end of the year, she is $10,000 short of the target. She faces all kinds of unreasonable pressure to meet that target, "no matter what it takes." (Clearly, buying the product herself and throwing it away is better than just missing the target and is by no means the most unethical choice!) Many of the cases in this chapter provide an opportunity to debate and decide the best decision for a manager in this situation, as well as an opportunity to explore the morality of that work situation—for example, how it might arise and how they as managers might correct it.

Fraudulent financial reporting has been at the center of debate over business ethics for several years. Enron and WorldCom were merely the most visible of frauds that seem to take place with alarming regularity. Because accounting rules are somewhat flexible (though not as flexible as WorldCom and others had evidently wanted them to be), the preparation of financial statements requires professional judgment. Therefore, a certain degree of discretionary aggressiveness (or conservatism) is legal and consistent with generally accepted accounting principles. Nevertheless, is it ethical? Does it make a difference if the flexibility is used solely to enhance management bonuses? To what extent do managers have the right to benefit themselves, within the rules of the control system, when they know that it is at the expense of the shareholders?

The Enron Corp. case provides documentation of one of the most spectacular and sudden corporate failures in recent American history. Arguably, Enron is not a good case for class discussion because all the evidence suggests that the actions taken by those responsible were clearly and unambiguously unethical. There is little to debate. Yet, it does raise some important questions. What is the responsibility of top management? Who is ultimately responsible for the financial statements, and how could an auditor detect financial statement irregularities? What obligation do managers have to ensure that the environment for which they are responsible minimizes the risk of fraud?

The Acme Hardware case provides an example of a probable accounting manipulation, from the point of view of an auditor. The auditor is planning the audit of its new client, Acme Hardware. While preparing the audit plan, he becomes aware of the possibility that certain managers might be using accounting flexibility to aid them in qualifying for incentive bonuses based on profitability. The areas are inventory and advertising. The case provides an opportunity to discuss the morality of the managers engaging in this behavior, the nature of the flaws in the reward system and the incentives they create, and the responsibility of senior managers. The auditor must decide what action, if any, to take. The Fardo Industries case also documents an ethical dilemma for an auditor in the context of flexibility in accounting rules and includes issues of personal versus professional relationships. The partner of an accounting firm must decide how to advise a client, who has not understood the implications of this flexibility, to amortize the goodwill involved in an acquisition. The decision will significantly affect the acquisition price to be paid to a former client, who is a friend of the accountant.

In the Ontario Capital Group case, the branch manager at a branch of the Ontario Capital Group has to decide what to do about one of his investment advisers. Over the past 3 months, an investment adviser had apparently been injecting his own capital into a client's account that had been losing value. However, the market had now recovered, and the client had made a profit. The branch manager takes a utilitarian view—he thought to himself, "How did this go unnoticed? But no harm has come to anyone—why should I do anything about it?" The main teaching objective of this case is to explore corporate responsibility for promoting ethical behavior. The role of control systems in promoting various types of behaviors and the scope of control applied can be discussed. Other objectives include the responsibility of the individual to various stakeholders in the organization. In the Jeffrey Verde Account case, also in the securities industry, a newly licensed futures investment adviser at Securities Trading Company has just received an order from Jeffrey Verde, a regular client of a colleague and of the company. The firm's research department is recommending that those contracts be sold. On further investigation, she realizes that the client has a high trading limit that he regularly exceeds and that he also has a high level of exposure. She must decide how to handle this situation responsibly. This case, written from public documents, is based on an actual court case, although the names of the persons and firm involved and the dates have been disguised. The case highlights ethical and compliance issues that arise in the securities industry; the dangers of failing to comply with regulations, even though they may constrain profit and be tiresome; and the challenges of having to deal with the consequences when things subsequently do go wrong.

REFERENCE

Friedman, M. (1970, September 1). The social responsibility of business is to increase its profits. *New York Times Magazine,* pp. 122–126.

NORTHEASTERN MUTUAL LIFE: PREPARING FOR EMPLOYEE TERMINATIONS

Prepared by Ken Mark under the supervision of Professor David Sharp

Version: (A) 2003-06-04

INTRODUCTION

On the 7th of March 2000, Gordon Gillingham, president and chief executive officer (CEO) of Northeastern Mutual Life, had to decide how to reduce costs at his company. Northeastern Mutual Life's return on equity had declined steadily in the past four years and had triggered calls for cost cutting measures. Gillingham knew that staff reduction at the Calgary head office would be a large component of the cuts and wondered how he would balance shareholder and employee interests.

NORTHEASTERN MUTUAL LIFE

From its beginnings in northern Alberta selling small life insurance policies, Northeastern Mutual Life now marketed a full range of financial service products across the country and in many parts of the world. Northeastern Mutual Life was the major subsidiary of the Calgary Insurance Group, which operated life insurance, reinsurance, general insurance and investment, and other activities in North America and internationally. Calgary Insurance Group was a publicly held Canadian corporation, which owned 98 per cent of the shares of Northeastern Mutual Life.

In Canada, the company had more than three million individual and business customers, and was one of the largest providers of life insurance to Canadians. The company also provided retirement savings and disability insurance to individuals, as well as group life, pension and health products to businesses in Canada. In 1996, a new subsidiary, the Trust Company of Northeastern Mutual Life, was established to broaden the range of retirement savings products for customers and strengthen the company's relationship with its customers.

In 2000, Northeastern Mutual Life's investments totaled more than $15 billion, and included mortgages for tens of thousands of Canadians. The company's investments also provided financial support for a wide variety of Canadian industries and governments. Significant investment subsidiaries included the National Care Corporation, which developed and operated retirement homes, Doran Properties Limited, which owned commercial properties and Edmonton Park Limited, an office, residential and hotel complex.

Almost 3,000 people were members of Northeastern Mutual Life's Canadian sales organization, the largest among insurance companies in Canada. Of approximately 9,000 employees, Northeastern Mutual Life had about 2,600 administrative staff. Northeastern Mutual Life relied heavily on its public image and reputation for new sales—selling insurance was difficult even in the best of times.

IMPETUS FOR CHANGE

Since 1996, Northeastern Mutual Life's return on equity had declined steadily from 11.5 per cent to seven per cent (see Exhibit 1). The dividends on profit participating whole life

policies were also declining, and as a result, sales were suffering. Whole life policies paid dividends to holders that were based on earnings on the whole life section of the business; in the case of Northeastern Mutual Life, this accounted for over 50 per cent of the total. An insurer's rate of dividend payments on whole life policies was a very important part of the sales pitch to sell whole life (policyholders) policies, as it allowed for comparison between insurers. As a result, a lower yield rate would directly affect sales. In early 2000, a meeting of Senior Management Partnerships (SMP), the management body of Northeastern Mutual Life, decided that administrative costs had to be cut by 20 per cent and that an acquisition of a U.S.-based rival would permit additional increased efficiencies. Since employee salaries formed the largest component of administrative expenses, staff terminations were being discussed by the SMP: who would they terminate and how would the terminations affect the pension plan fund surplus and liabilities?

	2000	*1999*	*1998*	*1997*	*1996*
Total revenue	$9,455	$8,345	$7,563	$6,702	$5,909
Income to common shareholders	$103	$113	$125	$128	$132
Returns to policyholders	$301	$317	$320	$334	$350
Net income	$108	$120	$133	$145	$150
Shareholders' equity	$1,497	$1,450	$1,398	$1,360	$1,306
Total assets	$18,925	$17,796	$16,413	$15,650	$140,029
Total assets under administration	$28,698	$27,031	$24,453	$21,541	$19,740
Life insurance in force	$101,605	$98,777	$100,398	$98,783	$99,653
Number of employees and field staff	9,010	6,927	6,795	7,334	7,499
Return on common equity	7.20%	8.20%	9.50%	10.60%	11.50%
Number of common shares outstanding (millions)	40	40	42	42	42

Exhibit 1   Financial Highlights (amounts in millions, except per share amounts)

Northeastern Mutual Life had a defined benefit pension plan with a 1997 surplus of Cdn$85 million and a 1999 surplus of Cdn$35 million. Under Alberta law, if a restructured company with a pension fund found itself with a substantial reduction in staff, it could voluntarily (or be required to) do a partial windup of the pension for all terminated staff or it can try to avoid the legislation. A partial windup involves the payment of a full pension at age 65 to any employee (known as a qualified employee) whose age plus years of service, on date of termination, is 55 or over. A partial windup also includes a payment of a substantive portion (or all) of the pension surplus to any employee whose position is terminated.

The cost of a partial windup is substantial. It requires an employer to assume (for the purposes of the pension) that qualified employees actually worked to age 65, notwithstanding their ages at date of termination. Also, the present value of the pension liability is much higher than the contribution amounts that the company would otherwise give to the employee on termination. A partial windup would also require that a share of the surplus be paid to qualified employees.

Pension Plans

Historically, pension plans were established because the plan sponsors (employers) expected to be in business indefinitely and a pension plan provided an incentive to attract and retain employees. As a result, the plan operates for the benefit of its members and the company, unless business circumstances warrant a windup of the pension plan.

Pension plans are of two types. A typical defined contribution plan simply collects contributions from employees and their employer and invests them. The employee bears the financial risk and benefits of the investment performance. In contrast, a defined benefit plan, such as the Northeastern Mutual plan, promised a pension based on a fixed percentage of final salary, based on years of service. Both the employee and employer contributed prescribed amounts (typically percentages of salary) to the fund. However, since the employer bore the financial risk, if insufficient contributions were collected to meet the expected pension liability (or returns on the fund were low), the employer would have to contribute additional funds to meet pension commitments. Conversely, if the fund was well managed and returns on the fund assets exceeded expectations, the fund would have a surplus. In such a case, there might be no need for the employer to contribute the prescribed amount for a period of time. Northeastern Mutual Life had been in this fortunate position for over 20 years.

Pension plans required careful investing by the plan manager to ensure that they could meet their future obligations to plan members. Normally, the present value of future pension obligations (from the employer's standpoint) was less than the cumulative value of contributions, until the employee reached approximately 10 years of service. After that point, the present value of future pension obligations to employees increased at a greater rate than the cumulative contributions for each additional year of service. This is illustrated in Figure 1.

Using the example given, if an employee were no longer employed with the company after three years of service, the present value of benefits would be much less than the cumulative contributions made by both parties. However, after 15 to 20 years of service, the present value of the employer's future pension obligations would be much higher than the contributions made to the fund. There is normally a contribution surplus versus pension liabilities for short-term employees and a contribution deficit for longer-term employees. Under a well managed plan, however, the cumulative value of contributions, in aggregate for all employees (compounded), should equal the future value of pension obligations to all employees at any moment in time. Therefore in practice, it was hoped that the returns from investing exceeded discount rates.

Most company pension plan benefits were paid out in the form of an annuity, a fixed monthly payment for the rest of the employee's life. The formula used to calculate company

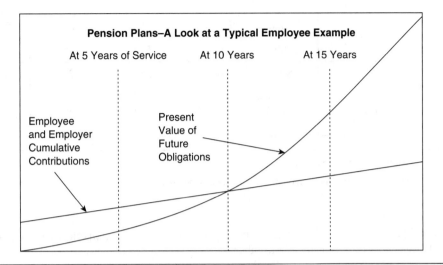

Figure 1   Cumulative Value of Contributions, Present Value of Future Obligations and Years of Service

pension plan benefits was typically the employee's final salary multiplied by years of service multiplied by a fixed percentage rate (often two per cent). Therefore, moving from job to job and plan to plan could be costly for employees and beneficial for employers. All else being equal, the "loyal company employee" was rewarded while the job-hopper suffered when this formula was used.

When employees left their jobs or were terminated, the company returned all cumulative contributions (the total of the employee's and employer's actual costs prescribed, whether or not they had actually been paid in) without (or with minimal) interest or compounding. Northeastern Mutual Life's pension plan terms were written so that terminated staff were given the contribution amounts plus nominal interest, which was much less than the present value of their future pension and health benefits. This was due to the fact that most terminated employees over the company's 125-year history had been fired with cause.

There was also considerable public debate as to whether pension surpluses belonged to the employer or the employees. In Northeastern Mutual Life's case, the company had not made any actual contribution to the pension since 1983, due to the outstanding investment performance of the fund. Their employees, for their part, had made no contributions since 1989. Prior to 1989, employees had contributed three per cent to four per cent of their salary and bonus per year into the pension plan. However, in 1989, the pension payout rate was also changed; the payout percentage was reduced substantially from two per cent of final salary to 1.4 per cent and employees were no longer required to contribute.

Choosing From the Pool of Staff

Administrative salaries at Northeastern Mutual Life averaged $45,000. Gillingham looked at the numbers that his team had generated, detailing the number of staff, tenure and percentage of managers within each group (see Table 1). As Sales staff were commission-based, they would not be included in the layoff decision. The administrative ranks included accountants, secretaries, investment operation managers, information system managers, vice-presidents—almost any employee who was not a salesperson. Many of the administrative staff performed duties that were

Tenure	<1 Year	1–5 Years	6–10 Years	11–15 Years	15+Years
Administrative Staff	800	600	500	400	300
Sales Staff (commission-based)	1,800*	600	375	125	100
Percentage of Administrative Staff in Management	10%	20%	30%	50%	80%

Table 1   Staff by Years of Service

Note: It was typical that within the first 12 months of being hired, approximately one-third of the sales staff would leave the company.

unique to Northeastern Mutual Life operations. These skills were not easily transferable to other companies within the Calgary region. Gillingham wondered if Northeastern Mutual Life was obliged to retain these longer-term employees because of the non-transferability of their skills.

Gillingham knew that Northeastern Mutual Life needed approximately 80 per cent of its staff to continue operations without substantially affecting service. However, Gillingham knew that even if 20 per cent of 2,600 administrative employees were chosen for termination, Northeastern Mutual Life might eventually need to look elsewhere for additional cost savings. Furthermore, he was aware of government regulations stipulating that if a substantial percentage of a company's staff were terminated or left voluntarily, the Alberta Pension Commission could order a partial windup of the pension fund.

If a windup was required, Northeastern Mutual Life would be forced to pay qualified employees the full pension of age 65. This was an amount whose present value was estimated to be worth substantially more than the cumulative nominal contribution of those employees.

Last, Gillingham was aware of regulations (independent of Alberta pension legislation) that stipulated a company had to file reports to the Alberta government if it planned to lay off more than 50 people per month. He wondered if there was a way to avoid this additional bureaucratic step.

THE PENSION COMMISSION OF ALBERTA

In 1987, Alberta's pension legislation was substantially revised and new measures were introduced to strengthen the employment pension system in Alberta. The reforms improved members' rights to benefits and the way benefits were funded. It gave members rights and entitlements, such as access to more information about their pension plan. The Pension Commission of Alberta oversaw and enforced these rulings.

Windups for pension plans occurred for a variety of reasons. Often a windup is caused when all or a significant number of members have ceased employment. When all employees cease employment, the entire pension plan must be terminated or wound up. When a significant number of pension plan members are terminated, the pension plan can be partially wound up voluntarily by the company or under an order of the pension commission. (Those members unaffected by the restructuring, who continue to be employed following the downsizing, are not included in the partial windup and their membership in the plan continues without change.) Some reasons for pension plan windups include:

- The employer has decided not to operate a pension plan and ceases to remit contributions to the pension fund.

- The employer fails to make contributions to the pension fund as required by pension law.
- There has been a plant closure or downsizing of operations and a significant part of the business at a specific location is discontinued (this may require a partial or full windup).
- Plan members cease to be employed as a result of the discontinuation of all or part of the business or reorganization of business operations.
- The employer has sold all or part of the business or the assets of the business to a purchaser, and the purchaser does not provide a pension plan for the members of the pension who become employees of the purchaser.
- The employer is bankrupt (or insolvent).

The pension commission legislation also required that terminated employees in a partial windup receive their share of any pension plan surplus. This penalized companies who might otherwise take advantage of the situation by terminating employees just prior to retirement.

Most employers involved in these situations voluntarily windup their pension plans. In some cases where the employer does not take steps to windup the plan voluntarily, the Pension Commission of Alberta may order the windup to comply with the requirements of Alberta's pension law. Simon Donato, vice-president of corporate lending, stated:

> But in every case, where the company does not voluntarily do a partial pension windup, the Pension Commission must be petitioned by the employees to order a partial windup, and the employees need to provide strong evidence of a lot of terminations and that the rules for a partial windup are met. The Pension Commission, which is an agent of the government, must then agree to a windup (and they don't do so very often, especially in a conservative, pro-business environment). The purpose of the mandatory windup legislation is to protect the interests of the long-term pension plan members and ensure the safety of their pension benefits.

It was estimated that if a partial windup was required at Northeastern Mutual Life, it would cost the pension fund an extra $62,500 per qualified employee that was terminated.

DECISION TIME

On average, there was a 30 per cent difference in salaries, between the older (at least six to 10 years in tenure) and the younger (less than six years in tenure) employees. Thus, excluding the potential extra cost to the pension account of the partial windup, Northeastern Mutual Life would reap the same nominal savings from either laying off 100 older employees or 130 younger employees.

Also, firing older employees and hiring new recruits to replace them would mean fewer layoffs in total, as the cost savings would be, on average, greater per person. This would be true unless a partial windup was voluntarily agreed to by the company or ordered by the Pension Commission. Gillingham did not wish to voluntarily order a windup of Northeastern Mutual Life's pension plan. A partial windup (without calculating the share of surplus issue) could add $25 million to $50 million to Northeastern Mutual Life's current pension liabilities (or $62,000 per employee on average) if the senior staff were terminated. If a substantial number of the employees was terminated, he might be required to submit the results to the Pension Commission for scrutiny. But if he did not submit the results (and did not voluntarily windup the pension fund or was not ordered to do so), he would reduce the company's current pension liability by $45,000 per employee (on average).

Many questions remained in Gillingham's mind. Could he stagger the terminations over a couple of years? Did Northeastern Mutual Life have a moral obligation not to terminate employees close to retirement? Would he ever have to explain the substantial numbers of terminated employees to the Pension Commission? And would he ever have to personally face the cost of a partial windup and the bad publicity? And how would he keep his senior executives enthusiastic throughout this period?

Ultimately, Gillingham knew that, in the interests of shareholders, he had to reduce costs now. He wondered what his plan of action would look like.

ENRON CORP.[1]

*Prepared by Karen Bong under the
supervision of Professor Claude Lanfranconi*

Version: (A) 2004-07-06

INTRODUCTION

In late 2001 and in 2002, investors, securities regulators, the energy industry and the capital markets watched as the details behind the collapse of Enron Corp. (Enron) came to light. Enron's was the largest corporate collapse in American history, with the company's share price losing almost all of its value in the ten months preceding its bankruptcy petition. George Calvert, like virtually all of Enron's shareholders, was very unhappy with his losses. He wanted to know how, in light of all the supposed checks and balances in the financial reporting system, this had apparently happened so suddenly and with so little warning. He depended upon management, the board of directors, its audit committee, the auditors and various financial analysts, among others, to protect his interests and, at the very least, to keep him appropriately informed. How had Enron seemingly fooled so many people so quickly? Calvert wondered, could the system be relied upon to protect him and what should he do in the future if he wished to continue investing in the capital markets?

THE U.S. NATURAL GAS INDUSTRY

The natural gas industry in the United States was regulated by the Federal Energy Regulatory Commission (FERC), an independent regulatory agency within the Department of Energy. FERC's mission was to regulate and oversee energy industries in the economic and environmental interest of the American public. FERC's vision was to have dependable, affordable competitive energy markets that would support a strong, stable national economy.[2] FERC was created in 1977 as part of President Jimmy Carter's response to the 1970s energy crisis; the new agency replaced the Federal Power Commission, which regulated electric power.

The natural gas industry underwent deregulation in the 1980s. The energy industry had been run as a regulated monopoly for decades; regulation started in the early 1900s when the electricity industry argued that its utilities were a "natural monopoly" because the economies of scale and the large capital investment needed to build multiple transmission and distribution systems made competition inefficient. Electricity also became regarded as a basic service to which the entire population should have guaranteed access. By the 1980s, pressure had grown to allow the market to determine energy prices. Deregulation was supposed to introduce competition to these industries; it was believed that in the long run, competition would force companies in the energy business to operate more effectively and efficiently than the regulated monopolies, thereby lowering the end price to consumers.

In 1985, pipelines essentially had a monopoly on the natural gas market. Their business of buying natural gas from producers and reselling to local distribution companies required a method of transporting the gas from one place to another. Only the pipeline companies could provide natural gas to the local distribution companies because other firms could not obtain approval from FERC to build their own pipelines and there was no other cost-competitive way to transport the gas. In October 1985, FERC Order 436 was issued. Pipeline companies were forced to become open-access transporters, allowing other companies to transport natural gas on their pipelines.

Deregulation further developed in the 1990s, with FERC's Order 636, enacted in November 1993. Order 636 required interstate pipeline companies to unbundle their sales and transportation services, and revised the method of determining rates for transportation services. One effect of Order 636 was the creation of a reseller market for transportation and storage capacity, enabling the marketing of unused or underutilized pipeline capacity.

A period of consolidation followed Order 636; by 2001, 14 corporations accounted for more than 85 per cent of interstate natural gas pipeline activity. Electricity deregulation also progressed in the 1990s. The electricity and natural gas industries began to converge, as companies with strong ties to the electric power industry acquired natural gas pipelines as natural gas explorers and producers divested themselves of pipeline assets. Natural gas was increasingly used to fuel electricity generation plants. In the United States, consumption of natural gas was 22.8 trillion cubic feet in 2000; projections for natural gas demand growth suggested that consumption could reach 29 trillion cubic feet by the end of the decade and 35 trillion cubic feet by 2020.[3]

ENRON'S HISTORY

Enron was formed in July 1985 when Houston Natural Gas merged with InterNorth, a natural gas company based in Omaha, Nebraska. This merger integrated several pipeline systems to create an interstate natural gas pipeline system. Kenneth Lay, who had been the chief executive officer (CEO) of Houston Natural Gas, was appointed Enron's chairman and CEO the following year. Enron's company vision at the time was "to become the premier natural gas pipeline in North America."[4] Through 1985 to 1990, Enron's revenues came mostly from its regulated pipeline business. Its activities were mostly the purchase of gas from producers and reselling the gas to local distribution companies while shipping the

gas through the company's pipelines. The natural gas pipeline business was under regulation that affected rates, accounts, records, the addition of facilities, the abandonment of services and facilities, the extension of services in some cases, in addition to other matters. The company's revenues in 1985 were less than $5 billion.[5]

As the natural gas industry was being deregulated, Enron set up separate businesses to buy, transport, sell, explore and produce gas. Pipeline companies at the time tended to be vertically integrated; with the separation of business functions, some of their functions remained regulated while others faced new regulations or became deregulated. Subsidiaries and affiliates allowed Enron to participate and take advantage of the newly unregulated markets for natural gas.

In the late 1980s, with deregulation changing the way natural gas was contracted in the wholesale market, Enron developed a host of services to help reduce the risk of price swings. A precursor of its massive trading operations in the future, GasBank was launched and Enron began trading natural gas commodities. GasBank allowed producers and wholesalers of natural gas to lock into long-term supplies of natural gas at fixed prices and to hedge price risk in the new spot market for natural gas.

Meanwhile, energy markets around the world were opening up and natural gas was gaining ground as a clean burning, cheap and plentiful fuel. In 1990, Enron's company vision changed; Enron's mission now was "to become the world's first natural gas major." Shortly after the United Kingdom had deregulated its energy industry, Enron began construction on a gas-fired heat and power facility in England. Enron also built or began construction on power plants in other countries, including the Philippines, Guatemala, China, India, Turkey, Brazil, Puerto Rico, Italy, Poland, Guam and Dominican Republic. Enron acquired a pipeline company in South America in 1992, with plans to expand its commercial presence on that continent. Enron's English power plant was operational in the spring of 1993; it was the world's largest gas-fired heat and power facility, and the second largest project financing ever completed in the United Kingdom.

In 1995, Enron adopted a new strategy and a new corporate vision: to become the world's leading energy company. This, Ken Lay explained, meant, "We don't necessarily mean to be the largest or the most profitable—at least not now. We just aim to be the leader in all the businesses we're in worldwide."[6] In 1995, Enron's business segments were Exploration and Production, Transportation and Distribution, Retail Energy Services, Wholesale Energy Operations and Services, and Corporate and Other.[7] Between 1995 and 2000, revenues from Exploration and Production declined, while revenues from Corporate and Other increased but continued to account for less than two per cent of total revenue. Transportation and Distribution and Retail Energy Services had modest revenue growth of several billion dollars per segment, but Enron's revenues from Wholesale Energy Operations and Services grew more than 1,200 per cent, with reported revenue growth of more than $87 billion in that period (see Exhibit 1).

ENRON'S WHOLESALE
ENERGY OPERATIONS AND SERVICES

Enron's dramatic revenue growth between 1995 and 2000 was fuelled by revenue growth in its Wholesale Energy Operations and Services business segment; this segment included its energy trading operations and its sales of risk-management products. Enron's natural gas commodity trading operation (financing for oil and gas producers [1989], trading of electricity [1994], power and gas trading in the United Kingdom [1995] and commodity transactions using weather derivative products [1997]) grew out of GasBank.

Prior to GasBank, standard gas contracts were traded on the New York Mercantile Exchange. The prices of these standard contracts were all based on delivery to one place (usually Henry Hub in Louisiana). Thus, these contracts were useful in hedging against changes in gas prices, but were not practical for the actual buyers and sellers of gas, whose transactions required natural gas to be physically delivered to or from various locations. Factors based on location that could influence price included regional differences in supply and demand and laws particular to a state or country. With the deregulation of the natural gas industry, producers, distributors and other parties now participating in the market required some way of managing the risk of price swings in natural gas. Through GasBank, Enron created a market for natural gas commodities that established future prices on long-term supply contracts through the trading of these forward commitments.

	1995	1996	1997	1998	1999	2000
Exploration and Production	$759	$824	$897	$884	$526	$408
Transportation and Distribution	$813	$725	$1,416	$1,849	$2,032	$2,955
Retail Energy Services	$400	$528	$685	$1,072	$1,807	$4,615
Wholesale Energy Operations and Services	$7,697	$11,904	$18,022	$27,725	$36,287	$94,906
Corporate and Other	$19	$14	$55	$516	$740	$(2,095)
Total Revenue*	**$9,189**	**$13,289**	**$20,273**	**$31,260**	**$40,112**	**$100,789**

Exhibit 1   Enron's Revenue by Business Segment (before restatement): 1995 to 2000 (in millions of dollars)

Source: Company annual reports.

*Intersegment eliminations account for the differences between total revenue and the sum of business segment revenue.

In 1999, Enron introduced, alongside its telephone-based trading system EnronOnline, the first global Internet-based commodity-trading site. EnronOnline revolutionized the energy-trading business, at huge risk to the company; rather than being a neutral forum as traditional exchanges were, Enron served as the counterparty to every transaction, guaranteeing the liquidity of every deal. This role of being the buyer or seller of every transaction accounted for Enron's spectacular revenue growth; whereas a neutral trading operation would only book its commissions as revenue, Enron, taking actual possession of the traded commodities, could book the entire value of each trade.

By 2001, Enron traded a wide variety of products, including oil, natural gas, electricity, coal, pulp and paper, plastics, metals, bandwidth, water commodities, energy-related derivatives and derivatives for weather-related insurance risk, pollution emission credits and commercial credit. By this time, its Wholesale Energy Operations and Services were generating more than 94 per cent of the revenue Enron was reporting. Enron's Transportation and Distribution activities, the company's standard regulated gas-pipeline business when it was formed in 1985, accounted for around 80 per cent of the company's revenues in 1990; by 2000, Transportation and Distribution was a mere three per cent of reported revenues.

After FERC Order 636, energy trading became a standard and important business for all of Enron's major competitors. Many interstate pipeline companies, forced to separate their transportation business from their buying and selling business, divided their marketing units into affiliated marketing subsidiaries. These subsidiaries then managed the buying and selling of natural gas to customers who, before Order 636, purchased gas directly from the pipeline company. As was the case with Enron, these energy marketers came to trade more than simple natural gas commodities; in 2001, the Department of Energy's Energy Information Administration reported that of the 14 companies that accounted for more than 85 per cent of interstate natural gas pipeline activity, all 14 had energy marketing activities that were an "important enterprise" within the company.[8]

While energy trading had become a common and significant business for all the major pipeline companies in the United States, Enron was considered the leader, being the world's largest marketer of natural gas and the first to introduce online trading.

GROWTH OF ENRON'S REPUTATION

Enron's transformation from a natural gas pipeline company to an online energy-trading giant was closely watched by investors and the capital markets; before its collapse, Enron was widely held as a model of how "old economy" firms could transform themselves into powerhouses of the technological, fast-paced "new economy."

Each of the six years from 1996 and 2001, Enron won *Fortune* magazine's "America's Most Innovative Company" award among the magazine's list of Most Admired Companies. Enron was also one of America's fastest growing companies; its double-digit revenue growth in the late 1990s became triple-digit revenue growth once EnronOnline was launched in late 1999. With this dramatic revenue growth, Enron vaulted up the Fortune 500 list of companies, jumping from 18th in 1999 to seventh in 2000. Despite declaring bankruptcy on December 2, 2001, Enron's reported revenues from its first three quarters still made it the fifth largest company on the Fortune 500 that year. Only Wal-Mart, Exxon Mobil, General Motors and Ford were larger.

Enron's revenue growth was accompanied by profit growth (see Exhibit 2). Management's communications about the company's performance and ambitions for the future were confident and positive. All this made Enron a true market darling; in 2000, when most technology stocks lost value, Enron shares returned around 90 per cent. Thirteen of the 18 analysts covering the stock in the spring of 2001 gave it a "buy" or "strong buy" recommendation; some of these positive analyst recommendations would continue right up until December 2, 2001, when Enron declared bankruptcy (see Exhibit 3). From 1998 through the end of 2000, Enron's stock price soared (see Exhibit 4).

	1997	1998	1999	2000
Revenue	$20,273	$31,260	$40,112	$100,789
Net Income	$105	$703	$893	$979
Earnings per Share* (basic)	$0.32	$2.14	$1.17	$1.22
Total Assets	$22,552	$29,350	$33,381	$65,503
Total Liabilities	$16,934	$22,302	$23,811	$54,033
Total Shareholders' Equity	$5,618	$7,048	$9,570	$11,470

Exhibit 2   Selected Data (before restatement) from Enron's Auditied Financial Statements: 1997 to 2000 (in millions of dollars)

Source: Company annual reports.

*Earnings per share calculations based on the following average number of common shares (millions): 272 (1997), 321 (1998), 705 (1999), 736 (2000).

Date (2001) and Relevant Events	# of Analysts Following Enron*	Recommendations			
		Strong Buy	Buy	Hold	Sell
Oct. 18—Two days after Enron announced its $618 million third quarter loss, $1.2 billion write-down of shareholders' equity and restatement of earnings through first half of 2001, and as scrutiny intensifies on Fastow's LJM1 and LJM2 partnerships.	15	12	3	0	0
Nov. 8—Enron has announced a upgraded, formal SEC investigation into its finances, that it is restating its financial results as far back as 1997 and that it is in merger talks with Dynegy.	15	11		3	1
Nov. 28—Enron is downgraded to junk bond status by major credit rating agencies; this triggers a merger agreement clause, causing Dynegy to terminate the deal.	14	3	3	7	1
Nov. 29—Second-last trading day before Enron files for bankruptcy. (Two analysts dropped coverage of Enron.) Enron now trading at $0.36.	12	2	1	7	2

Exhibit 3   Recommendations From Analysts Following Enron's Stock

Source: Dan Ackman, "Enron Analysts: We Was Duped," Thomson Financial/First Call, *http://www.forbes.com/2002/02/27/0227analystsprint.html,* June 25, 2002, and Matt Krantz, "Why Were Analysts So Slow to Downgrade Enron?," *http://www.usatoday.com/money/energy/2001-11-30-enron.htm,* June 25, 2002.

*As tracked by Thomson Financial/First Call.

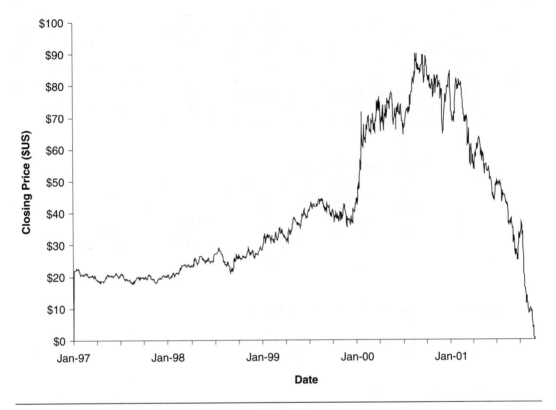

Exhibit 4   Enron's Share Price Performance 1997 to 2001

Source: Stock quotes from www.siliconinvestor.com, July 17, 2002.

Note: Chart shows prices until December 3, 2001, the first day of trading after Enron's chapter 11 bankruptcy filing on December 2, 2001.

Even before Enron became prominent for its leadership position in online energy trading, Chairman and CEO Ken Lay was respected in the business community and connected in political circles. Lay was known to President George W. Bush and Vice-President Dick Cheney, both former Texas oilmen. Enron and its executives were Bush's largest political patrons during his 2000 presidential election (see Exhibit 5). Lay served as formal energy advisor to former President George Bush and as informal advisor to the second Bush administration of George W. Bush.

On February 12, Enron's board approved Jeffery Skilling's promotion to CEO; Ken Lay would remain Enron's chairman. Skilling, long the second-in-command at Enron, had worked as a McKinsey consultant with Lay to craft Enron's vision in the 1980s; he joined Enron in 1990 and had been steadily groomed as Lay's successor.

ENRON'S FINANCING STRATEGY

Beginning with its gas-fired heat and power facility in the United Kingdom, Enron made

- From 1989 to 2001, Enron Corporation PAC, Enron executives, employees and their family members gave $5,951,570 in hard and soft money to federal candidates and parties. Republicans received 74 per cent of the donations ($4,404,162) while Democrats received 26 per cent ($1,547,408).
- As of 2001, Enron Corporation was the biggest contributor to George W. Bush's political career; from 1993 to 2001, Enron Corporation PAC, Enron executives, employees and their family members donated $736,800 to Bush. Enron was Bush's biggest patron in his 2000 presidential campaign.
- Ken and Linda Lay gave $276,500 to Bush from 1993 to 2000, including $100,000 to Bush's inauguration fund. Jeffrey Skilling and Enron each donated an additional $100,000 to the inaugural fund.[1]

Enron's hard money donations from 1989 to 2001

	Republicans	Democrats	Independent	Total
Senate	$417,480	$110,513	$2,500	$530,493
House of Representatives	$346,348	$257,140	N/A	$603,488

Ken Lay's hard money political donations from 1989 to 2001

Total Republicans	Total Democrats	Total Donations
$793,110	$86,470	$882,580

Exhibit 5   Enron's Political Donations

Source: Data from Center for Responsive Politics/Federal Election Commission; "Enron Timeline", http://news.bbc.co.uk/hi/english/static/in_depth/business/2002/enron/timeline/5.stm and http://news.bbc.co.uk/hi/english/static/in_depth/business/2002/enron/timeline/7.stm, June 25, 2002.

1. www.thedailyenron.com/enron101/political.asp, June 25, 2002.

many huge investments in power plants and pipelines around the world during its international expansion. EnronOnline was also growing, at its peak trading nearly $3 billion worth of contracts every day. Energy trading fuelled Enron's rapid growth, but required large amounts of cash. Since EnronOnline was structured so that Enron was the counterparty for every deal, Enron needed to secure its obligations with money to cover the possibility it was unable to find enough buyers to match with sellers, or vice versa. Consequently, more trading required more cash to secure Enron's counterparty obligations.

For the company's trading operations to continue, Enron needed an investment-grade credit rating. Without it, sources of debt to secure its trading obligations would be more expensive and difficult to acquire. If customers lost confidence that Enron could guarantee the liquidity of the market it made for energy commodities, customers would stop trading with Enron.

Enron financed its growth in part with debt; the company's on-balance sheet debt climbed from $3.5 billion in 1996 to $13 billion in 2001.[9] In the first nine months of 2000, Enron issued a net of $3.9 billion in debt.

The overriding importance of protecting Enron's credit rating meant that the company had to limit the amount of debt it took on. The company's growth required financing beyond what debt alone could provide; additional financing came from Enron's use of special purpose entities (SPEs) (see Appendix).

Enron had hundreds of SPEs. Merrill Lynch, J.P. Morgan Chase, Citigroup, Credit Suisse First Boston, General Electric, the MacArthur Foundation and the Arkansas Teacher Retirement System were among the SPE investors. Enron sold energy contracts and assets to some of the SPEs, sometimes at prices inflated above fair market value.[10] These transactions enabled Enron to move the sold assets off its balance sheet and to show income from the sales on its income statement. While the money Enron received for the sale of its assets was obtained by SPEs borrowing against the transferred assets, the money from these loans was counted as debt on the SPEs' books, but was recorded as income on Enron's books.

Among Enron's SPEs were four partnerships collectively known as the Raptors; the Raptors were created in 2000 and run by Andrew Fastow, Enron's chief financial officer (CFO). These SPEs had been formed to hedge Enron's market risk in its portfolio of volatile technology stocks; the effect was that roughly $504 million in losses from portfolio investments were kept off Enron's books. To finance the Raptors, Enron issued common stock in exchange for notes receivable from the Raptor SPEs. Essentially, Enron had sold its own shares to itself and paid for them with an IOU to itself. The Raptors ultimately resulted in the shareholders' equity on Enron's balance sheet being overstated by $1 billion and Enron's notes receivable being overstated by $1 billion.

Enron's SPEs had the effect of keeping debt off Enron's balance sheet, thus protecting the company's credit rating. The SPEs also kept losses off Enron's income statement, thus improving reported profit. Fastow's role in running numerous partnerships, including the Raptors, was approved by Enron's board of directors.

MANAGEMENT MOTIVATION

Some people wondered if the actions of Enron's management might have been motivated by the incentive scheme that was in place for managers. Under a four-year program called the Performance Unit Plan, Enron had set a series of stock-price targets in 2000, which, if met, would result in a one-time bonus for the company's executives. For meeting these stock-price targets, $320 million in bonuses, money that Enron executives said had been anticipated for several years, was paid out during the ten months prior to the company's collapse. In January and February of 2001, top executives received other bonuses whose amounts were determined largely by company earnings. CFO Andrew Fastow received three payments totaling over $3 million, then-president and chief operating officer (COO) Jeffrey Skilling received two payments totaling $7.5 million and then-CEO Ken Lay received two payments totaling $10.6 million.[11]

ARTHUR ANDERSEN

Enron's auditor since the company's formation in 1985 was Arthur Andersen LLP, the U.S. member firm of Andersen Worldwide and one of the American "Big Five" accounting firms. Andersen Worldwide, the co-ordinating entity for autonomous member firms around the world, had its roots in the accounting firm Andersen, DeLany & Co, established in 1913 in Chicago. In September 2001, Andersen Worldwide's individual member firms collectively employed approximately 85,000 people; Andersen Worldwide's revenues for 2001 were in excess of $9.3 billion.

Based in Chicago, Arthur Andersen LLP served Enron through its Houston office, with David Duncan as the office's lead partner and chief auditor for Enron.

In addition to auditing services, Andersen also acted as a consultant to Enron, providing advice and helping in the structuring of some of Enron's SPEs and transactions. Enron reported paying Arthur Andersen $52 million in fees for 2000,

$25 million for auditing services and $27 million for consulting services.

There were some early indications of accounting problems. Several years earlier, while auditing Enron's 1997 financial statements, Andersen proposed $51 million in adjustments to the statements; these changes would have reduced Enron's income for the year by almost 50 per cent, from $105 million to $54 million. When Enron refused to make the changes, Andersen decided the adjustments were not material and certified the company's accounts anyway.[12]

On February 5, 2001, David Duncan, Thomas H. Bauer (the other lead accountant on the Enron account), six colleagues and six Andersen executives connected by speakerphone held a meeting in which the handling of two of Fastow's partnerships—LJM1 and LJM2—was debated at length. The accountants resolved to suggest that a special committee of the Enron board be created to review the fairness of Enron and LJM's transactions; they also decided to confirm with Enron that the LJM partnerships met accounting rules that allowed the partnerships to be treated as separate entities and not as a subsidiaries whose financial results would be shown on Enron's books. One week later, when Enron's audit and compliance committee gave the auditors the opportunity to express any concerns they had, Duncan and Bauer raised neither of these points.[13]

UNRAVELLING

It had been suggested that the nature of Enron's business made it difficult to value; the value of its assets shifted continually and Enron utilized many off-balance sheet partnerships based on complicated derivatives transactions. Furthermore, the company was not required to, or did not adequately, disclose the details of these partnerships. Since some of the transactions Enron engaged in were difficult to assess, the revenue reported on them was based on the company's own aggressive estimates.[14] Despite bullish endorsements from analysts following Enron's stock, the consensus among those analysing Enron's businesses and financial results was that the company was very complex and difficult to understand. Enron kept many details about its Wholesale Energy Operations and Services confidential for "competitive reasons." Some analysts were at a loss to explain how the company made money.[15]

Even the financial statements and disclosures Enron released did not fully clarify its business activities and their results. "The ability to develop a somewhat predictable model of this business for the future is mostly an exercise in futility," wrote Bears Stearns analyst Robert Winters in a report shortly before Enron began to crumble.[16] Not having a good understanding of Enron's business, analysts admitted they took Enron's word on its numbers.[17]

In early 2001, James Chanos, president and founder of Kynikos Associates, a firm specializing in short selling, publicly raised questions about Enron's profitability, the level of risk associated with its trading business, the mysterious related-party transactions, the conflict of interest implied by having these entities run by "a senior officer of Enron," and the company's optimism about its plan to trade broadband capacity and its other investments in telecommunications, a sector that was in sharp decline. These types of concerns, compounded with analysts' existing complaints about the clarity and level of disclosure in Enron's financial statements, coincided with Enron's stock price drop.

Financed with Enron stock, Enron's transactions with the Raptors contained provisions requiring Enron's share price to remain above certain levels. The Raptors and the losses they covered could only be kept off Enron's books if the SPEs remained financially healthy enough to fulfill their obligations. As the value of technology stocks on the NASDAQ continued to drop, the losses that the Raptors were supposed to cover ballooned. At the same time, Enron's stock price was falling, hindering the Raptors' ability to cover these losses. There were provisions should the stock price fall too far; if the price declined too much, Enron would be forced to report a $504 million loss.

Enron's management tried to bolster the company's credibility to boost the share price; one share price trigger had already been breached near the end of the first quarter of 2001, but at the last minute, Enron found a way to refinance and prop up the Raptor SPEs. Late July, at the beginning of the third quarter, Enron's stock price dropped below $47, a second price trigger. In spite of management's efforts, the stock never rebounded.

On August 14, Skilling unexpectedly resigned after only six months as CEO. He left Enron citing "personal reasons," assuring investors that "there's nothing to disclose. The company's in great shape."[18]

WARNING[19]

The same day Skilling resigned, Ken Lay, who resumed the CEO position, tried to reassure employees through an e-mail:

> All of you know that our stock price has suffered substantially over the last few months. One of my top priorities will be to restore a significant amount of the stock value we have lost as soon as possible . . . I want to assure you that I have never felt better about prospects for the company . . . Our performance has never been stronger; our business model has never been more robust; our growth has never been more certain. . . . We have the finest organization in American business today.[20]

Two weeks later, in another e-mail to employees who received a stock options grant, Lay said, "one of my highest priorities is to restore investor confidence in Enron. This should result in a significantly higher stock price."[21]

After Skilling's resignation, Lay began meeting with employees and encouraging them to write about their concerns anonymously.

One unsigned letter he received pointed, with great detail, at problems with Enron's SPEs:

> I am incredibly nervous that we will implode in a wave of accounting scandals . . . Skilling is resigning for "personal reasons," but I think he wasn't

having fun, looked down the road and knew this stuff was unfixable and would rather abandon ship now than resign in shame in two years . . . the business world will consider the past successes as nothing but an elaborate accounting hoax.

The letter writer soon identified herself as Sherron Watkins, an accountant who had worked at Enron for eight years. She was laid off the previous spring and then brought back in June to work for Fastow. Watkins also expressed her concerns to David Duncan and two other accountants at Andersen, one of whom recorded her concerns in a memo in Enron's file.

Lay met with Watkins on August 22 and decided, along with Enron's general counsel, to assign an investigation to the law firm Vinson & Elkins, who had handled some of the legal documents for a number of the SPEs. Enron wanted quick results and instructed Vinson & Elkins not to spend time examining the propriety of the accounting treatment of Enron's SPEs, the heart of Watkins' warnings. The lawyers interviewed Fastow, Duncan and others involved in the SPE transactions and reported to Lay on September 21 that there was no reason for concern—Fastow's operations appeared to be proper and legitimate.

COLLAPSE

In preparing financial reports for Enron's third quarter, the company's auditors discovered that they had made a mistake more than a year earlier in the way they had accounted for the Enron shares used to finance the Raptor partnerships. Correcting the mistake would involve reducing Enron's assets by $1 billion that had mistakenly been added earlier. The Raptor partnerships were dismantled, necessitating the report of Enron's investment losses to shareholders and further reducing assets by $200 million. On October 16, an Enron press release announced a $618 million loss for its third quarter, the company's first quarterly loss in more than four years. Shareholders' equity was written down by $1.2 billion, and Enron announced it was restating earnings through the first half of 2001. The *Wall Street Journal* reported that of Enron's losses, $35 million alone had come from the two LJM partnerships run by Fastow; Fastow himself had made $45 million from the management of these two partnerships. The Securities and Exchange Commission (SEC) began an inquiry into some of the Fastow partnership transactions. Ken Lay and Enron's board of directors said they stood by Fastow, but on October 24, Fastow took a leave of absence and did not return to the company.

By the end of October, credit agencies were considering a downgrade on Enron's credit rating. On October 31, the SEC's inquiry was upgraded to a formal investigation into Enron's finances. On that same day, Enron announced its board of directors had formed an investigation committee of its own with the power to take disciplinary action against any Enron employee, officer or director who it determined had improperly participated in the limited partnership transactions.

LAST-DITCH EFFORTS

Ken Lay sought intervention from officials in various government agencies in Washington; on October 26, he phoned Federal Reserve Chairman Alan Greenspan. Later, spokespeople for the Federal Reserve would not disclose what was discussed during the conversation between Lay and Greenspan, but said Greenspan did not follow up the call with any action. "He did nothing in response to the call. It would have been inappropriate," the spokesperson said.[22]

On the same day, Lay phoned Donald L. Evans, the Commerce Secretary (reportedly one of President Bush's closest friends). Evans was out of town, and Lay did not reach him that day.

On October 28, Lay contacted Paul H. O'Neill, the Treasury Secretary. Lay described Enron's problems to O'Neill, suggesting that the company's collapse could put the entire financial system at risk. O'Neill consulted Peter R. Fisher, the Under Secretary for Domestic Finance; Fisher advised O'Neill that such aftershocks were unlikely.

Donald L. Evans was back at his office October 29 and returned Lay's call. Evans' spokesperson James Dyke later indicated that during the October 29 phone call, Lay "indicated that he would welcome any support the secretary thought appropriate" in dealing with the credit rating agencies.

Ultimately, both O'Neill and Evans decided against intervening.[23]

At around the same time, discussions began with rival company Dynegy over a merger that might save Enron. In the meantime, officials at Enron discovered another accounting mistake: a secret side deal had been drawn up during the formation of an SPE controlled by an Enron employee working under Fastow. The side deal shifted SPE ownership away from independent investors; these SPEs had never been independent entities and therefore did not meet the accounting requirements for off-balance sheet treatment. Accountants from Andersen informed the company that hiding the side deal might have been a criminal act.[24]

A tentative agreement to merge was reached by Enron and Dynegy's boards of directors on November 7. On November 8, Enron filed a report with the SEC, restating its earnings back to 1997. Enron disclosed $591 million in losses against previously reported profits and acknowledged that three of the SPEs should have been consolidated into Enron's financial statements all along. Enron's quarterly filing on November 19 revealed its depleted cash situation and a $690 million debt payment that had been accelerated due to its downgraded credit rating. Dynegy had received little warning about these revelations.

On November 28, Standard and Poor's downgraded Enron's credit rating to below investment grade, triggering the immediate repayment of almost $4 billion in off-balance sheet debt. Enron's downgrade to junk bond status triggered a clause in the merger agreement with Dynegy; on the same day as the credit downgrade, the merger with Dynegy fell apart. On December 1, Enron's board of directors unanimously supported a motion to declare bankruptcy. The petition was filed December 2.

RESULT

Following the filing of its bankruptcy petition, Enron laid off 4,000 of its 20,000 workers worldwide. Enron employees also suffered through their 401(k)[25] retirement plans; Enron contracted out the administration of the fund to an outside company, a process that froze the investment accounts being transferred. The frozen accounts kept Enron employees from dumping their Enron stock in late October as the share price plummeted. A feature of Enron's retirement fund involved matching 50 per cent of any contributions from employees, up to six per cent of their salary, with Enron stock. Employees were prohibited from selling any of the stock Enron gave them until the age of 50; however, they were free to sell any Enron stock they had purchased with their own money.[26] Of the assets in Enron's retirement system, approximately 62 per cent of the individual pensions were made up of the company's own stock.[27] The combination of frozen 401(k) accounts and Enron's restrictions on selling stock it had contributed forced employees to hold on to the company's stock even as the price collapsed. The 401(k) plan ended up losing more than $1 billion in October and November of 2001, rendering many of employees' 401(k) accounts worthless.[28]

Meanwhile, between 1999 to mid-2001, a group of Enron executives and directors sold 17.3 million Enron shares, pocketing approximately $1.1 billion. Lay's take was the second highest, selling 1.8 million shares for $101.3 million; Skilling received $66.9 million for 1.1 million shares; Fastow had a take of around $30 million for his Enron holdings.[29]

From its high of $90.75 on August 23, 2000, Enron shares closed at $0.26 on November 30, 2001, the last trading day before it declared bankruptcy. From a market capitalization of more than $60 billion at the beginning of 2001, by the end of the year Enron had destroyed all of its value. Shareholders' lawsuits were filed against Enron and against Arthur Andersen in an attempt to recover some of their losses.

CONCLUSION

The report released on February 2, 2002 by the special investigation committee formed by Enron's board of directors concluded

> the partnerships . . . were used by Enron management to enter into transactions that it could not, or would not, do with unrelated commercial entities. . . . Many of the most significant transactions apparently were designed to accomplish favorable financial statement results, not to achieve bona fide economic objectives or transfer risk.

The board of directors, technically elected by the shareholders, was responsible for overseeing management as well as ensuring that proper accounting reports were delivered to the shareholders. In fact, a company's financial statements were usually signed by two members of the board on behalf of all the board members. Enron's board and its audit committee (see Exhibit 6) were also being asked to explain what happened and to justify their actions in light of the consequences to the company and its investors and creditors. Carl Levin, the chairman of a U.S. Senate subcommittee investigating the Enron affair, made the following statement about the board of directors: "[the board] approved an awful lot of what happened. They can't duck their responsibility."[30] The question many asked was where were the board of directors and the audit committee when Enron was quickly deteriorating? What were their responsibilities? Did they act in the best interest of the shareholders?

Enron's collapse had damaged investors' faith in the corporate financial reporting system. What and where were all the checks and balances? What were the institutional and other safeguards? Which ones failed? Calvert, after his experience with Enron, wondered if anything could have been done to prevent his losses, and what, if anything could be done in the future to prevent a similar disaster from occurring.

Kenneth L. Lay
Houston, Texas
Chairman, Enron Corp.

Jeffrey K. Skilling
Houston, Texas
President and CEO, Enron Corp.

Robert A. Belfer
New York, New York
Chairman, Belco Oil & Gas Corp.

Jerome J. Meyer
Wilsonville, Oregon
Chairman, Tektronix, Inc.

John H. Duncan
Houston, Texas
Former Chairman of the Exec. Committee
of Gulf & Western Industries, Inc.

Frank Savage
Stamford, Connecticut
Chairman, Alliance Capital
Management International

Charles A. LeMaistre
San Antonio, Texas
President Emeritus, University of Texas
M.D. Anderson Cancer Center

Ken L. Harrison
Portland, Oregon
Former Chairman and CEO,
Portland General Electric Company

Norman P. Blake, Jr.
Colorado Springs, Colorado
Chairman, President and CEO,
Comdisco, Inc.
Former CEO and Secretary General,
U.S. Olympic Committee

Herbert S. Winokur, Jr.
Greenwich, Connecticut
President, Winokur Holdings, Inc.
Former Senior Executive Vice
President, Penn Central Corporation

John A. Urquhart
Fairfield, Connecticut
Senior Advisor to the Chairman, Enron Corp.
President, John A. Urquhart Associates
Former Senior Vice President of Industrial and
Power Systems, General Electric Company

The following members of Enron's Board of Directors also formed Enron's Audit Committee.

John Mendelsohn
Houston, Texas
President, University of Texas
M.D. Anderson Cancer Center

Ronnie C. Chan
Hong Kong
Chairman, Hang Lung Group

Robert K. Jaedicke
Stanford, California
Professor of Accounting (Emeritus) and
Former Dean, Graduate School of
Business, Stanford University

John Wakeham
London, England
Former U.K. Secretary of State for
Energy and Leader of the Houses of
Lords and Commons

Paulo V. Ferraz Pereira
Rio de Janeiro, Brazil
Executive Vice President of Group Bozano
Former President and COO, Meridional
Financial Group
Former President and CEO, State Bank
of Rio de Janeiro, Brazil

Wendy L. Gramm
Washington, D.C.
Director of the Regulatory Studies
Program of the Mercatus Center at
George Mason University
Former Chairman, U.S. Commodity
Futures Trading Commission

Exhibit 6   Enron's Board of Directors and Audit Committee

Source: Enron Corporation 2000 Annual Report, http://www.enron.com/corp/investors/annuals/2000/board.html#super
June 25, 2002.

NOTES

1. This case has been written on the basis of published sources only. Consequently, the interpretation and perspectives presented in this case are not necessarily those of Enron Corp. or any of its employees.

2. http://www.ferc.fed.us, April 8, 2002.

3. Annual Energy Outlook 2002 with Projections to 2020, Energy Information Administration, http://www.eia.doe.gov. Accessed April 17, 2002.

4. http://www.enron.com/corp/pressroom/mile stones/frameset.html, March 27, 2002.

5. All figures in U.S. dollars.

6. William H. Miller, "Vision Vanquisher," May 18, 1998. http://www.industryweek.com., April 3, 2002.

7. The Corporate and Other business segment included the operation of water, renewable energy businesses and clean fuel plants, as well as overall corporate activities.

8. Susanne Johnson and James Tobin, "Corporate Realignments and Investments in the Interstate Natural Gas Transmission System," *Energy Information Administration*, April 18, 2001.

9. Bethany McLean, "Why Enron Went Bust," *Fortune*, December 24, 2001, pp. 59 to 66.

10. Jeremy Kahn, "Off Balance Sheet—and Out of Control," *Fortune*, February 18, 2002, www.fortune .com, February 21, 2002.

11. Kurt Eichenwald, "Enron Paid Executives US$320M in Bonuses," *The New York Times*, March 1, 2002 www.nationalpost.com.

12. David S. Hilzenrath, "Early Warnings of Trouble at Enron; Accounting Firm Found $51 Million in Problems, but Still Signed Off on Books," *The Washington Post*, December 30, 2001, page A10.

13. Kurt Eichenwald and Diana B. Henriques, "Web of Details Did Enron in as Warnings Went Unheeded," *New York Times*, February 10, 2002.

14. Mathew Ingram, "How Aggressive Should an Accountant Be?," *The Globe and Mail*, April 3, 2002.

15. Bethany McLean, "Is Enron Overpriced?," *Fortune*, March 5, 2001.

16. Ibid.

17. Bethany McLean, "Why Enron Went Bust," *Fortune*, December 24, 2001, pp. 59 to 60.

18. James Flanigan, "Enron's Troubles Could Spur Securities Reforms," *The L.A. Times*, November 25, 2001.

19. Frank Pellegrini, "Person of the Week: 'Enron Whistleblower' Sherron Watkins," *Time.com*, January 18, 2002; Kurt Eichenwald and Diana B. Henriques,

"Web of Details Did Enron in as Warnings Went Unheeded," *New York Times*, February 10, 2002, p. 9.

20. "Enron Head Might Have Misled Staff," *Reuters*, January 14, 2002.

21. "Waxman Wants Explanation of Enron E-Mail," http://CNN.com, January 12, 2002.

22. "Enron's Lay called Greenspan in October," *Reuters News Service*, January 11, 2002.

23. Kurt Eichenwald and Diana B. Henriques, "Web of Details Did Enron in as Warnings Went Unheeded," *New York Times*, February 10, 2002.

24. Ibid.

25. A defined contribution plan that permits employees to have a portion of their salary deducted from their paycheck and contributed to an account. Federal (and sometimes state) taxes on the employee contributions and investment earnings are deferred until the participant receives a distribution from the plan (typically at retirement). Employers may also make contributions to a participant's account.

26. Michael W. Lynch, "Enron's 401(k) Calamity," *ReasonOnline*, December 27, 2001. http://reason.com/ml/m1122701.shtml, Accessed June 25, 2002.

27. "Enron Timeline," http://news.bbc.co.uk/hi/english/static/in_depth/business/2002/enron/timeline/11.stm, June 25, 2002.

28. Martine Costello, "Company Stock Slams 401(k)s," *CNN Money*, December 10, 2001. http://money.cnn.com/2001/12/10/401k/q_401k_lawsuits/

29. Leslie Wayne, "Before Debacle, Enron Insiders Cashed in $1.1 Billion in Shares," *The New York Times*, January 13, 2002.

30. Kathryn Kranhold and Michael Schroeder, "Senate report accuses Enron board of complicity," *The Wall Street Journal*, July 8, 2002.

APPENDIX: INTRODUCTION TO SPECIAL PURPOSE ENTITIES

A special purpose entity (SPE) is an organization with a limited purpose or life. Such vehicles are commonly used to manage risk and to access capital. A SPE is created by a sponsoring company that typically sells an asset to the SPE.[1] For an SPE to qualify for off-balance sheet treatment, an independent third party must invest at least three per cent of the fair value of the financial asset to be sold into the SPE as equity; the remaining 97 per cent is often in the form of loans from creditors. The third-party investor would control the SPE's activities and bear the substantial risks and rewards of the entity. The sponsoring company receives the money borrowed by the SPE as payment for the asset sold; the asset, now owned by the SPE, is used as collateral for the loans.

The benefits of using such an SPE come from isolating assets in an entity that is prohibited from undertaking any other business activity or from taking on additional debt. This isolation helps manage risk; should the sponsoring company go bankrupt, the transferred asset in the SPE could not be touched by the sponsor's creditors. Conversely, if the SPE became insolvent, the sponsoring company would only be responsible for what it had put into the SPE. Isolating the transferred asset also has the effect of protecting the asset from the risks of the sponsor's other business activities or claims from other creditors; consequently, credit risk is reduced. The SPE can borrow against the asset at a lower cost of capital than the sponsor would have been able to obtain borrowing against the same asset.

The theory behind SPEs is that the value of its assets (the loan collateral) should be equal or greater than the value of the SPE's debt; the debt risk is covered as the assets and liabilities effectively cancel each other out. If the assets have solid value that does not fluctuate dramatically, the SPE would be unlikely to become insolvent as a result of its own activities. Typically, SPE consolidation does not cause differences in reported income. Since the assets and liabilities in a SPE usually balance out, consolidation of an SPE into the sponsoring company's financial statements usually does not have much effect on the financial statements. This form of off-balance sheet financing might be used because other reasons exist for keeping assets or special projects off the consolidated balance sheet.

Having been created for a specific purpose, the SPE is structured with limitations on liabilities it can incur, with insulation from the liabilities of third parties, protection from dissolution risk and with measures to prohibit it from filing a bankruptcy petition while solvent. These measures ensure the SPE is adequately isolated from any of its related parties and does not engage in any business outside of that which it was created for.

Note

1. SPEs are used in various ways to manage risk or as a financing vehicle: an SPE can be a joint-venture partner in a special project with the sponsoring company co-signing the SPE's debts; a SPE can enter into leasing arrangements for large assets to enable the sponsoring company to avoid capitalizing the lease. Virtually all banks use SPEs to issue debt secured by pools of mortgages. SPEs are widely used for factoring (the generation of cash through selling off receivables). The SPE structure described above is known as an asset securitization.

ACME HARDWARE

Prepared by Alister K. Mason, Partner, Deloitte Haskins and Sells, Toronto, and Professor Claude Lanfranconi

Version: (A) 2003-05-25

INTRODUCTION

John Smith, C.A., was recently assigned the responsibility for the audit of Acme Hardware, a new client. He was wondering what action, if any, he should take about the way certain stores of Acme Hardware were accounting for inventory and advertising costs. As a result of his pre-audit review of the previous auditor's files, he had identified a situation where there was a probability that certain store managers, motivated by the company's management and control system, were taking advantage of discretionary accounting alternatives available to them. Any complete investigation would be disruptive and expensive and had to be considered in light of the fact that the impact of their actions on the company's financial statements might be immaterial.

THE COMPANY

Acme Hardware was a rapidly expanding chain of hardware stores which operated in southern Ontario. All stores were company-owned; there were no franchises.

By the beginning of the 1987/1988 fiscal year, Acme had 14 stores, four of which had been opened up in the previous five years. Total sales in 1986/1987 were $30.7 million (up from $21.4 million in 1982/1983), resulting in net income—after corporate expenses and income taxes—of $1.2 million ($650,000 in 1982/1983). Total assets as at March 31, 1987 were $17.4 million.

Acme's success was attributed to several factors, but the most important was usually considered to be the generous bonuses ($15,000), which were payable to the store manager when the budgeted net income for the year was met. Budgets were set by head office, after negotiations with store management. Net income was computed in accordance with accounting policies laid down by head office, and in the event of disagreement, Acme's auditors, who also reviewed each store's records, were to act as arbitrators. The predecessor audit firm had not been required to arbitrate any disagreements about the income computations in the preceding five-year period.

PREPARATION FOR THE AUDIT

Acme had recently engaged a new firm of auditors, AB&Co., and John Smith was the partner assigned to the engagement. In planning

the work to be performed for the first year—the year ended March 31, 1988—he reviewed the predecessor audit firm's working paper files. John found that the above-mentioned bonus arrangement had been identified by that firm as a potential "audit risk"[1] with regard to the pressure on store managers to achieve budgets.

John reviewed the budget and actual net income figures for the previous five years, to see how frequently the budgets had been met, and hence the bonuses paid. He noted that, for 10 stores he examined, because they had been in operation for some time, and therefore had an established pattern of operations, bonuses had been paid on 23 occasions (out of a maximum of 50). He also noted that, when a budget was met, the tendency seemed to be for it to be met by a narrow margin, but, when missed, by a much wider margin.

ANALYSIS OF INCENTIVE SYSTEM

To examine this issue more closely, John prepared a table setting out the budget and actual net income figures for the 10 stores over the five-year period (see Table 1). He separated the 10 stores into two groups:

1. Three stores (North York, Hamilton, and Waterloo) in which:
   a. budgets were met four times out of a possible 15 (27 per cent);
   b. the margins by which the budgets were met were $10,000, $3,000, $9,000 and $6,000 (average $7,000); and,
   c. on the 11 occasions when the budgets were not met, the margins ranged from $5,000 down to $1,000 (average $2,800).

2. The other seven stores, for which:
   a. budgets were met 19 times out of a possible 35 (54 per cent);
   b. the margins by which the budgets were met ranged from $2,000 to $5,000 (average $3,300); and,
   c. on the 16 occasions when the budgets were not met, the margins ranged from $7,000 to $18,000 (average $11,200).

	1982/1983 Income		1983/1984 Income		1984/1985 Income		1985/1986 Income		1986/1987 Income	
	Budget	Actual	Budget	Actual	Budget	Actual	Budget	Actual	Budget	Actual
Oshawa	$125	$129*	$136	$118	$132	$135*	$140	$132	$145	$147*
Scarborough	180	173	195	198*	212	217*	228	216	236	240*
Markham	76	65	84	88*	102	86	120	125*	138	121
North York	202	198	212	208	220	218	235	245*	250	247
Mississauga	168	171*	175	165	185	189*	197	186	202	205*
Hamilton	136	139*	142	137	148	146	158	167*	168	165
St. Catharines	94	85	98	100*	105	96	110	112*	114	102
Guelph	85	76	88	92*	95	98*	101	92	104	106*
Waterloo	148	146	154	160*	163	160	172	170	185	184
London	189	192*	195	184	198	201*	205	195	209	213*

Table 1   Budget/Actual Net Income Figures for 10 Stores (all figures in $000)

*Bonus paid to store management.

John concluded that there was a strong probability that the managers of seven stores were manipulating net income computations. Based on his experience, John thought that the most likely way of doing so would be by advancing or deferring—from one period to the next—the recognition of income and/or expenses. For example:

1. By deferring the recognition of income or advancing the recognition of expenses, it would be easier to meet the budget in the next period. Managers would be tempted to do this when it was apparent—say by the 10th or the 11th month of the fiscal year—that (a) the current year's budget could not be met, or (b) the budget had already been met.

2. By advancing the recognition of income or deferring the recognition of expenses, it would be easier to meet the budget in the current period. This would be particularly tempting when, without action of this kind, the budget would probably be missed by a fairly narrow margin.

John reviewed the monthly income statements for the individual stores, all of which followed a standard format (prescribed by head office), based on the income and expense accounts in the general ledger. He concluded that the two most likely areas for manipulation were:

1. Inventories

These were valued at the lower of cost (determined on a FIFO first in first out basis) and net realizable value. The write-down to net realizable value was largely a matter of judgment, particularly in respect of seasonal merchandise, e.g., garden supplies, and products for which expected new models might make the present ones obsolete, e.g., power mowers.

2. Advertising Expenses

Company policy required the costs of local advertising to be expensed in the period the campaign was run. However, store managers had discretion when a campaign should be run, and it would be quite possible to advance a campaign scheduled for the first week of April to the last week of March. (Experience had shown that some advertising campaigns result in increased sales over the next few weeks, rather than only in the period in which the advertisements are run.)

CONCLUSION

John was very familiar with these types of incentive schemes because of their use by many of his other clients. He was also aware that senior management recognized that any management control system had flaws. However, these systems motivated their operating managers to maintain a focus on net income and, in the process, to maximize revenues and minimize costs.

John also recognized that, unless several stores manipulated their results in the same direction in any year, the impact on the corporate financial statements would probably not be material. He now had to decide what, if any, action was necessary.

NOTE

1. "Audit risk" is the risk that the audit firm would fail to express a reservation in its opinion on Acme's financial statements if they were materially misstated. Such material misstatement would not have been prevented or detected by Acme's internal controls, and would not have been detected by the audit firm.

FARDO INDUSTRIES INC.

Prepared by Professor Jeffrey Gandz

     Version: (A) 1993-10-22

Ron Bellamy, senior tax partner for a large public accounting firm was preparing for a meeting with John Gardner, president and chief executive officer of Fardo Industries. Fardo was about to conclude an acquisition of Shorter Software, a small software company specializing in developing custom software for several large organizations. The only minor problem was not directly related to the acquisition at all but, rather, how Fardo should amortize the $1.5 million goodwill payment included in the purchase price.

FARDO INDUSTRIES INC.

Fardo Industries was a privately held company with an estimated market value of $20 million and 1,000,000 shares outstanding. John Gardner, the founder, held 31 per cent of the shares; two other corporate officers held 20 per cent between them; the remaining shares were held by 30 outside investors, none of whom held more than five per cent.

Since its inception ten years previously, Fardo had specialized in acquiring small firms in the information systems field. It had raised the equity capital for this from small investors, mainly professionals such as doctors and lawyers, and also had substantial lines of credit at two banks.

SHORTER SOFTWARE

Founded by two brothers, Ben and John Shorter, former systems analysts and programmers with large computer firms, Shorter Software had developed a specialized niche in the software market, developing customized software to tie together a number of frequently utilized and commercially available application packages.

THE ACQUISITION

Ron Bellamy had helped the Shorters set up their business six years ago and had acted as their accountant since its start. He had been surprised when, some three months previously, Ben had indicated that they would like to try to sell the business.

> It really needs more capital to expand and, quite frankly, John and I are not very good business people . . . we're much happier doing the technical stuff. Maybe if we could sell the business to someone, remain associated with it for a number of years, and then retire, we could see a much better business development and have our own retirement nest eggs.

Ron Bellamy had mentioned this conversation to John Gardner since he thought that Fardo Industries might be interested . . . they were. Bellamy immediately suggested to Ben Shorter that they get some independent financial advice since he could not really act for both the buyer and the seller in this kind of acquisition. Shorter retained George Miller, an old friend who was an accountant with a small firm.

Negotiations proceeded very smoothly and a deal was soon struck. The Shorters were to get ten Fardo shares for each of their shares, with Fardo issuing 100,000 new shares for the acquisition. Furthermore, after five years, the Shorters would have to tender their shares to Fardo for an amount equivalent to ten times the earnings per share in the best of the five years following the acquisition. Ben Shorter called Ron Bellamy after the deal was agreed to.

> We're real happy, Ron. This Gardner guy seems pretty good to us and we think the deal's a fair one. Thanks for your help in this.

Ron Bellamy's Concern

Ron Bellamy did not feel quite as excited as Ben Shorter about this deal. Of the acquisition price of $2 million, $1.5 million was for goodwill, representing the relationships built up between the Shorters and their customers over the years. Such goodwill was not deductible for Fardo, however. Furthermore, the conventional accounting practices allowed a very wide range of alternative methods and amounts for writing off such goodwill. It could be written off quickly, over five years, or much more slowly, up to forty years! (See Exhibit 3 for guidelines.)

	Before Acquisition	After Acquisition
Current Assets	5,000	5,500
Fixed Assets	25,000	25,000
Goodwill	0	1,500
Total Assets	**30,000**	**32,000**
Current Liabilities	2,500	2,500
Long-Term Debt	17,500	17,500
Total Liabilities	**20,000**	**20,000**
Shareholders' Equity	10,000	12,000
Total Liabilities & Shareholders' Equity	**30,000**	**32,000**

Exhibit 1 Balance Sheet December 31, 1987 (000's)

FARDO INDUSTRIES INC. (amortization period of 5 years)

	Year 1	Year 2	Year 3	Year 4	Year 5	Year 6
Revenue	30,000,000	31,500,000	33,075,000	34,728,750	36,465,1888	38,288,447
Oper. Expenses	25,500,000	26,775,000	28,113,750	29,519,438	30,995,409	32,545,180
Amort. Goodwill	300,000	300,000	300,000	300,000	300,000	
Net Income	4,200,000	4,425,000	4,661,250	4,909,313	5,169,778	5,743,267
Tax	2,025,000	2,126,250	2,232,563	2,344,191	2,461,400	2,584,470
Earnings A/T	2,175,000	2,298,750	2,428,688	2,565,122	2,708,378	3,158,797
# Shares O/S	1,100,000	1,100,000	1,100,000	1,100,000	1,100,000	1,100,000
E.P.S.	1.98	2.09	2.21	2.23	2.46	2.87
Shorter's Tender @ 10 × earnings	1,977,273	2,089,773	2,207,898	2,331,929	2,462,162	2,871,634

Exhibit 2 Projected Income Statement for Six Years Subsequent to Acquisition of Shorter Software

GOODWILL

.54 Goodwill is commonly considered to be a composite of all the factors which cannot be individually identified and valued and which contribute to or accompany earnings capacity of a company. In a business combination, goodwill is represented by the difference between cost and the acquiring company's interest in the identifiable net assets.

.55 There are various possible approaches that may be considered in accounting for goodwill including the following:

(a) retain as an asset indefinitely unless a reduction in its value becomes evident;

(b) retain as an asset but permit amortization as an operating expense over its estimated limited life or over an arbitrary but specified maximum or minimum period;

(c) retain as an asset but require amortization as an operating expense over its estimated limited life or over an arbitrary but specified maximum or minimum period;

(d) write off complete amount at time of acquisition;

(e) reflect as a deduction from shareholders' equity unless a reduction in its value becomes evident.

.56 The accounting treatments which do not involve the amortization of goodwill are based on the contention that the value of goodwill is not consumed or used to produce earnings in the same manner as various other assets and therefore net income should not be reduced by mandatory amortization of goodwill. Furthermore, it is contended that net income should not be reduced by both amortization of goodwill and the current expenditures that are incurred to enhance or maintain the value of acquired intangible assets. Amortization of goodwill is also criticized as being arbitrary, since it is contended that the life of goodwill is indefinite and an estimated period of existence is not measurable.

.57 In the opinion of the Committee, however, goodwill does not have a limitless life, and therefore, amortization of goodwill should have the same theoretical recognition as is presently afforded depreciation of tangible assets. Goodwill existing at the acquisition gradually disappears and may, or may not, be replaced by new goodwill. Furthermore, goodwill is a cost which is incurred in anticipation of future earnings, and should be amortized by systematic charges to income over the periods of those future earnings in order to produce a proper matching of costs against revenue. The straight-line method of amortization should be applied. An analysis of all pertinent factors should normally enable the company to assess a reasonable estimated life of such goodwill. However, the period of amortization should not exceed forty years.

.58 *The amount reflected as goodwill at the date of acquisition should be amortized to income by the straight-line method over the estimated life of such goodwill; however, such period should not exceed forty years. The period of amortization should be disclosed.*

[April 1, 1974*]

.59 Because Recommendations are not normally given retroactive effect, the Recommendation in paragraph 1580.58 is not intended to apply to goodwill arising from business combinations where the date of acquisition (see paragraph 1580.39) is prior to the effective date of these Recommendations.

.60 Since goodwill is an asset (see paragraph 1580.42), it would be accounted for as such both at the date of acquisition and in subsequent periods to the extent that it has not been amortized. It would not be written off in a lump sum at the date of acquisition or shown as a deduction from shareholders' equity. A subsequent permanent impairment in value would result in a writedown of goodwill which would be treated either as a charge against income before extraordinary items, or as an extraordinary item, depending on the circumstances.

.61 *The amount attributed to goodwill should be shown separately on the balance sheet as an intangible asset, to the extent that it has not been amortized or written down. It should not be shown as a deduction from shareholders' equity.*

[April 1, 1974*]

.62 *Where there has been a permanent impairment in value of the unamortized portion of goodwill, it should be written down. The write-down should be treated as a charge against income.* The charge against income will be shown either in income before extraordinary items or as an extraordinary item, depending on the circumstances which give rise to the impairment in value. (See EXTRAORDINARY ITEMS, Section 3480.)

[April 1, 1974*]

Exhibit 3   CICA Guidelines

Clearly, writing this off over five years—as John Gardner wanted to do—would depress the earnings-per-share of Fardo Industries significantly in those five years. This would affect the amount that the Shorters would actually get for their shares at the end of the five-year period. Beyond that, however, it would also affect the earnings-per-share and, presumably, the share price for all investors, including small minority shareholders, several of whom were either clients of Bellamy's firms or personal acquaintances.

Ron Bellamy had to give Gardner some clear advice about what to do in this situation, but he was uncomfortable about the impact on the Shorters and other minority shareholders. Before meeting with Gardner, he decided to discuss the matter with George Clarke, a senior auditing partner with his firm, who was known throughout the accounting profession as an expert in accounting ethics. He wondered what Clarke was likely to say to him and, indeed, what the case was for either a quick or slow write-off.

THE ONTARIO CAPITAL GROUP

Prepared by Niels Billou under the supervision of Professor David J. Sharp

Frederick Jones, branch manager at the London, Ontario branch of the Ontario Capital Group (OCG), was alarmed. It was late October 1997 and Jones had just finished a quarterly review meeting with one of his investment advisers, Dan Cooper. It appeared that since the previous July, Cooper had been injecting his own capital into a client's account that had been losing value, but which had now recovered and had made a profit. As Jones pondered his next move, he thought to himself, "How did this go unnoticed? But no harm has come to anyone—why should I do anything about it?"

THE ONTARIO CAPITAL GROUP—LONDON BRANCH

The Ontario Capital Group was a mid-sized brokerage house with offices throughout Southwestern Ontario. The London, Ontario branch had been a moderately successful operation throughout its 20-year history; however, its performance had suffered in the past two years as other branches posted higher trading volumes and assets under management.

The branch had been under pressure from the head office in Toronto to improve its results. The employees, many of whom had been at the branch since its opening, felt "under the gun" to improve their performance.

DAN COOPER

Dan Cooper was 50, married with three children and had been with the London branch of OCG for the past 15 years. His performance had been consistently average over the years. His quiet, reserved style attracted mostly elderly retirees. One of his colleagues commented:

Dan is a quiet, conservative person. He's not a high volume trader, and generally recommends established securities that yield a stable return. His clients are mostly pensioners and widowers in fixed incomes with a small nest egg. Many are quite elderly, and we joke with him that if he doesn't lower his minimum age requirement below 70 he's not going to have any clients left pretty soon. I think he must be getting tired of our ribbing because I've seen him advising some young professional types lately.

THE QUARTERLY REVIEW

All investment advisers had quarterly reviews with the branch manager to discuss performance for the past quarter as well as discuss targets for the upcoming quarter. Trading volumes, assets under management, number of existing and new clients and selling success rates were all examined.

As Jones was reviewing Cooper's file prior to the meeting, he noticed a number of trades in one particular account, under the name Gerry Marchisi, that struck him as odd, given Cooper's trading style and clientele.

THE MARCHISI ACCOUNT

Gerry Marchisi was 31 years of age, married, and the president of Marchisi Supermarkets, a family owned firm. He had an annual income of approximately $75,000 per year and a net worth of approximately $300,000. He opened a margin account in March of 1990 and listed his investment objectives as 30 per cent growth, 40 per cent growth with risk, and 30 per cent venture situations. The account was not approved as a discretionary or a margin account.

The following is a summary of the trading activity on the file for the period July to September 1997:[1]

- On July 3, 1,000 shares of Movie World shares were purchased at a price of $14.00.
- On July 21, the value of the Movie World shares had declined to a price of $3.25. Marchisi's account had a negative equity of $492 and was undermargined by $4,534. On that day, 1,000 shares were sold for $3.25, resulting in a loss of approximately $11,000. Despite the sale, the account still had a negative

equity of $552, and was still undermargined by $3,600, resulting in a margin call.

- On July 23, $4,500 was deposited into the account in order to satisfy the margin call. This resulted in a net equity of $3,600 and excess margin of $635.
- In August, the shares lost their option eligibility and the account was once again undermargined. Three more deposits were made between August 15 and August 30, for a total of $1,200.
- On September 5, Cooper bought 3,000 shares of Cable Communications for $3.25. At this point, the account was undermargined by $4,800.
- On September 12, the settlement date for the trade, Cooper sold the 3,000 Cable Communications shares for $5.50, resulting in a profit of approximately $6,000 (after commissions and interest). The account now had excess margin of approximately $4,500.
- On September 15, Cooper bought 5,000 shares of DT Technologies for $7.875. This resulted in a the account being undermargined by approximately $14,500.
- On September 20, two days before the settlement date, Cooper sold the 5,000 DT Technologies shares for $9.875, resulting in a profit of $8,500. The account now had excess margin of $14,000.

CURRENT SITUATION

Cooper seemed nervous and apprehensive from the beginning of the review. When Jones further questioned Cooper about these trades, Cooper hesitantly explained the story.

Gerry Marchisi was referred to me by his grandfather, Umberto, one of my long-time clients. He's a pretty aggressive young guy, wants to go for the risky stocks that have the potential for big gains. Not my sort of client, really, but with all the talk lately of getting the numbers up, he seemed like the new type of client that management wants us to go after. At first I bought him some equity mutual funds, but he wanted higher returns and was willing to take more risk. So I recommended Movie World—rumor had it that it was a takeover target and the stock was going to go through the roof. The rumors proved to be wrong, their second quarter results were disastrous, and the company was being sued for a breach of contract that could bankrupt the company if they lost. Marchisi blamed this all on me and told me he would not put any more money into the account to satisfy margin calls or settle trades. Given that he was undermargined, he was obliged to put in more money. I told him that we could make up the money, and he told me to do as I pleased, but he wasn't going inject any more cash into the account. I didn't really know what to do, so I put in my own money to satisfy the margin calls.

I then received these tips on these two stocks, so I bought them on the company's account and flipped them before the settlement date. Thankfully, the stocks went up and now Marchisi's original loss has been eliminated, and he's even made a profit.

As Cooper finished his story and left, Jones though to himself, "How could this go unnoticed? We should have controls to prevent such a situation from occurring. At the same time, to what extent is Cooper to blame? What kind of a message are we sending when an essentially decent guy like Cooper feels compelled to act the way he did?"

NOTE

1. During that period the Marchisi account included other securities that were not traded.

THE JEFFREY VERDE ACCOUNT

Prepared by Michelle Theobalds under the supervision of Professor David Sharp

Version: (A) 1999-02-12

On December 5, 1997, Sarah Robertson, an investment advisor at Securities Trading Company (STC), looked over Jeffrey Verde's recent transaction history and contemplated her next move. That morning, she had received a call from Verde to enter into six long March Standard and Poor's 500 (S&P 500) Index futures contracts. Mr. Verde had a history of temporarily exceeding his trading limits,[1] and this most recent order would once again put him over the limit.

Verde was actually the client of her colleague, David Simpson. However, Sarah, who had recently passed the Futures Licensing Course, was overseeing his accounts while he was away on sick leave. In response to Verde's request, Sarah informed him that STC's research department had issued a sell recommendation on those contracts in view of the continuing uncertainty in the Asian markets. Verde replied,

Yes I know . . . David already told me. However, I am convinced that your analysts are wrong. The market is heading for further gains and I want to be a part of it.

Sarah knew that Verde was an experienced speculator in the market and had been a client of Simpson's for almost 20 years. She responded, "OK, Mr. Verde, I'll see if I can put through the order."

As soon as she hung up the telephone, Sarah regretted her hasty decision. Although she knew of Mr. Verde's long-standing relationship with David Simpson and the firm, she did not know much else about him. She decided to check Verde's Futures Application Form and also printed his recent transaction history. Sarah also consulted Simpson's sales assistant to find out more details on Verde.

Jeffrey Verde

Simpson's sales assistant knew Jeffrey Verde very well. He had met and spoken with Verde on a number of occasions, and, therefore, he was able to fill in the details not included in Verde's application form.

Jeffrey Verde, aged 60, was a lawyer by profession. Over his 30-year career, he had practised with several large law firms, was an in-house counsel for a mutual fund, and then, finally, counsel for a consumer finance organization. Two years ago, Verde's employment was terminated, however, his employer continued to pay his salary until the end of last year. Since then, Verde had attempted to generate an income stream through consulting, writing a book and some highly speculative projects. Up until December, these attempts were largely unsuccessful.

In August 1997, Jeffrey Verde got married. While the marriage did result in Verde moving to a larger apartment, Mrs. Verde was not dependent on him for income. Although she had worked at a variety of jobs, her main vocation was exotic flowers. Shortly after they were married, the Verdes travelled to Florida to explore the possibility of opening a flower shop in a trendy section of Palm Beach. Although the initial plan fell through, it was their intention to look for other business opportunities in the area and to eventually move to Florida.

Jeffrey Verde was in Toronto in November and had since transacted several trades through Simpson. He had mentioned to Simpson that he was worried about his mother, who had been ailing for some time.

Relationship With David Simpson

Verde and Simpson met over 20 years ago when Simpson was an account executive at a rival brokerage. Simpson, who was also trained as a lawyer, inherited Verde's account from another broker. At that time, Verde had a small account, mostly in common shares. Verde was very interested in the markets, and, over time, became a more active trader. Verde and Simpson's relationship may be described as one of mutual respect. Jeffrey Verde viewed Simpson as a very knowledgeable and reliable broker, while Simpson described Verde as a "keen student of the market, always looking for opportunities for successful trading."

In the early days, Simpson and Verde dabbled in commodity futures contracts (hogs, cattle) on the Chicago Mercantile Exchange. Over time, Verde learned the business from Simpson and increasingly made decisions on his own. He always followed the markets in the daily newspapers and the financial network on television. He also subscribed to market oriented periodicals and believed in the Elliot Wave Theory of market cycles. Like a professional technical analyst, Verde kept charts of market activity and used the charts to make forecasts. He was particularly attracted to "hot equity new issues" and futures trading in order to make significant short-term gains. Clearly, Jeffrey Verde was not a conservative investor.

In 1992, Simpson moved to Securities Trading Company (STC) and Verde's accounts totalling $85,000[2] were transferred with him. According to the normal procedure, Verde filled out and signed the following documents: New Client Application Form, Customer Account Agreement, Futures Account Application Form, Risk Disclosure Statement and a Futures Trading Agreement. On the application forms Verde indicated an annual income of $52,000 and a net worth (and liquid net worth) of $225,000.

In the same year, Simpson introduced Verde to stock index futures contracts and in particular, S&P 500 Index contracts. Within one year, Verde was trading these contracts confidently, while relying less on the commodity futures and equities. At that time, Verde's trading in the markets increased significantly when his mother chose to distribute a portion of her estate. He received $120,000, which he put into his accounts at STC. From time to time, Verde would accumulate large cash balances from liquidated positions and realized profit. Simpson recommended an interest-bearing stock account to keep these cash balances until required. Verde agreed, understanding that the transfers to this account would be temporary until the funds were needed to enter into more futures contracts or to meet margin calls. As long as there were sufficient funds in the stock account, then margin calls would be satisfied without giving notice to Verde.

Verde was a "careful position trader." He would make an informed decision on the near term market prospects and hold that position regardless of daily fluctuations. Over the past three years, Verde had been successful with his trading. In fact, the profits on his accounts in the past two years had exceeded the annual income he had declared on his application form. In 1995, the year-end summary indicated that Verde had made a profit of US$83,870. While last year, his profits were US$114,860 for the year.

In January 1997, perhaps in recognition of his changed circumstances, Verde acquired a portfolio of Canadian and United States income-producing stocks. Therefore, the cash reserve in the stock account that was previously used to enter into futures contracts or to meet margin calls was depleted, leaving share assets in the account. By the end of March 1997, the cash position had declined from a credit balance of $233,000 as at December 31, 1996, to a debit balance of $35,000. However, Verde continued to trade in commodity and index futures on a regular basis.

While Verde had a good relationship with Simpson and STC, the relationship was by no means exclusive. Verde had accounts with several other brokerages in Canada and the United States. Recently, Verde had asked Simpson for a discount on stock trades. When Simpson told him that discounting was against company policy, Verde transferred a part of his portfolio to a local discount brokerage. It was not known exactly how much business Verde conducted with other firms.

Recent Transaction History

Now that Sarah knew some of the details of Jeffrey Verde's circumstances, risk profile and

trading experience, she turned to a summary of his recent trading transactions. Exhibit 1 shows Verde's transactions for the period November 1 to December 2.

Trading Limit

The first column Sarah looked at was the trading limit, which was set at $100,000. She thought this figure was high, given Verde's most recent Futures Account Application Form. In 1994, Verde had submitted financial information indicating net worth of $550,000, liquid net worth of $250,000 and an annual income of $65,000. STC's compliance manual, filed and approved by the Toronto Stock Exchange (TSE), stated that the "10-40 rule" would be applied in order to establish client trading limits. This rule stated:

> The trading limit for a client will not exceed a level of 10 per cent of the client's net worth or 40 per cent of liquid net worth **whichever is less**.

In the event that a net worth statement is not provided or can not be verified, the account can only be carried if the client provides excess margin or other collateral to eliminate the credit risk. The trading limit was established to minimize the risk of a loss that might endanger a client's standard of living or ability to meet obligations. According to the 10-40 rule, Sarah calculated that Verde's trading limit should not have exceeded $55,000. A total net worth of at least a million dollars was required for a trading limit of $100,000. The trading limit of $100,000 had been approved in February. Justification for the increase was US$281,000 held in Verde's Canadian accounts. A note from the credit manager indicated that the accounts should be "monitored regularly."

Even more disturbing was the "Original Margin Req." column. This column was the total margin required by STC based on the futures contracts held by the client. The original margin required should always be less than the trading limit. Over the past month, Verde had exceeded his trading limit every day except November 28,

Client: Jeffrey Verde

Date		(a) Closing Balance	(b) Gain (Loss) Unrealized	(c) Net Equity	(d) Actual Call (Excess)	(e) Funds in (Out)	(f) Trading Limit	(g) Original Margin Req.	(h) Purchase and (Sale)	(i) Gain (Loss) Realized
1-Nov	Tues	168,460	(80,115)	88,345	15,440	(18,400)	100,000	141,940	—	—
2-Nov	Wed	183,900	(89,095)	94,805	25	15,440	100,000	141,963	—	—
3-Nov	Thur	183,900	(103,542)	80,358	61,530	—	100,000	141,910	—	—
4-Nov	Fri	245,455	(125,597)	119,858	—	61,555	100,000	141,963	—	—
7-Nov	Mon	245,455	(131,876)	113,579	(818)	—	100,000	141,963	—	—
8-Nov	Tues	244,637	(141,702)	102,935	(2,725)	(818)	100,000	141,760	—	—
9-Nov	Wed	241,912	(148,145)	93,767	3,543	(2,725)	100,000	141,760	—	—
10-Nov	Thur	245,455	(125,130)	120,325	3,081	3,543	100,000	141,621	—	—
11-Nov	Fri	248,536	(96,722)	151,814	(11,113)	3,081	100,000	140,700	—	—
14-Nov	Mon	237,536	(98,162)	139,374	—	(11,000)	100,000	140,700	—	—
15-Nov	Tues	202,691	(94,050)	108,641	—	—	100,000	140,700	6(6) T-Bond	(34,845)
16-Nov	Wed	202,691	(116,319)	86,372	—	—	100,000	140,700	—	—
17-Nov	Thur	104,633	(7,117)	97,516	—	—	100,000	140,700	10(10) S&P	(98,058)
18-Nov	Fri	104,633	(562)	104,071	—	—	100,000	140,700	—	—
21-Nov	Mon	104,633	(27,902)	76,731	63,975	—	100,000	140,700	—	—
22-Nov	Tues	168,608	29,905	198,513	(57,812)	63,975	100,000	140,700	—	—
23-Nov	Wed	110,908	29,725	140,633	—	(57,700)	100,000	140,700	—	—
24-Nov	Thur	110,908	(14,680)	96,228	—	—	100,000	140,700	—	—

Exhibit 1   Summary of Commodity and Index Futures Trading Data

(Continued)

Date		(a) Closing Balance	(b) Gain (Loss) Unrealized	(c) Net Equity	(d) Actual Call (Excess)	(e) Funds in (Out)	(f) Trading Limit	(g) Original Margin Req	(h) Purchase and (Sale)	(i) Gain (Loss) Realized
25-Nov	Fri	110,908	26,422	137,330	—	—	100,000	140,700	—	—
28-Nov	Mon	144,174	12,730	156,904	(76,202)	—	100,000	80,700	(6) S&P	33,265
29-Nov	Tues	68,174	1,095	69,269	40,000	(76,000)	100,000	120,700	4 S&P	—
30-Nov	Wed	113,857	355	114,212	9,500	40,000	100,000	130,200	2 S&P 7(7) crude oil	5,683
1-Dec	Thur	156,122	(1,982)	154,140	(83,941)	9,500	100,000	70,000	(6) S&P	32,765
2-Dec	Fri	74,105	537	74,642	(8,041)	(83,700)	100,000	66,600	(4) Cdn. $	1,683

Exhibit 1   Summary of Commodity and Index Futures Trading Data

Explanation of Columns

(a) This represents the cash funds in the account.

(b) Unrealized gain or loss on open positions.

(c) Net equity is the balance plus or minus the unrealized gain or loss on futures contracts held.

(d) Variation margin call or excess generated due to market activity for that day. A margin call takes place if net equity falls below the maintenance margin level. If this happens net equity must be replenished back to the original margin level.

(e) Actual cash funds transferred into or out of the account.

(f) The trading limit is the maximum total original margin requirement the client is allowed to carry. The limit is set by the client in the Futures Trading Agreement.

(g) Total original margin required by STC based on the futures contracts held (e.g. $10,000 for each S&P contract).

(h) The number and type of contracts purchased or sold on a particular date. For example, 8 (8) indicates that on the same day, eight contracts were opened and then closed; 6 indicates the opening of six new contracts.

(i) The gain or loss from the offset of contracts.

December 1, and December 2. At the end of December 2, Verde's required amount stood at $66,600. Sarah quickly calculated that if she purchased the six S&P 500[3] contracts that Verde requested that morning, then the original margin required would rise to $126,600, once again exceeding his trading limit.

Margin[4] Calls

Sarah noticed that there had been eight variation margin calls in the past month. Virtually all of the margin calls had been satisfied via a transfer of funds into the futures/commodity account. On further investigation, Sarah realized that the source of the funds was the interest bearing stock account that Verde had opened some years previously. However, since his January stock purchases, the cash balance in that account had been depleted. Therefore, the "funds" that were being transferred from this account were really excess margin or loans from STC using the stock assets in the account as collateral. All of the stocks that Verde had in this account were option eligible securities,[5] therefore, he could borrow up to 70 per cent of the market value of these stocks from STC. As per the usual arrangement, Verde was not informed of the margin calls on his commodity account as long as there was sufficient margin in the stock account to cover the calls. On December 2, Verde had equity valued at $117,000 in the stock account.

This use of "margin to cover margin" was alluded to in the STC Customer Account Agreement signed by Verde:

Ten. Any and all securities and any credit balance held or carried by you to the delivery of which you are entitled under this agreement for the account of the undersigned shall stand as security for any and all of the indebtedness or obligations of the undersigned to you, however arising, and in whatever account appearing, as well as for any contingent liability to you by reason of any guarantee by the undersigned of the account of any other person. Whenever the undersigned shall carry more than one account with you, you may at any time, without notice to the undersigned, charge any one or more of said accounts with any sum upon crediting any other of the said accounts with the same sum.

Conclusion

As Sarah looked over the recent transactions and documentation, she pondered her next move. She had already spent over half an hour investigating the Verde account, and she had to make a quick decision. Since Sarah had recently completed the Futures Licensing Course, the regulations (see Exhibit 2 for an excerpt) regarding futures contracts and the standards of practice were fresh in her mind. However, she was reluctant to approach her supervisor. Her colleague who normally managed this account, David Simpson, was a well respected, experienced broker in the firm. He must have been aware of the status of the Verde account, yet he had continued to accept orders from his client. In addition, the credit and compliance staff at STC had not restricted Verde's trading and had even given him more leverage than provided for in the "10-40 rule." As Sarah thought about a suitable course of action, she was very aware that whatever she did may impact her long-term prospects at STC and her career.

Notes

1. Trading limits refer to the original margin required.

2. All dollar amounts are in Canadian dollars unless otherwise indicated.

3. Each S&P contract required an additional $10,000 in margin.

4. See Appendix for definitions of margin and related terminology.

5. An option eligible security qualifies as an underlying security for either Canadian or U.S. exchange-traded put and call options. To qualify, common shares must have a market price of five dollars or higher. In addition, the company must meet specific criteria as to the number of shareholders, number of publicly held shares outstanding and market capitalization.

1800.5 The designated futures contract principal or designated futures contract options principal of a Member designated pursuant to Regulation 1800.2 shall ensure that the handling of customer business relating to futures contracts or futures contract options, as the case may be, is in accordance with the By-laws, Regulations, Rulings and Policies of the Association. In this respect the Member shall have written procedures acceptable to the Director of Compliance describing the control, supervisory and delegation procedures used by the Member to ensure compliance with the By-laws, Regulations, Rulings and Policies. In the absence or incapacity of the designated futures contract principal or futures contract options principal or when the trading activity of the Member requires additional qualified persons in connection with the supervision of the Member's business, an alternate, if any, shall assume the authority and responsibility of such designated persons. Without limiting the foregoing, each designated futures contract principal and designated futures contract options principal shall be responsible for the following matters with respect to trading or advising in respect of futures contracts and futures contract options, respectively:

(a) opening all new contracts accounts pursuant to a new account application form approved by the Director of Compliance and the approval in writing on such form of all accounts prior to the commencement of any trading activity;

(b) using due diligence to learn and remain informed of the essential facts relative to every customer (including the customer's identity, creditworthiness and reputation) and to every order or account accepted, to ensure that acceptance of any order for any account is within the bounds of good business practice and to ensure that recommendations made for any account are appropriate for the customer and in keeping with the customer's investment objectives;

(c) obtaining prior to the commencement of any trading activity in any futures account the executed futures contract or futures contract trading agreement referred to in Regulation 1800.9 or the letter of undertaking referred to in Regulation 1800.10;

(d) imposing any appropriate restriction on futures contracts or futures contract options accounts and the proper designation of such accounts and related orders;

(e) the continuous supervision of each day's trading in futures contracts and futures contract options and the completion of a review of each day's trading no later than the next following trading day;

(f) reviewing on a monthly basis the cumulative trading activity of each futures contracts and each futures contract options account no later than the day of mailing of the monthly statement for each month;

(g) monitoring performance as necessary of any duties that have been delegated by the futures contract principal or futures contract options principal, as the case may be; and

(h) performing such other responsibilities as the Director of Compliance may prescribe from time to time.

A designated futures contract principal or designated futures contract options principal may delegate by written direction the performance of any of his or her duties under this regulation 1800.5 (except those described in clauses (g) or (h) unless permitted by the Director of Compliance and except those that are expressly stated not to be delegated) to any person whom he or she has reason to believe is capable of performing such duties; provided that futures contract principal or futures contract options principal shall remain fully responsible for the performance of such duties.

1800.9 Each Member shall have and maintain with each customer trading in futures contracts or futures contract options an account agreement in writing defining the rights and obligations between them on such subjects as the Director of Compliance may from time to time determine, and shall include the following:

(a) the rights of the Member to exercise discretion in accepting orders;

(b) the obligation of the Member with respect to errors and/or omissions and qualification of the time periods during which orders will be accepted for execution;

Exhibit 2   Excerpts From Investment Dealers Association of Canada Regulation 1800,
Commodity Futures Contracts and Options, 1994   *(Continued)*

(c) the obligation of the customer in respect of the payment of his or her indebtedness to the Member and the maintenance of adequate margin and security, including the conditions under which funds, securities or other property held in the account or any other accounts of the customer may be applied to such indebtedness or margin;

(d) the obligation of the customer in respect of commissions, if any, on futures contracts or futures contract options bought and sold for his or her account;

(e) the obligation of the customer in respect of the payment of interest, if any, on debit balances in his or her account;

(f) the extent of the right of the Member to make use of free credit balances in the customer's account either in its own business or to cover debit balances in the same or other accounts, and the consent, if given, of the customer to the Member taking the other side to the customer's transactions from time to time;

(g) the rights of the Member in respect of raising money on and pledging securities and other assets held in the customer's account;

(h) the extent of the right of the Member to otherwise deal with securities and other assets in the customer's account and to hold the same as collateral security for the customer's indebtedness;

(i) the customer's obligation to comply with the rules pertaining to futures contracts or futures contract options with respect to reporting, position limits and exercise limits, as applicable, as established by the commodity futures exchange on which such futures contracts or futures contract options are traded or its clearinghouse;

(j) the right of the Member, if so required, to provide regulatory authorities with information and/or reports related to reporting limits and position limits;

(k) the acknowledgement by the customer that he or she has received the current risk disclosure statement provided for in Regulation 1800.2 unless provided for by other approved means;

(l) the right of the Member to impose trading limits and to close out futures contracts or futures contract options under specified conditions;

(m) that minimum margin will be required from the customer in such amounts and at such times as the commodity futures exchange on which a contract is entered or its clearing house may prescribe and in such greater amounts at other times as prescribed by the By-laws and Regulations and as determined by the Member, and that such funds or property may be commingled and used by the Member in the conduct of its business;

(n) in the case of futures contract options accounts, the method of allocation of exercise assignment notices and the customer's obligation to instruct the Member to close out contracts prior to the expiry date; and

(o) unless provided for in a separate agreement, the authority, if any, of the Member to effect trades for the customer on a discretionary basis, which authority shall be separately acknowledged in a part of the agreement prominently marked off from the remainder and shall not be inconsistent with any By-laws or Regulations pertaining to discretionary accounts.

Exhibit 2   Excerpts From Investment Dealers Association of Canada Regulation 1800, Commodity Futures Contracts and Options, 1994

Source: Materials provided by the Canadian Securities Institute.

APPENDIX: MARGIN ACCOUNTS

Stock Margin Account

A stock margin account is a special brokerage account that allows a client to buy securities on credit, by borrowing part of the purchase price from the dealer, or to sell securities short. The word *margin* in this case refers to the amount of funds the investor must personally provide. The margin plus the amount provided by the dealer (the dealer's loan) together make up the total amount required to complete the transaction.

Interest on the margin loan is calculated daily on that month's debit balance. The exchanges regulate the amount of credit that a Member may extend to customers on the purchase of securities. Below are the maximum loan values allowed:

On Listed Securities Selling:	Maximum Loan Value
at $5.00 and over, qualifying as "Option Eligible Securities"	70% of market value
at $2.00 and over	50% of market value
at $1.75 to $1.99	40% of market value
at $1.50 to $1.74	20% of market value
under $1.50	No loan value

A margin call is generated on a stock margin account when the client's margin deposit is less than the gross margin requirement (30 per cent of market value in the case of option eligible securities).

Futures Margin Account

When a futures contract is initiated both the buyer and the seller must post margin with the Member firm through whom the transaction took place. The Member firm in turn submits the margin to the clearinghouse. The future margin represents a good faith deposit or a performance bond. It does not represent a partial payment or a loan from the Member firm as in the case of equity margin.

Futures exchanges set both original (initial) and maintenance (variation) margin levels. Original margin is the amount of capital the client must deposit when a futures position is first established. Maintenance margin, generally set at a level under the original margin, is essentially a threshold level. Once net equity (funds in the account plus open profit or minus open loss) in the account falls below the maintenance margin level, the client will receive a margin call that requires him/her to replenish the account back to the original margin level.

Minimum margin requirements for futures contracts are generally established by the exchange where the futures contract is traded. The exchange sets both the original and maintenance margin requirements. Member firms are allowed to levy more than the minimum requirements if they so choose. Margin requirements are based on several factors including the size of the contract, the volatility of the underlying security, the type of position, the type of customer (hedger or speculator), and whether the futures contract has entered its spot month.

Source: Materials provided by the Canadian Securities Institute.

2

ETHICS OF THE RELATIONSHIP BETWEEN THE FIRM AND ITS CUSTOMERS

Unethical marketing practices have possibly the longest history of any area of business ethics—after all, the term *snake oil* entered the English language before the advent of the public company. This chapter covers the rights and responsibilities of companies to their customers, as well as questionable selling and marketing practices. Ethical analysis uses ideas around ethical relativism (can an action be justified because it is common practice?), fairness, and egoism (invariably the self-interest of the decision maker).

One key problem in marketing is information asymmetry, particularly in retail marketing. The firm and its management know far more about a product and its potential uses and capability for harm than the public who buy it. Does this mean that a firm has a special obligation to communicate clearly to the customer the properties of the product it sells? A number of common marketing practices have been described as misleading at best, including making the packaging larger than necessary to give the appearance of more contents.

The Hayward & Guzman: Disposable Contact Lenses case provides an interesting dilemma. The company researches and develops contact lens products and has recently developed a new disposable contact lens. It has identified two market segments with different price sensitivity. To reach these segments, the products will need to be packaged and sold differently. A marketing representative for Hayward & Guzman must develop a marketing mix for the two segments and determine pricing for each product. Is there an ethical problem with selling a product at two prices in different markets, and, if so, what is it?

Another marketing area fraught with ethical problems is the relationship between buyer and seller, in which the seller is often under considerable pressure to meet sales targets. This places considerable power in the hands of the buyer, especially when the dollar amount of the sale is large, and several competing products have very similar specifications. This problem arises in the Cruickshank, Garth & Romano case. Richard Romano, a principal of a small real estate appraisal firm, faced an interesting ethical dilemma. A client had just stated that if the firm did not increase its appraised value of the client's commercial property by $4.5 million (15%), he would take his business elsewhere. Potentially, the client had a large volume of business that the young appraisal firm could certainly use. Romano must consider the firm's economic health in the short and long terms, his personal values, and the ethical guidelines of the Appraisal Institute of Canada in making this decision.

Sometimes, the approach made by the customer is more devious, as in the Grandview Excavators Ltd. case. Grandview Excavators is a privately owned company that prepares and excavates land for construction development. A recently promoted project estimator has prepared a quote for a project. He receives a phone call from the customer stating that the quote was too low and is asked to resubmit a new quote for a suggested higher amount. He makes the adjustment and submits the second quote. A few days later, the company is awarded the project, and work begins immediately. After the project is completed, the project estimator receives payment and discovers the payment is less than the original quote amount. It is not clear why the payment has been reduced, and he must decide whether to contact the client directly for an explanation or advise his boss. From a relativist ethical perspective, is this normal business practice, and even if it is, is it morally acceptable? The Peter Farber (A) case introduces a new angle on relativism, in that Peter Farber works in his father's investment advice business, and his father had apparently been bending industry regulations for decades to please one of his clients. Peter is now serving the client and wonders whether he should irritate the client, and possibly his father, by sticking to the letter of the regulations or to adopt a "customer is always right" approach. A subsequent case (Peter Farber [B]) is available separately, which explores some of the consequences of Peter's actual decision in the A case.

The ethical challenge becomes more difficult when the customer and seller are located in different countries, where cultural and ethical norms differ. These cases are included in Chapter 4.

HAYWARD & GUZMAN: DISPOSABLE CONTACT LENSES

Prepared by Eric Dolansky under the supervision of Professor Niraj Dawar

Version: (A) 2003-07-17

OVERVIEW

Nadine Palmer looked over the report on her desk once again. In two days, she would be expected to give a recommendation regarding the pricing of the new disposable contact lenses, and she was unsure of what to do. It was by far the most difficult decision that she'd had to deal with during her short time in Hayward & Guzman's eye care division. She knew that Shannon Cole, her superior in the marketing department, would look upon her recommendation with interest and not only as an informed opinion as to what should be done. The pricing decision had significant implications for divisional profitability over the short to medium term, as this was one of the two new product launches the company was counting on to generate growth.

Palmer understood the basic factors that should go into the pricing decision, but she was uncertain about the price differential that should be charged for the two versions of the product. It had already been determined that the new lenses would be offered as two distinct offerings: a two-week-use lens, and a 24-hour-use lens, targeted at two distinct segments that had been identified in the market. The physical lens in the two packages was identical, but its usage would be quite different, and the benefits each product would represent to users were distinct. Because the value of the lens to the consumers in the different segments was so different, Palmer knew that a different price could be charged. She would therefore need to develop specific pricing recommendations.

Contact Lenses

Until these new, short-term-use lenses were created and their use approved by regulatory bodies, the only vision correction options available to consumers were glasses, long-term-use contact lenses and, more recently, small proportions of the population were opting for corrective eye surgery. Glasses were the more traditional, durable and economical alternative, but contact lenses had gained in popularity over the previous 10 years, especially among younger consumers. About one-third of all those who needed vision

correction used contact lenses and supplemented their use with glasses. Laser eye surgery, while growing, remained confined to a small proportion of the total population, perhaps due to its high costs and perceived risk.

Lenses continued to grow in popularity. However, in their current form, traditional lenses presented a number of problems for consumers. The main problem with the existing lenses was the amount of care and cleaning they required. Various solutions and soaps were needed to keep the lenses free of deposits (the prices of these cleaning products are in Exhibit 1); unclean lenses could increase the chances of infection and damage to the eye. If the lenses were not kept in special solutions, they would be damaged and would need to be replaced. As well, the lenses could not be worn overnight or they would severely irritate the eyes. They had to be removed while swimming or they could be lost. Lenses could not be worn for too many hours per day or the eye could suffer damage. And finally, even with a great deal of care, on average the lenses needed to be replaced every 18 to 24 months, at a retail price of $60 per pair. Moreover, as stated above, most contact lens users wore glasses when not wearing lenses.

Despite these costs and inconveniences, contact lens use was gaining popularity all across North America. Users tended to prefer the way they looked without glasses. Also, contact lenses

Item	Average Retail Price	Frequency of Purchase	Approximate Annual Cost
Saline (Storage) Solution	$8	4 Weeks	$104
Contact Lens Soap	$5	Monthly	$60
Rinsing Solutions	$6	3 Weeks	$104
Contact Lenses	$60	18–24 Months	$35
Contact Lens Case	$6	24 Months	$3
Total Annual Cost of Lenses			**$306**
Glasses	$220	2–3 Years	$85

Exhibit 1   Breakdown of the Costs of Contact Lenses and Glasses

offered clear peripheral vision, whereas glasses could not offer this advantage, important especially to people who enjoyed sports. Although consumers were willing to put up with the demands of contact lens use, if an easier solution were available it would be perceived as a great value.

Customer Segments for Short-Term Contact Lenses

Hayward & Guzman had invested close to $18 million over the past five years developing an easier-to-use contact lens product. Their research had paid off, as they now had a contact lens approved for use that was considerably cheaper to produce than the existing contact lens and could be worn continuously for two to three weeks without cleaning, even during sleep. The solutions and soaps previously required would no longer be necessary. At the end of two weeks the consumer could discard the lenses and replace them with a new pair.

Based on the considerable market research that Palmer and Cole had reviewed the previous week, two distinct target segments had been identified. The first was users of traditional lenses who would switch to a more convenient product, and the second was a smaller, but potentially very lucrative segment of occasional users who normally wore glasses. It was estimated that about 50 per cent of traditional lens users would switch to Hayward & Guzman's lenses in the long term, with about 10 per cent to 20 per cent of these switching within the first year, depending on the first year promotional budget. The size of the occasional user market was more difficult to estimate, but the market research appeared to indicate that approximately 15 per cent of current glasses users would use the product on average six times per year. Palmer and Cole recognized that the market size for the second segment would be even more sensitive to marketing expenditures.

Traditional lens users would be attracted to the new lenses for their convenience. To these users, Hayward & Guzman needed to present the benefits of not having to constantly worry about one's lenses. The simplicity of the long-term wear disposable lenses would replace the daily complexity of traditional lenses.

Occasional users normally wore glasses. But for specific usage occasions, such as playing sports, or at times when they wanted to be seen without glasses, the disposable lenses could be purchased, used and disposed of, without too much trouble. An initial visit to the optometrist would allow them a reusable three-year prescription to purchase disposable lenses.

Palmer and Cole had agreed that the new product was to be presented, in effect, as two products. One would be a two-week continuous use contact lens, targeted at traditional contact lens users as well as those who had considered buying contacts in the past but decided against it because of the rigorous care involved. The other would be a 24-hour-use disposable contact lens, targeted at those who do not currently use contact lenses and do not want to use them on a regular basis, but would like to sporadically replace their glasses on special occasions, such as to engage in sports or for a date. The primary difference in positioning for the two segments would be the label on the packaging. The product package targeted at the traditional lens wearers would indicate that the lens was a two-week lens, while the other occasional lens would read "24-hour" lens. The managers believed that this difference, coupled with differences in packaging color, and perhaps differences in multiple packs (e.g., six packs) would differentiate the offerings sufficiently for the two segments.

The Pricing Decision

Palmer had been asked to provide a recommendation for the pricing of the two product offerings, as well as a suggested package size (i.e., how many lenses would be bundled together under one price). Cole had made it clear that she wanted only one bundle offered for each of the two products.

The cost of producing a pair of disposable lenses was $2. This amount included production costs (raw material, labor, allocated overhead). A budget for marketing costs had not yet been established, but it would be a function of the pricing and projected market shares of the two types of lenses. A separate budget would be established for each of the two segments. Hayward & Guzman expected sales to increase by 10 per cent to 20 per cent annually for five years, at which point they would more or less level off.

Palmer felt the way to arrive at pricing was to consider the value being delivered to customers. First, she took the price of permanent lenses into consideration. These would no longer be required and provided a starting point for her calculations. Next, she factored in the solutions and soaps that consumers would no longer need to buy. Then, more qualitatively, she estimated the value of convenience to customers. She conducted this analysis for both segments.

Nadine Palmer's Pricing Decision

Less than 48 hours before she was expected to present her recommendation to Shannon Cole, Palmer still had not decided on a price for the new products. The disposable lenses had the potential to be a blockbuster product, and their profitability to the company would be greatly affected by the pricing decision. Success or failure of this product would determine Hayward & Guzman's capability to fund the development of new products and, consequently, the future of the company.

CRUICKSHANK, GARTH & ROMANO[1]

Prepared by Daniel Sinclair under the supervision of Professor John Haywood-Farmer

Version: (A) 2002-06-24

$30.5 million! Are you crazy? I know the property is worth more than that! Even last year, Allied Property Services' $31 million appraisal was low. That's why we came to you this year. If you can't come up with a value of $35 million when you send me your final report in two days, then you can forget about our business too!

Richard Romano, a principal of Cruickshank, Garth & Romano, was rather taken aback by that outburst from John Mortimer of Watson & Musico Developments. Richard put down the phone in the Ottawa, Ontario office of his new real estate appraisal and consulting firm, and began to ponder the dilemma he now faced. Richard had just completed a preliminary evaluation of a property for Watson & Musico, a new client, and had estimated a value of $30.5 million. Richard and two other appraisers had formed their company just over three months earlier. The action he took on the Watson & Musico estimate could have a far-reaching impact on the new business' success and its ability to develop new clients. Richard wanted to complete the appraisal according to his best estimate of the current market value of the property. On the other hand, Watson & Musico was a major developer in the Ottawa area. Landing it as a client could provide a major boost to Cruickshank, Garth & Romano, which the young firm could ill-afford to pass up. Richard wondered what he should do.

THE OTTAWA REAL ESTATE MARKET

The City of Ottawa lay within the National Capital Region (NCR), which included territory in both Ontario and Quebec. The NCR's population of approximately 905,000 made it Canada's fourth largest urban centre, after Toronto, Montreal, and Vancouver.

Government accounted for approximately 30 per cent of employment in the NCR; other services accounted for an additional 30 per cent. The real estate industry made up approximately five per cent. In addition to dominating employment, the Government of Canada was by far the largest landowner and tenant in the NCR, accounting for approximately 35 per cent of all leased space in the area. Consequently, the NCR was more resistant to economic fluctuations than other urban areas. This situation made the NCR real estate market very attractive to large institutional investors. Pension funds and real estate mutual funds owned many properties.

However, the NCR was not entirely immune from the poor real estate market affecting the rest of Ontario. Because the commercial office market had been significantly over-built during the real estate boom of the previous decade, it had been particularly hard hit. Vacancy rates were very high, and revenues and profits very low. Thus, many of the smaller single project developers had been forced out of the market. Large developers' costs had increased because they held large amounts of vacant space.

The NCR real estate market had three main segments: commercial, residential, and industrial. A few major landowners and developers dominated both the development and rental markets in the commercial and residential sectors. The industrial market was highly fragmented, with a large number of small owners and developers. Generally, the costs of industrial land and buildings were significantly lower than those of commercial developments, permitting the entry of a number of small players into the market. Construction of residential units was the least costly of the three, but the large scope of residential developments required that developers possess a significant amount of capital.

To attract new tenants, developers had reduced rents for commercial office space from an average of $35 to about $25 per square foot. In addition, they had offered attractive packages, such as rent free periods. Occupancy rates decreased as a number of firms amalgamated their office locations to decrease rent costs, and other firms became bankrupt. The downturn had less severely affected industrial and residential properties.

This situation had effectively shut down the private commercial market; most demand came from government tenders. With major developers looking for ways to increase revenue, competition for government contracts intensified, and profitability decreased. Industry observers did not expect the all-important commercial market to recover for approximately two years.

THE REAL ESTATE APPRAISAL INDUSTRY

Background

The appraisal industry's basic function was to evaluate clients' properties for financing or reporting purposes. The evaluation process involved analyzing relevant zoning by-laws, local demographic and economic conditions, and the physical condition of the property; and estimating the property's value.

Appraisers used four approaches to estimate value:

- cost, which used the estimated replacement cost of the property;
- direct sales, which compared the subject property to the sale prices of similar properties, perhaps on a value per square foot basis;
- direct capitalization, which used the next year's income and a capitalization rate; and,
- discounted cash flow, which used the estimated cash flows from the property, discounted at an appropriate discount rate.

The method used for any particular property depended on the type of property and the reliability of market information. Evaluations became less reliable as the dependence on judgment increased and the dependence on facts decreased. The direct capitalization and discounted cash flow approaches were commonly used for commercial properties.

Although appraisers were primarily property evaluators, many often also acted as consultants to real estate development firms in areas of investment and feasibility analyses. Appraisal firms were typically composed of certified partners (see below), who were assisted by candidates for certification and research assistants. Partners in large, well respected firms could often make up to $100,000 annually. Salaries for uncertified appraisers started at around $25,000; many generally earned $50,000 to $75,000 per year by the time they became certified.

The Appraisal Institute of Canada

The Appraisal Institute of Canada (AIC) was a professional body which regulated the industry and served its members. AIC's professional activities included publication of a technical journal (*The Canadian Appraiser/L'Évaluateur Canadien*) and a newsletter (*Appraisal Institute DIGEST*) containing news and articles on relevant topics, and education programs for members. AIC accredited appraisers in two categories. Holders of the Accredited Appraiser Canadian Institute (AACI) designation were fully-accredited AIC members who could use their certification in connection with the appraisal of any type of property within the limits prescribed in AIC's Code of Ethics. Holders of the Canadian Residential Appraisers (CRA) designation could use their certification only regarding the appraisal and evaluation of individual undeveloped residential dwelling sites and dwellings containing three or fewer self-contained family housing units.

AIC had about 6,000 members (individuals) divided approximately as follows:

	Active	Retired
AACI	31%	4%
CRA	20	1
Candidate	43	

AIC did not allow its retired members to use their professional designation to issue appraisals.

AIC members were active in every Canadian province and territory, and, except for Quebec, were distributed roughly in proportion to population: 40 per cent operated in Ontario, 20 per cent in British Columbia, and eight per cent in Quebec. About one per cent of the members operated outside Canada. Annual fees for active members were $265 to $305, depending on membership status. Retired members paid a fee of $25.

The AACI and CRA designations were valuable because, although anyone could appraise a property, the vast majority of third parties, particularly lending institutions, required that the appraiser be appropriately certified. Quebec had an independent provincial certification program which reduced AIC membership in that province. It was common practice in the industry for a non-certified individual, possibly a candidate for certification, to do the evaluation and then have the final report signed by a certified appraiser. Appraisers had to remain AIC members to retain their AIC certification.

AIC Certification

AACI or CRA certification candidates were sponsored by an AIC member. Candidates had to take AIC-sponsored courses, article for three years (or have sufficient relevant experience), and complete one or more comprehensive evaluation reports. AIC required CRA candidates to complete six courses and an ethics seminar. AACI candidates had to take an additional nine courses. Each course involved about 40 hours of classroom activity. The evaluation report for CRA candidates involved an evaluation of a residential property. AACI candidates had to complete two evaluation reports, one of which had to be on an income-generating property. The final evaluation reports were much more comprehensive than reports normally submitted to clients and often required up to a year to complete. Although a candidate could be certified in three years, it normally took him or her five years. AIC required its members to continue to take courses and to be recertified periodically.

AIC required candidates to meet university entrance requirements and to complete the first AIC course before articling. Most of the required background courses, such as economics, real estate law, and real estate analysis, were university credit courses; some could be taken at community colleges. AIC was actively trying to upgrade its standards and the profession's image. It would soon require AACI candidates to have a university education and had recently started a public relations campaign.

Professional Standards

AIC published a Code of Ethics, Rules of Professional Conduct, and Standards of Professional Practice to govern appraisers' actions. Exhibit 1 presents selected excerpts from AIC's regulations. The AIC established acceptable minimum standards against which AIC judged complaints. Because AIC had no audit procedures, the "product" and its quality varied greatly among firms, individuals, and jobs. The appraiser's judgment and his or her firm's standards were significant factors in estimating a property's value and determining the appraisal's quality. Appraisal firms could try to improve turnaround time by ignoring the requirements of a report (see Exhibit 1).

AIC had procedures to deal with breaches of its regulations. In Ontario, written complaints from clients or members were taken up by a provincial investigation committee that fully examined the alleged offence. If the outcome warranted, the investigation committee made recommendations to a provincial adjudication committee which decided what action to take. Members found guilty by this body could appeal to a national board of appeal. The adjudication committee could penalize transgressors; warnings, censure, suspension for a period of time, remedial education, and expulsion were options available. Censure, suspension, and expulsion penalties were accompanied by publication of the individual's name, violation, and penalty in the *Appraisal Institute DIGEST*. Canada-wide, investigation committees dealt with 100 to 150 cases per year.

Appraisers were supposed to develop their evaluations independently. The appraisal assignment might be subject to certain limiting conditions affecting value. Such factors might be specified by the client and should be identified in the report. An example is a property subject to a change in zoning. Appraisers could be under heavy pressure to adjust values to meet client needs. The process generally involved extensive negotiation. The ability of appraisers to meet their professional obligations depended on their experience, the reputation of their firm, the importance of the client to their firm, and the general conditions of the real estate market. Because negotiating power was often in the client's favour, some outside observers had cynically redefined AACI certification to stand for: "Appraised According to Client's Instructions." Appraisals were often subject to third party requirements; adjusted values that were not supportable might result in a complaint to AIC. The conflict between professional responsibility and client satisfaction was most evident in startup firms.

Starting Up in the Industry

Two factors strongly influenced a startup firm's chances of success. Because an appraiser's reputation was a marketable asset, many clients were loyal to an individual appraiser, rather than to the firm. Thus, appraisers who left a firm were often able to take their clients with them. A firm's first report for a new client was a critical factor in forming the future firm-client relationship. Angering a new client might not only prevent a relationship from forming, but also create a reputation that would preclude the firm from attracting other clients. Also, the business required appraisers to develop strong relationships with lending institutions, which could refuse to accept an appraisal that did not meet their standards. Thus, no matter how much an evaluation pleased a client, acceptance by a lending institution could mean the difference between success and failure. New appraisal firms had to meet both industry norms and ACI standards.

Ethical Rule 1

Members of the Institute pledge to conduct themselves in a manner that is not detrimental to the public, the Institute, or the real property appraisal profession. Members' relationships with other members and the Institute shall be characterized by courtesy and good faith and shall show respect for the Institute and its procedures.

Ethical Rule 2

Members pledge to assist the Institute in carrying out its responsibilities to the public and users of appraisal services.

Ethical Rule 3

Members pledge to avoid advertising or solicitation which is misleading or otherwise contrary to the public interest

Ethical Rule 4

Members pledge to uphold the confidential nature of the appraiser-client relationship.

Ethical Rule 5

Members pledge to develop, support and communicate each analysis and estimate of value without regard to any personal interest.

Ethical Rule 6

Members pledge to comply with the Institute's Standards of Professional Practice.

Standards of Professional Practice

Standard Rule 1

Members shall, upon undertaking, and developing an appraisal analysis or estimate of value, employ recognized appraisal methods and techniques and, further, shall communicate each analysis and estimate of value in a manner that is not misleading.
An appraisal report must include the following:

a. An adequate description of the real property being appraised;

b. The purpose of the appraisal and a definition of the rights and value estimated;

c. The effective date of the value estimate and date of inspection;

d. Pertinent land use regulations as of the effective date of the value estimate;

e. A discussion and statement of the highest and best use;

f. A documented and factually supported value conclusion based on at least one approach to value considered most applicable to the type of property being appraised;

g. Reasoning supporting the value conclusion;

h. The final estimate of value;

i. Assumptions and limiting conditions;

j. The appraiser's certification and signature. . .

Exhibit 1   Excerpts From the Appraisal Institute of Canada's Regulations

Source: Appraisal Institute of Canada Directory.

Local Conditions

In the NCR, appraisers, as the rest of the real estate industry, had been affected by the economic downturn. However, they had maintained some strength in earnings because of the stabilizing effect of the government on demand, and because of the downward trend in mortgage rates which led to continued demand for refinancing appraisals. In the past two years, the portion of evaluations for refinancing had increased from 15 per cent to 40 per cent; over the same period, the portion of new development evaluations had fallen from 25 per cent to 10 per cent. Evaluations for reporting, the government, and other client-specific purposes accounted for the remaining 50 to 60 per cent. Economic downturns made evaluations more difficult because there were few transactions of comparable sales upon which appraisers could rely to determine appropriate discount rates and sale prices.

The NCR had 85 to 100 AACIs, 65 to 75 CRAs, and over 100 candidates. The area also had about 40 real estate appraisal firms, including three real estate brokerages with multiple offices, and approximately 30 real estate consulting firms. Two firms advertised themselves as being in both the real estate appraisal and the real estate consulting business. Four firms, which held 80 per cent of the market, dominated commercial appraisal in the NCR. Their strong relationships with private developers, the government, and lending institutions were significant entry barriers for new firms. Their reputations were attributable to their individual appraisers; thus, a new firm composed of appraisers from an existing firm would stand a higher chance of success.

CRUICKSHANK, GARTH & ROMANO

Chris Cruickshank, Wayne Garth, and Richard Romano formed Cruickshank, Garth & Romano to provide residential, industrial and commercial evaluations, as well as consulting services and feasibility analyses in the NCR. The firm's offices were in a restored house on the outskirts of Ottawa's core. The principals decided to offer a service that was similar in quality to that offered by the NCR's top four firms but aimed primarily at owners of smaller properties who normally would not deal with the top four. They had low overheads and could provide relatively fast turnaround. They were confident that their personal reputations and satisfied clients would serve to promote the business.

The three principals had worked for one of the four major NCR firms and were well known in the local real estate community. They had decided to start their own firm because they wanted to be independent and they had not enjoyed working for their previous boss. Because he had made it difficult for them to depart and establish their own firm, their relations with him remained strained. Chris and Wayne were AACI certified; Richard was an AACI candidate. Chris had 10 years of appraisal experience and concentrated on mid-size commercial properties ($1 million to $5 million). Wayne had six years of experience and concentrated on industrial and small commercial properties ($1 million and less). Richard had eight years of experience and was recognized by industry insiders as one of Canada's leading real estate experts. He concentrated on large commercial properties, complex appraisals, and the consulting aspect of the business.

The three principals were responsible for typing their own reports, and planned to divide the business' anticipated profits evenly and to share administrative duties to keep overhead to a minimum. Exhibit 2 shows a *pro forma* income statement.

The three principals had had some success in attracting clients. The clients that they had originally brought into their previous firm formed the nucleus. However, these clients were generally smaller developers and property holders and would not provide a sufficient revenue base alone to ensure Cruickshank, Garth & Romano's success. Thus, although the firm's primary target clients were owners of smaller properties,

Revenues:	
Commercial	$200,000
Residential	100,000
Industrial	100,000
Total	**$400,000**
Expenses:	
Partner Salaries	$135,000
Rent	22,000
Supplies	12,000
Secretary	15,000
Travel	4,000
Advertising	5,000
Other	7,000
Total	**$200,000**
Profit Before Tax	$200,000
Taxes	80,000
Net Income	$120,000

Exhibit 2 Projected First Year Statement of Income for Cruickshank, Garth & Romano

Source: Company files.

the principals considered it crucial also to develop some business with some of the NCR's larger developers and to build relationships with lending institutions. Although each partner had a strong reputation, the institutions were unsure of their ability to prepare appraisals and run their business simultaneously. Richard had spent his first three months since incorporation conducting an extensive marketing campaign, meeting with mortgage officers, and cold calling prospective clients. His efforts had begun to pay off; a number of the major local developers had engaged the company's services.

THE WATSON & MUSICO DEVELOPMENTS PROPERTY

Watson & Musico Developments was one of the NCR's major developers and property owners. Its total portfolio of properties was worth approximately $250 million, 90 per cent of which was in the NCR; it also had holdings in Montreal. Watson & Musico had started 30 years earlier as a residential developer and had been active in the commercial market for 15 years. John Mortimer controlled the firm; he was well-known in the NCR real estate market for his abrasive style and aggressive approach in business dealings.

Watson & Musico had been the most aggressive NCR developer in attracting clients to its properties. However, the depressed real estate market had forced it to provide extremely attractive packages to clients. Such packages generally involved a two-year rent holiday on a five-year lease which was structured to allow Watson & Musico to recover property expenses in full. Watson & Musico often achieved such rent abatements through side agreements which were not part of the lease, and allowed the firm to preserve its face rental rates[2] when seeking financing. A property evaluation based on face rental rates could result in an estimate significantly higher than one which fully reflected all side agreements. This value would allow Watson & Musico to receive a higher level of financing from its bank. Potentially, a developer could borrow up to 75 per cent of the appraised value.

Watson & Musico was rumoured within NCR real estate circles to have a highly restricted cash flow because of its aggressive leasing policy. With interest and mortgage rates declining steadily in response to a relaxation of the Bank of Canada's monetary policy, Watson & Musico was refinancing all of its properties to reduce its debt service requirements and to generate cash. Successful refinancing required that a property be evaluated at a value at least as high as the previous year.

The Watson & Musico property was an office building of 200,000 square feet located in the prime commercial office area of Ottawa. It was the first property in Watson & Musico's portfolio to be appraised. It was 85 per cent occupied with tenants committed to five-year leases, but, as was common in the market, about 15 per cent of the tenants would pay no rent for the next eight to 12 months. Exhibit 3 presents an outline of the property's revenues and expenses. Although mortgage rates had fluctuated, they had been showing a downward trend for some time; currently, they were about three per cent lower than the rate of the existing $23.25 million mortgage on the property.

Richard decided to use the direct capitalization approach to evaluation. Because this was a large income producing property, the cost and direct sales approaches were not suitable for this evaluation. He ruled out the discounted cash flow approach because of the uncertainty of predicting cash flows beyond five years in such an uncertain environment, the leases of the current tenants, and his experience that showed that the two methods would usually give a value within about five per cent of each other. He accepted Watson & Musico's statement of revenues and expenses (Exhibit 3) which showed the annual net income at $2.7 million from leases which were fixed for five years. Similar buildings had recently sold within the range of 10 to 12.5 times the annual net income, which implied a capitalization rate of eight to 10 per cent. Consequently, Richard decided to capitalize the Watson & Musico property at nine per cent. He divided the annual net income of $2.7 million by 0.09 to give an estimated value of $30.0 million. He then rechecked his figures and increased the value by $500,000 after adjusting for the recovery of

Gross revenue potential @ 100 per cent occupancy	
Lease contract rental revenue	$3,800,000
Parking	149,000
Total	**$3,949,000**
Add: Recovery income[1]	1,377,000
Total	**$5,326,000**
Less: Vacancy @ 15 per cent	799,000
Effective gross income	$4,527,000
Less: Operating expenses	
Rent abatements	$450,000
Realty taxes	470,000
Utilities	344,000
Insurance	20,000
General repairs and maintenance	230,000
Cleaning	60,000
Systems maintenance	79,000
Professional fees	16,000
Security services	16,000
Management fees	142,000
Total	**$1,827,000**
Net operating income	$2,700,000

Exhibit 3   Income Statement for the Watson & Musico Property

Source: Watson & Musico Developments files.

1. Operating expenses less rent abatements.

some operating expenses. Last year, Allied Property Services, one of NCR's top four firms, had evaluated the property at just over $31 million using an income of $2.65 million and a capitalization rate of 8.5 per cent. Because of the condition of the NCR real estate market, this change was not surprising. He then telephoned Mr. Mortimer.

The Decision

After gingerly replacing the telephone, Richard pondered his options. He knew that if Mr. Mortimer was satisfied with this report, he would likely give Cruickshank, Garth & Romano the contract to appraise Watson & Musico's remaining properties. This contract would be for a fee of $35,000 to $40,000, which could raise revenues by 10 per cent.

Richard could refuse to raise the value, in which case Watson & Musico would likely take its business elsewhere and give Cruickshank, Garth & Romano a reputation as being hard to deal with.

Alternatively, he could raise the value to $35 million, as Mr. Mortimer had requested, by ignoring the side agreements and using the full face rental rates in his calculations. The bank would likely never know about the side agreements. Even if the agreements did become public, Richard could plausibly deny that he had ever seen them. Further, Richard knew that some appraisal firms in the city would agree to this approach. He wondered whether this was the correct time to make a stand.

The third option was a compromise, which would give a value between $30 million and $35 million, and could be accomplished by incorporating the increase in cash flows once the side agreements had expired. Although appraisers did not commonly use this method, Richard was confident that he could convince Watson & Musico's bank of the property's incremental value. However, Richard expected that it would be difficult and time-consuming to convince Mr. Mortimer.

Richard was confident that his partners would fully support whatever he decided to do.

Notes

1. The authors acknowledge the editorial help of Ray Kaduck and the financial assistance of the William Pickard Fund.

2. Face rental rates are the rates that are detailed in the body of the lease contract.

Grandview Excavators Ltd.

Prepared by Michael LeBoldus under the supervision of Professor James A. Erskine

                    Version: (A) 2003-04-23

Taking a second glance at the October 7, 2002, payment invoice, Andrew Kenworth, project estimator at Grandview Excavators Ltd. in Edmonton, Alberta, could barely believe his eyes. Only six weeks previously, Phil Donaldson, a project manager at Brentwood Construction, had asked Kenworth to increase his quote for Grandview's potential involvement in the construction of a new supermarket from $126,000 to $166,000. After Grandview won and completed the majority of the excavation, Kenworth was puzzled as to why Grandview had received payment from Brentwood for only $113,000.

COMMERCIAL CONSTRUCTION

In Edmonton, as in many other cities in Canada, the construction of commercial real estate essentially involved three parties. First, the individual or group who wished to construct the commercial property, along with the help of an architect, sought, through a tender process, a suitable construction management company to oversee and manage the construction of the project. Second, this construction management company sought, also through a tender process, to subcontract pieces of specific work to third-party, specialized construction companies. For example a construction management company would seek the assistance of a company like Grandview Excavators to perform its specialized excavation and land leveling work in the initial stages of site construction. The construction management company would also seek to subcontract any electrical, plumbing, and structural development components of the overall construction project to other specialized construction firms.

The construction business in Edmonton was primarily driven through relationships and reputation within the industry. As such, the 80/20 rule applied for rewarding the majority of the construction work in the city. For example, the management construction companies with a proven track record, like Brentwood, won the largest commercial construction contacts. In turn, the most reputable subcontractors were chosen by construction management companies to complete the actual construction. With fewer than 10 construction management companies overseeing the majority of the commercial construction in Edmonton, most of the substantial players knew of the work of their competitors through direct relationships with their counterparts at competing firms. With this in mind, it was not uncommon for other construction management firms to know the kind of work managed by their competitors as well as their competitors' selection of subcontractors.

As with Brentwood, most construction management companies sought quotations through an open tender for the completion of a predefined piece of work; these quotes would be sought from a number of subcontractors prior to beginning work on the project. Based on the open tender bid, the management construction company would then make recommendations to a project architect for specific subcontractors to complete the work based on the price and the reputation of the subcontractor. The combined quotes of all the subcontractors, in addition to the management firm's fee, became the price charged to the real estate owner for the work's completion. Once an agreeable price was reached between the management company and the real estate owner, it was in the best interest of the management firm to closely manage all construction costs. Any underestimates often resulted in the management company and the subcontractor eating potential margin.

ANDREW KENWORTH'S QUOTATION

Established in 1973, Grandview Excavators was a private enterprise that focused on the preparation and excavation of land for construction development. With revenues of approximately $6 million, the company's market share for site work preparation placed Grandview as one of the top three firms of its kind in the Edmonton area. As a seasonal business, a small office of four project estimators, an office manager and an equipment dispatcher supported over 40 seasonal operators during peak construction periods.

During his university education, Kenworth worked most summers as a laborer and equipment operator in the construction industry. After graduating in 2000 with a business degree from the University of Alberta, Kenworth joined Grandview as a field superintendent in the summer of the same year. During his time with Grandview, Kenworth worked on and reported back to his boss on the largest and most complex contracts. As a field superintendent, Kenworth's responsibilities included organizing equipment and men for projects, conducting field surveys, and safety management. After approximately two and a half years in this role, Kenworth was promoted to estimator in the office.

Phil Donaldson of Brentwood Construction had approached Grandview Excavation to provide a quote for land excavation and leveling work for the proposed construction of an Agora Food's IGA supermarket in North Edmonton. Paul Smith, a project director for Grandview, had decided to give this assignment to Kenworth as his first project as an estimator with the company. The project was viewed by Kenworth's superiors as a valuable means to introduce him to his new role, while building Grandview's relationship with Brentwood through a substantial piece of work. Ready to take on the task, Kenworth researched the proposed project, interacted with fellow Grandview colleagues and completed a quotation for the work on the tender bidding closing date of August 7th. Kenworth believed his initial quote for $126,000 was an accurate reflection of Grandview's cost to complete the proposed work, in addition to incorporating a standard 25 per cent profit. After a quick review of the quote by his immediate supervisor, Kenworth faxed the estimate to Donaldson at Brentwood (see Exhibit 1).

Grandview Excavators Ltd.
12520 – 157th Street
Edmonton, Alberta T5V 1L9

Facsimile Transmittal

To: Brentwood Construction   **Fax:**   539-3129

Attn: Phil Donaldson   **Date:**   August 7, 2002

From: Andrew Kenworth   **Pages:**   1

Re: North Edmonton IGA

We are pleased to quote the above mentioned project. Our price of **$125,990.00** includes the following.

Scope of work:

- Removal of fill and black organics as indicated in engineering dated August 1, 2002.
- Removal of exposed concrete structures.
- Import of low to medium plastic clay to achieve grading fills.
- Bonding, Surveying and Layout, Dewatering. Soils testing.
- Ramp excavation and tailing removal (12 cu. m.).
- Safety supplies and equipment.

Not included:

Handling or removal of material generated by others, mechanical/electrical excavation or backfill, sawcutting, permits, first call, signage, GST.

Regards,
Andrew

CONFIDENTIAL

07-08-2002—2:01:04 pm

Exhibit 1   Quotation

Later the same day, after forwarding Grandview's quote to Brentwood, Donaldson telephoned Kenworth and inform him that Grandview's quote was substantially less then those of other subcontractors. As such, Donaldson asked Kenworth to re-examine his figures and to resubmit a new quote. Donaldson instructed Kenworth that he should increase his quote by approximately $40,000 and fax the new quote to Donaldson as soon as possible. Donaldson was scheduled to meet with the project architect later that same day, and he wanted a complete list of quotes so he could provide his recommendations for subcontractors and so the construction work could begin soon as possible. Kenworth agreed to re-examine his estimate and informed Donaldson that he would fax the new quote to Brentwood's office if an error was recognized in the initial assessment of work.

Upon reviewing the original quote, Kenworth believed he had accurately reflected the resources, time and costs required to complete the work. With that in mind, however, Kenworth began to doubt his ability to accurately estimate the work as this was his first attempt at developing a quotation. In addition, he wondered whether he had interpreted the land survey documentation correctly, especially as his quote was substantially less then those of the other subcontractors. Accordingly, Kenworth adjusted the quote to reflect a new cost of $166,000 and faxed the new version off to Donaldson later that afternoon (see Exhibit 2).

The following day, Kenworth telephoned Donaldson to confirm Brentwood's receipt of the new quote. At this time, Donaldson informed Kenworth that he had received Grandview's new quote and that the architect had agreed with Brentwood's recommendation to have Grandview complete the land excavation work for the proposed supermarket site. In addition, Donaldson informed Kenworth that Grandview could begin its work immediately.

The work took approximately four weeks for Grandview to complete and basically followed the proposed timeline and resource requirements set forth in Kenworth's initial assessment

of the work. Kenworth's boss, Paul Smith, was impressed with his efforts in developing the quote. The $166,000 in revenue that Kenworth had outlined in his quote was viewed by Smith as a substantial amount. In addition, Kenworth's superiors viewed the work as a good means of strengthening Grandview's relationship with both Brentwood Construction and Agora Foods. In fact, Kenworth believed Grandview was in a strong position to win follow-up work on any future Agora projects. He had overheard that Agora was currently in direct negotiations with the president of Grandview to purchase approximately 20 acres of land that Grandview owned directly adjacent to Agora's Western Canada Distribution Centre. With Agora wishing to expand its distribution facilities on the Grandview-owned land, Kenworth overheard the current negotiations between Grandview and Agora, and he knew the value of land to be over a million dollars.

CAUSE FOR CONCERN

Less than two weeks following the completion of the land excavation and leveling work on the supermarket site, Kenworth received an adjusted payment invoice from Brentwood Construction for Grandview's excavation work. As was customary at Grandview, the contract and all correspondence regarding the project was forwarded to the project estimator. In general, all cheques where first sent to the office manager before being forwarded to the estimator.

In the case of Brentwood's adjusted invoice, Kenworth was surprised to realize that the value of the invoice was worth only $113,090 (see Exhibit 3). Kenworth could hardly believe his eyes. While he understood that the invoice reflected a reduction of $12,000 for components of the initial work assessment that were not necessary and therefore not performed by Grandview, Kenworth could not understand why Brentwood had based its payment on what appeared to be the original quote of $126,000.

Grandview Excavators Ltd.
12520 – 157th Street
Edmonton, Alberta T5V 1L9

Facsimile Transmittal

To: Brentwood Construction

Attn: Phil Donaldson

From: Andrew Kenworth

Re: North Edmonton IGA

Fax: 539-3129

Date: August 7, 2002

Pages: 1

We are pleased to quote the above mentioned project. Our price of **$165,990.00** includes the following.

Scope of work:

- Removal of fill and black organics as indicated in engineering dated August 1, 2002.
- Removal of exposed concrete structures.
- Import of low to medium plastic clay to achieve grading fills.
- Bonding, Surveying and Layout, Dewatering. Soils testing.
- Ramp excavation and tailing removal (12 cu. m.).
- Safety supplies and equipment.

Not included:

Handling or removal of material generated by others, mechanical/electrical excavation or backfill, sawcutting, permits, first call, signage, GST.

Regards,
Andrew

CONFIDENTIAL

07-08-2002—5:31:56 pm

Exhibit 2   Quotation

CONCLUSION

Kenworth had promised his superiors that the work would generate $166,000 in revenues for Grandview. He wondered what Donaldson had done with the requote, speculating that Donaldson may have charged Agora Foods the full $166,000 while realizing the profit from the difference it paid back to Grandview. Further to that, Kenworth was concerned that if Agora learned of this incident, the relationship that had developed during the negotiations between Grandview and Agora executives could be damaged.

Kenworth's initial instinct was to phone Donaldson and ask him about the discrepancy. He was reluctant, however; he remained unsure about the effect this would have on the Grandview's relationship with Brentwood. In addition, he did not want his superiors, or other construction management companies, to learn of his altering of the original quote. He began to sweat as he contemplated his next move.

October 2, 2002

Grandview Excavators Ltd.
12520 – 157th Street
Edmonton, Alberta T5V 1L9

Attention: Andrew Kenworth

Project: Iga Garden Market—North Edmonton

Please be advised that your invoice #00005201 in the amount of **$164,786.00** has been reduced to **$113,090.00** for the following reasons:

- This invoice exceeded total value of your subcontract.

Your invoice will be held until we receive a credit invoice in the amount of the reduction. Please expedite the credit invoice to avoid delays in payment.
Yours truly,

BRENTWOOD CONSTRUCTION INC.

Phil Donaldson
Project Manager

EDMONTON - CALGARY - VANCOUVER

Exhibit 3   Invoice

PETER FARBER (A)

Prepared by Niels Billou under the supervision of Professor David J. Sharp

Copyright © 1998, Ivey Management Services   Version: (A) 1999-07-20

"What a week," thought Peter Farber, investment adviser at the Toronto, Ontario branch of Reese, Gordon, and Company (RGC). It was 3:30 p.m. on a Friday, in late February 1997, and Peter was finally getting close to the bottom of the pile of orders he had received that day. One order in particular caused Peter to pause. The order was from Leonid Strovsky and called for a transfer of his wife's pension plan from her previous employer to an RRSP account in her name at RGC. As well, Strovsky wanted the entire amount put towards the purchase of common stock of Reltec Pharmaceuticals. This was the fifth trade Strovsky had ordered on his wife's account in the last few weeks. Peter thought to himself:

> Although Mr. Strovsky opened the account, it is in his wife's name and he technically doesn't have any trading authority over the account. He keeps telling me his wife is too busy at the moment to send in a trading authorization form.

With the markets set to close in a half-hour, Peter Farber wondered what to do next.

PETER FARBER

Peter Farber was 24 years old, married, and had been with RGC since he had graduated from university two years ago. His father, James Farber, had a successful 30-year career in the industry and rose to the rank of vice-president at RGC before retiring to Florida six months prior. James Farber had passed along a considerable client list to his son, and Peter was anxious to continue where his dad had left off. At the same time, Peter acknowledged that it would not be any easy task:

> My dad had a long and successful career at this firm—he was well-known and well-liked by clients and colleagues alike. He got his accounts with a combination of salesmanship and street smarts. I don't have his salesman personality or his street smarts quite yet—but people expect me to. Being James Farber's son can be a bit of a double-edged sword, but on the balance, I guess I'm lucky to be able to ride on his coattails.

THE STROVSKY ACCOUNT

Leonid Strovsky was referred to Peter Farber by his mother, a long-time client of Peter Farber's father, James Farber. Strovsky opened an RRSP account in his wife's name at the beginning of January. Peter filled out the new client information form without ever meeting Mrs. Strovsky; indeed, he had to wait several days to receive her signature on the form via mail. Mrs. Strovsky was listed as a sophisticated investor and her stated investment objectives were as follows: mutual funds 40 per cent, growth 30 per cent and income 30 per cent. No one other than Mrs. Strovsky was given authority for the account. Since the account was opened the following trades were effected:

January 3	Buy	Industrial Growth fund	$25,000
January 9	Buy	Canada Treasury Bill	$5,000
January 17	Buy	Canada Treasury Bill	$5,000
February 20	Sell	Canada Treasury Bill	$5,000

All of the above trades were effected with instructions from Leonid Strovsky. When Peter asked for written authorization from Strovsky, he would say that his wife was busy at work at the moment and would get to it at a later date. As well, Strovsky would remind Peter that Stovsky's mother had had an account with Peter's father for nearly 20 years, and Strovsky's father had made all the trades without any problem.

CURRENT SITUATION

Strovsky's latest request involved the transfer of his wife's entire pension plan with her former employer, worth just over $25,000, to her RRSP account with RGC. Furthermore, he wanted the entire amount of the pension fund plus $5,000 that was in a cash account, invested in Reltec Pharmaceuticals, which was trading at $0.80 per share. Peter felt a certain amount of apprehension:

> It's quite a big order for this account and the trade is a little risky. As well, I have still not talked to Mrs. Strovsky regarding any of her trades. But then again, my father handled the elder Strovsky's account the same way for 20 years and never did have any problems.

It was now 3:30 p.m. on Friday afternoon. Peter had to make a decision soon before the markets closed for the weekend.

3

ETHICS OF THE FIRM'S RELATIONSHIP WITH ITS EMPLOYEES

This chapter explores the range of moral obligations that exist between an employer and employee. At one moral extreme, the relationship could be viewed as nothing more than an arm's-length market transaction, in which employees sell their services to the employer at the market rate, and the employer pays for the services, thereby meeting all obligations. The classical legal and economic analysis of employee relations is based on agency theory, in which an employee has a duty to work to achieve the goals of the firm, and the firm's only obligation is to provide compensation in exchange for its employees' services. In practice, of course, the relationship is far more complex. Employers are organizations, not markets, and the employment relationship creates a variety of legal and moral long-term obligations on both sides. Many aspects of the employee-employer relationship—confidentiality, working conditions, hiring and layoff rights, for example—are prescribed in legislation, but as is usually the case, legislation leaves plenty to management discretion.

For example, collective agreements often stipulate that employees must be permitted to return to their previous job, even after a long sick leave. In Matt Moreau's Dilemma, however, a newly appointed manager of customer services for a department store must decide whether to offer a job to an employee who was recovering from a serious illness. The employee might experience a relapse of her illness if she took on this high-stress position. Another case that introduces stress in the workplace is Coastal Uniforms, which provides an interesting chronicle of one company's attempt to improve shareholder profitability by setting higher performance targets. It permits discussion of both the rights of shareholders as covered in Chapter 1, the utility and effectiveness of very stressful performance targets, and the limits on the moral rights of an employer to require them.

The CXP Publishing Inc. series of cases deals with a sensitive issue—the potential conflict of interest created by personal relationships in the workplace. The newly promoted director of sales and marketing at CXP has just inherited an employee conduct issue. In her previous position, she became aware that a sales representative was having sexual relations with the company's clients, but the company's president was dealing with the issue. In her new role, she discovers that issue persists, and this employee now reports to her. She realizes that this is a "hot issue" and needs to determine the best way to handle the situation. There is more to consider than just dealing with the employee because she does not want to put the company's relationship with the client in jeopardy.

The digital revolution has transformed workplaces and created a number of ethical issues, including pornography on the Internet. The Canadian Imperial Bank of Commerce: Digital Employee Privacy case explores a closely related ethical issue— the justification under which an employer is entitled to read employee e-mail. What rights do an employer and employee have in this situation? If the employer discovers personal or private information on e-mail, what are the rights and responsibilities of the two parties, given that everyone knows that e-mail is not secure and therefore, to some extent, in the public domain? The Canadian Imperial Bank of Commerce (CIBC) had implemented word recognition software, Assentor, in its U.S. brokerage arm to ensure that its employees were not acting inappropriately in their dealings with customers and to protect company systems from viruses. This software scans e-mails for flagged "business words" and archives the e-mails in a central database. The manager of compliance at CIBC's head office in Toronto found that the decision to implement the Assentor software was much easier than deciding what to do in the event the software found something improper. Issues related to company ethics and employee privacy were raised. Acknowledging that occasional personal e-mails would be sent and received, he wondered what the legal ramifications would be if a manager found out about a private situation because Assentor had found a flagged word in a personal e-mail. He felt that clear communication with and upfront understanding from employees would help prevent negative impressions of this process, so he had to determine the best way to inform employees about the e-mail scanning while enforcing CIBC's e-mail policy.

Maintaining an ethical workplace is difficult enough, but the practice of management provides more challenges than merely maintaining a healthy corporate culture. For example, an important managerial skill is the ability to manage the communications process between the firm and the media. These often arrive in a phone call from a well-informed and aggressive media correspondent, with no warning. The Stamford Machine Corporation: Allegations of Racism case provides an opportunity for a class to address some of these communications challenges with respect to accusations of unethical behavior. Stamford Machine Corporation is a market leader in the manufacturing of photocopiers and office equipment. The director of corporate business ethics and compliance has been notified that the company is being served with a discrimination lawsuit. A newspaper announcement was released to the public outlining details of the charges, but before the director could leave his office, he receives a call from a journalist asking for the company's comments. He must determine if there has been a breach in the company's policy on discrimination and plan how the company will deal with the media.

Matt Moreau's Dilemma

Prepared by Professor Jeffrey Gandz

 Version: (A) 1999-07-15

Matt Moreau, newly appointed manager, customer services for Bantings department stores, picked up the telephone:

> We think we have the perfect person for you, Matt. She's a manager in one of the medium-sized suburban stores—been with the company for 15 years, ambitious, smart, on-the-ball and, what's more, I think that she'd jump at the chance of moving into the head office environment.

Customer Service Department

The voice on the other end of the phone was that of Steven Judson, corporate personnel manager. Moreau had asked him to help in the staffing of his newly created department. It had been set up to improve the quality of customer service, developing new programs that would have organization-wide impact on how stores were designed and laid out, how staff were trained, and how customer satisfaction could be measured and factored into the company's merchandising and marketing programs.

The task that lay ahead for Moreau was a difficult and demanding one. The stores were managed through a strong line operations department which reported up to the president of the corporation. His department would be "staff"—hopefully well-respected and influential, but with very little real power or authority. It was critical for him to get good people, preferably those with some line management experience who had developed credibility with the operations types.

Sally Armitage

Moreau asked Judson to tell him a little more about his "find":

Judson: Well, I've just been through her personnel records—by the way, her name is Sally Armitage. She's been with the company a number of years, always had good or excellent performance appraisals. She started fresh out of high school as a clerk but, after a couple of years, started bugging her manager to be put onto the management development program. As you know, we usually just put university and college grads on that program, but in this case we made an exception. I think that her manager really went to bat for her on this one.

Worked out great! She completed the program and then went into the Thunder Bay store as assistant manager in the white goods department. Rotated through a number of departments, then . . . let me see. . . . Oh yes, she moved to the Toronto region as assistant manager of the Eastland Mall store—one of the biggest and, at that time, the worst performer. Well, she and Tony Abbott turned the thing around and I have a note attached to a performance appraisal from Tony which gives her much of the credit.

Two years ago we gave her the Chute Hill store—it's small but she's doing a good job of enlarging it and also increasing profitability. As you know, Tony Abbott is the regional manager out there and I know he thinks the world of her. In fact, he'd be hopping mad if he even knew I was talking to you about her.

Moreau: Why are you talking to me, Steve? What makes you think that she's the least bit interested in moving into a head office job?

Judson: Well, I was just looking over the results of her last performance appraisal and see that she indicated that she'd like to get some head office experience. And when Chuck Mackness (the president of Bantings) was on his last field visit, he called on her store and she mentioned to him that she saw her career at Bantings benefiting from some head office experience. He mentioned it to me and so I got out her file. So there it is, I think she's well worth looking at.

Moreau: What's the next step, Steve?

Judson: You should contact Tony Abbott and get a first-hand impression from him. He'll not be pleased but he's always been a booster of Armitage. Try not to tell him you heard of her through me!!

DISCUSSION WITH TONY ABBOTT

The following day Matt Moreau called Tony Abbott and told him over the telephone that he was interested in talking with him about any personnel in his region who might be candidates for a position in the newly formed customer service group. He arranged to meet with Tony early the following week at the regional office.

"I bet that it's Sally you're interested in," were the first words that greeted Moreau after he sat down in Abbott's office. "The ungrateful, ambitious, disloyal . . . highly competent, super-achiever," he added with a grin. "How I'd hate to lose her."

Abbott and Moreau talked for about 30 minutes about Sally Armitage and during the conversation Moreau outlined some of the challenges that lay ahead for his group.

As you know, Tony, we have our work cut out for us. The public are getting pretty annoyed with the kind of service they've been getting at all department stores and ours is no better than most of the others. We have to improve. The president has detached me from my normal function to get this thing done and he wants to see results by Christmas. We can do it, but it's going to take maximum effort. Late nights, lots of tension and stress, tough decisions, meetings, travel—a lot of old-fashioned blood, sweat and tears.

As he went through this, Moreau noticed some worry on Abbott's face. He asked,

Abbott: How much do you know about Sally's background? Do you know much about her personal circumstances?

Moreau: No, at least no more than appears in her personnel file. Apart from some fairly extensive absences about three years ago—for medical reasons I think—it seems to point to a first-class person.

Abbott: Let me give you some additional background. The absences that Sally had a few years ago were serious—not many people know this but she had cancer, I think it was cancer of the lymph glands. She was off work for several weeks and then went for chemotherapy for over two years. I don't know how she managed it . . . for a couple of days after the treatments she looked like the walking dead. But she seemed to bounce back okay. She still goes in once every three months or so for regular check-ups.

In her current position I think she can cope with the situation. She lives with her teenage daughter—she was divorced about six years ago—just about 10 minutes away from the Chute Hill store. She's got a good staff and on those days when she's not feeling 100 per cent, she can coast a little bit.

The job that you could offer her would change all that. First, she'd have a long commute into the city to work—maybe an hour each way unless she moved much closer to downtown and I doubt you guys would pay her that much extra to make that affordable. Second, it looks as if the job is very high stress and will require all sorts of extra work. I'm not sure Sally is up to that, that it wouldn't cause her condition to deteriorate. Oh, you'd never know it. Sally is just one of those people who always looks cheerful, never lets on that anything is wrong.

By the way, I'm sure that if you offered her the job—even if you explained the situation to her, really pointed out all the problems and difficulties—she'd take it. One of the ways she has coped with her illness is to push even harder, show herself that she can do anything. This would be another challenge for her.

But I wonder if it's the right thing to offer it to her. What if she took it and it did cause her situation to deteriorate? What good would that have done her? Or you, for that matter. Could you afford to have someone with a health problem on your staff, especially now?

It's not like you're running a store where you can get someone else to fill in when a manager or employee is off ill. You know what it's like with cancer—it can recur any time.

THE DILEMMA

As he rode back to head office, Moreau mulled over this conversation. What options did he have? Should he even pursue the possibility with Armitage? Should she be given the option, knowing how tough things would likely be? Should he take the risk of promoting an employee who—despite high performance and apparent good health—had such a medical history? How would he explain his decision—no matter what it was—to Tony Abbott? To Steven Judson? To Chuck Mackness?

COASTAL UNIFORMS

Prepared by Ken Mark under the supervision of Professor David Sharp

Version: (A) 2004-12-07

INTRODUCTION

Andrew Vilas was thinking about his next moves at Coastal Uniforms (Coastal). It was April 3, 2002 and Vilas was concerned about the way the company was being managed. On a cool day in Boston, Massachusetts, Vilas reviewed the sequence of events that had led to the degradation of ethics at his company.

COASTAL UNIFORMS

Boston-based Coastal Uniforms was a publicly traded U.S. company, with $200 million in sales and 2,000 employees. Until 1999, Coastal had achieved steady growth for the past 22 straight years. During this period, its sales had grown at a compound rate of 21 per cent and its profit had grown at a rate of 25 per cent. On several occasions, it was named one of Massachusetts's best employers by leading local business magazines. While working at the company, many of its shareholding employees had become quite wealthy through share price increases.

Coastal had a dozen locations in Massachusetts, New Hampshire and Rhode Island. It provided work uniforms and uniform cleaning services to manufacturing and services industries. Many of its clients were sheet metal fabrication plants, automobile repair shops, and tool and die firms. It recently launched new initiatives, including a Flame-Resistant Clothing Division, a First Aid Supplies Division and the Custom Uniform Apparel Division, to cater to high-end hotels and casinos.

1999: Signs of Trouble

Coastal's issues started in 1999 when several small competitors, through skillful negotiation, wrested a handful of key contracts from Coastal. These companies, previously dismissed by Coastal management as being serious competitors, because they were perceived as being unorganized and somewhat incompetent, surprised Coastal with their renewed sense of purpose. Coastal management soon found out that a new crop of leaders was at the helm of these enterprises and were driving sales at a furious pace.

In 1999, for the first time in Coastal's history, sales and profit were flat versus 1998; and even then, preventing a decline from occurring required a huge effort from Coastal's sales and operations teams.

Coastal had been focused on hitting pre-established profit and growth levels at each location. Its management had ingrained a concept termed "Rule 35," which stipulated that profit and revenue growth increases had to add up to 35. For example, if revenue grew by 20 per cent, profit had to grow by 15 per cent; if revenue grew by five per cent, profit had to grow by 30 per cent. General managers of each location were heavily rewarded to achieve these levels, even forming discussion groups to share revenue- and profit-growth ideas with each other. It was no surprise that 1999's zero-profit growth and zero-revenue growth was of huge concern—none of the general managers received any bonus for that year. Typically, a bonus constituted up to 40 per cent of a general manager's total compensation.

Management was not looking forward to 2000, as they knew that they would have to redouble their efforts. Amidst this chaos, several key managers left the company to start ventures in unrelated businesses.

2000: The Beginning of the Decline

During the first nationwide sales representatives meeting, the 12 general managers collectively pressured the sales representatives to beat their previously established sales targets by 20 per cent. Despite outward signs of discontent, not one salesperson objected. After the meeting, two general managers tacked on new tasks for their delivery personnel: Instead of just delivering cleaned uniforms and new uniform sales to customers, delivery personnel in these two locations would have to sell catalog items to the customers on their route. Although the target was small ($300 a week in sales), delivery reps that did not meet this target would be dismissed.

Products were re-examined for cost savings. In addition to ordering lower quality cotton and polyester uniforms (while keeping the price to customers the same), Coastal management decided to reduce what they believed to be unnecessary features on uniforms, in order to save costs. Extra buttons were taken off; coveralls were ordered without snaps on the cuffs, name patches were sewn on with wider stitches. In addition, during a gasoline price increase in 2000, the company added a "delivery surcharge," about $15 on top of a $300 weekly contract, to the bottom of the invoice. Only a dozen out of 300 customers called to complain, at which point the surcharge was removed for those that called. When gasoline prices dropped in late 2000, the surcharge remained unchanged.

As a result of these initiatives, profit and revenue growth resumed, with the former growing 10 per cent and the latter growing 10 per cent. Once again, the general managers did not receive their bonus.

2001: More Initiatives Are Put in Place

At the start of 2001, the sales quotas for delivery personnel were increased from $300 a week to $800 a week. In addition, the other 10 locations adopted this "best practice" after the two general managers who instituted it shared the idea with their colleagues midway through the fiscal year. Sales quotas for salespeople remained very aggressive, and turnover in sales staff increased to 20 per cent. Fortunately, due to the amount of goodwill the company had built up in its community, recruiting efforts more than made up for the attrition; overall company employee strength increased by 10 per cent. An unexpected gain for the general managers was the fact that these new sales recruits eagerly accepted the aggressive sales targets—they appeared eager to please. In addition, the new recruits were half the cost of experienced sales people.

During the first quarter of 2001, an environmental charge was added to invoices. In an explanation to customers, the environmental fee contributed to the cost of cleaning the garments in an environmentally friendly fashion. In reality, no change to the cleaning process was made.

Again, only a small subset of customers, about six to 10 out of every 300, would complain. Dutifully, the complaints were noted, and the charges were dropped for those customers.

In mid-2001, a Hazardous Analysis Critical Control Points (HACCP) charge was added to all invoices going to customers in the food industry. HACCP was a set of regulations in the food-processing industry that required industry participants to adhere to certain sanitation standards. Although Coastal Uniforms had no special method of washing food-processing garments (generally, soiled garments from the food industry were washed along with the rest of the soiled garments), an HACCP charge of $30 per $300 weekly invoice was added. Few customers complained. For several customers, this additional charge amounted to $500 a week for essentially the same service.

These initiatives, implemented by the general managers, were communicated to the rest of the company to be "steering mechanisms" to guide locations to their "correct" profit and revenue growth targets.

For the first time since 1999, the company hit its "35" target. This target was reached despite the slowdown in the industry that occurred in late 2001 as a result of the terrorist attacks in the United States. After much celebration, most employees breathed a sigh of relief, thinking that 2002 would be an easier year.

Unfortunately for Coastal, the start of 2002 was heralded by the departure of another five key customers, who had suddenly discovered an extra thousand dollars a week of extra charges on their invoices. Furious and unwilling to accept an "apology" from Coastal, these customers had voiced their complaints in public forums—at the Better Business Bureau office, at City Council business meetings and to any journalist willing to listen. All of a sudden, an easy 2002 seemed impossible.

2002: More Efforts to Drive Revenue and Profits

The general managers assured anxious Coastal employees that these clients were mistaken and that their company was, as always, doing the right thing. During the national sales meeting, sales targets were set, and an additional challenge was put to sales reps: Lose any customer you signed and you lose your entire bonus for the year. To delivery reps, sales targets were increased, yet again, to $1,200 a week.

The number of customers calling to complain that deliveries were late, product was missing, improper sizes were delivered, etc. was increasing. Up to 25 per cent of customers were "dissatisfied" or "somewhat dissatisfied" with Coastal's service.

Many delivery reps confided to their sales counterparts that, in order to meet their weekly targets, they had resorted to leaving product at the client's location (without the client's knowledge) and charging them for it. So far, this indiscretion had gone unnoticed.

ANDREW VILAS'S DECISIONS

Vilas was one of the sales reps in whom the delivery reps confided. He was not surprised to hear of their practices. After all, many of these reps were in their mid-stage of life and had families to take care of. None could risk losing a job at this stage of their career. Vilas was feeling tremendous pressure too. He had been able to hit 50 per cent of his targets during the past few years. He noticed himself beginning to get visibly angry with prospective clients (if they were too slow to sign up for contracts). Due to the publicity Coastal's practices had received, old customers were calling Vilas to cancel contracts signed just months before. Although Vilas was owed a bonus of $20,000 for 2001, he had not received it. His general manager had even expressed surprise that a bonus was owed to Vilas. Vilas suspected that this reaction was a ploy to either delay or cancel the bonus owed to him.

Vilas considered legal action but wondered about the effects it would have on his career in the uniform business. If he were labeled a pariah, he would never find work. He wondered about quitting his job, but with the purchase of a new house and car, he was stretched to the limits with regard to finances. He really had been counting on that bonus.

To make matters worse, a recession was hitting Massachusetts, and the effects were amplified in Boston, where many of the factories saw huge drops in customer orders. Companies large and small were laying off workers, and economic recovery was not thought to be around the corner, at least not in the next 12 months.

Vilas wondered what he should do.

CXP PUBLISHING INC. (A)

Prepared by Ken Mark under the supervision of Professor Lyn Purdy

Copyright © 2001, Ivey Management Services

Version: (A) 2002-12-09

INTRODUCTION

"Do her sexual activities affect our business or is this matter personal?" Helen Tilmant, newly promoted director, sales and marketing, of CXP knew she had to handle the employee conduct issue she had just inherited. It was mid-October at the head office of CXP Publishing Inc., and Tilmant, the centre of senior management's attention, sensed that she had a hot issue on her hands.

BACKGROUND

Founded in 1975, CXP Publishing had grown from its home base into a number of regional offices, employing nearly 100 personnel. Unionized since 1990, the company was a publisher of advertising inserts. An advertising insert was a four-color set of stapled advertisements, containing mostly local,

targeted advertisements. These inserts were delivered to households by CXP's network of delivery persons. CXP did not have significant competitors in the advertising insert business as it had been able to out-compete or acquire its major competitors in its market area. It was estimated that CXP captured 80 per cent of the market share allocated for insert advertising.

THE ISSUE

In July, the president of CXP approached the marketing director, Mark Biel, and requested that Biel follow up on a rumor that the president had heard at a golf tournament the weekend before. At the informal monthly peer group meeting held between Biel and his management team (the directors for business development, finance, systems, marketing, customer services, as well as the production managers and the vice-president of directory services) to discuss issues faced by their business units, Biel recounted,

> The president just walked up to me and blurted out that he was concerned about a sales representative having intimate relations with one of her customers, who was married with a wife and two children. He even named the employee, Sheila McMaster, who was in charge of northern region sales. I felt a bit uncomfortable, and my immediate reaction was that it was none of our business.

"I'm glad that it's not my responsibility," thought Tilmant, silently. "I already have enough to deal with in my current job as sales manager." She did not attempt to counsel Biel, saying that she wanted to put more thought into the matter. During the following peer group meeting in August, Biel announced to the group that he had decided to leave the matter alone and inform the president only if the issue arose again. Before long, the story had leaked out to the rest of the employees from their friends in the business community. There was a range of emotion expressed amongst employees: some were angry, some disappointed, some embarrassed, others thought it was a joke, and some were thinking "Thank God it's not my problem."

In mid-October, CXP announced a reorganization of its senior management ranks and promoted Tilmant to director of sales and marketing, with new responsibilities for northern sales. Shortly thereafter, Biel, the incumbent, left CXP to pursue other professional opportunities.

HELEN TILMANT

In her new role, Tilmant would manage all aspects of the sales process, including researching targeted revenue objectives, the "paper flow" of sales documentation, profit and loss, and the management of customer relations. In addition to the change, CXP hired two extra sales representatives, who also reported to Tilmant, to manage the southern markets. Tilmant reported to the vice-president of directory services who in turn reported to the president. In addition to her sales

team, she had two marketing managers involved with advertising communication and product development.

Tilmant preferred to have an "open door policy" when dealing with her employees. She enjoyed working in a team environment that emphasized collaboration. Before giving her opinion on business matters, Tilmant listened and observed the situation, looking for a rationale as to what action to take, and how the action could be implemented. Typically, she would ask her subordinates for their recommendations for a course of action. Similarly, if Tilmant's subordinates were involved in a conflict, she would discuss the issues with the parties involved, find out the needs of the employees, and then prompt them to resolve the issues on their own. Tilmant explained,

> For problem employees, for example, I would ask, "What is it you want out of this job, and how would you get it?" If the current job was not what they were looking for, I would say "Obviously you need to see if your values meet the values of this company." I'd get them to buy in, to realize the situation they're in, and that helps to move the discussion in the right direction.

Upon realizing that the McMaster issue was hers to resolve, Tilmant's initial reaction was, "The business community is small, and this could have potentially adverse effects if the relationship turned sour. But then again, this issue is personal. Should I get involved?"

SHEILA MCMASTER

McMaster started with CXP as a telemarketer seven years ago. She had been promoted three times and was currently in the position of northern sales representative. Despite these promotions, McMaster's job performance had not always been excellent. Her first manager, Allan Souris, had noted in her employee record that she had been on sick leave three times in her first year of employment, due to stress on the job. It was also noted that she had been warned about her confrontations with fellow employees when she was refused support from CXP's in-house creative and production department—the department that designed and produced the advertising inserts. This department worked on a set schedule to meet its delivery deadlines. Occasionally, it was possible to circumvent this schedule in order to accommodate a special client request; however, it was generally accepted that the department would provide this "rush" service only if timing and resources existed. Souris also noted in his remarks that McMaster performed "the minimum amount of work possible, sometimes meeting, sometimes not meeting expectations, but never exceeding expectations."

When the "major accounts" position became available five years after her initial hiring, McMaster was the employee next in line for promotion, based on her seniority. In assessing McMaster's performance, her current manager noted that McMaster "was unprofessional, and known to have high and low emotional points, and was very aggressive, even towards people in her support team. McMaster was not a model employee." There were three documented incidents of conflict between McMaster and her women colleagues disputing allocation of company time resources. In addition, McMaster had filed two grievances with the union, alleging that her performance as an employee was incorrectly assessed. Despite these issues, McMaster received the promotion because of her seniority.

When the position of northern sales representative became open earlier in this year, it was filled by an employee from the external relations department. Not satisfied by this decision, McMaster filed a grievance with the union, arguing that because of seniority, she should be given the post. The union sided with her demand and ordered CXP to promote McMaster, reversing the previous decision. In this new role of selling advertising space to clients in the northern region, she reported to the director of marketing, Biel. Biel noted that McMaster could not be counted upon to deliver "paper flow," the record of advertising and administrative contracts between CXP and its advertisers. Fortunately, noted Biel, McMaster had good rapport with both her male and female advertising clients.

THE CURRENT SITUATION

Now that Tilmant had taken over the position of director of sales and marketing, she had to decide what to do about the McMaster situation. Tilmant had just finished reading McMaster's work history. Before she had a chance to conclude if the issue should be best left alone, Biel walked into her office. "Helen, I want you to know about the latest rumor in town. McMaster is now sleeping with *two* of her clients."

CANADIAN IMPERIAL BANK OF COMMERCE: DIGITAL EMPLOYEE PRIVACY

Prepared by Ken Mark under the supervision of Mike Wade

INTRODUCTION

"We could have a lively situation on our hands if some of these e-mail privacy scenarios come

true," remarked Bob Jones, manager, Compliance at Canadian Imperial Bank of Commerce (CIBC). It was May 16, 2000, and Jones was aware that Toronto-based CIBC had implemented word recognition software in its U.S. broker to comb e-mail messages sent by employees for specified business words. What if these routine searches flagged an e-mail message that also contained personal information about an employee? In the wake of an e-mail "worm" that crippled corporate networks in the first week of May 2000, use of e-mail at work was a hot topic of discussion in management circles.

CANADIAN IMPERIAL BANK OF COMMERCE

As of May 2000, Canadian Imperial Bank of Commerce had 45,000 employees worldwide serving six million individual customers, 350,000 small businesses, and 7,000 corporate and investment banking customers. The bank had total assets of $250 billion, and a net income of $1.029 billion in 1999.

Formed out of a 1961 merger between The Canadian Bank of Commerce and Imperial Bank of Canada, CIBC was one of North America's leading financial institutions offering retail and wholesale products and services through its electronic banking network, branches and offices around the world.

Customer Privacy in the Banking Industry: The Tournier Case

Privacy practices in the banking industry could be traced back to the landmark 1924 "Tournier Case" (Tournier vs. the National Provincial and Union Bank of England). Common law and guidelines resulted from that decision, and thus the case had become necessary background for management employees in the banking industry.

The Tournier Case concerned a bank customer with a £10 overdraft, who, having no fixed address, gave his bank branch manager the name and address of his new employers. When he defaulted on repayments, the branch manager telephoned those employers to ask if they knew his customer's address. In the course of doing so he disclosed the overdraft and default, and expressed his opinion that his customer was

betting heavily. As a result, Tournier lost his job, sued the bank, and won his case upon appeal.

What came out of the decision was a set of four exceptions on the banker's contractual duty of confidentiality where customer information could be disclosed without their consent:

a. Where disclosure is under compulsion by law;

b. Where there is a duty to the public to disclose;

c. Where the interests of the bank require disclosure;

d. Where the disclosure is made by the express or implied consent of the customer.

Since the Tournier decision, banks have become extremely sensitive about protecting customer information. Strict privacy policies have been put in place, and systems containing personal information have been protected from unauthorized use and manipulation. Recent advances in security and encryption technology allowed banking customers to access their accounts and conduct simple transactions though online and telephone banking systems.

Employee Privacy in the Banking Industry

Employee privacy was somewhat different than customer privacy. By design, in most banks, customers were provided with the best level of privacy protection available. However, there were legitimate reasons why banks might want to monitor what employees were doing on company time and with company equipment.

For banks like CIBC, providing employees with access to company e-mail had become a strategic necessity. However, with e-mail access came the possibility of unwittingly receiving or transmitting an e-mail worm or virus, much like the ones which swept across the world in early 2000. (For an explanation of worms and viruses, see Exhibit 1.) Computer Economics Inc., a research firm based in Carlsbad, California, reported that the ILOVEYOU virus alone had infected three million computers around the world, causing US$2 billion in direct economic losses and a further US$6.7 billion in

---

VIRUSES

A virus is a piece of programming code usually disguised as something else that causes some unexpected (and often undesirable) event, and which can automatically spread to other computer users. Viruses can be transmitted by diskette or CD, by sending them as attachments to an e-mail message or by downloading infected programming from the Internet. The source of the e-mail note, downloaded file, or diskette is often unaware of the virus. Some viruses wreak their effect as soon as their code is executed; other viruses lie dormant until circumstances cause their code to be executed by the computer. Some viruses are playful in intent and effect, while others can be harmful.

Generally, there are four main classes of viruses.

File infectors

Some file infector viruses attach themselves to program files, usually selected .COM or .EXE files. Some can infect any program for which execution is requested, including .SYS, .OVL, .PRG, and .MNU files. When the program is loaded, the virus is loaded as well. Other file infector viruses arrive as wholly contained programs or scripts sent as an attachment to an e-mail note.

System or boot-record infectors

These viruses infect executable code found in certain system areas on a disk. They attach to the DOS boot sector on diskettes or the Master Boot Record on hard disks. A typical scenario is to receive a diskette from an innocent source that contains a boot disk virus.

Macro viruses

Macro viruses are the most common form of viruses. Each macro virus can only be spread through a specific program. The most common types are Microsoft Word and Excel viruses. These programs contain "auto open macros" and "global macro templates." Virus writers recognize that any macros stored in the global file will automatically execute whenever something is opened. Macro viruses exploit these two aspects to enable themselves to replicate.

WORMS

A worm is a special type of virus that transfers itself from one computer to another via a network. Worms can replicate themselves very quickly (often through e-mail address books) and thus carry the potential to overload host systems. Normally, worms cannot attach themselves to other programs, and thus do not pose a threat to files or data.

Exhibit 1   Explanation of Worms and Viruses

---

lost productivity. Insurer Lloyd's of London announced on May 8, 2000, that computer viruses would prove to be the biggest insurance risk in upcoming years, prompting business analysts to call for a widespread change in company e-mail policies.

In addition to protecting company systems from viruses, employers like CIBC had obligations to ensure that employees were not acting illegally, for example in perpetrating frauds, or immorally. E-mail could be used by employees to make inappropriate or defamatory comments. It could also be used to transmit sensitive corporate information, without appropriate security.

CIBC's Electronic Communication Policy

E-mail and voice mail were both included in Section 4.6 of CIBC's *Principles of Business Conduct*. CIBC recognized that occasional personal use could not be avoided.

E-mail and voice mail are essential ways to communicate with employees, customers, suppliers, and other parties. Although all e-mail and voice mail facilities supplied by CIBC are its property, CIBC recognizes that incidental or occasional personal use of both is unavoidable.

CIBC reserved the right to access and monitor both internal and external e-mail and voice mail, including stored messages, and to restrict the use of both, without prior notice. The company also reserved the right to produce all office communications in legal proceedings.

Assentor Software

To ensure that its brokerage employees were not acting inappropriately in their dealings with customers through e-mail communications, CIBC relied on software to screen and archive e-mail messages in a central database. The software had the ability not only to screen key words, but combinations of words and sentences (so called natural language technology). The software allowed CIBC to "flag" and hold potentially inappropriate e-mail communications, such as high pressure sales tactics, insider information, as well as other potentially litigious issues, such as sexual harassment. These flagged e-mails were then held for human analysis and review before being sent.

The market for e-mail screening software was worth $17 million in 1999, and was growing at a rate of 45 per cent per year. According to a report by the Tower Group (www.towergroup.com), natural language technology was a significant improvement in screening technology allowing for more flexible and accurate monitoring than keyword or phrase search alone.

An excerpt from a news release from SRA International Inc. (which markets Assentor e-mail screening software), dated Feb. 22, 1999, read:

> (Tower Group) predicts that natural language functionality will become the technology of choice for e-mail compliance tools. . . . Securities firms of all sizes are using Assentor to apply technology to the compliance review process and take advantage of the many benefits of e-mail

technology for communicating with their clients. Assentor uses a sophisticated, linguistics-based natural language pattern matching engine and highly refined compliance patterns developed closely with securities industry associations, compliance experts, and major broker/dealers to ensure that the technology is effective for all types of compliance requirements.

Companies in the financial services industry which used Assentor included CIBC, A.G. Edwards, BancBoston, Southwest Securities, and the National Association of Securities Dealers. Many others used other, mostly less powerful, e-mail screening methods.

Call centers typically tape conversations for quality control, and most organizations announce to the customer at the beginning of the call that the conversation will be taped. Employees working at call centers knew when they arrived at work that their conversations would be taped due to the possibility of disputes—for example, replaying a taped call would confirm if the customer requested a "buy order" of 500 shares instead of a "sell order" for 5,000 shares of the same stock. It was much easier, on the other hand, to forget that e-mail use could be monitored.

CIBC had recently developed an "Electronic Mail Policy," which went into more detail than the previous entry in its *Principles of Business Conduct* document. This policy outlined appropriate and inappropriate use of this company resource. A short summary of the policy read:

> Electronic mail (e-mail) systems, provided by the CIBC Group of Companies (CIBC Group) are its property. Employees are to use these systems for company business primarily within the boundaries of this policy and its standards. Business information, and the ability to freely communicate it, are valuable assets that play a significant role in CIBC's success. The protection and appropriate use of these assets is everyone's responsibility.

> All messages sent or received by electronic mail are CIBC records and must be handled in a manner consistent with CIBC record management policies and practices. Caution and discretion should be used in the nature and content of all messages sent, stored or distributed.

CIBC recognizes that incidental or occasional use of e-mail for personal communications is unavoidable. However, all users with access to CIBC e-mail systems should be aware that the CIBC reserves the right to access, to monitor and to archive all e-mail messages, transmitted, received or stored on its systems, without further prior notice.

"E-mail use is often similar to casual conversations rather than formal written communications," stated Jones, "because employees forget that it is recorded and can be monitored." Jones went on to stress that e-mail is a business resource covered by a separate e-mail policy. He concluded by asking, "How should employees be discouraged from inappropriate language, content and usage?"

Jones knew that these were not easy questions to answer. Recent articles in newspapers and trade journals on e-mail privacy, such as the following excerpt, had brought the issue to CIBC's attention once more.

"Prying Times: Those Bawdy E-Mails Were Good for a Laugh—Until the Ax Fell," *The Wall Street Journal,* Feb. 4, 2000.

In the course of their inquiry, workers say, managers found a number of potentially offensive e-mails, some of which had been sent by or forwarded to other employees in the office. That led to a wider investigation, and ended Nov. 30th 1999 when the Times fired 22 people in Norfolk, plus one in New York. Roughly 20 more workers, who the company determined had received offensive messages but didn't forward them to others, got warning letters. Most of the fired employees were otherwise in good standing; one had just received a promotion, and another had recently been commended as "employee of the quarter."

Some corporations, like CIBC, used e-mail screening to catch e-mail misuse, but since these filters tended to slow down network traffic, the practice was not universal. A second option, according to Jordan Worth, an Internet Analyst with International Data Corporation, an Internet research firm, was to put in place policies that banned certain "types" of attachments. A third approach was to archive e-mail, but only access it in the event of a complaint.

WHAT SHOULD CIBC DO?

Jones found that taking the decision to implement the Assentor software was a lot easier than deciding what to do in the event that the software found something improper.

"What if an employee sends a personal message using a business 'word' flagged by Assentor and his or her direct manager finds out about a private situation?" wondered Jones. "What are the legal ramifications if the employee is reassigned or fired and subsequently claims bias on the part of the manager? What about the question of company ethics? Should we be reading personal e-mail from employees?"

Jones was wondering how to best reinforce the e-mail policy at CIBC.

The employee should know that e-mail is a business resource that *could* be monitored by the employer. But how would we enforce it?

If we were to cease monitoring e-mail, it might seem to be a viable solution, but remember that we have a responsibility to our customers, shareholders, and the regulatory agencies to ensure proper records are kept and to monitor business e-mail use. It is also a regulatory requirement in the securities industry. Should we consider taking that risk and not having an e-mail screen? Probably not. There are things that an employee legally can't say, and some things they shouldn't say. Assentor "sniffs" this out for us and our employees should understand this.

I believe it is all about how we present it to our employees. To best implement our Principles of Business Conduct, clear communication and upfront understanding from our employees will go far to prevent negative impressions. We want to be as upfront and clear as possible to them. How best, then, to do that?

Should we inform our employees once? Inform them once per year? Have them sign a code of conduct? Or inform the employee every time he or she logs on to a company computer?

Stamford Machine Corporation: Allegations of Racism

*Prepared by Ken Mark under the
supervision of Professor Christina A. Cavanagh*

Introduction

It was May 2001, and Allen Douglas, director of corporate business ethics and compliance of Connecticut-based Stamford Machine Corporation (SMC), received a call from Michael Weisberg, senior partner in New York law firm Weisberg Coltin. Douglas was advised that SMC was being served with a racial discrimination lawsuit from current and former black sales representatives.

The lawsuit was filed on behalf of six salespeople from California, Georgia, New York and Texas, and alleged that white sales managers would routinely exclude black salespeople from opportunities that would allow them to earn higher commissions and promotions. Douglas requested full details from Weisberg, and then sat down to chart a course of action. He knew that Weisberg's next call was to the press.

Stamford Machine Corporation

Founded in 1925, Stamford Machine Corporation had a long history of prevailing against seemingly impossible odds in the office products market: surviving the Great Depression, technology change, entrance and dominance of Japanese and Taiwanese competitors.

SMC designed, manufactured and marketed a range of typewriters, photocopiers and overhead projectors to businesses. With sales approaching US$1 billion in 2000, Stamford senior management believed it had achieved a major milestone. In the 1980s, Asian competitors had entered the

fray, changing the sedentary pace of the industry almost overnight. Faced with year after year of large losses, Stamford knew it had to reorganize its business practices.

Throughout the 1990s, Stamford embarked on an ambitious program to overhaul its sales force, rewarding successful salespeople with increasingly larger territories, and transferring or dismissing poor performers. The company avoided its competitor's strategies of promoting successful salespeople into management positions, where they were often ineffective. Rather, Stamford chose to richly compensate salespeople, keeping them in their preferred environment.

The program bore fruit in late 1999, when Stamford became the market leader in the U.S. copier market. With high positive cash flow and growth, Stamford looked poised to remain the leader for years to come.

The Public Announcement by Weisberg Coltin

Weisberg announced in a press release:

> Our clients have described a system where Stamford Machine routinely assigns white salespeople to profitable territories and expeditiously promotes them through ranks, while assigning minority salespeople to traditionally less profitable territories. Our clients charge, furthermore, that no matter how well minority salespeople perform in their territories, Stamford Machine rarely, if ever, promotes them to more profitable positions and territories.

In a press interview, another attorney in the case, James Fulton, continued:

> Basically, the company would send white salespeople to Wall Street and all the black salespeople to Harlem or the Bronx. The whites would sell 30 copiers at Morgan Stanley, and the black salesman was lucky if he sold one machine at a little mom-and-pop business. There was racial steering here, and there was an incredible difference in pay.

Before Douglas could even leave his office, the telephone rang again. It was the state newspaper's business affairs journalist, asking for comment. The journalist, who did not give his name, alluded to the fact that several employees had already voiced their opinion in separate interviews. Douglas was furious but tried not to show it. He calmly reserved comment and thanked the journalist for his interest. Out of concern, he asked the journalist what the employees had told him in their interviews:

- Cory Jameson, who sold for SMC in Atlanta, charged that the company took away his most lucrative accounts in late 1999 as part of a reorganization, giving the accounts to white salespeople. Jameson claimed that many of the representatives who gained control of his accounts not only had less tenure at SMC but also received commissions on several sales that were pending at the time. Jameson had filed charges with the Equal Employment Opportunity Commission in 1998 and received a notice from the commission earlier in 2001 that said he had enough of a case to sue.
- Ferran Ferguson, another black salesperson, said he was assigned a territory in the Bronx, New York, that required a car. When Ferguson notified the company that the territory would be hard for him to cover because he did not have a car, Ferguson alleges that a vice-president told him he was assigned to the Bronx because "blacks and the Bronx go hand-in-hand."

Douglas thanked the journalist again and sat down.

4

ETHICAL ISSUES IN INTERNATIONAL BUSINESS

No other type of corporate entity has attracted so much opprobrium for its perceived lack of morality as has the multinational corporation. Multinationals are large, and therefore conspicuous, and often operate in industries fraught with ethical problems—notably resource development. Whether they (or their managers) are in fact less moral than other organizations is an open question. What is not in doubt is the complexity of the moral dilemmas they face because they operate in many countries with different ethical norms and legal systems.

The perennial problem in international business is ethical relativism—under what circumstances should a manager "do in Rome what the Romans do," that is, follow local norms versus parent country norms? Cultural differences (i.e., values and acceptable norms of behavior) give rise to different business practices and different legal standards in different parts of the world. Developing countries often have lower standards of regulation (pollution and worker safety, for example) than those in developed countries. The absence of regulation makes these countries attractive for those industries in which regulations are costly for firms. Is it ethically sufficient for the multinational to meet local regulatory requirements, or should it be required to meet a higher standard? If it has to meet a higher standard, it might not be able to justify the investment.

If a particular business practice—for example, paying bribes or "facilitating payments" to customers—is considered normal business practice in a host country but is either illegal or unethical at home, what should a company do? The Foreign Corrupt Practices Act (FCPA) made the *legal* answer to this question easier, in that it extended the reach of American law (at least as far as the law relating the payment of bribes to foreign government officials is concerned) to the rest of the world for American corporations. If paying bribes is illegal, then must it not also be immoral? Does the magnitude of payment make any difference? Does the influence of the recipient matter? Does it make any difference if the recipient is underpaid and very poor? Does it matter that the recipient is underpaid because it is commonly understood in a particular country that most of their income will be earned in the form of bribes? The moral questions are endless!

Most writers would agree with Tom Donaldson (1996), who says that a relativist argument that it is acceptable to pay bribes where it is common practice is flawed. However, applying the same ethical rules abroad that apply at home (ethical imperialism) is also inadequate. He proposed three guiding principles: a respect for core human values (an absolute universal moral threshold), respect for local traditions, and recognition that context does matter when deciding what is right and wrong. However, following these guidelines is costly; some American companies claim that the FCPA (which many see as an example of ethical imperialism) has handicapped their competitiveness in international markets. To invoke another ethical argument, is the FCPA fair to U.S. multinationals?

The Siam Canadian Foods Co., Ltd., case explores the dilemma of whether a company should do business in a country whose government does not follow the rule of law, which is the case in several developing countries. Notwithstanding the attractiveness of low labor costs in developing countries (and the corresponding benefit to shareholders), foreign investment can also bring benefits to workers in those countries, but the investment is considered by many to be tacit support for a corrupt regime. The managing director and founder of Bangkok-based Siam Canadian Foods Co., Ltd., was considering the emerging business opportunities in neighboring Burma (also known as Myanmar). Although relatively undeveloped compared to the rest of Southeast Asia, Burma had been experiencing increasing levels of foreign investment activity in recent years. Siam, which had considered entering Burma in the past but declined, needed to determine if the time was now appropriate for the company to enter the market and, if so, what ethical questions should be resolved.

The NES China: Business Ethics (A) case addresses the problem of different ethical standards in China and Germany. NES is one of Germany's largest industrial manufacturing groups. The company wants to set up a holding company to facilitate its manufacturing activities in China. It has authorized representatives in its Beijing office to draw up the holding company application and to negotiate with the Chinese government for terms of this agreement. To maximize its chances of having its application accepted, the NES team in Beijing hires a government affairs coordinator who is a native Chinese and whose professional background has familiarized her with Chinese ways of doing business. NES's government affairs coordinator finds herself in a difficult position when she proposes that gifts should be given to government officials to establish a working relationship that will better NES's chance of having its application approved. This method of doing business is quite common in China. The other members of the NES team are shocked at what would be considered bribery and a criminal offence in their country. The coordinator must find a way to bridge the gap between working within accepted business practices in China and respecting her employers' code of business ethics. The complementary (B) case, available separately, gives a brief summary of the eventual solution to this problem but raises even more questions of ethics.

The N.K.Builders and Contractors-India case provides a somewhat different context, in which an investor already has a considerable amount of money at stake and is wondering whether he should abandon it because he has been told that questionable ethics will be necessary to bring the project to a successful completion. As in the NES case above, a local partner plays an important role. N.K.Builders and Contractors was a construction company newly formed by an experienced contractor and a young project manager. The project manager was very knowledgeable of the construction industry but not familiar with the bidding process for contracts; for this, he relied heavily on the experience of his partner. The company's first project was a government contract that required the partners to go to the divisional office to apply for the tender, where they found out they were one of 15 interested in the highway project. The bidding process was similar to an auction; the highest bid won. Money generated from the highest bid was shared equally among the remaining contractors, and the higher the bid, the more "commission" government officials received. Winning the contract was only the beginning. Once a company received the project, it was expected to begin work within a month; however, many things can happen between winning and completing the contract, and he would discover there would be a number of times when it was necessary to pay various officials to proceed with the project. The project manager was disappointed by the way the government awarded the contract to his company and must decide if he should quit and lose the money he invested in the company or remain with the business.

Differences in ethical and business norms provide particularly interesting material for discussion in the global banking industry when issues of confidentiality, secrecy, extraterritoriality, and possibly unethical transactions come together, and this book provides two examples. In the first case, Citibank Mexico Team: The Salinas Accounts, the head of a bank's Mexico Team must consider her options when confronted with the task of aiding in the arrest of one of her clients. She had just returned from Switzerland, where Swiss narcotics agents were encouraging her to lay a trap for the wife of one of her clients, the brother of a former Mexican president, who had been arrested in Mexico a few months earlier on charges of murder, illegal enrichment, and laundering money for the Mexican drug cartel. As she pondered her options, the fate of one of her former employees, who had recently been sentenced to 10 years' imprisonment for managing the account of a convicted money launderer, provided food for thought.

In the second case, Bank of Nova Scotia (Brady Subpoena), the laws of two countries conflict. The Bank of Nova Scotia, a Canadian bank, possesses documents subpoenaed by a grand jury in the United States, which is deliberating whether to issue an indictment against two U.S. citizens (clients of the bank) for drug trafficking and tax evasion. The documents are located in the Bahamas and the Cayman Islands. The bank has not been able to get permission from the islands to release the documents, and complying with the subpoena would mean violating the bank secrecy laws of the islands. The bank is caught in a bind. Its choices seem to be breaking the laws of the Cayman Islands and the Bahamas or the laws of the United States. A sequel to this case, Bank of Nova Scotia (Brady Subpoena) (B), available separately, describes the decision made by the bank.

The Internet is the ultimate conduit for international transactions and already provides enough material in business ethics for a book of its own. However, this book contains only one case, but one with an intriguing range of issues: Yahoo v. Survivors of the Holocaust. Yahoo Inc. was the second largest Internet portal worldwide and the leading Internet portal in France. After Nazi-era memorabilia were posted on one of its English-language auction sites, the company was ordered under a French law to block access to neo-Nazi content. Yahoo filed a countersuit, alleging that compliance would violate free speech, as guaranteed under U.S. and international laws. Angered by the company's response, survivors of the Holocaust charged the chief executive officer with war crimes for supporting the atrocities of the Nazi regime through its Web site. The borderless nature of the Internet raises many issues for the company: conflicting laws and cultures of other countries, differing views on freedom of speech and suppression of objectionable material, ethical considerations, and the impact of extraterritoriality.

No casebook including international business ethics would be complete without a case of a multinational company involved in resource development. Talisman Energy Inc. spent several years under the intense sustained scrutiny of the global media and environmental groups with respect to its activities in Sudan. This case, written with the cooperation of a member of the board, provides detailed insight into senior management's challenges as they saw them. Talisman Energy is the largest Canadian oil and gas producer, with main business activities in exploration, development, production, and marketing of crude oil, natural gas, and natural gas liquid. At a special board of directors meeting, the management and board of Talisman conducted a review of the Sudan operation to assess its fit within the current business portfolio. After years of direct and often angry criticism by human rights groups and the fact that the U.S. government was threatening to restrict firms operating in Sudan from listing their securities on American markets, the board was considering its options in the region. The Sudan project had good economic value for Talisman, with good prospects and future production possibilities. In addition, the company had gone to considerable lengths to develop and implement socially responsible policies and programs in Sudan. Senior management believed that they had contributed to an increased quality of life for the people of Sudan. Despite this, activist groups had continued to attack Talisman for its role in Sudan. The continued pressure from activists and governments was believed to be responsible for a steady decrease in the company's share price. The issue before the board in conducting this review was to question whether continuing operations in Sudan was compatible with Talisman's mandate to operate in the best interests of the company and its shareholders.

REFERENCE

Donaldson, T. (1996, September/October). Values in tension: Ethics away from home. *Harvard Business Review,* pp. 48–62.

SIAM CANADIAN FOODS CO., LTD.

Prepared by Tom Gleave under the
supervision of Professors John Kennedy and Tony Frost

Version: (A) 2002-10-17

In July 1996, Jim Gulkin, Managing Director and founder of Bangkok-based Siam Canadian Foods Co., Ltd., was considering the emerging business opportunities in neighbouring Burma (also known as Myanmar). Although relatively undeveloped compared to the rest of Southeast Asia, Burma had been experiencing increasing levels of foreign investment activity in recent years. Gulkin, who had considered entering Burma in the past but declined, needed to determine if the time was now appropriate for him to enter the market.

COMPANY PROFILE

Siam Canadian Foods Co., Ltd. (SC) was a brokerage business based in Bangkok, Thailand. It was started in April 1987 after Canadian Jim Gulkin quit his job in the oil industry and invested his life savings of Cdn$130,000 in the business. Gulkin was raised in Montreal where he remained until he graduated from grade 11 "with a stratospheric 51 per cent average." With school out of the way, he began travelling and working in various parts of the world and became enamoured with Thailand after holidaying there in 1979. SC's role as a food broker was to identify overseas customers, usually food importers, and negotiate sales with them on behalf of food processors in Thailand. SC's initial activity was limited to brokering canned pineapple and tuna; however, it gradually expanded its offerings to include a wide range of products such as frozen seafood, frozen poultry, canned and frozen fruit and vegetables as well as dehydrated fruit and juice concentrates. Over time, SC also began to source various products from both Burma and India on an ad hoc basis.

When first starting out, Gulkin was admittedly very inexperienced in the food brokering business. He commented:

> I didn't have a clue what I was doing . . . I didn't know what a letter of credit, invoice or cross-check was. I didn't even have a business plan or a marketing plan.

Adding to this inexperience, Gulkin found that local processors were reluctant to deal with him, despite the fact that he spoke fluent Thai. As a newcomer to an industry tightly controlled by Thailand's highly assimilated Overseas Chinese community, Gulkin struggled to develop comfortable levels of trust and confidence with the processors.

The food brokerage business generally operated on low margins, thus necessitating movements of large volumes of goods in order to achieve profitability. As the business evolved, SC began to focus mainly on brokering frozen seafood because the commissions were the most attractive. The company earned an average commission revenue of 1.25 per cent on sales contracts, usually denominated in U.S. dollars, that it negotiated on behalf of the food processors. During the late 1980s and early 1990s, the frozen seafood business was in a state of expansion in North America and Europe. At the same time, Thailand was quickly becoming a globally recognized source of frozen seafood, largely on the strength of overseas market acceptance of Black Tiger Shrimp. Gulkin estimated that Thailand harvested about 200,000 tons of Black Tiger shrimp in 1995, 90 per cent of which came from aquaculture facilities.

The following is an estimate of Thailand's recent fresh and frozen shrimp exports:

Year	1990	1992	1994
Baht (Billions)	20.5	31.7	49.2

25 Baht = US$1.00

In 1991, Gulkin opened up a representative office in Vietnam with the help of Philippe Vo. Vo was born in France to a French mother and Vietnamese father and, prior to moving to Vietnam, managed a seafood exporting business in California. The purpose of the representative office was to procure frozen seafood products for sale to overseas importers. Several months later, Gulkin, Vo and another local partner started a separate importing and distribution business, SC Food Services, in Ho Chi Minh City.

In 1992, Gulkin began to investigate the possibility of setting up a representative office in Burma but decided against it because he felt "very uncomfortable" with the local players in the seafood industry. This investigation made him realize that, apart from the necessary start-up capital which would be required, he also needed "connections" to people favoured by the ruling military junta, SLORC. He returned to Burma in 1994 when he discovered that new activity in the seafood industry was being generated by independent, non-politically connected business people. Discussions with the new players gave him a much higher level of comfort that business could be done in Burma without the need for buying favours. However, Gulkin also found that these new players were "sincere but incompetent" given that his attempt to export US$100,000 of frozen seafood collapsed due to insufficient raw material supplies of acceptable quality, resulting in a net loss to SC of about US$30,000. He later recalled that "it was a cheap lesson for the market knowledge we gained."

In 1994, SC secured one of the most significant contracts in the company's history on the strength of the relationship it had established with one of its key German importers. The contract called for SC to procure 600 tons of breaded shrimp to be shipped for ultimate sale to McDonald's Restaurants in Germany. A second contract for 450 tons was awarded to SC in 1995, with shipments this time going to McDonald's in Germany and Austria. The trading value of the 1995 shipment was US$7 million to US$8 million. Under the terms of the contracts, SC received a commission from the processor as well as a supervision fee paid by the importer. The latter was paid because SC dispatched quality control personnel to the processor's site to oversee the production and packaging of the breaded shrimp.

SC first achieved profitability in 1991 and had remained in the black ever since. In 1995, SC's trading volume was valued at about US$85 million, 90 per cent of which was attributable to frozen seafood. By 1996, SC employed 15 staff who were involved in sales, quality control and administration. The main destinations for the company's shipments were importers from the following countries, in descending order of sales value: United States, France, Germany and Canada.

The combination of increasing success in the food brokering business and the growing affluence in Bangkok in recent years, led Gulkin to form a separate sister company, Siam Canadian Gourmet Ltd., in early 1996. This importing and distribution business was initially focused on importing wines and coffees for sale to hotels,

restaurants and specialty food retailers. It was later expected to expand its product range to include imported cheeses, sauces and other gourmet cuisine items. Initial results were considered "very promising."

SC's VIETNAMESE EXPERIENCE

Gulkin's motivation for entering Vietnam in 1991 was largely based upon his assessment that, as an undeveloped country with a large, intelligent and hard-working population, many opportunities were becoming available to small firms with limited resources such as SC. As well, entering Vietnam was also consistent with Gulkin's view that in order to succeed in the food brokering business, firms had to adopt a diversification strategy in terms of both supply sources and product line offerings. Furthermore, the amount of foreign investment in Vietnam had been escalating, due largely to the implementation of the Vietnamese government's so-called "doi moi" or "renewal" policy, which was designed to attract foreign investment. This meant that there would be a limited window of opportunity for SC to enter the market before being shut out permanently by bigger players. Therefore, with the help of Vo, Gulkin opened up Siam Canadian Foods (Vietnam) in order to gain access to frozen seafood for shipment overseas. Apart from Vo, SC (Vietnam) employed four quality control staff and an administrative assistant. Gulkin held 100 per cent ownership of SC (Vietnam) while maintaining a 50 per cent profit-sharing arrangement with Vo. Later, Gulkin, Vo and a local Vietnamese partner opened up SC Food Services, a separate distributorship that imported meats and dairy products, and sourced local fruits and vegetables, for sale to hotels and restaurants in the Ho Chi Minh City area.

Gulkin's view on the performance of SC Foods (Vietnam) was mixed. The business had experienced modest profitability since its inception, something that he felt was "very good, all things considered." On the other hand, daily operations were frustrating, particularly with respect to the honoring of contracts by food processors. Gulkin offered the following as a simple, typical example of a Vietnamese contract gone bad:

> We enter into a contract with a Vietnamese processor to supply us with 30 metric tonnes (mt) of frozen cuttlefish tentacles per month for 12 months. We, in turn, contract to sell this quantity of product to a European buyer. One month into the contract the Japanese, all of a sudden, become interested in this particular commodity. The raw material price, therefore, goes up and out of 360 mt contracted, we might get to ship 15 or 30 mt. The Vietnamese processor has absolutely no intention of honouring our contract if it means that he loses money or even makes less than he originally hoped. The contract is meaningless to him. It is nothing more than a piece of paper. His word or his reputation are not tangible concepts to him. My company, however, has to find a way to pacify our buyers who are none too happy. Sometimes it costs some money but fortunately our relationships with our buyers are strong. We do tend to make it very clear to our buyers beforehand that a contract in Vietnam is basically worthless and we, therefore, give ourselves a very wide notwithstanding clause in any contract we involve ourselves in.

These frequent experiences left Gulkin with the impression that local processors only considered the short-term implications of their business, often leading him to ponder the question "why bother?"

BURMA

Burma, also known as The Union of Myanmar, was the largest mainland country in Southeast Asia and had a population of about 47 million. The country bordered on Bangladesh and India in the northwest, China in the northeast, Laos in the east and Thailand in the southeast. It was a diverse nation with over 135 distinct cultural groups, the predominant one being the Bamars, representing about 69 per cent of the population. The country was considered by the World Bank to be among the poorest in the world, with a per capita income of US$676, based on purchasing-power parity. The capital city of Rangoon (also

known as Yangon) had a population of approximately six million and was the nation's main port through which over 90 per cent of all ocean going trade passed. The physical geography of the country was a mixture of tropical mountains, plains and delta lowlands. Burma had a coastline that totalled over 2,830 kilometres bordering along the Andaman Sea and the Bay of Bengal. The country was thought to have abundant natural resources, particularly in teak wood, oil and seafood. (See Exhibit 1 for a Regional Map of Southeast Asia and Exhibit 2 for Recent Economic Indicators on Burma.)

Burma's seafood resources were plentiful given its exclusive economic fishing zone of 486,000 square kilometres along its coastline. Prior to 1994, the Myanmar Fisheries Enterprise, a state-run company controlling the nation's seafood harvesting and processing, was the dominant player in the Burmese fishing industry. This company was dissolved in 1994 in an effort to improve the industry through attracting private investment. The total marine harvest for Burma was estimated to be as follows:

Year	1990	1992	1994
Tonnes (Thousands)	645.7	650.7	689.0

Gulkin estimated that the total current annual harvest of all shrimp species in Burmese waters was about 20,000 tons. Given that the state of development within the seafood industry was relatively low, he felt that the placement of modern fishing fleets and aquaculture facilities, spurred on by recent measures to liberalize the industry, would increase Burma's seafood output considerably over the next several years, but not to the extent that it would match Thailand's output.

In 1988, Burma passed the Foreign Investment Law which, much like Vietnam's "doi moi" policy, was designed to attract foreign capital to industries which would promote exports and provide for the acquisition of new technologies. This Law was seen by the Burmese government as a market oriented measure because it allowed 100 per cent foreign ownership of firms, repatriation of capital and an "unequivocal guarantee" against the

Cambodia, Myanmar, Laos

Exhibit 1   Map of Southeast Asia

Source: E-I-U Country Report, first quarter 1995.

	1991/1992	1992/1993	1993/1994
Nominal GDP (kyat—billions)	187	248	339
Real GDP* (kyat—billions)	50	55	58
Real per Capita GDP (kyat—millions)	1,202	1,289	1,341
Real GDP Growth Rate (%)	−0.6	+9.3	+6.0
Consumer Price Index (1986 = 100)	349.30	460.49	541.51
Total Exports (kyat—millions)	2,932	3,655	4,071
Total Imports (kyat—millions)	5,337	5,365	7,218
GDP Area of Economic Activity (%)			
Agriculture	37.5	38.5	38.3
Trade	22.1	22.1	22.1
Processing/Manufacturing	8.9	8.8	9.2
Livestock/Fishing	7.6	7.3	7.2
Social Administration	7.2	6.7	6.7
Rental and Other Services	4.8	4.5	4.4
Transportation	4.0	4.0	3.9
Construction	2.9	3.0	3.0
Other	5.0	5.1	4.2

Exhibit 2   Recent Economic Indicators—Burma

Source: Investing in Myanmar, Union of Myanmar Investment Commission, 1995.

*Real GDP figures given use 1985/1986 fiscal year as benchmark.

1994 exchange rates: US$1.00 = 5.08 kyat; Cdn$1.00 = 3.78 kyat.

nationalization or expropriation of businesses. Firms operating under the guidelines of the Law paid a flat tax of 30 per cent; however, there existed numerous provisions which could be used to lessen a firm's tax burden, including the following:

- a tax holiday period of three consecutive years inclusive of the year of start-up with a possible extension if the Myanmar Investment Commission deemed it appropriate

- exemption or relief of tax paid on profits which were held in reserve and re-invested into the firm within one year
- accelerated depreciation of capital assets
- exemption or relief from customs duties paid on various equipment and instruments imported during the start-up phase of the firm

By 1994, 113 enterprises involving foreign ownership were engaged in a variety of agricultural, seafood processing, manufacturing, mining, energy and transportation activities in accordance with the provisions of the Law, eight of which were directly related to the seafood industry. (See Exhibit 3.)

Recent Political History

In April 1947, Burma took a significant step towards gaining independence from British colonization by having its first free elections after WWII. The winner of the election was Aung San, the leader of the Anti-Fascist People's Freedom League (AFPFL). On July 19, 1947, Aung San, along with six of his senior cabinet colleagues, was assassinated. This became known as Martyr's Day. U Nu, the ranking AFPFL politician remaining, took over the leadership of the country and gained Burma's independence from Britain in early 1948. During these early years, U Nu attempted to establish his party's concept of Buddhist based socialism. However, in March 1962, General Ne Win led a left-wing military takeover of Burma in support of the Burmese Socialist Programme Party (BSPP) and subsequently imprisoned U Nu and his supporters. In July 1962, several students who protested this takeover were shot to death at Rangoon University. These killings were followed by the complete destruction of the student union building on the campus. In the ensuing years, Ne Win began to direct the country towards the "Burmese way to socialism" in accordance with the doctrine of the BSPP. As a consequence, virtually all businesses were nationalized and there was a gradual closure of trade with most of the outside world. This eventually led to the collapse of the Burmese economy.

In 1987 and 1988, many Burmese organized mass demonstrations protesting the legacy of incompetence of the Government and calling for the removal of Ne Win. In July 1988, Ne Win

Firm	Activity	Origin of Foreign Investor
1. Myanmar Bangladesh Fisheries Ltd.	Shrimp farm management	Bangladesh
2. Myanmar American Fisheries Co., Ltd.	Fish and marine products	United States
3. General Fisheries Co., Ltd.	Fishing, breeding, processing of fresh and saltwater products	Thailand
4. Myanmar Niino Joint Venture Co., Ltd.	Culturing and marketing of high quality pearls	Japan
5. Hanswaddy Fisheries Co., Ltd.	Fishing, prawn farming, processing and marketing of fresh and saltwater products	Thailand
6. Myanmar P.L. International Ltd.	Prawn farming, processing and marketing	Singapore
7. Myanmar Garming Fisheries Ltd.	Shrimp cultivation, fish processing and marketing	Hong Kong
8. Myanmar Seafoods Ltd.	Procurement, processing, handling and marketing of fresh and saltwater products	Singapore

Exhibit 3   Recent Joint Venture Investments in the Burmese Fisheries Sector

stepped down following six weeks of bloody confrontations between pro-democracy demonstrators and the military, in which an estimated 3,000 people were killed. The BSPP did not relinquish power, however. In September 1988, a BSPP-backed military coup was staged resulting in the establishment of the new State Law and Order Restoration Council (SLORC), under the leadership of General Saw Maung, Commander-in-Chief of the armed forces. Saw Maung immediately imposed a state of martial law while promising to hold a democratic election in the near future. This quickly led to the forming of the National League for Democracy (NLD), a coalition of parties opposed to the BSPP, under the leadership of Aung San's daughter, Aung San Suu Kyi. The NLD went on to win the election which was held in May 1989, despite allegations that SLORC had attempted to manipulate the outcome. After the election, SLORC refused to allow the NLD to assume the role of government and arrested the party's leadership and soon after placed Suu Kyi under house arrest.

On July 10, 1995, Suu Kyi was released from house arrest after six years of detainment, and four years after she had won the Nobel Peace Prize, in absentia, for her dedication to democratic reform in Burma. Despite SLORC's warning that Suu Kyi should abstain from political activism, she continued to hold press conferences and political rallies outside of her housing compound on University Avenue in Rangoon. Furthermore, she repeatedly called upon the United States and the European Community to impose economic sanctions against Burma as a means to force democratic reform in the country and was successful to some degree. During 1995, the four U.S. cities of Santa Monica and Berkeley, California, Ann Arbor, Michigan and Madison, Wisconsin passed "selective purchasing" legislation which barred these cities from buying goods and services from companies doing business in Burma. Similar legislation had also been tabled and was awaiting ratification by the cities of Oakland, San Francisco, New York and Colorado Springs.

By July 1996, several recent events had caused the issue of human and democratic rights in

Burma to gain political attention and press coverage worldwide. Two months previously, in May, the Burmese government arrested 262 NLD members, thus preventing them from holding their first national congress since the 1990 election. This incident was followed by the mysterious death of James Nichols, a Burmese resident and former honorary consul in Burma for Denmark, Finland, Norway and Switzerland, who died in jail under vague circumstances. The 69-year-old Nichols, a close friend of Suu Kyi, had served two months of a three-year prison sentence for possessing an unlicensed fax machine.

These events led Suu Kyi to escalate her call to the Western powers for sanctions against Burma. At one point, she was able to have a video-taped speech smuggled out of the country. The message, which was played to members of the European Parliament, prompted the European Union to support Suu Kyi's position that economic sanctions were needed in Burma in order to move the democratic reform process forward. The culmination of these events led Heineken to announce on July 1 that it would divest itself of its interest in its Burmese joint venture. Soon after, Carlsberg announced that it had cancelled its plans to develop a brewery in the country. These announcements occurred about four months after Pepsi sold off its 40 per cent stake in a Burmese joint venture.

That same July (1996), leaders from the Association of Southeast Asian Nations (ASEAN), whose members included Thailand, Vietnam, Malaysia, the Philippines, Brunei, Singapore and Indonesia, met in Jakarta for their annual conference. ASEAN was a forum used to discuss issues that were of mutual interest to its members, including political, economic, security and environmental concerns. Burma had been invited to the conference as an observer for the first time, a move that was seen by many as the first step towards eventually granting it full membership status. Interestingly, by the time the conference concluded in late July, the United States Senate had passed a bill approving the use of sanctions against Burma if SLORC engaged in any acts which suppressed the pro-democracy movement of the NLD. The only hurdle which remained for full passage of the bill was the signature of President Clinton who, only several months previously, approved the Helms-Burton Bill, a measure designed to penalize firms and firm managers who continued to conduct business with Cuba.

The issue of democratic and human rights abuses in Burma was very prominent at the conference. However, while the United States and the European Union considered applying economic sanctions on Burma, ASEAN's policy position called for "constructive engagement" with SLORC. ASEAN's view was that the region's economic and security interests would be better served if Burma was not isolated. To this end, many ASEAN firms were encouraged by their governments to invest in Burma. In fact, Singapore-based Fraser and Neave immediately offered to take over Heineken's ownership stake in its Burmese joint venture. Similarly, discussions about building a new brewery between the Golden Star Group, Carlsberg's former Burmese partner, and Malaysia's Asia-Euro Brewery were already under way, less than three weeks after Carlsberg announced its pull-out.

GULKIN'S PERSPECTIVE ON BURMA'S POLITICS

In considering his position on the question of democratic and human rights in Burma, Gulkin offered the following:

> Aung San Suu Kyi is a decent, intelligent, well-intended, brave and selfless person. I realize that the politically correct trend is to call for sanctions against Burma, but economic isolation simply does not work. Take a look a Cuba, Chile, North Korea and Iraq. All of those countries have experienced economic sanctions of varying degrees, but their leaders still remained. People will often use South Africa as an example that sanctions work, but their case was unusual. The new South Africans were an island of Europeans isolated both within their own country and from the rest of the world.

> Economic empowerment raises hope for democracy. Just take a look at Taiwan, South Korea and even here in Thailand. All of these countries went from dictatorships to democracies as their level of wealth increased. In 1992, when the Thai military tried to take over the government, the people said "No!" and what happened? Democracy prevailed. Many Thais had started to enjoy the benefits of increased economic power and were not going to give them up. It is the economically deprived that lack money and education. These people are easy to keep in place.

> On the question of human rights, Burma is no worse than Indonesia or China. The Indonesian government has brutally occupied East Timor for over 20 years. As for China, there are tens of thousands of executions happening there each year, some even for economic crimes. Amnesty International is constantly citing China as a major human rights offender but I don't see Pepsi or Carlsberg pulling out of there.

RECONSIDERING BURMA IN 1996

Gulkin recognized that time was of the essence if he was going to finally commit to Burma. On the positive side, Rangoon had seen the development of at least five new seafood processing plants in past two years financed by independent firms. Having had preliminary discussions with some of the independents, Gulkin's instincts led him to believe that corruption would not be a problem and that he would be able to quickly develop relationships of trust and confidence with them. As well, the lack of economic development within the country meant that smaller firms such as his own might be able to gain a sustainable foothold before many larger, well-financed firms entered the market. It was Gulkin's view that bigger multinational corporations could afford to be "politically correct," while smaller firms needed to take advantage of the windows of opportunity while they existed. A further incentive for establishing operations in Burma was his belief that, given the underdeveloped state of the Burmese seafood industry, he would be able to realize significantly larger commission margins than he was currently receiving in Thailand or Vietnam.

Investment in Burma was also consistent with Gulkin's business philosophy of developing and managing diverse supply sources and product ranges. This was particularly important when he considered that the Thai seafood market was simultaneously experiencing increased levels of competition as well as dwindling supplies of raw materials. He estimated that the seafood industry in Thailand had reached the saturation point in terms of the number of processors operating and that raw material supply levels would gradually deplete to the point where the industry would be in definite decline within ten years. At the same time, relations between Thailand and Burma had moved in a decidedly favourable direction in recent months. In March 1996, Banharn Silpa-archa became the first Thai Prime Minister in 16 years to visit Burma. The primary objectives of the trip were twofold: first, to re-establish border trade between the two countries, given that cease-fires between insurgent ethnic groups along the border had been sustained, and second, to give Thai business interests a chance at gaining a stronger foothold in the country given the recognition of increased interest that other nations in the region were showing in Burma.

Gulkin's view was that most of the other nations in the region did not offer the same potential for developing his seafood exporting business further. For instance, although neighbouring Cambodia had a sizeable coastline along the Gulf of Siam and thus strong potential as a seafood exporter, the country was still experiencing the devastating effects that years of brutal war and governance under the Khmer Rouge had brought to the country. A strong consensus among many business people living in Thailand was that Cambodia was not a secure place to travel, let alone conduct business. Evidence of this insecurity was shown by the recent kidnapping of a British landmine disposal expert, along with 20 Cambodian colleagues who were working on behalf of the Mines Advisory Group. Additionally, in a highly publicized incident in 1994, three foreign backpackers were kidnapped and subsequently murdered by the Khmer Rouge.

Gulkin had also dismissed the possibility of entering Malaysia because it had experienced very strong economic growth in recent years which, in turn, allowed the seafood exporting industry to become well-developed. Gulkin viewed Indonesia as having potential, given that it was a large, resource rich archipelago; however, he dismissed this option because of its considerable distance from Thailand. Furthermore, Indonesia was currently experiencing political turmoil of its own, brought on by the arrest of Megawati Sukarno, daughter of Indonesia's founding President Sukarno and the principal political foe of the current President, General Suharto.

Several factors existed which were working to dissuade Gulkin from making the leap to Burma, however. First, Gulkin was concerned about competing against PL Corporation, a local seafood exporting company controlled by General Ne Win's son-in-law, particularly since local companies were often shown preferential treatment by local suppliers and producers. Additionally, there was increased interest in the region from two of SC's key competitors, the Hong Kong-based Sun Wah Trading Company and a sourcing division for the Japanese trading giant, Mitsui. Sun Wah was a well-financed firm which maintained its own fleet of transport ships and had a well-established reputation in the seafood trading business. Its solid financial position allowed the firm to extend million dollar financing arrangements to processors, thus enabling them to remain open in times when cash flow was squeezed, something SC was not able to do for its customers. Mitsui's sourcing division was interested in Burma's raw material supply so that other members of the Mitsui keiretsu would be assured of having inputs for their value-added food processing operations. Gulkin viewed Mitsui, as well as the increasing interest of Japan's other big trading companies, as his largest threat in Burma. This was because the Japanese giants would be able to outbid many of the smaller players, and in turn, limit their ability to secure reliable supply sources. Additionally, the recent trend of the Japanese Yen was also cause for some concern because its rising value gave the Japanese greater purchasing power throughout the world.

The recent political attention given to Burma also worried Gulkin. While Gulkin viewed economic isolation as harmful, he also needed to consider the view of his overseas customers.

He remained cautiously optimistic that his customers would not view his possible foray into Burma as unduly harmful. At the same time, however, he realized that if the economic sanctions movement gained momentum, some of SC's customers might "black list" Burma. Adding further confusion to this situation was the recognition that an increasing number of Asian firms were making inroads into Burma, despite the calls for sanctions elsewhere in the world. It was quite clear that Asia's view of Burma was considerably different from that of the Western powers.

The level of development of Burma's infrastructure was also cause for some concern. It would clearly be difficult to conduct business in a country which lacked an adequate system of roads or communication linkages. The port facility in Rangoon was especially problematic and was considered to be the biggest bottleneck in the country. It was not uncommon for vessels to wait for several days or even weeks before they could be loaded or unloaded. The matter was so grave that it prompted several foreign investors from Singapore and Hong Kong to begin the development of a new port across the river from Rangoon; however, it was expected to be about a year before the port became operational.

DECISION

In considering his Burmese investment decision, Gulkin had to consider several trade-offs. Could he afford to take a "wait and see" approach to Burma while other Asian firms started to tap into the market? Similarly, could he afford to allow this opportunity to pass him by given that other seafood exporting opportunities in the region were quite limited? Alternatively, if Gulkin entered Burma, could he be assured that his investment was secure given the state of political governance in the country? At the same time, would he run the risk of losing some key clients who would discontinue doing business with him because of his involvement in Burma?

NES CHINA: BUSINESS ETHICS (A)

Prepared by Xin Zhang under the supervision of Professor Joerg Dietz

Version: (A) 2002-08-30

By April 1998, it had been almost a year since the Germany-headquartered multinational company NES AG had first submitted its application to the Chinese government for establishing a holding company in Beijing to co-ordinate its investments in China. The application documentation had already been revised three times, but the approval by the government was still outstanding. Lin Chen, government affairs co-ordinator at NES AG Beijing Representative Office, came under pressure from the German headquarters and had to find a way to obtain approval within a month.

During the past year, Chen had almost exclusively worked on the holding company application. In order to facilitate the approval process, she had suggested giving gifts to government officials. But her European colleagues, Steinmann and Dr. Perrin, disagreed because they thought such conduct would be bribery and would violate business ethics. Confronted with the cross-cultural ethical conflict, Chen had to consider possible strategies that would satisfy everybody.

COMPANY BACKGROUND

NES and NES AG

NES was founded in Germany in 1881. Over the following 100 years, by pursuing diversification strategies, NES had grown from a pure tube manufacturer into one of the largest industrial groups in Germany, with sales of US$14 billion in 1997. NES built plants and heavy machinery, made automotive systems and components, manufactured hydraulic, pneumatic and electrical drives and controls, offered telecommunications services and produced steel tubes and pipes.

NES was managed by a holding company—NES AG—that implemented value-oriented portfolio management and directed its financial resources to the areas with the greatest profit potentials. In 1997, NES AG owned NES's 11 companies in four business segments: engineering, automotive, telecommunications and tubes. These companies generally operated independently and largely at their own discretion, as NES AG was interested in their profitability and not their day-to-day operations.

NES had always been committed to move along the road of globalization and internationalization. Headquartered in Germany, NES had businesses in more than 100 countries with over 120,000 employees. In the process of globalization and internationalization, NES established a business principle that demonstrated its responsibilities not only to shareholders, employees and customers, but also to society and to the countries where it operated. As an essential part of the company's corporate culture, this principle pervaded the decentralized subsidiaries worldwide and guided the decision-making and conduct of both the company and its employees.

NES China Operations

NES's business in China dated back to 1889, when it built the flood barrages for the Canton River. In 1908, NES supplied seamless steel tubes for the construction of a waterworks in Beijing. Through the century, NES continued to broaden its presence. From the mid-1950s to 1997, NES supplied China with an enormous 5.2 million metric tons of steel tube and 1.6 million tons of rolled steel.

Since China opened up to foreign trade and investment in the late 1970s, NES's presence had grown dramatically. From 1977 to 1997, NES had completed more than 40 technology transfer and infrastructure projects. It had also set up 20 representative offices, six equity joint ventures and three wholly owned enterprises.

In developing business links with China, NES adhered to its business principle. Most NES enterprises in China had highlighted this principle in their codes of conduct in employment handbooks (see Exhibit 1). These codes required employees to pursue the highest standards of business and personal ethics in dealing with government officials and business customers, and to avoid any activities that would lead to the involvement of the company in unlawful practices. Instead of tendering immediate favors or rewards to individual Chinese officials and customers, NES relied on advanced technology, management know-how and top quality products and service as a source of its competitive advantage. NES emphasized long-term mutual benefits and corporate social responsibility. Since 1979, NES had trained more than 2,000 Chinese engineers, master craftsmen, technicians and skilled workers in Germany. It had also offered extensive training programs in China. Moreover, NES was the first German company to adopt the suggestion of the German federal government to initiate a scholarship program for young Chinese academics to study in Germany. As a result, NES had built a strong reputation in China for being a fair business partner and a good guest company.

NES Beijing Representative Office

In 1977, NES was the first German company to open its representative office in Beijing. Along with NES's business growth, the Beijing Representative Office continued to expand. In 1997, it had 10 German expatriates and more than 40 local staff in nine business units. One unit represented NES AG. This unit was responsible for administrative co-ordination and office

---

Article 3 Employment and Duties

3.1 The Company employs the Employee and the Employee accepts such employment in accordance with the terms and conditions of the Employment Contract and this Employment Handbook.

3.6 The Company expects each Employee to observe the highest standards of business and personal ethics, and to be honest and sincere in his/her dealings with government officials, the public, firms, or other corporations, entities, or organizations with whom the Company transacts, or is likely to transact.

3.7 The Company does business without favoritism. Purchases of materials or services will be competitively priced whenever possible. An Employee's personal interest or relationship is not to influence any transaction with a business organization that furnishes property, rights or services to the Company.

3.8 Employees are not to solicit, accept, or agree to accept, at any time of the year, any gift of value which directly or indirectly benefits them from a supplier or prospective supplier or his employees or agents, or any person with whom the Company does business in any aspect.

3.9 The Company observes and complies with all laws, rules, and regulations of the People's Republic of China which affect the Company and its Employees. Employees are required to avoid any activities which involve or would lead to the involvement of the Company in any unlawful practices and to disclose to the proper Company authorities any conduct that comes to their attention which violates these rules and principles. Accordingly, each Employee should understand the legal standards and restrictions that apply to his/her duties.

3.10 All Employees are the Company's representatives. This is true whether the Employee is on duty or off duty. All Employees are encouraged to observe the highest standards of professional and personal conduct at all times.

Article 13 Discipline

13.1 The Company insists on utmost discipline. The Employee's misconduct or unsatisfactory performance will be brought to the attention of the responsible Head of Department or Member of the Management when it occurs and will be documented in the Employee's file.

13.2 Some offences are grounds for immediate dismissal and disciplinary procedures will apply to other offences.

13.3 Offences which are grounds for immediate dismissal include:
  (i) Breach of the Company's rules of conduct.
  (j) Neglect of duties, favoritisms or other irregularities.

Exhibit 1   Excerpt From the Employment Handbook of One of the NES's Enterprises in China

Source: Company files.

---

expense allocation. The other eight units worked for the German head offices of their respective NES companies in the engineering, automotive and tube segments.

Chinese legal restrictions severely limited the activities of the Beijing Representative Office. It was allowed only to engage in administrative activities, such as conducting marketing research for the German head offices, passing on price and technical information to Chinese customers, and arranging for meetings and trade visits. Moreover, it could not directly enter into employment contracts with its Chinese employees. Instead, it had to go through a local labor service agency designated by the Chinese government and consult with the agency on almost all personnel issues including recruitment, compensation and dismissal. As a result, the German managers of the Beijing Representative Office found it difficult to effectively manage their Chinese employees. In the absence of direct employment contracts, the managers had to rely on an internal reporting and control system.

CURRENT SITUATION

Establishing China Holding Company

In early 1997, NES AG had decided to establish a holding company in Beijing as soon as possible after carefully weighing the advantages and disadvantages of this decision. Establishing a China holding company was advantageous because, unlike a representative office, a holding company had its own business licence and could therefore engage in direct business activities. In addition to holding shares, a holding company could co-ordinate many important functions for its enterprises, such as marketing, managing government relations, and providing financial support. As a "country headquarters," a holding company could also unite the NES profile in China and strengthen the good name of NES as a reliable business partner in the world's most populous country. Moreover, it could hire stàff directly and thus retain full control over its own workforce. In light of these advantages, NES AG expected substantial time and cost efficiencies from the China holding company.

Several disadvantages, however, potentially outweighed the advantages of a China holding company. First, Chinese legal regulations still constrained some business activities. For example, a Chinese holding company could not balance foreign exchange accounts freely and consolidate the taxation of NES's Chinese enterprises, although this might be permitted in the future. Second, the setup efforts and costs were high. To establish a holding company, NES had to submit a project proposal, a feasibility study, articles of association and other application documents to the local (the Local Department) and then to the central trade and economic co-operation departments (the Central Department) for examination and approval. Third, there was only a limited window of opportunity for NES AG. Once the China holding company had received its business licence, within two years, NES AG would have to contribute a minimum of US$30 million fresh capital to it. The Chinese regulations prescribed that this capital could be invested only in new projects, but otherwise would have to remain unused in a bank

account. NES currently was in a position to invest the capital in its new projects, but the company was not certain how much longer it would be in this position.

Working Team

NES AG authorized the following three individuals in the Beijing Representative Office to take up the China holding company application issue:

Kai Mueller, 58 years old, had worked for NES in its China operations since the 1970s and had experience in several big co-operative projects in the steel and metallurgical industries. He would be the president of the holding company.

Jochen Steinmann, 30 years old, was assigned to Beijing from Germany in 1996. He would be the financial controller of the holding company.

Dr. Jean Perrin was a 37-year-old lawyer from France who had an in-depth understanding of Chinese business laws. He would work as the legal counsel. His previous working experience included a professorship at the Beijing International Business and Economics University in the 1980s.

The trio had advocated the idea of a China holding company to NES AG for quite some time and were most happy about NES AG's decision, because the future holding company would give them considerably more responsibilities and authority than did the Beijing Representative Office.

Considering the complexity and difficulty in coping with the Chinese bureaucratic hurdles, Mueller decided in March 1997 to hire Lin Chen as a government affairs co-ordinator for the working team. Chen, a native Chinese, was a 28-year-old politics and public administration graduate who had worked four years for a Chinese state-owned company and was familiar with the Chinese way of doing business. Mueller expected that Chen would play an instrumental role in obtaining the holding company approval from the Chinese government. He also promised that Chen would be responsible for the public affairs function at the holding company once it was set up.

Chen's View of Doing Business in China

Chen officially joined the Beijing Representative Office in June 1997. She commented on doing business in China:

> China's economy is far from rules-based; basically, it is still an economy based on relationships. In the absence of an explicit and transparent legal framework, directives and policies are open to interpretation by government officials who occupy positions of authority and power. In such circumstances, businesspeople cultivate personal *guanxi* (interpersonal connections based implicitly on mutual interest and benefit) with officials to substitute for an established code of law that businesspeople in the Western society take for granted.
>
> In building and nurturing *guanxi* with officials, gifts and personal favors have a special place, not only because they are associated with respect and friendship, but also because in today's China, people place so much emphasis on utilitarian gains. In return for accepting gifts, officials provide businesspeople with access to information about policy thinking and the potentially advantageous interpretation of the policy, and facilitate administrative procedures. Co-operation leads to mutual benefits.

Although an existing regulation forbids government officials to accept gifts of any kind,[1] it remains pervasive for businesspeople to provide officials with major household appliances, electric equipment, "red envelopes" stuffed with cash, and overseas trips. There is a common saying: "The bureaucrats would never punish a gift giver." Forbidding what the West calls bribery in a *guanxi*-based society where gift giving is the expected behavior can only drive such under-the-table transactions further behind the curtain.

While sharing benefits with officials is normal business conduct in China, it is interpreted as unethical and abnormal in the West. Faced with their home country's ethical values and business rules, Western companies in China cannot handle government relationships as their Asian counterparts do. They often find themselves at a disadvantage. This dilemma raises a question for a multinational company: Should it impose the home country's moral principles wherever it operates or should it do what the Chinese do when in China, and, if so, to what extent?

Different Opinions on Bribery

When Chen started working in June 1997, Mueller was sick and had returned to Germany for treatment. Steinmann and Dr. Perrin told Chen that NES had submitted the holding company application to the Local Department in April 1997 and that the Local Department had transferred the documents to the Central Department at the end of that month. But nothing had happened since then. Chen felt that she had to fall back to her former colleague, Mr. Zhu, who had close personal *guanxi* with the Central Department, to find out first who had the authority in the Central Department to push the processing and what their general attitudes towards the application were.

In July, Chen reported her findings to Steinmann and Dr. Perrin:

> The approval process at the Central Department is difficult. Because holding companies are a relatively new form of foreign investment in China, the officials are unsure whether they are a good idea for China. They have been very prudent to grant approval. Hence, we don't have much negotiating leverage, although we are a big company and have products and technologies that China needs. The officials say that they will consider a holding company's application within 90 days of its submission. They issue approval however, only when the application is deemed "complete and perfect" (in that all issues have been resolved to the Central Department's satisfaction). The Central Department is under no real obligation to approve any holding company application. They can always find some minor issues. So the approval procedure may be lengthy. The legal basis for establishing holding companies is provided by the Holding Company Tentative Provisions, Supplementary Rules and some unpublished internal policies. This provisional and vague status allows the officials to be flexible in authorizing a holding company. In such circumstances, maintaining close connections with the responsible officials is absolutely critical.

Chen suggested:

> The quickest and most effective way to build such connections is to invite the responsible officials to dinner and give gifts. It won't cost the company too

much. But what the company will gain in return—efficiency in obtaining approval and flexibility in the interpretation of the wording within the scope permitted by law—is worth much more.

Upon hearing Chen's report and suggestion, Steinmann was shocked:

That would be bribery. In Germany bribing an official is a criminal offence for which both the briber and the bribed are punished. NES is a publicly traded company with a board of directors that reports to shareholders and monitoring authorities in Germany.

We have met the criteria for setting up the holding company. What we should do now is organize a formal meeting with the officials and negotiate with them. This is the way we have done it in the past, and it has always worked. I am not aware that we ever had to use bribery. NES does not have a history of wrongdoing.

Knowing how critical it was to follow China's customary business practices in tackling such issues, Chen argued:

Yes, it is correct. NES did not have to give gifts of this kind in the past. But don't forget: virtually all of NES's projects or joint ventures in the past were approved by agencies responsible for specific industries or local governments that were very keen on having access to NES's technology. As a result, NES always has had considerable bargaining power. It is different this time: we need to found a holding company, and we have to deal with the Central Department that we have never contacted before. Even Mueller does not have relations in this department. Moreover, our contacts at the industrial and local levels won't help much because they have very limited influence on the Central Department and, hence, the holding company application issue.

Moreover, you can't equate gifts with bribes. The approval letter doesn't have predetermined "prices" and no one forces us to pay. We give gifts just to establish relationships with officials. We develop good relationships, and favorable consideration of these officials comes naturally. According to Chinese law,[2] to give gifts to government officials and expect them to take advantage of

their position and power to conduct *illegal* actions is bribery. Our intent is to motivate officials to handle our application legally but without delay. I see no serious ethical problem.

In some ways it's also hard to blame officials for feathering their nest because they are poorly paid. Whether they process our application quickly or slowly has absolutely no impact on their US$200 monthly income. Then, how can we expect them to give our case the green light? They are not morally wrong if they accept our gifts and don't create obstacles for us in return.

Negotiation doesn't help much. Unless we have close relationships with them, they will always find some minor flaws in our documents. After all, they have the authority for interpreting the regulations. Therefore, we have to be open-minded and get accustomed to the Chinese way of doing business.

Chen hoped that Dr. Perrin would support her, as she had a feeling that the French were more flexible and less ethically sensitive than the Germans. Dr. Perrin, however, shared Steinmann's view. Perrin said:

We should not give officials anything that has some value, with the exception of very small objects (pens, key holders, calendars and the like) given mainly for marketing and advertisement purposes. I also think that these officials should not accept any gifts. It's unethical and illegal. If we think it is unethical, we should combat it and refrain from it.

Nonetheless, Dr. Perrin understood the importance of *guanxi* as an informal solution to Chinese bureaucracies. So he agreed that Chen could invite one of the two responsible officials to dinner through Mr. Zhu and present a CD player to this official as an expression of respect and goodwill, although he thought it went too far and was approaching bribery.

On a Saturday evening in July, Chen met the official at one of the most expensive restaurants in Beijing. At the dinner, the official promised to work overtime the next day on NES's documents and give feedback as soon as possible.

The following Monday, Chen got the government's official preliminary opinion demanding a revision of 16 clauses of the application documents. Steinmann and Dr. Perrin found it difficult to understand this. NES had drafted the documents with reference to those of another company, whose application had been approved by the Central Department a few months ago. Why didn't the Central Department accept the similar wording this time? Chen again contacted her former colleague Zhu, who told her:

> You should never expect to get things done so quickly and easily. It takes time to strengthen your relationships. I can ask them to speed up the procedure without changing too much of the wording. But you'd better offer them something generous to express your gratitude since they would consider it a great favor. RMB3,000 (US$360) for each of the two will be OK. Don't make me lose face anyway.

Steinmann and Dr. Perrin thought it was straightforward bribery even if gifts were given through a third party. If they agreed to do so, they would run high personal risks by violating the corporate business principle and professional ethics. As controller and lawyer, they were expected to play an important role in implementing strict control mechanisms in the company and keeping the corporate conscience. Moreover, they were worried that the potential wrongdoing might damage the strong ethical culture of the Beijing Representative Office and the good corporate image among the Chinese employees of the office, although it likely would not affect the whole company because NES was so decentralized.

However, Chen thought that *renqing* (social or humanized obligation) and *mianzi* (the notion of face) were more important and that NES's business ethics and social responsibility could be somewhat compromised. In Chen's eyes, Steinmann and Dr. Perrin were inflexible and lacked knowledge of the Chinese business culture. Steinmann and Dr. Perrin told Chen that she needed to learn Western business rules and values in order to survive in a multinational company.

Recent Developments

In August 1997, the vice-president of NES AG led a delegation to visit China. Chen arranged a meeting for the delegation with a senior official of the Central Department. It turned out just to be a courtesy meeting and did not touch upon the details of the holding company approval issue.

In November, Steinmann and Dr. Perrin met the two responsible officials in hopes of negotiating with them such that the officials would allow NES to leave some clauses unchanged. But the officials insisted on their original opinion without giving a detailed explanation of the relevant legal basis. The negotiation lasted only half an hour, and Steinmann and Dr. Perrin felt that it accomplished nothing.

Because of the limited window of opportunity (that is, new investment projects required an immediate capital injection), they felt that they had no choice but to modify the documents according to the officials' requirements. Modifying the documents was an administrative struggle with NES AG, because due to company-internal policies, the German headquarters had to approve these modifications. The application was resubmitted at the end of November. When Chen inquired about the application's status in December, the officials, however, said that the case needed more consideration and then raised some new questions that they said they failed to mention last time. This happened once again three months later in February 1998.

What Next?

In April 1998, Steinmann, Dr. Perrin and Chen submitted the newest revision of the application. As NES AG could not defer funding the new projects, it demanded that the Beijing working team obtained approval within a month so that NES AG could use the China holding company's registered capital of US$30 million. Otherwise, NES AG would have to re-evaluate the China holding company and might abandon it all together. In that case, Mueller, Steinmann and Dr. Perrin would miss opportunities for career advancement. As for Chen, she was concerned about her job because the Beijing Representative Office would no longer need her position.

Being very anxious about the current situation, Mueller decided to come back to Beijing immediately. Chen wanted to be able to suggest a practical approach that would gain the co-operation of the bureaucrats while conforming to the German moral standards. Chen also contemplated some challenging questions. For example, what constituted bribery? When ethical values conflicted, which values should people follow? How could these differences be resolved? To what extent should a multinational company like NES adapt to local business practices? Should the future China holding company develop special ethical codes to recognize the Chinese business culture? The answers to these questions were very important to Chen, because she expected to face similar ethically sensitive issues in the future.

NOTES

1. The China State Council Order No. 20 promulgated on 1988.12.01. Article 2 Any State administrative organization and its functionary shall not give and accept gifts in activities of domestic public service. The China State Council Order No. 133 promulgated on 1993.12.05. Article 7 Gifts accepted in activities of foreign public service shall be handled properly. Gifts above the equivalent of RMB200 (about US$24) according to the Chinese market price shall be . . . handed over to the gift administrative department or acceptor's work unit. Gifts of less than RMB200 belong to the acceptor or to the acceptor's work unit. P. R. China Criminal Law (revised edition) promulgated on 1997.03.14. Article 394 Any State functionary who, in his activities of domestic public service or in his contacts with foreigners, accepts gifts and does not hand them over to the State as is required by State regulations, if the amount involved is relatively large, shall be convicted and punished in accordance with the provisions of Article 382 and 383 of this law. (Article 382 and 383 regulate the crime of embezzlement.)

2. The China State Council Order No. 20 promulgated on 1988.12.01. Article 8 Any State administrative organization and its functionary who give, accept or extort gifts for the purpose of securing illegitimate benefits shall be punished in accordance with relevant state law and regulations on suppression of bribery. The P. R. China Criminal Law (revised edition) promulgated on 1997.03.14. Article 385 Any State functionary who, by taking advantage of his position, extorts money or property from another person, or illegally accepts another person's money or property in return for securing benefits for the person shall be guilty of acceptance of bribes. Article 389 Whoever, for the purpose of securing illegitimate benefits, gives money or property to a State functionary shall be guilty of offering bribes.

N.K.BUILDERS AND CONTRACTORS-INDIA

Prepared by Nipun Chaudhary under the supervision of Professor James A. Erskine

Version: (A) 2002-04-26

In early May 2002, N.K.Builders and Contractors (NKBC) was successful in getting its first construction contract for a highway on the outskirts of New Delhi, India. Success in this field had been a lifelong ambition for Aditya Dahiya, one of the two partners at NKBC. However, winning the contract did not make him happy. NKBC had bought out the other contractors for five per cent of the contract amount. Dahiya, deep down, knew that this payment would be the first of many. He was not certain how far he would have to go, how many more compromises he would have to make and what other actions he would be forced to take in completing the contract. Dahiya was torn: should he proceed against his better judgement or get out while he still could?

CITY OF NEW DELHI

New Delhi, the capital of India, was officially established in about 3000 BC. Throughout the last century, the ancient and the modern times remained in juxtaposition here, not only in the legacy of a succession of empires, but equally in social structure and lifestyles. Delhi exuded a true picture of India. It housed people from all of the corners of India, a unique country of over 300 languages and as many cultures within a population of about one billion. The population of New Delhi was about 10 million. Delhi, the political hub of India, was among the top five business cities in the developing economy of India. It had the largest road network among all the major cities (see Exhibit 1).

THE CONSTRUCTION INDUSTRY OF DELHI

New Delhi was host to a number of government construction departments. The construction industry comprised various departments such as the Delhi Development Authority (DDA), Central Public Development Works (CPWD), the Public Development Works (PWD) and the Municipal Corporation of Delhi (MCD). These departments operated in their geographically specified areas with their own specified budgets. The work undertaken by each of these departments was different in nature. DDA mainly constructed residential apartments; CPWD maintained the major highways and drainage pipelines connecting New Delhi with the other States. PWD undertook work of a technical nature relating to electricity and telephone cables. MCD maintained the roads in New Delhi. News about two of these departments had recently appeared in New Delhi newspapers. The Hinduston Times reported that the Central Bureau of Investigation had registered a case against an executive engineer of NCD on charges of possessing assets disproportionate to his known sources of income. The Times of India also carried a story in which the DDA's former land commissioner claimed that "the DDA is the most corrupt institution in the country." And he added, "The majority of the DDA workers are

not corrupt; it's a handful of officers who are giving the organization a bad name."

Most of the contractors generally did work for only one department and rarely for more than one department. The main reasons for this were the high barriers to entry. The existing contractors did not welcome new entrants, as that would increase competition. Second, many government officials preferred to work with only certain contractors. Third, networking was the most critical factor for success in the construction business. Working in two departments would make it harder for a contractor to maintain business contacts. Lastly, it was very difficult to get a licence for one department, let alone getting licences to operate in two. The licence application process was slow and cumbersome because of the prevalent bureaucratic practices.

THE MCD DEPARTMENT AND THE TENDER PROCESS

The MCD had 10 divisions (offices) in Delhi (see Exhibit 2). Each division had a specific area under its jurisdiction. A division's primary responsibility was to maintain the roads in its area. The MCD Department, like all the other departments when awarding a contract, published the Notice Invited Tender (NIT) in three different newspapers as required by law. The NIT included all the necessary information about the contract—including the tender amount, the location, type of work and the tender calling date. In practice however, sometimes in case of "emergencies," the department, after contacting a particular contractor, would publish a tender in a newspaper and "call" it on the same day, not leaving much time or opportunity for other contractors to respond and apply for the tender. This practice, though rare, happened when the contractor and the government officials were on good terms and mutually agreed on what was to be done.

After becoming aware of the contract, the contractor had to submit a written application in person at the respective division[1] on a company letterhead with an income tax clearance (ITC) certificate. The application certified the eligibility of the contractor to undertake projects. The

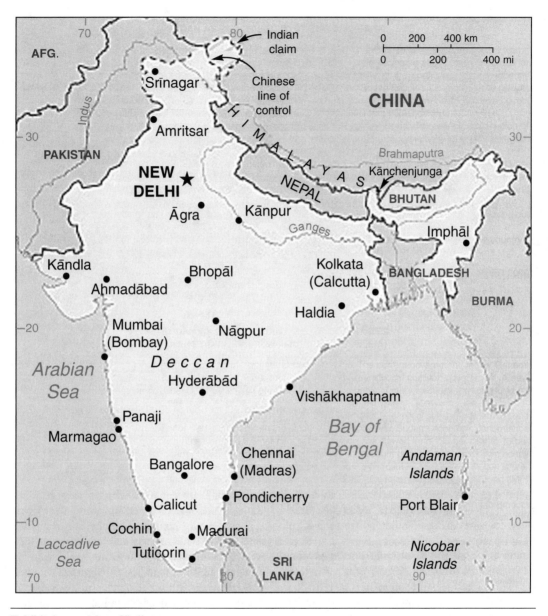

Exhibit 1   Map of India

Source: http://www.odci.gov/cia/publications/factbook/country.html

government office then issued a tender form for the respective project. If there was no pool,[2] the contractor had to submit a formal application on the due date, which included a deposit of two per cent of the tender amount in cash. This two per cent was the tender fee and was mandatory for all contractors. Eighty per cent of the fee was refundable if the contractor did not win the tender. A list was then formed of all interested parties. The department kept a record of all the contractors who applied for the contracts in the MCD database. The data was required for the

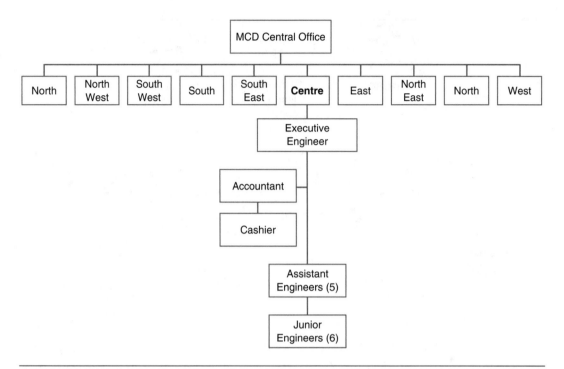

Exhibit 2   The 10 Divisions of MCD

Source: NKBC records.

Description: The 10 divisions of MCD in Delhi all had their own areas and operated on their independent budgets allocated be the Central office. NKBC operated at the Centre office. The head of each division is the executive engineer. An executive engineer normally had four to five assistant engineers under him. An assistant engineer had five to six junior engineers under him. The accountant and the cashier worked independent of the assistant engineers and junior engineers under the executive engineer.

renewal process of the licences of various contractors. The contractors had to undertake at least three contracts per year to qualify for renewal of their licences.

On the tender date, all the interested contractors submitted the tender forms with their quotation rates. All the submissions were then evaluated, and the company with the lowest quote was awarded the contract. After the contractor was awarded the contract, the respective division issued a work order and a specific time period within which the work had to be completed. There was a 10-day grace period to start the work after receiving the work order.

A legal document was drawn up between the contractor and the MCD department at the time the work order was issued. After the work started,

the junior engineer and assistant engineer regularly came to the site to check the work in progress. The executive engineer and the superintendent engineer also visited the site, especially if there was a complaint regarding the work from the junior engineer or the assistant engineer. The quality control department also made surprise visits. If the quality control department found the quality of material sub-standard, they had the authority to stop all the work that was being undertaken by the particular firm anywhere in the MCD.

Aditya Dahiya

Aditya Dahiya's family had been a part of the construction industry for a long time. His father manufactured road rollers and hot mix plants.[3] His main customers were the contractors of the construction industry of North India (which included Delhi). Though the family business was lucrative, Dahiya had always wanted to do something on his own. He wanted to be self-made and self-sufficient. From the start, he was attracted to the construction industry. He had never thought of doing anything else in his life. Dahiya loved the enormous machines that were used. To him, they were not made of steel, but were extensions of the minds of some very intelligent people. Every part of the machine was an embodied answer to "why" and "what for." The machine for him was a moral code caste in steel. To him, the machines symbolized perfection—something he admired and respected.

Dahiya was an ambitious 20-year-old. He valued success from a very early point in his life. After finishing school, Dahiya was accepted at the University of Delhi where he was pursuing an undergraduate degree in arts. He also found work after school as an assistant project manager in a large construction firm. The firm, V.K. Builders, was an esteemed company in the construction industry of Delhi. Dahiya spent his mornings at the university and the rest of the day at work.

Construction was Dahiya's passion. He enjoyed his work thoroughly. He often worked seven days a week without any overtime pay. He was one of the most disciplined workers in the firm and was promoted to project manager after a short stint with the company. He was learning about the business every day and was becoming "street smart" with time.

N.K. BUILDERS AND CONTRACTORS

As project manager at V.K. Builders, Dahiya had made many business contacts. The most useful one was Vikrant Sangwan. Sangwan was an old-time player and a guru when it came to possessing knowledge of the MCD construction industry. He had been involved in this industry for his entire life and knew how things worked. Dahiya gained a lot from his conversations with

Sangwan. As a tyro, he wanted to learn as much as he could from Sangwan on the modus operandi of the construction industry. Sangwan, on the other hand, admired Dahiya's enthusiasm and energy. The structure of their conversations was always the same, with Dahiya asking a plethora of questions and Sangwan making his best effort to answer them.

Dahiya was the one who proposed to Sangwan that they should go into business together. Sangwan had good experience and knowledge about the construction industry but was cash starved. This was mainly because the government was sometimes late in paying final bills, which left contractors in financial disarray, especially if they had borrowed the capital and were paying interest. Sangwan had been a victim of this casualty and had suffered a few losses in the recent past. Dahiya, on the other hand, had saved some money, which would be sufficient to start a firm. He could also borrow money from his father whenever he fell short. After working with V.K. Builders for two years, Dahiya formed a company with Sangwan in January 2002 and named it N.K.Builders and Contractors (NKBC).

Dahiya and Sangwan were equal partners. Both partners decided to specialize in road construction (mainly highways) with the MCD. This was because Sangwan had worked in the MCD all of his life in the area of road construction. As well, there was less investment required as most of the machinery could be leased and investment was required only in purchasing construction materials. The labor was outsourced to independent contractors. The firm directly employed only about 20 people. However, at times of maximum workloads, the number of people employed could go up to 200.

The government regulated four categories of construction firms. The categories were divided on the basis of a firm's experience in the industry. New firms were listed in category four and could tender for small contracts only (under the tender amount of Rs10,000,000).[4] As a firm gained more experience, it could apply for higher accreditation. Generally, it took about five years to move from one category to another.

Dahiya's father and Sangwan had enough political clout to register the new firm in the class 2 category. Less than one per cent of contractors had the power and influence to make such a thing happen. The higher classificatioin was beneficial, as the partners could immediately jump into the big contract tender game could apply for contracts under the tender amount of Rs100,000,000. The presence of economies of scale in bigger contracts created some very lucrative propositions.

THE POOL

Soon after NKBC was registered, both the partners began to seek out contracts. Finally, Sangwan came across a good project and NKBC made a pitch for its first contract. The two partners went to the division office to apply for the tender. They reached the office at 1:30 p.m. The tender calling time was as always 3 p.m. They discovered there were about 15 other companies interested in the same tender. Most of them were present and were evaluating their tender quotes. Other contractors who had applied for the contract were expected shortly. It was uncertain at this point who would win the contract. They mingled with the other contractors. As Sangwan introduced Dahiya to the fellow contractors, Dahiya felt a degree of animosity in the air since new players were not easily welcomed. It was difficult for a new player to enter the industry without the support of an existing player. The only reason Dahiya could apply for a tender with the MCD was due to his partnership with Sangwan who was well known in the industry circles.

As time went by, everyone started to form a group. Finally, it was signaled that a "pool" was to start. "Pool" was a negotiating exercise among all the contractors. It was similar to an auction. All the contractors assembled and the tender was auctioned to the highest bidder. Two types of contractors came to the tender bidding: those who were interested in the contract and those who pretended to be interested just to get their

portion of the pool money. The money generated from the highest bid was divided equally among the remaining contractors. The successful bidder could now quote a favorable rate, which would guarantee him a lucrative deal.

The government officials were happy with the practice as they received commissions[5] on the contract amount from the contractor. A pool enabled the contractor to quote the highest possible rate, which increased the value of the contract, in turn increasing the commissions. A pool was thus a practice in which all the stakeholders were winners.

A pool was always easy to run if the number of contractors was small. It was difficult to organize a pool if there were a large number of contractors. A larger group meant more egos and less control, which could prove to be detrimental for contractors and government officials. In normal circumstances, the contractor who won the tender could submit the tender with the most favorable rate. This rate was better for the contractors and for the government officials as it increased the total value of the contract. Though the quotation rate was higher than usual competition rates, it had to be less than the "justification" rate.[6] The assistant engineer prepared the justification rate.

If the quotation rate was higher than the justification rate, the firm was not awarded the contract. If there was little difference between the quotation rate and the justification rate, then the superintendent engineer would summon the contractor for negotiations, which were held between the executive engineer, superintendent engineer and the contractor. The negotiation depended heavily on the relationship of the contractor with the government officials, and especially the executive engineer. If the contractor agreed to reduce his rate, he would get the tender; otherwise, the tender would be recalled and the same procedure would have to be repeated.

NKBC was the winner of this pool. NKBC had bought out the competition after paying them five per cent of the contract amount. Five per cent was the standard pool amount in the industry with a range from two per cent to eight per cent of the contract amount. This particular contract had a duration of two years, and work was supposed to start within a month.

WORK ON SITE

The contractor was supposed to start the work within a month of receiving the contract, but a lot could happen between winning and completing of the contract. One of the profit areas in the road construction contracts for both parties (the contractor and the government officials) was the "charcoal" item on the schedule. In the case of a road contract, this item constituted about 35 per cent of the total tender cost. In a standard project, only 40 per cent of the requisite amount of charcoal was used in the construction process. The rest was divided amongst the junior executive, assistant engineer and the contractor. The split between the contractor and the government officials was even. The same thing was done with cement, which was the main input item in the construction of footpaths alongside the roads. On average, only 33 per cent of the requisite amount of cement was used in the construction. The rest was equally divided between the contractor and the government officials. In most cases, the income earned from these two activities financed the running costs of the contract. Both the cement and charcoal were easy to sell. There was a huge demand in the market, and there were many agents in the market who would organize everything from start to the finish. All the contractor had to do was make a telephone call. In most cases, the contractor got the cash payment from the sale of charcoal and cement on the same day.

The contractors also made substantial compromises on the quality of the other raw materials. This enabled them to pay commissions to the various engineers. The going commission rate in the department for a junior executive was three per cent; assistant engineer, two per cent; and executive engineer one per cent of the contractual amount. The executive engineer took care of the officials above him. Although the percentages decreased in moving up the

hierarchy, the officials at the top had a broader base. An assistant engineer had up to four junior engineers under him. Similarly, an executive engineer also had four to five assistant engineers as subordinates. Samples[7] of raw materials used on site had to be sent to the MCD laboratories. The purpose was to test the quality of the raw materials. The contractor had to pay 0.2 per cent to the person who collected the samples from the site. This payment would enable the contractor to send the best possible sample and ensure a positive result.

The various officers had specific roles during the construction process. The role of the junior engineer was to supervise the work and enter the bills in the measurement book. The assistant engineer, after reviewing the measurement book, had to submit a test report of the work in the measurement book. A junior engineer was a civil engineer by qualification. Some of them also had PhDs. The ultimate losers in the game that was played by the government officials and the contractor were the common citizens, as they were provided with lower quality roads and other facilities. The contractors did not lose financially by paying the government officials. They compromised on quality in order not to incur losses from paying the government officials. There was a positive correlation with the level of corruption prevalent in the government and the profits earned by the contractors.

After the measurement book was checked and forwarded from the assistant engineer, it was transferred to the accounts clerk. The accounts clerk was paid 0.5 per cent commission. His job was to check the bill, tally the justification rate with tender rates and forward the measurement book to the accounts officer. The accounts officer was paid a one per cent commission. This was the last step after which the measurement book was transferred to the executive engineer who, after signing the measurement book, took it to all the other officials. After this cumbersome process, a bank cheque was paid to the contractor. The cashier was paid a 0.2 per cent of the amount on the bank cheque. The nature of this process could vary slightly and depended on the relationships the contractor had with each of the officials. Most of the time, the contractors did not know who was in possession of their measurement book and hence could not pursue the officials. Paying more to the government officials could influence the speed of this process.

Saurabh Singh

Saurabh was a junior engineer in the MCD. Dahiya had dealt with him many times when he worked at V.K. Builders as a project manager and knew him quite well. Singh and Dahiya shared a good relationship. Dahiya once causally asked Singh whether he realized that the practice of accepting commissions from contractors was unethical and illegitimate. He asked Singh if he felt guilty and whether he was afraid that one day he might be caught and charged for bribery. Singh replied,

> I do realize that accepting commissions is illegitimate according to the law. But accepting bribes is just something I have to do. I do not have the capacity or freedom to change how things are done in this department. After all these years, I have realized that the only freedom a man has is the freedom to think. Other than that, a man has no freedom. He cannot do whatever he wants to. He is always bound by historical, emotional and material circumstances.

> When I was young, I strongly believed that there was no such thing as a compromise. As there can be no compromise between food and poison, there can be none between business and ethics. But look around you; you will find that everyone has to make innumerable compromises every day in their lives. We see politicians who are mere salesmen and have no principles. We come across scientists who practice science without humanity; there are people who claim to make sacrifices without any pain; there are people who indulge in hedonistic pleasures without a conscience. It's not hard to find people who have knowledge but no character and hence can't use their knowledge for their own good or for the good of our society. This is the society we live in. This is the society that tells us what is ethical and unethical. Those who accept the state's influence over this society and allow it to define the course of their life go far; others have no choice but to live a wasteful existence. They are unable to earn what they deserve and do not intend to earn what they can glibly negotiate. As a result, in your so-called "ethical" society, nothing is more common than unsuccessful men with talent.

> Ethics is a very strong word, Aditya, the meaning of which not many people understand. Those who do are, in most cases, too weak to live by it. They have given up the fight and live in guilt, pain and insecurity. If I would ask you to define what ethics was and to give me an example of a person who lives or has ever lived with that definition, will you have an answer for me? Ethics is just a word with little or no meaning in our modern society. It is merely used to support our conceptions about people, which in most cases are biased.

> People call individual actions "ethical" or "unethical" irrespective of their motives but solely on account of their useful or harmful consequences. They tend to ignore the origin of these designations and believe that the quality of good and evil is inherent in the actions themselves, irrespective of their consequences—that is to say, by taking for cause that which is effect. Then people consign the act of being ethical or unethical to the motives and regard the deed in itself as morally ambiguous. They go further and accord the predicate ethical or unethical no longer to the individual motive but to the whole nature of a man out of whom the whole motive grew. People say "government officials" are corrupt using the same logic. Thus, people successively make men accountable for the effects they produce, then for their actions, then for their motive and finally for their nature. No one accepts that man's nature cannot be held accountable. It is a mere consequence and assembly of the elements and influences of the past and present and nothing can change that. Socrates and Plato were right when they said: whatever man does he always does the good, that is to say: that which seems to him good (useful) according to the relative degree of his intellect, the measure of his rationality.

The word ethics is merely used in the adjectival sense these days to either praise people or ridicule them. For people these days, ethics is perceived as nothing other than obedience of historical customs. This is the benchmark we use to label people as ethical or otherwise. If they adhere to our established norms and customs, they are dignified; otherwise, they are accused as being unethical. The free human being is therefore unethical in all cases because in all things he is determined to depend upon himself and not upon a tradition or custom.

We either call someone ethical or a hypocrite without understanding the meaning of either of the two. We put these labels on people because it makes it easier for us identify them and deal with them in the way we think is appropriate. The simple truth is that no one among us or anywhere in the world is purely ethical. We respond to different situations in different ways, keeping our interests in mind. Sometimes we act like a lion and other times like a fox.

Let me tell you my story: I had an A-class[8] civil engineering degree, which proved to be insufficient to get me a job, the job that I most deserved. My father had to pay US$120,000 under the table in order for me to get this job. Our house was mortgaged, as my father couldn't pay this huge sum even after pledging most of his life savings. If we did not pay the money, the job would have been offered to someone who could have afforded to pay the sum. The world would have carried on and I would have been left behind. After the way I got this job, I feel it's imperative for me to clear my family debt. I can't do it with my meagre salary. Therefore, I take bribes. I have chosen to take bribes not because I want to grow rich unscrupulously but to clear the burden of the debt. That is my main objective and motivation.

If you judge me on face value, you'll probably say I'm unethical. If you try understanding the cause and effect, maybe you'll form a different perspective. I have no freedom. I have no choice. If I was alone, I would have perhaps challenged the system. Now, I have a lot at stake and cannot accommodate the risk of being iconoclastic. I am a realist in means and an idealist in the ends. I am a slave to the system, but not to the society and traditions.

Therefore, I accept bribes, without any guilt, pain and fear.

THE FIRST CONTRACT

All the happiness and pride that Dahiya felt upon winning his first road construction contract was tarnished by the fact that NKBC paid five per cent of the contract amount to the other contractors who were interested in the tender. Dahiya had, so far, relied on intelligence and hard work to earn a living. He had never indulged in such practice before and was disappointed with the way his firm was awarded the tender. Deep inside, he knew that this was just the start. He would have to undertake more illegitimate practices as the contract progressed. Dahiya contemplated how far he would have to go. How many more compromises would he have to make? He could quit now if he wanted. He would, at most, lose the money he had paid to buy the competition and establish the company. The decision to stay in business or quit weighed heavily on his mind.

NOTES

1. The MCD had 10 divisions in Delhi. Work was divided among these divisions on a geographical basis.

2. See description of the pool process on page 104.

3. A plant used to mix charcoal with stone aggregate, also known as premix.

4. Indian currency is the rupee (Rs). In January 2002, Rs1 = Cdn$0.035.

5. Within the construction industry in India, the word "commission" was synonymous with bribe.

6. The maximum rate specified by the government at which it would agree to award the contract to the bidder.

7. A sample was a small amount of raw material, e.g., a small amount of concrete mix that had to be sent to the MCD laboratories.

8. A-class degree is a degree earned by the top five per cent of the class.

CITIBANK MEXICO TEAM: THE SALINAS ACCOUNTS[1]

*Prepared by David T. A. Wesley under
the supervision of Professor Henry W. Lane*

Copyright © 1999, Ivey Management Services   Version: (B) 1999-05-17

> *Mexico was . . . a country of smoke and mirrors, where yesterday's heroes are today's villains and today's champions of justice may be tomorrow's crooks.*
>
> —Andres Oppenheimer, Senior Correspondent, Miami Herald[2]

On July 4, 1995, Amy Elliott, head of Citibank's Mexico Team, had just returned from Switzerland, where Swiss narcotics agents were encouraging her to lay a trap for the wife of one of her clients,[3] Raul Salinas, who had been arrested in Mexico a few months earlier on charges of murder, illegal enrichment and laundering money for the Mexican drug cartel.

The fate of one of her former employees, who had recently been sentenced to 10 years imprisonment for managing the account of a convicted money launderer, provided food for thought. If she co-operated with narcotics agents, perhaps she could avoid the same fate. On the other hand, she had to considered her obligation to her client, who, as the brother of Mexico's most popular president in recent history, was believed by some to have been falsely accused by his political enemies. Another consideration was whether, by co-operating with authorities, Citibank could be liable for violating Swiss bank secrecy laws.[4]

COMPANY PROFILE

Citibank was established in 1812, and by the end of the 19th century had grown to become the largest bank in the United States, and the first to establish a foreign trading department.

In 1914 the bank established its first overseas office in Buenos Aires, Argentina, and shortly thereafter began to aggressively expand across South America and Asia. In 1929, Citibank became the largest bank in the world.

By the early 1990s, Citibank had grown to more than 3,400 branches in 100 countries, and was considered the world's most global bank. Of the company's 90,000 employees, more than 50,000 resided outside the United States.

In Mexico, Citibank had more than 65 years of history, and was the only foreign bank permitted to operate in that country following the nationalization of Mexico's banks in 1982. In the 1990s, more than 20 per cent of the bank's revenues came from Latin America.

THE MEXICO TEAM

Amelia Grovas Elliott, a Cuban American, began working for Citibank in 1967. In 1983 she became head of the bank's Mexico Team, consisting of 10 private bankers, at Citibank's New York office. The Mexico Team specifically sought out clients with a net worth of at least $5 million and at least $1 million of available liquid assets to invest with the bank. In the early 1990s, the Team managed accounts for about 250 Mexican clients.

Private banking services included deposit taking, mutual fund investing, personal trust, estate administration, funds transfers, and establishing offshore accounts and trusts. Service was very personal. Bankers typically knew their clients well and understood their specific needs. Elliott explained:

We visit our clients 10 to 12 times a year in their country. They come back three or four times to New York. We see our clients a lot. It's obviously a growing kind of thing and not just in knowing your customer, but making sure you know what's going on. Because the relationship can grow deeper the more you know the person, we go to their homes, visit their family, go to their business, and remember birthdays. It just increases the depth.[5]

RAUL SALINAS

On May 11, 1992, Elliott received a phone call from the Mexican Minister of Agriculture, Carlos Hank Rhon, one of the wealthiest men in Mexico and a long-standing client of Citibank. He wished to arrange a meeting between Elliott and Raul Salinas, brother of Mexican President and Harvard educated economist, Carlos Salinas. Salinas was in need of private banking services, and the agriculture minister had recommended Citibank.

John Reed, CEO of Citibank, was a personal friend of President Carlos Salinas, and Citibank had been working for some time to further its Mexican operations.[6] Securing the account of the president's brother could only serve to advance the Mexico Team's profile and possibly Elliott's career.

Later in the week, Salinas flew to New York to discuss his financial needs. There, Salinas stated that he had recently sold a construction company and needed a bank to provide confidential investment of the proceeds. Salinas explained:

> I do not want anyone in Mexico to know that I am moving large amounts of money out of the country. If the public finds out that I am not reinvesting the money in Mexico, it could harm my brother's political career.[7]

As such, confidentiality was a prime consideration. Rhon told Salinas that he believed Citibank could provide the type of confidentiality that Salinas was seeking. Apparently, Salinas was assured that indeed it could.

Normally when new accounts were opened, the bank followed strict procedures that made the process somewhat bureaucratic. Elliott explained:

> The relationship manager would be discussing the prospective client with his or her supervisor throughout the entire process. It's a complex kind of sale, so it has a fairly long lead-time, especially if you're not physically located in Mexico.[8]

In order to smooth the way as much as possible for Salinas, bank references and background checks were waived. Citibank policy allowed for such exceptions. In Salinas' case the waiver was allowed on grounds that he was a "known client and referred by a very valuable client of long standing." In most cases bank references did not provide useful information anyway and were viewed as a mere formality. Furthermore, this was the president's brother. Elliott noted:

> You can trust some Mexican officials, some not. If you get to know them, it's fairly obvious if they can be trusted. Public figures in Mexico are talked about a great deal. Generally speaking, it's a fairly small and tight upper crust.[9]

On May 26, 1992, Salinas was approved as a Citibank client. A chequing account was opened at the New York office under the name of his accountant, Juan Guillermo Gomez Gutierrez.

THE SALINAS ACCOUNTS

An "investment optimization" strategy had to be devised that would both conceal the identity of the account holder and produce a superior return on investment. In order to avoid a potential information leak, nobody at Citibank Mexico would be advised about the accounts.

Deposits made in Mexico would be done in the name of Salinas' fiancée, Patricia Rios Castañon. Rios delivered cheques, denominated in pesos, of between US$3 million and $5 million. The teller delivered the cheques, which were made payable to Citibank, to a manager at the branch, who then wired the money to New York.

Five corporations were opened in the Cayman Islands on behalf of Salinas. The main corporation was Trocca Private Investment Company, and the others were created to act as shareholders and directors of Trocca (see Exhibit 1). The principal shareholder, Tyler Ltd., received the transferred funds in a concentration account in New York where they were converted from Mexican pesos to U.S. dollars. The concentration account was designed as a transfer point of funds wired from Mexico to offshore corporations, and allowed the holder to mix both personal and business deposits in one account. The only record that showed Salinas as the owner of the company was held in Cayman where bank secrecy laws could protect his identity.

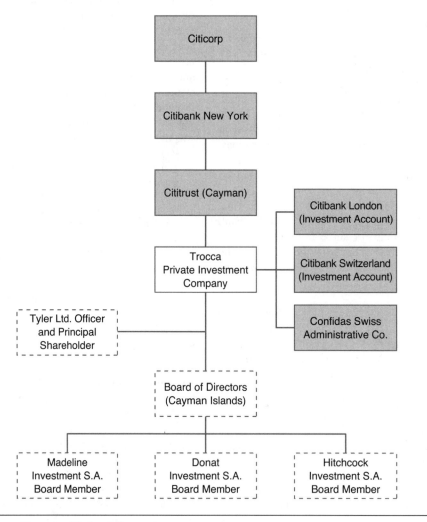

Exhibit 1   Trocca and Related Companies

Source: U.S. General Accounting Office.

From Trocca, funds were transferred to Citibank Switzerland. Salinas was assured that, while the scheme was complicated, it provided the best protection of his identity. She explained:

> By using a corporation in Cayman as the account holder, the source of ownership will be concealed from people who have no reason to know.
>
> The reason for the account in Switzerland is their very strict secrecy laws. A Swiss banker can be put in jail if they divulge the confidentiality of the name of an account.[10]

Salinas understood the value of the Swiss accounts. He had visited Switzerland on many occasions to take part in equestrian competitions in Lucerne, and to visit his two nephews who were attending school there. Salinas was well aware of Switzerland's international reputation for secrecy, and since his identity would be held in confidence, he could have direct contact with the banks and bankers involved.

In Switzerland, funds were deposited at various banks, including Citibank Zurich, Banque Pictet and Julius Baer Bank. Trocca, not Salinas, officially held the funds at Citibank Zurich. Funds were transferred back and forth between Zurich and London in order to take advantage of higher money market rates in the United Kingdom. Citibank London was not made aware that Salinas was the beneficial owner of the account.

Over the next two years, a total of $100 million was transferred through Citibank to accounts in Switzerland. Patricia Rios Castañon, who, in 1993, became Salinas' third wife, handled most of the transactions. A large portion was transferred on November 30, 1994, the last day of Carlos Salinas' presidency.

OFFSHORE BANKING SECRECY

While the United States had its own bank secrecy laws, these laws provided less protection than most offshore jurisdictions (see Exhibit 2). Federal law required that banks report all financial transactions above $10,000 to the Internal Revenue Service (IRS). If the bank deemed any transaction to be suspicious in nature, the bank was also required to contact the Criminal Investigation Unit of the IRS. As a result of these reporting requirements, banks operating in the United States were exempted from liability to their customers for reporting account information, even without customer consent.[11]

Investors have used the services of offshore banking in jurisdictions that provided greater protection of privacy, as well as tax advantages and limited legal liability. U.S. banks used offshore branches to hold information about the beneficial owner of accounts, where bank secrecy laws protected the client from disclosure. This provided a competitive advantage that allowed banks with offshore branches to attract clients who did not wish banking regulators and others to know about their substantial wealth. While such accounts were usually used for legitimate and legal purposes such as estate planning, tax shelters and reduced legal liability, they have also attracted those engaged in illegal activity, such as money laundering, investment fraud and tax evasion.

The main instrument for concealing wealth was the Private Investment Company (PIC). These were shell companies registered by banks in the offshore jurisdictions and used solely to hold the funds of clients. PICs, since they were not in the client's name, could be used to transfer funds in any country of the world without drawing the attention of regulators or others to the beneficial owner. Information about the beneficial owner was held secretly and safely in the offshore branch.

While many offshore jurisdictions provided the aforementioned benefits, the U.S. General Accounting Office[12] identified nine where U.S. bank subsidiaries and branches held substantial accounts (in excess of $1 billion). These were the Bahamas, Bahrain, the Cayman Islands, the Channel Islands, Hong Kong, Luxembourg, Panama, Singapore and Switzerland.

All of these locations, with the exception of Bahrain, had regulations that required the reporting

---

The Right to Financial Privacy Act of 1978

. . . as amended, the Privacy Act provides that it shall not preclude any financial institution, or any officer, employee, or agent of a financial institution from notifying a government authority that such institution, or officer, or employee, or agent has information that may be relevant to a possible violation of any statute or regulation. Such information may include only the name or other identifying information concerning any individual or account and the nature of any suspected illegal activity.

The Bank Secrecy Act and the Currency and Foreign Transactions Reporting Act, 1970

. . . all domestic and foreign currency transactions of more than US$10,000 must be reported within 15 days.

. . . Financial institutions must file a Currency Transaction Report (CTR) for each deposit, withdrawal, exchange of currency, or other payment of transfer, by, through, or to such financial institution which involves a transaction of currency of more than $10,000.

. . . the Report of International Transportation of Currency or Monetary Instruments (CMIR). Every person or entity must file a CMIR who physically transports, mails, or ships, or causes to be physically transported, mailed, or shipped, currency or other monetary instruments in an aggregate amount exceeding $10,000 on any one occasion.

. . . financial institutions are required to maintain for a five-year period a variety of records, such as copies of signature cards, bank statements, and checks drawn for more than US$100.

Violation of the Bank Secrecy Act provides for jail terms up to 10 years and fines from US$1,000 to US$500,000.

Exhibit 2   Relevant Bank Secrecy Laws: United States[1]

1. Campbell, D., *International Bank Secrecy,* Sweet and Maxwell, London, 1992.

---

of suspicious transactions to local authorities. And, in most jurisdictions, U.S. law enforcement could gain access to individual accounts to investigate certain criminal acts. Only Bahrain, Luxembourg and Singapore did not allow access for these purposes. On the other side, without a legal mandate to provide information, bankers could face fines or imprisonment for violating secrecy laws in several jurisdictions, including the Cayman Islands and Switzerland (see Exhibits 3 and 4). Furthermore, Switzerland allowed for third parties to take civil action against banks, and as a result, many bank officials expressed concern over the liability to their banks of breaching confidentiality in these jurisdictions.[13]

A Swiss judge had the power to overturn secrecy obligations for the purpose of criminal investigations conducted in Switzerland. Under most conditions, the same was true for crimes committed outside of Switzerland, provided that international law enforcement officials formally requested assistance, and the crime was also considered illegal in Switzerland (i.e., drug trafficking). A 1977 treaty signed between Switzerland and the United States allowed for co-operation between these countries, even when the crime was not considered illegal in Switzerland.[14]

U.S. banking regulators relied heavily on self-monitoring by banks to prevent offshore accounts from being used for illegal purposes. A "know your customer" (KYC) policy was considered the most effective of the self-monitoring measures implemented by the banks. Most banks stipulated under a KYC policy that clients had to submit bank references and other information related to the origin of their wealth. Banks also monitored accounts for unusual or large transactions that could be a sign of illegal activity. However, a study by the Federal Reserve Bank of New York concluded that "in general . . . client profiles contained little or no documentation on the client's background, source of wealth, expected account activity, and client contacts and visits by bank representatives,"[15] even though such information was believed to be critical in preventing the illegal use of offshore accounts.

Banks and Trusts Companies Law, 1989

. . . provides for the preservation of secrecy on the part of the Inspector of Banks and Trust Companies and any person authorized to assist him in his functions.

It prohibits the disclosure of any information, by the Inspector or his staff, of the affairs of a licensee or any customer of a licensee and provides a penalty of a fine not exceeding CI $10,000, or a term of imprisonment not exceeding one year, or both for contravention of this law.

Confidential Relationships Law, 1976

. . . as amended, provides that, if any person in possession of confidential information, however obtained, divulges it or attempts, offers, or threatens to divulge it to any person not entitled to possession, or who willfully obtains or attempts to obtain confidential information is guilty of an offense and is liable on summary conviction to a fine not exceeding CI $5,000, or for imprisonment of a term not exceeding two years, or both.

In addition, where such person solicits such information for himself or another for reward or being a professional person entrusted with such information, the above mentioned penalties are doubled.

Section 3(2)(b) of the Law provides a number of cases in which the law has no application. These are as follows:

1. Any professional person acting in the normal course of business or with consent, express or implied, of the relevant principal;

2. A constable of the rank of Inspector or above investigating an offense committed or alleged to have been committed within the jurisdiction;

3. A constable of the rank of Inspector or above, specifically authorized by the Governor in that regard, investigating an offense committed or alleged to have been committed outside the Islands which offense, if committed in the Islands, would be an offense against its laws; or

4. The Financial Secretary, the Inspector, or in relation to particular information specified by the Governor, such other person as the Governor may authorize;

5. A bank in any proceedings, cause, or matter when and to the extent to which it is reasonably necessary for the protection of the bank's interest, either as against its customers or against third parties in respect of transactions of the bank for, or with, its customer, and

6. The relevant professional person with the approval of the Financial Secretary when necessary for the protection of himself or any other person against crime.

. . . as amended, provides in section 3A that, where it applies, the following provisions shall apply:

Whenever a person intends or is required to give in evidence in, or in connection with, any proceeding been tried, inquired into, or determined by any court, tribunal, or other authority, any confidential information within the meaning of the Law, he shall, before doing so, apply for directions. . . . Upon hearing an application under subsection (2), a judge shall direct:

1. That evidence be given; or

2. That evidence shall not be given, or

3. That the evidence be given subject to conditions which he may specify whereby the confidentiality of the information is safeguarded . . .

. . . a bank should disclose information. . . . Where disclosure is under compulsion by . . . the Mutual Legal Assistance Treaty (signed by the United Kingdom, United States, and Cayman Islands), or the Misuse of Drugs Law (of the Cayman Islands).

Exhibit 3   Relevant Bank Secrecy Laws: Cayman Islands[1]

1. Campbell, D., *International Bank Secrecy*, Sweet and Maxwell, London, 1992.

... the right to privacy refers to a person's right to protection of his or her person in the sense referred to by article 28(1) of the Swiss Civil Code. . . . Violation of the right to privacy is also tantamount to a tort under articles 41 *et seq.* of the Code of Obligations. Thus a bank can not only be held liable on contractual grounds but also toward third parties.

Article 47 of the Federal Law on Banks and Savings Banks of November 8, 1934

As amended,

1. Whoever divulges a secret entrusted to him or of which he has become aware in his capacity as officer, employee, mandatory, liquidator, or commissioner of a bank, as representative of the banking commission, officer, or employee of a recognized auditing company and whoever tries to induce others to violate professional secrecy, shall be punished by imprisonment for not more than 6 months or by a fine of not more than 50,000 Swiss francs.

2. If the act was committed by negligence, the penalty shall be a fine not exceeding 30,000 Swiss francs.

3. The violation of secrecy remains punishable even after termination of the official or employment relationship or the exercise of the profession.

4. Remaining reserved are federal and cantonal provisions concerning the duty to testify in court to give information to a government authority.

Swiss Penal Code, Article 305 bis

1. Whosoever undertakes actions which lend themselves to defeat the ascertainment of origin, the discovery or collection of assets which, as he knows or must assume, emanate from crime, will be subject to punishment by imprisonment or a fine.

2. In severe cases punishment is penal servitude up to five years or imprisonment. Added to this penalty of detention is a fine of up to 1 million francs. A severe case is if the perpetrator:
   a) acts as a member of a criminal organization;
   b) acts as a member of a criminal organization whose purpose is the continued practice of money laundering;
   c) realizes a large turnover or considerable profit from professional money laundering activities.

3. The perpetrator will also be subject to sentencing if he commits the principal act of violation abroad and such act is also punishable in the place of perpetration.

Lack of Due Diligence in Financial Transactions

Whosoever professionally accepts, keeps in safe custody, assists in the investment or transfer of assets which are the property of others and fails to apply the relative due diligence called for in establishing the identity of the economic beneficiary, is subject to punishment by imprisonment of up to one year or a fine.

Exhibit 4   Relevant Swiss Bank Secrecy Laws and Regulations[1]

1. Campbell, D., *International Bank Secrecy,* Sweet and Maxwell, London, 1992.

THE HOBBS ACT

The Hobbs Act was a federal law enacted in the United States in 1951 to allow prosecution of corrupt American government officials. Specific unlawful activities under the Hobbs Act included extortion, fraud against a foreign bank, kidnapping, narcotics and robbery. The law could be used against foreign nationals and institutions if any aspect of illegal activity occurred in the United States. Therefore, if the proceeds of drug trafficking were either held in the United States or transferred through the United States, the law's jurisdiction would become extra-territorial.[16]

In 1994 Antonio Giraldi, a former banker in Elliott's Mexico Team, was arrested and tried for violations of the Hobbs Act. At the time, Giraldi was employed by American Express Bank International. In 1989, Giraldi secured a client who deposited $21 million over a very short period and was later discovered by U.S. federal agents to be laundering money for the Mexican drug cartel. Elliott was asked to testify against her former employee.

Elliott explained to the federal court that it was a banker's responsibility to know the client, and that an experienced banker should be able to spot irregularities in an account. Citibank had specific guidelines used to protect the bank from becoming an instrument for drug money laundering:

> "Know your client," at least in our bank, is part of the culture. It's part of the way you do things. It's part of the way you conduct yourself. If you come in with a prospect or the name of a prospect, you will be sure to be asked, "Who is this person, what do they do, who introduced them to you," by at least three or four people higher than you. It's just the way it is. . . . It's too risky to not do the due diligence, not to know who you are dealing with.[17]

No direct evidence was provided that proved Giraldi knew of the illicit origins of the money. Nevertheless, the court convicted Giraldi and sentenced him to 10 years imprisonment on the grounds that he had been negligent in not determining the source of his client's wealth. In Giraldi's case, "willful blindness" was deemed the same as having knowledge.[18] A female colleague who helped Giraldi with the accounts was also sentenced to three years in prison.[19]

THE MURDER INVESTIGATION

On February 13, 1995, the lead story in the Mexican news briefs that were delivered daily to Elliott's office by e-mail reported that Raul Salinas was under investigation for the murder of his brother-in-law, Jose Ruiz Massieu. As Salinas was one of Elliott's most important clients, she called him. Salinas claimed:

> Those allegations are absolutely false. They are lies made up by my brother's enemies. He made some

unpopular decisions in order to modernize Mexico and this attack against me and my family is a result of that.[20]

Although it seemed unlikely that the former president's brother could be formally charged, she decided to prepare a profile which, under bank policy, should have been completed when Salinas first became a client. Filling out the form, it became apparent that she had very little information about Salinas and the sale of his construction company. She had never visited the company, and did not even know its name.

On February 27, Salinas was arrested and formally charged with murder by Mexican authorities. A few days later, Mario Ruiz Massieu, the victim's brother and former chief investigator in the case, was arrested by U.S. Customs agents at the Newark Airport, also in connection with the murder. Ruiz Massieu, a professional civil servant, had somehow amassed millions of dollars, which had recently been deposited in a Texas bank. Within days allegations began to surface that both men had developed close ties with the Mexican drug cartel.[21]

In early March, Citibank's vice-president of legal affairs was contacted by a senior official at the bank and asked to investigate the Salinas accounts. Elliott was instructed to immediately report any activity on Salinas' accounts to the vice-president of legal affairs.

During the summer, the Swiss federal prosecutor and agents of the Swiss Central Narcotics Division contacted the executive vice-president of Citibank's office in Switzerland. They reported that at one of Salinas' residences in Mexico City, Mexican authorities had discovered phony identification which linked Salinas to a safety deposit box at Citibank Switzerland. The safety deposit box was believed to contain documentation valuable to the investigation that was being conducted by Mexican authorities.

Citibank Switzerland referred the matter to Elliott, who met with Swiss narcotics agents shortly thereafter. A senior agent asked Elliott to make arrangements with Patricia Rios de Salinas to remove any documents that were being held in the safety deposit box. She was to use the pretext that they were no longer secure due to an internal investigation by the bank. Since the agents, under Swiss law, were not permitted to enter the bank in order to seize the contents of the box, they planned to arrest Rios, documents in hand, while she was leaving the bank. The Swiss federal prosecutor asked Elliot to not discuss the matter with Citibank's vice-presdient of legal affairs, among others.

An article in the June 24 *New York Times*, "Score One for Salinas,"[22] revived doubts about Salinas' guilt. "We will get Mario!" began the fifth paragraph, which quoted a Mexican government official. The article continued:

> The [June 22] ruling of the U.S. magistrate in Newark, Ronald J. Hedges, also revived broader questions about the case against Raul Salinas. . . . Most of the witnesses whose credibility Hedges challenged in New Jersey when they implicated Mario Ruiz Massieu are lined up in Mexico to testify against Raul Salinas. . . . Hedges sharpened the public focus on doubts that have long existed about changes, gaps and contradictions in the testimony. . . . The most important witness left against Salinas is a congressional aide . . . [who] was probably the first person Hedges had in mind when he complained of being handed testimony from witnesses who changed their stories, contradicted themselves and said they had been tortured into confessing.

The U.S. magistrate further criticized Mexican prosecutors for having "picked and chosen" from testimony given against Salinas, and for having "glossed over" testimony that called into question the credibility of the witnesses.

Perhaps Salinas had been telling the truth. Perhaps this was a ploy by his family's enemies to undo the reforms begun by Raul's brother. Furthermore, neither Mexican nor Swiss authorities could offer any evidence linking Raul, or anyone in his family, to drug trafficking.

However, any feelings of vindication had to be balanced with knowledge of the fate of Giraldi and Elliott's testimony against him. The court, when passing sentence, had declared:

A rational jury could have found it incredible that carelessness and honest mistakes could account for the complexity required to give the transactions the appearance of legitimacy.

The court's opinion was largely based on Elliott's testimony about Citibank's meticulous "Know Your Customer" policy, a policy that she herself may have violated.

NOTES

1. This case has been written on the basis of published sources only. Consequently, the interpretation and perspectives presented in this case are not necessarily those of Citibank or any of its employees. Many of the events documented in this case were adapted from "Private Banking: Raul Salinas, Citibank, and Alleged Money Laundering," *United States General Accounting Office,* October 1998.

2. Oppenheimer, A., *Bordering on Chaos,* Little, Brown & Co., New York, 1996.

3. Raul Salinas' Testimony, "Murder, Money, and Mexico: The rise and fall of the Salinas Brothers," *The Corporation for Public Broadcasting,* 1998. Also see "How a Mover and Shaker Manoeuvred His Millions," *The New York Times News Service,* June 2, 1996.

4. Under article 28(1) of the Swiss Civil Code, a bank could be held liable, both on contractual grounds and by third parties, for violating a client's right to privacy.

5. Amelia Elliott quotations throughout this case were adapted from official testimony given by Amelia Elliott in United States vs. Antonio Giraldi, May 12, 1994, cited in "Murder, Money, and Mexico: The rise and fall of the Salinas Brothers," *The Corporation for Public Broadcasting,* 1998.

6. "How a Mover and Shaker Manoeuvred His Millions," *The New York Times News Service,* June 2, 1996.

7. Raul Salinas quotations throughout this case were adapted from official testimony given by Raul Salinas to Swiss prosecutors on December 6, 1995, cited in "Murder, Money, and Mexico: The rise and fall of the Salinas Brothers," *The Corporation for Public Broadcasting,* 1998.

8. United States vs. Antonio Giraldi, May 12, 1994, cited in "Murder, Money, and Mexico: The rise and fall of the Salinas Brothers," *The Corporation for Public Broadcasting,* 1998.

9. Ibid.

10. Ibid.

11. Campbell, D., *International Bank Secrecy,* Sweet and Maxwell, London, 1992.

12. The General Accounting Office is the investigative arm of the U.S. House of Representatives.

13. "Money Laundering: Regulatory Oversight of Offshore Private Banking Activities," *United States General Accounting Office,* June 1998.

14. EWJ Newsletters, Grendelmeier, Jenny, and Partners, Switzerland, 1998.

15. "Money Laundering: Regulatory Oversight of Offshore Private Banking Activities," *United States General Accounting Office,* June 1998.

16. "U.S. Laundering Law Applies in Salinas, other Corruption Case," *Money Laundering Alert,* January 1996.

17. United States vs. Antonio Giraldi, May 12, 1994, cited in "Murder, Money and Mexico: The rise and fall of the Salinas Brothers," *The Corporation for Public Broadcasting,* 1998.

18. "Business crime: Appeals court thumps money-launderer," *International Commercial Litigation,* London, November 1996.

19. "Legal Guide to White Collar Crime," *International Financial Law Review,* London, July 1995.

20. Official testimony given by Raul Salinas to Swiss prosecutors on December 6, 1995, cited in "Murder, Money and Mexico: The rise and fall of the Salinas Brothers," *The Corporation for Public Broadcasting,* 1998.

21. Real-life soap opera, *Time,* March 20, 1995.

22. "Score One For Salinas," *The New York Times News Service,* June 24, 1995.

BANK OF NOVA SCOTIA (BRADY SUBPOENA) (A)[1]

*Prepared by Associate
Professors Henry W. Lane and Errol Mendes
with the assistance of Douglas J. Powrie*

Version: (A) 2004-01-07

OVERVIEW

For eight months, the Bank of Nova Scotia had been trying to find its way through a legal maze which was beginning to look like it had no way out. A grand jury in the United States had subpoenaed documents located in the Bahamas and Cayman Islands relating to a client of the Bank. The Bank had not been able to get permission from those countries to release the documents, and complying with the subpoena would mean violating their bank secrecy laws. On October 10, 1983, a U.S. District Court denied an appeal from the Bank and presented it with a choice: comply with the subpoena or face a contempt of court hearing.

THE SUBPOENA

In early 1983, a U.S. federal prosecutor was attempting to convince a federal grand jury in West Palm Beach, Florida that there were reasonable grounds to believe that Frank and Paula Brady had been involved in smuggling marijuana into the United States, and also had evaded U.S. taxes on their drug-related profits.[2]

On March 1, 1983, this grand jury issued a subpoena to the Bank of Nova Scotia requesting documents maintained by the Bank in the Bahamas, the Cayman Islands, and Antigua. On March 4, 1983, the Bank was served with the subpoena at its agency in Miami, Florida.[3]

The Bank operated in Miami through an agency, which can be thought of as a branch with restricted activities. The subpoena served on the Bank's agent in Miami is considered in law to be served on the Bank itself. In this situation, the agency could have been making loans to U.S. and foreign companies in Florida and financing trade and, therefore, could have had substantial assets in the United States. However, the bank is considered to be present in Miami by reason of having an agent there, even if it does not have any substantial assets there.

Before American prosecutors can bring a person to trial for an offence punishable by over one year in prison, they must first convince a grand jury to bring an indictment. A *grand jury* is a group of ordinary citizens (the number varies) who hear and view evidence of an alleged crime compiled by the prosecutors. Their duty is to examine the prosecutors' evidence and to determine whether that evidence shows probable cause for believing that a crime has been committed. If they find probable cause, the grand jury will issue an indictment. An *indictment* is a formal written accusation of the crime which allows the prosecutor to bring the accused before the courts in a criminal trial. The grand jury only determines whether to accuse someone of a crime; it does not determine guilt. The proceedings of a grand jury are completely secret, similar to the deliberations of a jury in the more familiar jury trial.

During its proceedings, the grand jury is empowered by law to compel the appearance of witnesses to give testimony and to compel the presentation of documents. The written command to appear or to present is called a *subpoena*. Failure to comply with a subpoena is considered *contempt* of court (since non-compliance obstructs the administration of justice). U.S. courts have the power to punish contempt by fine or imprisonment.

The scope of subpoenas can be far reaching. The subpoena served on the Bank required production of virtually all papers, documents and records for all financial transactions, savings accounts, chequing accounts, trust accounts, and other financial accounts, maintained by the Bank of Nova Scotia, at any of its main or branch offices in the specified locations relating to Frank J. Brady, Paula Brady, Frank J. Brady Enterprises, Inc., Brady Farms, Inc., and/or Clay Island Farms, Inc. Moreover, the subpoena required that all documents be originals except where such were not available.[4] The subpoena gave no indication of how the documents would be relevant to the investigation.[5]

THE BANK'S RESPONSE

Upon receiving the subpoena, the Bank's attorneys contacted the U.S. attorney and expressed the Bank's intention to produce the documents in a lawful manner. The U.S. attorney was also informed of the financial privacy laws in effect in the Bahamas and the Cayman Islands.[6] The Bank also expressed its intention to apply for disclosure in accordance with the laws of the Cayman Islands and provided copies of the applicable Cayman Islands statute and a statement from the Cayman Islands court which explained the type of information necessary to file a successful application. The information necessary to satisfy the Cayman courts was available only from the U.S. government.[7]

Unfortunately for the Bank, it was a criminal offence under Cayman secrecy law to divulge confidential information originating in the Cayman Islands, including bank information and documents about client activities. The penalty for breach of the secrecy law was a fine of up to US$6,100, up to two years' imprisonment, and suspension of banking licenses. The penalty could be applied to the Bank itself and to the employee who broke the law on the Bank's behalf.

The U.S. prosecutor had two alternatives to a subpoena, either of which could have procured the documents. First, he could have applied directly to a Cayman court, requesting that it use its power to waive the secrecy laws and procure the documents to assist the U.S. investigation. Such an application is called *letters rogatory* and would have required the U.S. prosecutor to present evidence before the Cayman court showing that the secrecy laws were being used to shield criminal activity.

Second, he could have applied directly to the Cayman government for an executive method of disclosure. The direct application was provided for by a U.S.-Cayman Islands inter-governmental agreement under which evidence similar to that required by the Cayman courts would have to be supplied before disclosure could be obtained. The U.S. prosecutor would have to explain the materiality and necessity for the documents. The U.S. prosecutor did not choose either of these alternatives, claiming that the processes were too time consuming, expensive and unreliable.

In the Cayman Islands, production of the documentation could also be obtained if the customer agreed to the release of the documents. The Bank did not keep records of customer addresses, and therefore was not able to contact the individuals under investigation to obtain their consent to the production of the documents.[8] Although it probably could have found a way to contact the Bradys through further investigation, such action poses a potential dilemma from the Bank's perspective. On one hand, if it does not contact the customer to obtain consent, it could later be accused of not acting in good faith. On the other hand, if it does contact the customer and he refuses, he can go to court to get an injunction to prevent the Bank from making any disclosures. The Bank could then be accused of "courting the impediment," or creating the situation that reinforces its position that it cannot release the information. It is a potential no-win situation.[9]

The Bank also provided details on how to obtain the documents located in the Bahamas and was willing to cooperate with the United States to have the documents released.[10] Under Bahamian law, the release of such information was primarily through the traditional system of letters rogatory. However, the Bank of Nova Scotia could not initiate this procedure. Only the United States authorities could initiate the letters rogatory, but they refused. The United States authorities refused to produce affidavits of materiality similar to those required under the Cayman Islands' bank secrecy laws.[11]

On March 22, 1983, the Bank's Miami agency sent telexes to the Bank's branches in Antigua, the Cayman Islands and the Bahamas, requesting that the branches (a) determine whether they had the type of documents sought by the subpoena and (b) transmit any of the documents sought to the Miami agency no later than March 25, 1983.[12] There were 10 branches in the Bahamas alone that had to be searched.

Affidavits were received from the Bank's Cayman Islands' and the Bahamas' attorneys which stated documents covered by the subpoena had been located at two branches. However, financial privacy laws made it a criminal offense for the Bank or its employees to disclose the documents.[13] The Antigua branch responded that it did not have any of the documents sought by the subpoena. Apparently, the U.S. prosecutors accepted the Antigua branch's statement.[14]

BACK TO COURT

Since the United States was not cooperating in securing the release of the documents, on March 29, 1983 an agent for the Bank appeared before the grand jury and declined to produce the documentation sought.[15] On April 4, the Bank made a motion to quash the subpoena; or, alternatively, for more time to respond, particularly to get the Bahamian and Cayman Island governments' permission to disclose the confidential information; or, alternatively, to have the U.S. prosecutor provide information which supported the necessity of the documentation for the investigation of the grand jury.[16]

The two critical legal arguments raised by the Bank in the motion to quash the subpoena were as follows: First, the Bank argued that it had acted in good faith, and had done everything in its power to comply with the subpoena, but had not been able to produce the documents because of the lack of cooperation from the U.S. attorney's office. A number of U.S. court decisions seemed to be based on the principle that if you acted in good faith, you could be excused for not complying with a subpoena.[17]

The second argument was that before enforcing the cross-border subpoena, the District Court should balance interests as prescribed by Section 40 of the *U.S. Restatement (Second) of Foreign*

Relations, which had been applied by several federal courts and the Supreme Court in deciding cross-border subpoena cases.[18]

Restatements of the U.S. law are written by prominent legal scholars in an attempt to clarify the state of the law as passed by the U.S. legislatures and as interpreted by the U.S. courts. In the course of producing a restatement, a series of tentative drafts are circulated among interested scholars, allowing their views and comments to be incorporated. A restatement, then, is a consensus of expert opinion and can be influential in arguments before the U.S. courts. They are not, however, the law. Restatements are updated periodically to reflect developments in the law.

Section 40 of *Restatement (Second) of the Foreign Relations Law of the United States (1965)* states:

> Where two states have jurisdiction to prescribe and enforce rules of law and the rules they may prescribe require inconsistent conduct upon the part of a person, each state is required by international law to consider, in good-faith, moderating the exercise of its enforcement jurisdiction, in the light of such factors as:
> a. Vital national interests of each of the states.
> b. The extent and nature of the hardship that inconsistent enforcement actions would impose upon the person.
> c. The extent to which the required conduct is to take place in the territory of the other state.
> d. The nationality of the person, and
> e. The extent to which enforcement by action of either state can reasonably be expected to achieve compliance with the rule prescribed by the state.

The Bank argued that the most recent draft of the *Restatement* listed specific factors which also should be considered by U.S. courts:[19]

> In issuing an order directing production of documents or other information located abroad, a court in the United States must take into account:
> 1. The importance to the investigation or litigation of the documents or other information requested.
> 2. The degree of specificity of the request.
> 3. In which of the states involved the documents or information originated.
> 4. The extent to which compliance with the request would undermine important interests of the state where the information is located, and
> 5. The possibility of alternative means of securing the information.

The Bank also called attention to the notes to this section of the tentative draft of the *Restatement:*[20]

> No aspect of the extension of the American legal system beyond the territorial frontiers of the United States has given rise to so much friction as the request for documents associated with investigation and litigation in the United States.

Applying the balancing test in the *Restatement,* the Bank argued that the U.S. prosecutors had shown no valid reason why the District Court should provoke international friction by forcing a peaceful trader in the United States to violate the criminal laws of a foreign state.[21]

On April 27, the United States District Court of the Southern District of Florida denied the Bank's motion to quash the subpoena on extremely formalistic grounds, citing an earlier case involving the Bank of Nova Scotia in the same judicial district when, under similar circumstances, the Bank produced documents from branches in the Bahamas and the Cayman Islands. However, the District Court made two concessions to the Bank. First, it granted a time extension to May 31, to comply with the subpoena. Second, it required the United States' authorities to "provide any reasonable assistance, especially in dealing with foreign governments; however, the government is not required to forward letters rogatory."[22]

Soon after the District Court's decision, the Bank's counsel in Miami requested United States authorities to provide affidavits of materiality so that documentation could be released from the Cayman Island branches. The Bank offered to retain a Nassau solicitor who had acted successfully on behalf of the U.S. government in the past in obtaining documents in conformity with the

Bahamian bank secrecy laws. At one stage, Bank officials even asserted that in a telephone conversation, the assistant U.S. attorney agreed to provide such affidavits.[23]

On learning of this asserted oral agreement, Assistant U.S. Attorney Blair took a very adversarial stance and denied he had ever agreed to provide such affidavits. He claimed that he could not do this even if he wanted to, as this would breach the confidentiality of the grand jury proceedings. He claimed that his only duty under the April 27 Order of the District Court was to let the Caribbean authorities know that the grand jury investigation was proceeding. It seemed that the U.S. refusal to help came from a belief that any such assistance would be futile in getting the information requested from either Caribbean jurisdiction.[24]

The Bank, seemingly frustrated at the apparent lack of cooperation from the U.S. prosecutors, asked the Grand Court of the Cayman Islands on May 27 for permission to deliver the documents without the affidavit of materiality in view of the U.S. District Court Order of April 27, 1983. The Grand Cayman Court responded on May 31, by issuing its own injunction against disclosure, but stated it would rehear the matter, if and when the Bank received more information about the materiality of the documents to the investigation.[25] The Bank did not appeal, fearing any such action would be "futile" and "doomed to failure."[26]

On June 1, the Bank again sought an order in the District Court directing the U.S. authorities to act, or for more time, or to be relieved from further obligations under the subpoena.[27] The Bank presented a status report of events to that date.[28] It argued that:

a. The Bank was making a good faith effort to comply with the subpoena.

b. The Bank needed assistance from someone if it was ever to be in a position to apply to the Grand Court of the Cayman Islands for production of the required documents. It further asserted that this was especially appropriate when the scope of the grand jury's subpoena was so broad.

c. The U.S. authorities had to be given explicit directions to provide the Bank with assistance in light of the April 27 Order of the District Court, including deadlines to provide such assistance. The Bank asked for a partial waiver of any grand jury confidentiality requirements if such requirements existed.

d. U.S. authorities should be required to utilize letters rogatory in the Bahamas, as the Bahamian Supreme Court had expressly declared that method to be the appropriate procedure and the Bank had been willing to obtain Bahamian counsel to assist in the letters rogatory procedure.

e. In the absence of such assistance from the U.S. authorities, it should be relieved from further obligations to respond to the subpoena.[29]

The U.S attorney responded in a similar fashion. He asserted that:

a. The Bank had flagrantly refused to comply with the subpoena despite being given extra time to do so between April 27 and May 31, 1983.

b. The Bank had *procured* an order of the Grand Court of the Cayman Islands so that it could reinforce the argument that it could not disclose information under the Cayman bank secrecy laws.

c. The Bank was still asking for the U.S. authorities to go through the letters rogatory procedure when the District Court in its April 27 Order had expressly stated that such authorities need not issue such a request for judicial assistance in the Bahamas.[30]

The United States attorney requested that the Bank be fined $5,000 per day until the subpoenaed documents were produced, and he specified a particular employee of the Bank in Miami to be jailed for a period not to exceed the term of the grand jury, with the provision that the employee could purge himself of contempt by producing the subpoenaed documents.[31]

At the June hearing,

... the government submitted to the District Court for its in-camera review (i.e., the Bank was excluded) on the question of materiality and relevancy, an affidavit by I.R.S. Special Agent McCall as to the known existence of five negotiable instruments which were sought pursuant to the subpoena and further offered the in-camera testimony of Agent McCall with regard to a sixth, which was discovered after the affidavit was drafted.[32]

The U.S. attorney apparently had no qualms about providing evidence of the materiality and relevancy of the documents requested to the U.S. District Court, while denying the same to the Grand Court of the Cayman Islands. Any such disclosure by the U.S. authorities in the Grand Court of the Cayman Islands would also have been on an in-camera basis. The only individual who could leak the in-camera confidential testimony of the U.S. authorities would be the Judge of the Grand Court of the Cayman Islands.[33]

District Court Judge Paine on October 10, 1983 granted the U.S. authorities' motion to compel compliance with the subpoena. The Court was of the opinion that the government had done all that it was required to do by law and by the Court's Order of April 27, 1983. Judge Paine again cited the earlier case involving the Bank of Nova Scotia in 1982 as a precedent.[34]

Judge Paine denied the Bank's requests under their initial motion and he directed the Bank to comply with the subpoena no later than October 17, 1983. Furthermore, he stated that a contempt hearing would be held on October 21 unless the Bank complied with the subpoena before that time.[35]

THE BIND

The Bank was caught in a bind. Its choices at this point seemed to be to break the laws of the Bahamas and Cayman Islands, face contempt charges in the United States, or try to appeal the latest ruling.

What about international law? International law anticipates such a conflict and apparently offers a solution. The international standard is that the law which purports to affect conduct beyond the borders of a nation (like the U.S. subpoena of documents located outside U.S. borders) should defer to the law of the nation within whose nation the conduct will occur (the Cayman secrecy laws affecting documents in Cayman). Unfortunately for the Bank, there is no way to enforce international law. There are no international police of jails, and countries, including the United States, ignore the World Court when they want to.

DÉJÀ VU?

The previous Bank of Nova Scotia case to which Judge Paine referred twice was settled on November 29, 1982. A subpoena had been served on the Bank in Miami on September 23, 1981 requesting documents from its branches in the Cayman Islands, the Bahamas, and Antigua relating to a customer of the Bank. A federal grand jury was conducting a tax and narcotics investigation.

The Bank did not produce the documents, claiming that without the customer's assent or an order from the Bahamian courts, the Bank would be violating the Bahamian secrecy laws.[36]

A hearing was held on the U.S. government's request to compel the Bank to comply with the subpoena. Most of the arguments were similar to those in the Brady subpoena discussed earlier. Another issue that emerged in this hearing was the degree of control the Miami agency had over the Nassau Branch. The United States argued that all banking transactions for the Nassau branch could be done in Miami and the Bank argued the Miami agency was a one-way conduct for customer communication with Nassau. The District Court required compliance with the subpoena and the Bank appealed.[37]

The judge's conclusion:

Absent direction from the legislative and executive branches of our federal government, we are not willing to emasculate the grand jury process whenever a foreign nation attempts to block our criminal justice process. It is unfortunate the Bank of Nova Scotia suffers from differing legal commands of separate sovereigns, but as we stated in *Field* (at 410):

In a world where commercial transactions are international in scope, conflicts are inevitable. Courts and legislatures should take every reasonable precaution to avoid placing individuals in the situation [the Bank] finds (it)self. Yet, this court simply cannot acquiesce in the proposition that United States criminal investigations must be thwarted whenever there is conflict with the interest of other states.

For the reasons stated above, the judgment entered by the District court was affirmed.

The Bank turned over the documents in apparent violation of Bahamian law after the U.S. Supreme Court refused to quash the subpoena and the day after the fine was increased from $500 per day to $25,000 per day.[38]

INFORMATION ABOUT TAX HAVENS AND THE BANK'S STRUCTURE

Tax Havens—Use and Misuse

A tax haven is defined "loosely to include any country having a low or zero rate of tax on all or certain categories of income and offering a certain level of banking or commercial secrecy."[39] If this definition is applied literally, most developed countries fall within its scope—including the United States. However, there are degrees to which a country offers shelter or refuge from taxes and secrecy. There are four general types of tax haven.[40]

   a. *No-Tax Havens.* There are virtually no taxes in the Bahamas, Cayman Islands, Turks and Caicos, Nauru, and Vanuatu.

   b. *Tax on Local Income Only.* Liberia, Panama, Costa Rica, and Hong Kong do not tax income from foreign sources.

   c. *Low Tax with Treaty Benefits.* These countries offer a special, low tax rate (such as three per cent in the Netherlands Antilles) and are party to favorable income tax treaties (such as low withholding tax on dividends) with other countries. Jersey, Guernsey and the Isle of Man fall into this category.

   d. *Special Privileges.* Countries in this category allow corporations to be managed, controlled, and earn their income from abroad. Corporations

meeting these conditions pay a fixed annual fee in lieu of income tax. This category includes Luxembourg, Netherlands, Switzerland, Liechtenstein, Jersey, Guernsey, Isle of Man, Gibraltar and Barbados.

In these countries where it is possible to avoid taxes, an industry comprised of accountants, tax consultants, lawyers, bankers and trust officers has developed to help individuals and corporations avoid taxes.[41] There clearly are legal uses of tax havens, like tax avoidance and participation in the Eurodollar market free from U.S. control. However, features of tax havens like secrecy laws also lend themselves to an illegal use such as tax evasion; and for the laundering of money from illegal sources. (Note: At the time of the events in the case, the actual processing of money by a bank from illegal activities of others was not illegal in the United States or Canada.)

Most tax havens encourage foreign banks into offshore banking, usually by distinguishing between resident and non-resident banking. Non-resident banking usually does not have reserve requirements; is not subject to exchange controls; and is taxed differently, if at all.[42] Foreign banks are important to the economies of tax havens. The Gordon Report stated:[43]

One test of the importance of banking to an economy is the relationship of foreign assets of banks in a country to that country's foreign trade. When compared to foreign trade, foreign assets of deposit banks in tax haven jurisdictions were substantially greater than foreign assets of deposit banks in non-tax havens. Special statistics developed to measure the excessive holdings of foreign assets of tax haven banks indicate that these excess assets[44] are very large, and have been growing at a rapid rate. For all tax havens surveyed,[45] excess foreign assets grew from $16.7 billion in 1970 to $272.9 billion in 1978. During the same period, excess foreign assets in tax havens, as a percentage of foreign assets held worldwide, grew from 12.5 per cent to 29.1 per cent. When all jurisdictions were compared, only 13 out of 126 have foreign assets which are excessive relative to the world average in 1979. These 13 are the tax haven jurisdictions studied and the United Kingdom and France. The United Kingdom is an offshore financial center itself, and its data include the tax havens of the Channel Islands and the Isle of Man, which could not be separated from all other U.K. data. France has excess deposits, largely because export financing aid is handled through private banks.

The importance of U.S. banks to the major Caribbean financial centers is growing. For example, from 1973 to 1979, total assets of U.S. bank branches increased nine times in the Cayman Islands, eight times in the Bahamas, and four times in Panama.[46]

The banking industry has a significant effect on the economy of the tax haven. Financial business yields revenues in the form of fees and modest taxes on financial institutions. The tax haven also benefits from employment of personnel and rental of facilities. The Bahamas Central Bank estimated that expenditures of banks and offshore branches in the Bahamas in 1975 was $32,886,000, including $18,330,000 for salaries. Licenses and other fees amounted to $1.5 million, and the banks employed 1,890 (1,650 Bahamian) people.[47] Informed sources estimate that by early 1978, the banking sector may have employed 2,100 people (1,897 Bahamians), paying them salaries in excess of $26 million per annum. An additional 10,000 jobs may have been indirectly supported.

A comparable survey of the Cayman Islands indicates that, in 1977, total operating expenditures by Cayman branch banks were $10.2 million, of which $5.3 million were for salaries. These branches paid $1.6 million in fees and employed 433 people, of whom 298 were local citizens.[48]

The Gordon Report also provided the following information:

a. Total deposits in banks (U.S. and foreign) at year-end 1978 in tax havens in the Western Hemisphere[49] was $160 billion. $100 billion was in branches or subsidiaries of U.S. banks.

b. Total deposits in all banks (U.S. and foreign) at year-end 1978 in all tax havens surveyed[50] was $385 billion, of which $131 billion was in U.S. branches or subsidiaries.

c. Growth in deposits was most rapid in the Bahamas, Cayman Islands and Panama.

The Gordon study was not able to estimate the level of use of tax havens by drug traffickers and tax evaders. However, it did find 250 criminal cases that were active, or closed within the previous three years, involving offshore transactions. It stated that "this number of cases is an indication of a significant level of use." Another indication of the magnitude of the problem is the estimate of the money involved in the narcotics trade—up to $60 billion.[51]

The Bank of Nova Scotia—Structure and Operation[52]

In 1983, the Bank reorganized around its four core business areas:

a. *Retail Banking and Operations.* This division is responsible for consumer loans, mortgages, credit cards, savings and checking accounts, cashstop machines, branch operations, and administrative systems and support.

b. *Canadian Commercial Banking.* This division provides credit and non-credit (cash management, payroll preparation, etc.) commercial services to small and medium sized Canadian companies.

c. *North American Corporate Banking.* This division manages the Bank's relationships with large national and multinational corporations in Canada and the United States. The corporate office is in Toronto, and the division maintains offices in three other Canadian cities and nine U.S. cities (Atlanta, Boston, Chicago, Cleveland, Houston, Miami, New York, Portland, San Francisco). The 1984 annual report stated that the Bank maintains "a leading position among foreign banks in U.S. corporate relationships. Our activities included lead positions in major acquisition financing, letter of credit supported tax exempt transactions and project financings."

The *Treasury* coordinates the activities of the Treasuries in Europe, the Middle East, the Pacific and in North America. It also includes a new merchant banking activity.

d. *International.* The Bank maintains 174 offices in 51 countries to serve clients around the world. It provides a wide range of financial services to its clients—retail, commercial, corporate, wholesale and trust. The division is divided into four regions: Caribbean (Regional Office in Toronto; offices in 20 islands/countries); Central and South America (Regional Office in Toronto; offices in five countries); Europe, Middle East and Africa (Regional Office in London; offices in 15 countries); and Pacific (Regional Office in Manila; offices in 11 countries). The Bank operates through a network of branches, representative offices, agencies, subsidiary and affiliated companies. In 1981, it had a total of 211 offices outside Canada, of which 157 were located in the Caribbean Region.[53] The Bank's international retail activities are primarily located in the Caribbean, where it has been represented since 1889.[54] (Note: It is believed that the Bank is the largest financial institution, in terms of offices, in the Caribbean.)

Some selected statistics on the Bank's financial performance are shown in Tables 1 to 4.

	1980	1981	1982	1983
Domestic	93	118	92	152
International	142	126	181	196
Total	235	244	273	348

Table 1   Net Income ($millions)

	1980	1981	1982	1983
Domestic	19.9	24.2	28.5	28.3
International	18.5	21.1	24.5	25.7
Total	38.4	45.3	53.0	54.0

Table 2   Average Total Assets ($billions)

	1980	1981	1982	1983
Domestic	0.47	0.49	0.32	0.54
International	0.77	0.60	0.74	0.76
Total	0.61	0.54	0.51	0.64

Table 3   Return on Assets (%)

Source: 1984 Annual Report.

	$	% of Total Earning Assets
Middle East, Africa	$525	1.0
Japan	1,712	3.4
Other	1,634	3.2
Asia	3,346	6.6
Mexico	988	2.0
Brazil	807	1.6
Venezuela	549	1.1
Other Latin American	1,154	2.2
Total Central & South American	3,498	6.9
Jamaica	792	1.6
Other Caribbean	1,592	3.1
Total Caribbean	2,384	4.7
United Kingdom	2,348	4.7
France	1,925	3.8
West Germany	934	1.9
Belgium	662	1.3
Netherlands	596	1.2
Other Europe	2,467	4.9
Total Europe	8,932	17.8
Total Above	$18,685	37.0
United States	7,065	14.0
Canada	24,700	49.0
Total	$50,450	100.0

Table 4   Geographic Distribution of Major Earning Assets* ($millions) 1983

Source: 1984 Annual Report.

*Major earning assets are loans, deposits with banks other than the Bank of Canada, and securities. Location is based on geographic area or country of residence of the borrower or the residence of the guarantor. Countries exceeding one per cent of assets are reported separately.

NOTES

1. The legal events presented regarding the Brady subpoena have been taken from a legal record of the case entitled *"The Bank of Nova Scotia Case: A Case of U.S. Extraterritorial Information Gathering"* (unpublished). It was compiled by Errol P. Mendes, Faculty of Law, The University of Western Ontario from public documents. Footnotes 1–7 and 9–34 were also taken from that record.

2. Jud Harwood, "Bank of Nova Scotia (Brady Subpoena): U.S. Government Lawyers Deceive the Courts" (March 1985) 65, *Taxes International,* p. 3.

3. "Subpoena to Testify Before Grand Jury 83-1 (WPB)." In "The United States District Court for the Southern District of Florida; Selected Court Documents Pertaining to: *The United States of America* vs. *The Bank of Nova Scotia* (Brady)." Prepared by the Economic Law and Treaty Division, Department of External Affairs, Volume I (hereafter referred to as "Volume I").

4. "Attachment to Subpoena: The Bank of Nova Scotia." In Volume I (see n. 2).

5. Supra n. 1., p. 4.

6. Jud Harwood and Bruce Zagaris, "Judge Paine Socks-It-To The Bank of Nova Scotia" (April 1984) 54, *Taxes International,* p. 12.

7. Ibid., p. 12.

8. Ibid., pp. 5–8.

9. R.J. Marshall, Senior International Counsel Bank of Nova Scotia, Personal Communication.

10. Jud Harwood and Bruce Zagaris, "Judge Paine Socks-It-To The Bank of Nova Scotia" (April 1984) 54, *Taxes International,* pp. 12–13.

11. "Memorandum of Law in Support of the Bank of Nova Scotia's Motion Directed to Subpoena 83-1" 1–19, p. 4. In Volume I (see n. 2).

12. "Memorandum of Law in Support of the Bank of Nova Scotia's Motion Directed to Subpoena 83-1," p. 2. In Volume I (see n. 2).

13. Ibid., p. 2.

14. Ibid., p. 2.

15. "Government's Motion to Compel Compliance with Grand Jury Subpoena and Answer to Movant's Motion to Quash Grand Jury Subpoena," p. 2. In Volume I (see n. 2).

16. "Memorandum of Law in Support of the Bank of Nova Scotia's Motion Directed to Subpoena 83-1," pp. 1–2. In Volume I (see n. 2).

17. Ibid., pp. 7–14.

18. Ibid., pp. 8–13.

19. "Memorandum of Law in Support of the Bank of Nova Scotia's Motion Directed to Subpoena 83-1," p. 9. In Volume I (see n. 2).

20. *Restatement of Foreign Relations Law of the United States* (Revised), S420, reporters' notes at 18 n-1 (Tent. Draft 3, 1980). In Ibid., p. 15.

21. Ibid., p. 15.

22. "United States District Court, Southern District of Florida, Case No. 83–1 (WPB), April 27, 1983, Order pp. 1–2." In Volume I (see n. 2).

23. "Correspondence Between Bank's Attorney and U.S. Department of Justice" (March-June 1983), pp. 1–12. In Volume I (see n. 2).

24. Ibid., p. 9–10.

25. Supra n. 5, p. 13.

26. "Bank's First Appeal Reply Brief, p. 8." In Supra n. 5, p. 13.

27. "Motions of the Bank of Nova Scotia for Order Containing Findings, Directing Government to Act, For Further Enlargement of Time or, Alternatively, to be Relieved from Further Obligations Under Order and Subpoena," p. 1. In Volume I (see n. 2).

28. "Status Report and Memorandum of Law, In Support of the Bank of Nova Scotia's Motions for Orders Making Findings, Directing Government to Act, for Further Enlargement of Time or Alternatively, to be Relieved from Further Obligations Under Subpoena," pp. 3–8. In Volume I (see n. 2).

29. Ibid., pp. 9–19.

30. "Government's Answer to Defendant's Motion for Order Containing Facts, Directing Government to Act, For Further Enlargement of Time or, Alternatively, to be Relieved from Further Obligations Under Order and Subpoena," pp. 1–3. In Volume I (see n. 2).

31. Ibid.

32. "U.S. Attorney's First Appeal Brief, p. 12, footnote 9." In Supra n. 5, p. 13.

33. "The Bank of Nova Scotia's Reply to the Government's Answer to Defendants' Motion for Order Containing Findings, Etc." 1–8. In Volume I (see n. 2). See also Supra n. 1, pp. 28–29.

34. "United States District Court, Southern District of Florida, Case No. 83–1 (WPB): Order, October 10, 1983" 1–3. In Volume I (see n. 2).

35. Ibid.

36. *40 Taxes International,* February 1983, p. 4.

37. Ibid.

38. Jud Harwood, "Bank of Nova Scotia (Brady Subpoena): U.S. Government Lawyers Deceive the Courts" (March 1985), *65 Taxes International,* p. 4.

39. *Tax Havens and Their Use by United States Taxpayers—An Overview.* A report to the Commissioner of Internal Revenue, the Assistant Attorney General (Tax Division) and the Assistant Secretary of the Treasury (Tax Policy), by Richard A. Gordon, Special Counsel for International Taxation; January 12, 1981. Chapter 2.

40. *Practical International Tax Planning.* Marshall J. Langer. Practicing Law Institute, New York: Third Edition, 1985, pp. 3–3, 3–4.

41. Ibid., p. 3–4.

42. *Tax Havens . . .* p. A29.

43. Ibid., pp. A29 and A30.

44. Excess assets are those above the worldwide average of foreign assets of deposit banks to worldwide foreign trade. The amount above what this ratio would yield was the excess assets for that jurisdiction. For example, 1978 total foreign assets held by deposit banks in the Bahamas were $95.2 billion. Based on the worldwide average of deposits to world trade, $1.8 billion was needed to finance the foreign trade of the Bahamas. The difference, $93.4 billion, represents excess international assets and is an indication of assets attracted because of the tax haven status of the jurisdiction.

45. Bahamas, Bermuda, Cayman Islands, Hong Kong, Luxembourg-Belgium (the foreign trade data for the two countries could not be separated), Netherlands Antilles, Panama, Singapore, and Switzerland.

46. *See* Hoffman, *Caribbean Basin Economic Survey.* Federal Reserve Bank of Atlanta, May/June/July 1980, at 1.

47. C.Y. Frances, *Central Banking in a Developing Country with an Offshore Banking Centre,* Central Bank of the Bahamas (1978).

48. Cayman Islands, Department of Finance and Development.

49. Bahamas, Bermuda, British West Indies, Barbados, Costa Rica, Cayman Islands, Netherlands Antilles and Panama.

50. In addition to those countries listed in (48), add Bahrain, Hong Kong, Luxembourg, Singapore, and Switzerland.

51. *Crime and Secrecy: The Use of Offshore Banks and Companies.* Hearings before the Permanent Subcommittee on Investigations of the Committee on Governmental Affairs, United States Senate, Ninety-Eighth Congress, First Session, March 15, 16 and May 24, 1983; p. 67.

52. Bank of Nova Scotia Annual Reports 1984, 1985.

53. *Offering Circular,* "US$25 million, The Bank of Nova Scotia, 15½ per cent Deposit Notes Due June 15, 1986," dated May 27, 1981, p. 7.

54. Ibid.

YAHOO V. SURVIVORS OF THE HOLOCAUST[1]

Prepared by David Wesley under the supervision of Professor Henry W. Lane

Copyright © 2002, Northeastern University, College of Business Administration

Version: (A) 2002-11-12

The Net interprets censorship as damage and routes around it.

—John Gilmore, founder of the Electronic Frontier Foundation

On January 29, 2001, Timothy Koogle, chief executive officer (CEO) of Yahoo Inc. (Yahoo), learned that a group of French Nazi concentration camp survivors had charged him with war crimes for allegedly justifying the Holocaust through his company's Web site, Yahoo.com. The Association of Deportees of Auschwitz and Upper Silesia filed the charges in French criminal court after Yahoo executives refused to obey a French court order requiring the company to block access to neo-Nazi content on its U.S.-based servers. Yahoo claimed that the court order violated U.S. and International laws protecting freedom of speech. Holocaust survivors were angered by Yahoo's apparent support of content that demeaned their suffering and that of millions who died at the hands of Adolf Hitler's Nazi regime. If Koogle were found guilty, he potentially faced incarceration in France.[2]

COMPANY BACKGROUND

In 1995, two Stanford University students posted their Internet bookmarks on a Web site that they called Yahoo.com. The site was simple compared to other Internet search engines, but that simplicity made it popular with new users. By 1999, Yahoo had become the second most popular destination on the Net, behind America Online.

As Yahoo continued to expand its Web index, the company also began offering auxiliary services, such as news, e-mail, shopping, auctions and Web hosting. In May 1999, Yahoo acquired GeoCities for $55 million. This popular free Web hosting service was primarily supported through advertising revenues (see Exhibit 1).

In the late 1990s, the Internet had grown from a mainly English-speaking U.S.-based information service to a multilingual global communications and commerce industry. Most analysts expected the number of online users to approach one billion within a few years. The highest levels of growth were expected in non-English speaking countries throughout Europe, Asia and Latin America. While English speakers represented a clear majority among Internet users, their majority was quickly diminishing.

Components of the consolidated results of operations of Yahoo and the acquired companies, prior to their acquisitions by Yahoo (in thousands):

	2000	1999	1998
Net revenues:			
Yahoo!	$1,104,921	$543,732	$198,981
broadcast.com	—	28,748	17,392
GeoCities	—	12,984	18,227
eGroups	5,257	3,178	32
Others	—	3,144	10,500
	$1,110,178	$591,786	$245,132
Net income (loss):			
Yahoo!	$93,156	$86,766	$30,216
broadcast.com	—	(7,617)	(14,290)
GeoCities	—	(17,249)	(19,759)
eGroups	(22,380)	(13,322)	(967)
Others	—	(767)	(8,841)
	$70,776	$47,811	$(13,641)

The following table sets forth net revenues and gross property and equipment assets for geographic areas (in thousands):

	United States	International	Total
2000			
Net revenues	$941,266	$168,912	$1,110,178
Long-term assets	119,100	62,375	181,475
1999			
Net revenues	$532,731	$59,055	$591,786
Long-term assets	88,500	4,842	93,342
1998			
Net revenues	$228,929	$16,203	$245,132
Long-term assets	45,372	1,938	47,310

Exhibit 1   Selected Financial Data for Yahoo and Acquired Companies

Yahoo developed 24 international sites[3] in 13 languages. In each of its international markets, Yahoo built independent directories of local language Web sites and other content. By 2001, approximately 40 per cent of Yahoo users were located outside the United States, although no single international location accounted for more than 10 per cent of total company revenues.

Yahoo's international success could be traced back to early efforts, by founders David Filo and Jerry Yang, to hire qualified executives to build the company. One of their hires was Timothy Koogle, a former Motorola executive, who joined Yahoo in March 1995 as company president. After receiving his bachelor of science degree in mechanical engineering from the University of Virginia, Koogle went on to earn master of science and doctor of engineering degrees from Stanford University. In 1999, he was named one of the "Top 25 Executives of the Year" by *Business Week* for his instrumental role in building Yahoo into a $21.4 billion company. That same year, Koogle was elected company chairman. By January 2001, Koogle had accumulated stock options worth $365 million, in addition to receiving a $295,000 annual salary.[4]

As an Internet portal, Yahoo derived most of its revenues from online advertising (see Table 1). In the wake of the dot-com stock market crash in 2000, many companies cut advertising budgets in order to reduce costs. Worse still, 40 per cent of Yahoo's advertisers were other Internet companies, many of which faced bankruptcy. By the time Yahoo announced a 42 per cent decline in advertising revenues on April 11, 2001, company shares had already fallen 92 per cent.[5]

The decline of Yahoo's fortunes prompted a mass exodus of the company's leading executives in early 2001. Fabiola Arredondo, managing director of Yahoo Europe, resigned on February 15 following a sharp downturn in European advertising revenues. Savio Chow of Yahoo Asia resigned one day later. Three more Yahoo executives also quit: Mark Rubinstein, managing director of Yahoo Canada, Dennis Zhang, Yahoo's general manager in China and Jin Youm, chief executive officer (CEO) of Yahoo South Korea. Finally, on March 7, 2001, Timothy Koogle announced that he too would be replaced, albeit not on such voluntary terms as his international counterparts.[6]

YAHOO FRANCE

Established in 1996, Yahoo France, a 70 per cent-owned subsidiary of Yahoo Inc., was the first major French-language Internet portal.[7] The company housed its 56 French developers and company support staff in a spacious three-storey

	Q1 2001	Q4 2000	Q3 2000	Q2 2000	Q1 2000
Avg. Daily Page Views (millions)	1,100	900	780	680	625
Active Users (millions)	67	60	55	47	
Number of Advertisers	3,145	3,700	3,450	3,675	3,565
Avg. Revenue per Advertiser	$48K	$76K	$77K	$67K	$58K
Retention of Top 200 Advertisers	92%	93%	80%	98%	96%
Avg. Length of Contract (days)	285	252	235	225	230
Percentage of Non-U.S. Revenue	18%	15%	16%	15%	14%
Percentage of Non-U.S. Traffic	33%	29%	29%	27%	22%
Dot-com advertisers—% of Revenue	30%	33%	41%	47%	46%

Table 1   Yahoo Advertising and User Trends
Source: Deutsche Banc Alex. Brown.

office building in an upscale Paris suburb. Despite competition from France Telecom and other leading European media and telecommunications companies, Yahoo had grown to become the most popular portal in France, with 63 per cent of France's 7.7 million Internet users accessing the site on a daily basis.[8]

Content was organized in much the same way as the company's U.S. parent. In fact, all of Yahoo's international sites had the same look and feel, but each tailored its content to suit local tastes. In France, sports categories focused on the Tour de France, World Cup soccer and the French Decathlon; while in the United Kingdom, these categories focused on rugby, cricket and equestrian events. The challenge was to determine what should remain uniform for global brand building and what should be adapted to suit local tastes.

Yahoo v. La Ligue Contre le Racisme et L'Antisemitisme

> *As the most participatory form of mass speech yet developed, the Internet deserves the highest protection from government intrusion.*
>
> —Justice Stewart Dalzell,
> Panel Member, Communications
> Decency Act (U.S.)

From the start, France presented unique challenges, compared to other countries where Yahoo had local operations. Chief among these was the country's myriad regulations and a tradition of centralized bureaucracy (an artifact of the French Revolution that had been revived following the Second World War by the protectionist policies of Charles de Gaulle). One example was a language law that required the use of French, even when anglicisms were commonly used among the French population. As such, computers, by law, had to be referred to as "ordinateurs" in all official and commercial documents. Another example was a labor law that made dismissing employees an extremely difficult and involved process. The head of a French business organization did not hold out much hope for the future. "Things are going to change slowly," he noted. "Some companies have moved out of France for this reason."[9]

Although Yahoo was perhaps better prepared to enter France than many other Internet companies with less international experience, no one in the company could have envisioned that Yahoo would become embroiled in the most significant legal dispute over Internet jurisdiction in history. But that is what happened. In April 2000, La Ligue Contre le Racisme et L'Antisemitisme (LICRA), together with the Union of French Jewish Students, filed suit against the U.S. company for allowing users to post Nazi-era memorabilia for sale on Yahoo's auction site.

Yahoo executives believed that they had complied with a French law that prohibited the display or sale of items that incite racial hatred (including most historical items associated with Nazi Germany) by excluding such items from the company's French-language portal (www.yahoo.fr). For LICRA, however, Yahoo had not gone far enough. In LICRA's view, the availability of Nazi content on the company's U.S.-based English-language site constituted a violation of French law, as the items could be displayed on computer screens in France. Yahoo also maintained more than 150 neo-Nazi Web sites through its GeoCities Web hosting service.[10]

On April 5, 2000, LICRA sent a letter to Yahoo's U.S. headquarters in Santa Clara, California, demanding that all Nazi items be removed from the company's auction site within eight days. When Yahoo failed to comply, LICRA filed suit with the Tribunal de Grande Instance de Paris, alleging that Yahoo had violated the Nazi Symbols Act.[11]

Yahoo's lawyers argued that the French court lacked jurisdiction over a U.S. Web site operated from the United States and directed toward U.S. customers. The court disagreed. On May 22, 2000, it ruled that the availability of Nazi items on the company's U.S. English-language site constituted a violation of the law because French users could access the U.S. site. The court ordered Yahoo to block French users from accessing banned content. In the order, Presiding Judge Jean-Jacques Gomez stated:

> . . . YAHOO is currently refusing to accept through its auctions service the sale of human organs, drugs, works or objects connected with pedophilia, cigarettes or live animals, all such sales being automatically and justifiably excluded with the benefit of the first amendment of the American constitution guaranteeing freedom of opinion and expression;
>
> Whereas it would most certainly cost the company very little to extend its ban to symbols of Nazism, and such an initiative would also have the merit of satisfying an ethical and moral imperative shared by all democratic societies;
>
> Whereas it is true that the "Yahoo Auctions" site is in general directed principally at surfers based in the United States having regard notably to the items posted for sale, the methods of payment envisaged, the terms of delivery, the language and the currency used, the same cannot be said to apply to the auctioning of objects representing symbols of Nazi ideology which may be of interest to any person.
>
> Whereas, furthermore, and as already ruled, the simple act of displaying such objects in France constitutes a violation of Article R645-1 of the Penal Code and therefore a threat to internal public order.
>
> Whereas, in addition, this display clearly causes damage in France to the plaintiff associations who are justified in demanding the cessation and reparation thereof;
>
> Whereas YAHOO is aware that it is addressing French parties because upon making a connection to its auctions site from a terminal located in France it responds by transmitting advertising banners written in the French language;
>
> Whereas a sufficient basis is thus established in this case for a connecting link with France, which renders our jurisdiction perfectly competent to rule in this matter.[12]

Yahoo initially argued that the court's measures were not technically feasible since users were not identified by nationality, but by an anonymous Internet Protocol (IP) number. However, a court-convened panel of experts reported otherwise, namely that a number of startup companies had developed geolocation software for the purpose of delivering localized advertising. Such software could be adapted to selectively block 70 per cent of French users. If Yahoo were to also ask users for their nationality, the panel concluded that 90 per cent of French users could be prevented from viewing Yahoo's questionable content.[13]

On November 20, 2000, the court reconfirmed the May 22 decision, and further stated:

> We order YAHOO Inc. to comply within 3 months from notification of the present order with the injunctions contained in our order of 22nd May 2000 subject to a penalty of 100,000 Francs[14] per day of delay effective from the first day following expiry of the 3 month period;
>
> 1/ YAHOO Inc.: to take all necessary measures to dissuade and make impossible any access via yahoo.com to the auction service for Nazi merchandise as well as to any other site or service that may be construed as an apology for Nazism or contesting the reality of Nazi crimes.
>
> 2/ YAHOO France: to issue to all Internet surfers, even before use is made of the link enabling them to proceed with searches on yahoo.com, a warning informing them of the risks involved in continuing to view such sites;
>
> 3/ continuance of the proceeding in order to enable YAHOO Inc. to submit for deliberation by all interested parties the measures that it proposes to take to put an end to the trouble and damage suffered and to prevent any further trouble.[15]

Yahoo voluntarily began screening items on its auction sites worldwide to exclude some Nazi-era memorabilia,[16] but refused to screen users by nationality. Yahoo also continued to both host anti-Semitic Web sites on its GeoCities Web hosting service, and to provide Web links to similar sites hosted on third-party servers.

LICRA intended to file similar suits against Amazon and EBay. "The combat is only beginning," announced LICRA representative Marc Knobel.[17] In response, Amazon claimed that the display and sale of Nazi products wasn't "an issue" and that the company followed "all the rules of countries" in which it operated.[18]

In reality, both Yahoo and Amazon offered fresh English- and German-language copies of *Mein Kampf* on their U.S. Web sites, as well as used copies on their German auction sites, apparently in violation of German law prohibiting the sale of the book.

That such products were used by hate groups to promote their views was undeniable. Amazon even posted white supremacist reviews for *Mein Kampf* on its Web site, one of which read:

> This is a must-read book for every self-respecting white person to understand why Hitler had to start WWII and stop communists in Russia, which were mostly of Jewish origin. . . . If Hitler hadn't stopped them, then today the whole of Europe and probably most of the world would be living under the terror of Bolshevik communists. . . . Overall, the book shows that [Adolf Hitler was] very smart.[19]

Another reviewer maintained that *Mein Kampf* was an "ingenious work straight from one of the most intelligent minds of our century."

On May 17, 2001, EBay, the most popular auction site on the Internet with more than $5 billion in annual revenues, instituted a policy prohibiting the listing of items "likely to incite violence or perpetuate hate crimes" on its Web site. A company spokesperson stated that EBay was committed to following the laws of the countries where it conducts business. "It's a matter of respecting the communities where we live and work."[20] Despite EBay's policy, hate-crime items continued to find their way onto the auction site. A June 20, 2001 search of the term "Nazi" revealed 3,694 items (about one per cent of EBay's total listings), including a mix of historical artifacts and neo-Nazi paraphernalia.

THE YAHOO COUNTERSUIT

In Cyberspace, the First Amendment is a local ordinance.

—John Perry Barlow,
Electronic Frontier Foundation

On December 21, 2000, Yahoo filed a countersuit against LICRA with the U.S. District Court for the Northern District of California. Yahoo argued that compliance with the French order would violate constitutionally protected free speech in the United States.[21] Yahoo also argued:

> The Orders exercise an unreasonable, extraterritorial jurisdiction over the operations and content of a U.S.-based Web service belonging to a U.S. citizen. The Paris Court has extraterritorially imposed on a U.S. corporation the drastic remedy of a prior restraint and penalties that are impermissible under U.S. law, instead of simply enforcing the French Penal Code against French citizens who break French law.[22]

According to Yahoo, the French decision violated a U.S. federal law. The Communications Decency Act provided Internet hosts with immunity from liability for content posted by third parties (see Exhibit 2).[23] It also violated Article 19 of the International Covenant on Civil and Political Rights, Article 10 of the Convention for the Protection of Human Rights and Fundamental Freedoms, and Article 19 of the Universal Declaration of Human Rights (see Exhibit 3).

LICRA responded that the U.S. court did not have jurisdiction over the French organizations, and that defending itself in a U.S. court would result in an undue financial burden. District Judge Jeremy Fogel disagreed. On June 7, 2001, he declared that his court did indeed have jurisdictional authority over the French defendants. In his order, he stated:

> There can be little doubt that most people in the United States, including this court, find the display and sale of Nazi propaganda and memorabilia profoundly offensive. However, while this fact may cause one to sympathize with the Defendant's efforts before the French Court, it is immaterial to this Court's jurisdictional determination. As Yahoo! and others have pointed out, a content restriction imposed upon an Internet service provider by a foreign court just as easily could prohibit promotion of democracy, gender equality, a particular religion or other viewpoints which have strong support in the United States but are viewed as offensive or inappropriate elsewhere.[24]

Other factors that favored U.S. jurisdiction included LICRA's use of a U.S. marshal to serve

Sec. 230. Protection for private blocking and screening of offensive material

1. Policy
   It is the policy of the United States—

   (1) to promote the continued development of the Internet and other interactive computer services and other interactive media;

   (2) to preserve the vibrant and competitive free market that presently exists for the Internet and other interactive computer services, unfettered by Federal or State regulation;

   (3) to encourage the development of technologies which maximize user control over what information is received by individuals, families, and schools who use the Internet and other interactive computer services;

   (4) to remove disincentives for the development and utilization of blocking and filtering technologies that empower parents to restrict their children's access to objectionable or inappropriate online material; and

   (5) to ensure vigorous enforcement of Federal criminal laws to deter and punish trafficking in obscenity, stalking, and harassment by means of computer.

2. Protection for "Good Samaritan" blocking and screening of offensive material

   (1) Treatment of publisher or speaker
   No provider or user of an interactive computer service shall be treated as the publisher or speaker of any information provided by another information content provider.

   (2) Civil liability
   No provider or user of an interactive computer service shall be held liable on account of -
   (A) any action voluntarily taken in good faith to restrict access to or availability of material that the provider or user considers to be obscene, lewd, lascivious, filthy, excessively violent, harassing, or otherwise objectionable, whether or not such material is constitutionally protected; or
   (B) any action taken to enable or make available to information content providers or others the technical means to restrict access to material described in paragraph (1).

3. Effect on other laws

   (1) No effect on criminal law
   Nothing in this section shall be construed to impair the enforcement of section 223 or 231 of this title, chapter 71 (relating to obscenity) or 110 (relating to sexual exploitation of children) of title 18, or any other Federal criminal statute.

   (2) No effect on intellectual property law
   Nothing in this section shall be construed to limit or expand any law pertaining to intellectual property.

   (3) State law
   Nothing in this section shall be construed to prevent any State from enforcing any State law that is consistent with this section. No cause of action may be brought and no liability may be imposed under any State or local law that is inconsistent with this section.

   (4) No effect on communications privacy law
   Nothing in this section shall be construed to limit the application of the Electronic Communications Privacy Act of 1986 or any of the amendments made by such Act, or any similar State law.

Exhibit 2   Communications Decency Act Title 47 (abridged)

Source: Federal Communication Commission.

notice on Yahoo to appear in the French court, sending a cease and desist letter to Yahoo's headquarters in Santa Clara, California and accessing the U.S. Web site to gather evidence. The order further explained:

If the non-resident defendant's contacts with the forum state are substantial or continuous and systematic, the defendant is subject to general jurisdiction on the forum state even if the cause of action is unrelated to the defendant's activities within the state.

International Covenant on Civil and Political Rights

UN General Assembly (1972)

Article 19

1. Everyone shall have the right to hold opinions without interference.

2. Everyone shall have the right to freedom of expression; this right shall include freedom to seek, receive and impart information and ideas of all kinds, regardless of frontiers, either orally, in writing or in print, in the form of art, or through any other media of his choice.

3. The exercise of the rights provided for in paragraph 2 of this article carries with it special duties and responsibilities. It may therefore be subject to certain restrictions, but these shall only be such as are provided by law and are necessary:
   (a) For respect of the rights or reputations of others;
   (b) For the protection of national security or of public order, or of public health or morals.

Convention for the Protection of Human Rights and Fundamental Freedoms

Council of Europe—Rome (1950)

Article 10—Freedom of expression

Everyone has the right to freedom of expression. This right shall include freedom to hold opinions and to receive and impart information and ideas without interference by public authority and regardless of frontiers. This article shall not prevent States from requiring the licensing of broadcasting, television or cinema enterprises.

The exercise of these freedoms, since it carries with it duties and responsibilities, may be subject to such formalities, conditions, restrictions or penalties as are prescribed by law and are necessary in a democratic society, in the interests of national security, territorial integrity or public safety, for the prevention of disorder or crime, for the protection of health or morals, for the protection of the reputation or rights of others, for preventing the disclosure of information received in confidence, or for maintaining the authority and impartiality of the judiciary.

Universal Declaration of Human Rights

UN General Assembly (1948)

Article 19

Everyone has the right to freedom of opinion and expression; this right includes freedom to hold opinions without interference and to seek, receive and impart information and ideas through any media and regardless of frontiers.

Exhibit 3   International Covenants on Free Speech

Source: UN Office of the High Commissioner for Human Rights.

Fogel also stated that, beyond the direct circumstances, the case was "ripe for adjudication" as precedent to determine future litigation against U.S. Internet companies by foreign jurisdictions. "California has an interest in providing effective legal redress for its residents," particularly in matters that "might infringe upon the First Amendment to the United States Constitution," he argued. Furthermore:

Many nations, including France, limit freedom of expression on the Internet based upon their respective legal, cultural or political standards. Yet because of the global nature of the Internet, virtually any public Web site can be accessed by end-users anywhere in the world, and in theory any provider of Internet content could be subject to legal action in countries which find certain content offensive.

Finally, LICRA unsuccessfully argued that Yahoo should have challenged the order in a

French court. Fogel replied that U.S. courts were a "more efficient and effective forum" for addressing questions of U.S. laws and constitutional concerns. Furthermore, had Yahoo argued its case in the French court and lost, international law would have prohibited Yahoo from resubmitting its case in a U.S. court at a later date. Yahoo's only redress would then have been to appeal the decision to a higher court in France.[25]

PURVEYORS OF HATE

The Internet is a shallow and unreliable electronic repository of dirty pictures, inaccurate rumors, bad spelling and worse grammar, inhabited largely by people with no demonstrable social skills.

—Chronicle of Higher Education,
April 11, 1997

In the early 1980s, neo-Nazis and white supremacists began using computer bulletin boards to disseminate their views. Donald Black, the leader of one of the largest of these groups, had learned to use a computer while serving prison time for plotting to overthrow the government of Dominica in order to establish an Aryan state. After his release in 1985, Black launched the first white supremacist Web site. Black's "Stormfront" was one of the largest hate sites on the Internet, hosting skinheads, Ku Klux Klansmen and neo-Nazis. By 1999, Black reported more than one million hits to his Web site, with more than 2,000 Internet users accessing the site on a daily basis.[26]

The National Alliance was another of the more popular hate sites. It hosted a fictional novel titled "The Turner Diaries" in which an all-white army successfully establishes a world government and exterminates blacks, Jews and other minorities. The novel was also available in French and German, and was believed to have inspired several acts of violence, including the April 1995 bombing of the Oklahoma City federal building in which 168 people lost their lives.

Several neo-Nazi sites posted bomb-making formulas that were linked to at least 30 bombings between 1985 and 1996.[27] In April 2001, law enforcement agents uncovered a Neo-Nazi plot to destroy Boston's Holocaust Memorial, using the same explosive formula used in the Oklahoma City bombing.[28]

All told, some 800 Web sites promoted Nazism, the majority of which were physically located in the United States. Besides offering anti-Semitic literature, neo-Nazi sites also distributed computer games directed at children. These included KZ, a concentration camp simulator, and Manager, a game in which players selected victims for Nazi gas chambers.[29] More sophisticated sites offered multimedia content, including videos and rock music. Of the 50,000 white supremacist rock CDs sold annually in the United States, most were targeted toward teen listeners and included lyrics that advocated murdering blacks or committing other acts of violence.[30]

White supremacists claimed that the Internet has been very effective for recruiting new members. "We don't have money to have TV and newspaper ads," admitted one neo-Nazi Web publisher. "The Net has allowed us to reach people in a way we never could with our limited resources."[31] Some attributed the increasing popularity of such sites for the year-over-year increase in hate crimes against minorities.[32]

International Outrage

Hateful speech did not enjoy the same protection in most countries as it did in the United States. Germany, France, the United Kingdom, Denmark and Canada have all brought charges against individuals and organizations for posting racist and hateful content on the Internet.

Germany was one of the first countries to vigorously prosecute publishers of electronically delivered hate propaganda. Dr. Frederick Toben, an Australian citizen of German origin, operated a Web site in Australia in which he denied the Holocaust and railed against the supposed "forces of Zionist evil." Although many sites made similar claims, Toben was one of the few to direct his activities toward German users.

Toben published German-language pamphlets that advertised the site and distributed them in Germany. On December 12, 2000, Germany's highest court held that the Australian Web site was subject to German laws against denying the Holocaust, thus confirming a lower court ruling that sentenced Toben to 10 months in prison. A Georgetown University law professor, John Schmertz, explained:

> German criminal law may punish a foreign national if he publishes statements that constitute incitement of hatred among people on a foreign Internet server that is accessible to German Internet users within Germany. Such actions are considered "capable of disturbing the peace in Germany."[33]

Australian lawyer Ronald S. Huttner not only agreed with the German decision, but supported similar measures in Australia:

> In Australia we do not have any legislative equivalent of the First Amendment. On the contrary, we prefer the view that, even in the most free of democracies, the right of minorities to be protected from racial bigotry, vilification and abuse is more important than the so-called "right" of Nazis.[34]

The German interior minister, Otto Schily, criticized the United States for sheltering 90 per cent of the Web's hate content publishers. Although illegal under international law, the German government was exploring electronic countermeasures, such as spamming and denial-of-service attacks, against foreign sites that violated Germany's hate laws. In early 2001, in one of its first actions against a commercial site, German prosecutors charged Yahoo Germany for hosting *Mein Kampf* on its GeoCities Web hosting service.[35]

In the United States, anti-hate organizations, such as the Anti-Defamation League (ADL) and The Simon Wiesenthal Center, sought to combat hate and racism through education. These organizations took the position that many Internet users were unable to distinguish between legitimate Web sites, and those posting fallacious historical commentary in order to incite hatred toward minorities. They hoped to counter some of the progress made by hate groups by posting their own Web sites to expose the fallacies in Nazi propaganda.

The ADL also developed a filtering program, called the "Hate Filter," that could be downloaded by users. Whenever someone using the filter tried to access a blocked hate site, the user would be redirected to related ADL educational material. Filters were often employed by parents, schools and libraries, to counter groups intent on capturing "the minds of youngsters."[36] Critics of filters complained that they encouraged young users to access prohibited sites by bypassing the filter. Filters also blocked access to legitimate sites by historians providing information about the Second World War because these sites contained banned keywords such as "Nazi."

EXTRATERRITORIALITY

Until the 18th century, most nations maintained control over citizens and property within their borders, while lacking authority over persons or things outside their borders. When one government wished to assert its authority over another, it usually had to go to war. The Industrial Revolution and mass migrations of the 19th and 20th centuries changed that. Long before the advent of the Internet, the increased mobility of populations and the creation of multinational corporations necessitated the development of internationally accepted rules for cross-border legal disputes.

Extraterritoriality commonly referred to the practice by which one state exercised legal power over conduct that occurred in another state. Nations that exerted these powers usually did so to secure the safety and well-being of its citizens against criminal actions in foreign countries. Such would be the case when a country prosecuted foreign nationals involved in terrorist acts against its citizens. The nation initiating the case relied on the goodwill of the foreign state to enforce its judgements.

Problems of extraterritoriality occurred when both nations had an interest in the outcome of a case. The Internet vastly increased the complexity of these decisions, as content providers usually transacted, in one way or another, with individuals or organizations in multiple states simultaneously. An auction site in the United States, for example, may list an item from a seller in Japan, and then re-list that item through several online partner sites in Europe. As different jurisdictions may hold different opinions about who is actually responsible for the content, decisions over whose laws should apply remained unclear.

Prior to the Internet, businesses had to make an effort to generate sales in foreign markets. They had to set up distribution channels, advertise through local media and create local infrastructure to transact sales. Internet content providers, on the other hand, had to make an effort to *not* have their businesses accessed by foreign users. Suddenly the default market had become global and Web businesses had become subject to the laws of each country in which they transacted business. This could include a single act, such as the sale of a product to a foreign address, or a continuous presence, such as a foreign-language Web site targeted to residents of a foreign country.

The liability of the Web content provider substantially increased when the site intentionally targeted foreign users, either through the use of local languages or regionally specific content. If a Web site offered content in Malay, for example, one could be certain that it targeted Malaysian Internet users. A common interpretation of extraterritoriality suggested that the site provider could then be required to comply with Malaysian law. The U.S. Department of Justice applied this interpretation when it convicted an Antigua-based sports gambling site of violating U.S. gambling laws in early 2000.[37] The crux of the case rested on the fact that the gambling site knowingly accepted bets placed by U.S. Internet customers, even though sports gambling is legal in Antigua.[38]

A few courts, however, maintained that simply having a site accessible in a given jurisdiction was sufficient for the Web content provider to be subject to the laws in that jurisdiction. In the United States, a Connecticut-based firm sued a Massachusetts firm for using its trademark on the Internet, even though both companies had similar names and could justify claim to the trademark in their respective states. The court reasoned:

> The Internet, as well as toll-free numbers, is designed to communicate with people and their businesses in every state. Advertisement on the Internet can reach as many as 10,000 Internet users within Connecticut alone. Further, once posted on the Internet, unlike television and radio advertising, the advertisement is available continuously to any Internet user. [The company] has therefore, purposefully availed itself of the privilege of doing business within Connecticut.[39]

Under the Connecticut court's reasoning, any company doing business through the Internet would be subject to the laws of every jurisdiction where the Internet was accessible, even if the Web provider did not target the foreign state and did not derive any benefit from access to its site by foreign users. Increasingly, regulators in the United Kingdom and several other European Union (EU) nations began to adopt such an interpretation, namely "that if the Web site can be accessed in a particular jurisdiction, the laws of the place where the access takes place will apply and the Web site provider must comply with those local laws."[40]

Protection of Free Speech

The United States, however, did not extradite individuals for engaging in constitutionally protected speech, even if the activity was a clear violation of another country's law. For this reason, some experts believed that, as more countries began to enforce laws against promoting hatred, the United States would become an offshore haven for foreign hate groups. In at least one case, Ernst Zündel, a German resident of Canada, posted his anti-Semitic views on a California-based Web site in an attempt to avoid prosecution in Canada.[41]

The First Amendment's protection of speech did not prevent Internet companies from instituting an "acceptable use" policy for users.

Typically, when users signed up for a service, they signed contracts that included "terms of service." Private contracts of this type were entered into between an individual and a company and therefore did not involve government protected free speech. An "acceptable use" policy could prohibit users from sending racist messages, or posting questionable content on Web pages. Internet providers relied on company employees and public users to report violations of company policy. When companies banned individuals from using their services, most customers could easily find more liberal Internet providers willing to host their activities.

International Conventions on Jurisdiction

The international nature of the Internet created a plethora of jurisdictional problems for legislators. Since 1968, Europeans resolved international disputes using a mechanism known as the Brussels Convention. The convention dictated that all EU nations respect and enforce civil and commercial legal decisions handed down by other EU nations. New rules approved in 2000 extended the right of consumers to sue companies in other EU nations that used the Internet to market products in multiple jurisdictions.[42]

The Hague Convention on Jurisdiction and Foreign Judgments was broader still. In the early 1990s, the Convention's 52 member nations, including the United States, sought greater cooperation in international law enforcement. Later, the treaty was expanded to include Internet disputes. If passed, the Convention would require member states to enforce commercial laws of other member states even when the actions were considered legal in local jurisdictions.[43]

NOTES

1. This case has been written on the basis of published sources only. Consequently, the interpretation and perspectives presented in this case are not necessarily those of Yahoo Inc. or any of its employees.

2. "Yahoo's Timothy Koogle," *Forbes,* January 29, 2001.

3. This figures includes localized versions of Yahoo in Argentina, Asia, Australia and New Zealand, Brazil, Canada, China, Denmark, France, Germany, Hong Kong, India, Italy, Japan, Korea, Mexico, Norway, Singapore, Spain, Sweden, Taiwan, the United Kingdom and Ireland.

4. "Yahoo's Timothy Koogle," *Forbes,* January 29, 2001.

5. "Inside Yahoo!," *Business Week,* May 21, 2001.

6. "Out of Yahoo!'s hot seat," *Ad Age Global,* March 1, 2001.

7. SOFTBANK, a Japanese software distribution company, held a 30 per cent share.

8. "Yahoo France," *Fortune,* October 16, 2000.

9. "Yahoo France," *Fortune,* October 16, 2000.

10. The author's June 2001 search of Yahoo's GeoCities Web server using keywords such as "Aryan" and "White Pride" revealed multiple pages of links to GeoCities sites promoting hatred and violence toward minorities. (See www.geocities.com).

11. Le Nouveau Code Penal Art. R.645–2.

12. The County Court of Paris, N° RG: 00/05308 N°: 1/kl Interim Court Order, November 20, 2000. Translated by The Center for Democracy and Technology (www.cdt.org).

13. "Welcome to the Web. Passport, Please?," *The New York Times,* March 15, 2001.

14. 1 French Franc = US$0.13 (July 21, 2001).

15. The County Court of Paris, N° RG: 00/05308 N°: 1/kl Interim Court Order, November 20, 2000. Translated by The Center for Democracy and Technology (www.cdt.org).

16. Excluded items included flags, uniforms and badges, but not stamps and coins.

17. "Yahoo Ordered to Bar the French from Nazi Items," *The Wall Street Journal,* November 21, 2000.

18. Ibid.

19. Review from Amazon.com. June 2001.

20. "Yahoo! Decision in France Fuels E-Commerce Sovereignty Debate," *New York Law Journal,* December 12, 2000.

21. "Yahoo! Files Suit Over French Ruling," *Mealey's Cyber Tech Litigation Report,* January 2001.

22. "Cited in First Amendment: Yahoo! v. La Ligue Contre Le Racisme et L'Antisemitisme," *Computer and Online Litigation Reporter,* January 3, 2001.

23. Communications Decency Act, 47 U.S.C. § 230.

24. Yahoo! Inc., v. La Ligue Contre Le Racisme et L'Antisemitisme, Case No. 00–21275 JF, June 7, 2001.

25. "Achieving Legal and Business Order in Cyberspace: A Report on Global Jurisdiction Issues Created by the Internet," *American Bar Association,* Unpublished Draft.

26. Statement of the Anti-Defamation League on Hate on the Internet Before the Senate Committee on the Judiciary. September 14, 1999.

27. Ibid.

28. "Police: Suspect Wanted To Start Racial War," *WCVB TV,* June 21, 2001.

29. "A German and U.S. Clash Over Efforts to Crack Down on Neo-Nazi Web Sites in the U.S.," *International Enforcement Law Reporter,* February 2001.

30. "Web of Hate," *Salon,* October 16, 1998.

31. "Net Group Stalks LA Gunman," *Wired News,* April 11, 1999.

32. "Hate crimes reported to the FBI: 8,759 in 1996, 7,947 in 1995 and 5,932 in 1994. Web of Hate," *Salon,* October 16, 1998.

33. "German High Court decides novel issue . . . ," *International Law Update,* January 2001.

34. GigaLaw.com Discussion List, January 5, 2001 (www.gigalaw.com).

35. It's a Brave New World of On-Line Liabilities, *New York Law Journal,* May 1, 2001.

36. Statement of the Anti-Defamation League on Hate on the Internet Before the Senate Committee on the Judiciary. September 14, 1999.

37. Federal Wire Wager Act, 18 U.S.C. § 1084.

38. "Yahoo! Decision in France Fuels E-Commerce Sovereignty Debate," *New York Law Journal,* December 12, 2000.

39. 937 F. Supp. 161 (D. Conn. 1996) cited in "Achieving Legal and Business Order in Cyberspace: A Report on Global Jurisdiction Issues Created by the Internet," *American Bar Association,* Unpublished Draft.

40. "Thinking Twice About Your Web Site," *Corporate Risk Spectrum,* January 2001.

41. Statement of the Anti-Defamation League on Hate on the Internet Before the Senate Committee on the Judiciary. September 14, 1999.

42. "Thinking Twice About Your Web Site," *Corporate Risk Spectrum,* January 2001.

43. "Global Treaty-Threat to the Net?," *ZDNet News,* June 22, 2001.

TALISMAN ENERGY INC.

*Prepared by Gail Robertson under
the supervision of Professor Larry Tapp*

Copyright © 2002, Ivey Management Services   Version: (A) 2004-12-13

At the August 2001 Talisman Energy Inc. (Talisman) meeting, the board of directors was updated on the company's activities in Sudan. Chief executive officer (CEO), Jim Buckee, and the board of directors (the board) participated in an ongoing review of the Sudan asset and its role in Talisman's portfolio. Throughout the three-year period during which Talisman had operated in Sudan, it had been criticized repeatedly by human rights, religious and social responsibility groups. On June 13, 2001, the United States House of Representatives had voted on a bill that would prevent Talisman and other foreign companies engaged in the development of oil and gas in Sudan from selling securities in the U.S. market. This action was the culmination of a broader-based effort resulting from pressure applied by various lobby groups in the United States.

The Sudan project continued to have good economic value and good production possibilities. As well, the contribution income from Talisman's interest in the Sudan project had been disproportionately high when compared to other Talisman properties; however, some downdrafts in the share price could be linked to events associated with Talisman's involvement in Sudan.

A portion of the drop in the stock price in June and July of 2001 could be directly linked to the heating up of the Sudan issue and to the latest threat from the U.S. government directed at Talisman and other companies operating in Sudan. The question remained, however, whether the share price would continue to be adversely affected as issues pertaining to Talisman's Sudan interests unfolded. It was disturbing to Talisman's management that the entire company could be under attack due to decisions involving only 10 per cent of the business.

Talisman had gone to considerable lengths to develop and implement socially responsible policies regarding Sudan and believed the company had made a positive contribution toward improving the quality of life for the people of Sudan. In Sudan, the majority of the population was illiterate and access to the basics, such as clean water, was severely limited. Talisman executives believed that the economic development of Sudan was better left in the hands of ethical companies such as Talisman. It was the belief of Talisman executives that few companies would have contributed more to the economic development of Sudan than Talisman. While Talisman was not the sole operator of the Sudan operation, but rather a 25 per cent shareholder in the Greater Nile Petroleum Operating Company (GNPOC) operations, the influence of Talisman had prevailed with other shareholders in effecting socially responsible business practices in Sudan related to the GNPOC oil project.

Talisman's CEO was quoted in a Canadian national newspaper on June 19, 2001 as saying that Talisman was reconsidering its decision not to sell its interest in Sudan. This article was somewhat misleading as Talisman had always maintained that, in keeping with its role as a public company, at the right price, any asset, including its interest in the Sudan project, was for sale. The Sudan project had been highly successful to date, with substantial growth potential, and it had continually outperformed all plans. A key driver for the project was production growth, which was outstanding in this project. As a result, Talisman had continued to hold the asset to date.

The Sudan project had also outperformed expectations regarding political risk. The Talisman board of directors and management team had expected "typical" friction with local government in Sudan, but had not anticipated the degree of domestic and North American political risk that had materialized since the acquisition. Nor had they anticipated the extent of public outcry seen to date. The political system in the United States had provided Talisman with its greatest challenges to date. Some observers of the Talisman situation in Sudan were heard to speculate that Talisman, a Canadian company, was an easy target. It was suggested that by attacking Talisman, American politicians could take a stand on human rights issues in developing countries without hurting American corporations and important votes.

At the August 2001 board meeting, senior management and the board, in light of the external pressures brought to bear on the Sudan project, continued to be diligent as they sought to behave in a socially responsible manner. The board and management also continued to question whether the decision to operate holdings in Sudan was compatible with Talisman's mandate to operate in the best interests of the company and its shareholders.

THE ENERGY INDUSTRY

Total energy costs in the world were approximately US$2 trillion annually in 2001, with the world consuming 28 billion barrels (bbls) of oil per year. Approximately two-thirds of the world's oil and gas reserves were located in the Middle East. Oil consumption accounted for 40 per cent of energy costs. New exploration discoveries replaced significantly less than half of this amount, though oil and gas were projected to provide two-thirds of the growth in energy demand over the next decade. Throughout the 1990s, oil prices averaged US$20 per barrel (/bbl), with global demand increasing by almost 10 million barrels per day. The majority of the increased supply came from the Organization of Petroleum

Exporting Countries (OPEC). With world oil demand growing and production from major fields declining, it was felt that the long-term trend for oil prices was upward with dependence on the OPEC, especially in the Persian gulf, increasing.[1]

OPEC, a major force in the oil industry, was an international organization of 11 developing countries, all of which relied heavily on oil revenues as their main source of income. Membership was open to any country that was a substantial net exporter of oil and that supported the ideals of the organization. In 2001, OPEC members included: Algeria, Indonesia, Iran, Iraq, Kuwait, Libya, Nigeria, Qatar, Saudi Arabia, the United Arab Emirates and Venezuela. Members met regularly to determine the organization's oil output level and to look at future considerations. OPEC collectively supplied about 40 per cent of the world's oil and was in possession of more than three-quarters of the world's total proven crude oil reserves.[2]

Talisman's corporate strategy was based on the following beliefs about the oil and gas industry:

- The demand for oil and gas would continue to increase with population and economic growth.
- World-scale hydrocarbon discoveries were becoming increasingly rare; exploration risks could be mitigated by focusing on proved hydrocarbon basins.
- Corporate and asset acquisitions were viable ways to add value as long as they provided incremental exploration and development opportunities.
- Significant new oil developments would require a high level of technical, commercial and project management skills.[3]

Oil in Sudan was considered to be high quality oil. Canadian oil, in contrast, was heavier and had high sulfur content. Talisman's project in Sudan had been very successful by industry standards, as there had been less than two years' lead-time from the Arakis Energy acquisition in 1998 to production. The Sudan project had exceeded Talisman's expectations to date. Given that ownership of the pipeline would potentially gain incremental tariff revenues from third-party discoveries, the Sudan operation was desirable for Talisman, with the huge oil exploration potential in Sudan. Thus, the Sudan project was considered to be a good fit with Talisman's corporate strategy.

HISTORY OF TALISMAN ENERGY

Talisman, headquartered in Calgary, Alberta, was established in 1953 as BP Canada. The parent company, British Petroleum PLC, sold off its Canadian interests in 1991. The new entity was renamed Talisman in 1992 and became an independent Canadian oil and gas producer, rather than a subsidiary of a major international corporation. Talisman continued, however, to have a major BP slant with its international management skills base. Talisman was listed as an independent on the Toronto Stock Exchange (TSE) in Canada, having previously been listed as BP, and was later listed on the New York Stock Exchange (NYSE) in the United States. Talisman was included in the Standard and Poor (S&P)/TSE 60.

Talisman had been successful and was now the largest Canadian oil and gas producer, with production growth averaging 17 per cent annually from 1995 to 2000 and cash flow per share growth averaging 27 per cent annually in the same period. Talisman's main business activities included exploration, development, production and marketing of crude oil, natural gas and natural gas liquid. The company's main operating areas were Canada, the North Sea, Indonesia and Sudan. In 2001, Talisman directly employed more than 1,100 people and contracted services from approximately the same number of people.

Approximately half of Talisman's growth had been generic growth in production, with the other half based on acquisitions. Talisman's acquisition interests were:

- Encor (1993)
- Bow Valley Energy (1994)
- Goal Petroleum PLC (1996)
- Pembina Resources (1997)
- Arakis Energy (1998)
- Highridge Exploration Ltd. (1999)
- Rigel Energy Corporation (1999)
- Petromet Resources Limited (2001)
- Lundin Oil (2001)

The 1993 Encor purchase gave Talisman its first international interests, in Algeria and Indonesia. Talisman entered Sudan in 1998 through the acquisition of Arakis Energy Corporation, a move that resulted in Talisman obtaining a 25 per cent interest in the Greater Nile Petroleum Operating Company (GNPOC). In the summer of 2001, Talisman had its key international interests in Algeria, Colombia, Indonesia, Malaysia, Papua New Guinea, Trinidad, the United Kingdom, the United States and Vietnam.

Talisman had pursued international markets for growth as there was no significant growth potential in North America. The dilemma for smaller independents, such as Talisman, was that any new projects or acquisitions had to fit within the technical expertise of the organization as well as the financial capabilities. Such opportunities were limited.

TALISMAN BOARD OF DIRECTORS AND MANAGEMENT

The role of Talisman's board of directors in relation to the role of management was stated as follows:

> The principal role of the board of Directors is stewardship of the company with the creation of shareholder value including the protection and enhancement of the value of its assets, as the fundamental objective. The stewardship responsibility means that the board oversees the conduct of the business and supervises management, which is responsible for the day-to-day conduct of the business. The board must assess and ensure systems are in place to manage the risks of the company's business with the objective of preserving the company's assets. In its supervisory role, the board, through the Chief Executive Officer (CEO), sets the attitude and disposition of the company towards compliance with applicable laws, environmental, safety and health policies, financial practices and reporting. In addition to its primary accountability to shareholders, the board and the CEO are also accountable to government authorities, employees and the public.[4]

The board of directors of Talisman was elected annually by shareholders and consisted of a minimum of four directors and a maximum of 20 directors, as determined by the directors, the majority of whom were to be Canadian residents. At this time, the number of directors to be elected at shareholder meetings was fixed at nine, with four directors comprising a quorum at any meeting.

At Talisman, the role of chairman of the board had been separated from the role of president and CEO. It was intended that the chairman should be independent from management and free from any interest and any business or other relationship that could interfere with the chairman's independent judgment other than interests resulting from company shareholdings and remuneration.

The CEO was responsible for leading Talisman. The CEO's primary function was the development of a long-term strategy for the company. The CEO's leadership role also entailed ultimate responsibility for all day-to-day management decisions and for implementing the company's long- and short-term plans. The CEO, through the chairman, acted as a direct link between the board and management of the company and acted as spokesman for management to the board. The CEO was also the ultimate spokesman on behalf of the company to government authorities, the public, shareholders, employees and other stakeholders and third parties.[5]

Chairman of the board in August 2001 was David Powell. Peter Widdrington had been chairman of the board during the time of the Arakis acquisition and for much of the Sudan controversy. Members of the board of directors were:

- Douglas Baldwin
- James Buckee (CEO of Talisman)
- Al Flood
- Paul Hoenmans
- Dale Parker
- Roland Priddle
- Larry Tapp
- Stella Thompson

All but Larry Tapp and Douglas Baldwin had been directors under Peter Widdrington's leadership (see Exhibit 1).

BOARD OF DIRECTORS

David Powell—Calgary, Alberta, Chairman, Talisman Energy, Inc. since 1998

Chairman of the Board of the Company; Director of various corporations; Chairman of the Board of Petroleum Industry Training Service; from 1991 to 1995, President and Chief Executive Officer of Home Oil Company Ltd.

Douglas D. Baldwin—Calgary, Alberta, Corporate Director since 2001

Director of various corporations; from 1999 to 2001, President and Chief Executive Officer of TransCanada PipeLines Ltd.; from 1992 to 1998, Senior Vice-President and Director of Imperial Oil Ltd.; from 1988 to 1992, President and Chief Executive Officer, Esso Resources Canada Ltd.

James W. Buckee—CEO, Talisman Energy Inc.

BSc Honors in physics from the University of Western Australia with first class honors; and a PhD in Astrophysics from Oxford University. Dr. Buckee held various petroleum engineering positions with Shell International and Burma Oil Company in the U.K. North Sea, Norway, Australia and New Zealand from 1971 to 1977. From 1977 to 1983, Dr. Buckee held various petroleum engineering posts with British Petroleum in Canada and the Middle East. In 1983, he became the Chief Reservoir Engineer with BP Exploration in London, England. In 1987, Dr. Buckee became Operations Manager for British Petroleum in Norway, and was subsequently appointed Vice President Development Programs for BP Alaska where he stayed until May 1989 when he moved back to London as Manager, Planning for BP Exploration. In September 1991, Dr. Buckee was appointed President and Chief Operating Officer for Talisman Energy Inc. and he was appointed President and Chief Executive Officer for Talisman Energy Inc. in May 1993.

Al Flood, C.M.—Thornhill, Ontario, Corporate Director since 2000

Director of various corporations; from 1999 to 2000, Chairman of the Executive Committee of Canadian Imperial Bank of Commerce (CIBC); prior to June 1999, Chairman and Chief Executive Officer of CIBC and held various positions in the domestic and international operations of CIBC.

Paul Hoenmans—Director since 1998; Aspen, Colorado, Corporate

Director of various corporations; prior to September 1997, Executive Vice-President of Mobil Oil Corporation and Director and Member of the Executive Committee of Mobil Corporation and Mobil Oil Corporation; from 1986 to 1996, President, Exploration & Producing Division, Mobil Oil Corporation.

Dale Parker—Director since 1993; Vancouver, British Columbia

Public Administration and Financial Institution Advisor; Director of various corporations and public administration and financial institution advisor; prior to January 1998, President and Chief Executive Officer of Workers' Compensation Board of British Columbia; prior to November 1994, President of White Spot Ltd. and Executive Vice-President of Shato holdings Ltd.; prior to November 1993, Executive Vice-President and Chief Financial Officer of Shato Holdings Ltd.; prior to November 1992, Chairman and Chief Executive Officer of British Columbia Financial Institutions Commission.

Roland Priddle—Director since 2000. Saanich, British Columbia, Consultant

Consultant to public and private sector entities on policy and regulatory issues in oil and gas; advisor to the Energy Institute at the University of Houston; director of various corporations; prior to 1998, Chairman, National Energy Board of Canada.

Larry Tapp—Director since 2001; London, Ontario

Dean of The Richard Ivey School of Business, The University of Western Ontario since 1995; from 1992 to 1995, Executive in Residence of the Faculty of Management and Adjunct Professor, University of Toronto; from 1985 to 1992, Vice Chairman, President and Chief Executive Officer of Lawson Mardon Group Ltd.

Exhibit 1   Board of Directors   *(Continued)*

Stella Thompson—Director since 1995, Calgary, Alberta

Principal, Governance West Inc.; President of Stellar Energy Ltd.; Director of various corporations; prior to June 1991,Vice-President, Planning, Business Information & Systems of Petro-Canada Products.

SENIOR MANAGEMENT

James W. Buckee

President and Chief Executive Officer; See Talisman Board of Directors.

Edward W. Bogle

Vice-President, Exploration. PhD in Geology from Queen's University in 1980. Dr. Bogle joined Talisman Energy Inc. (formerly BP Canada Inc.) in May, 1980. He has held positions of progressively increasing responsibility in the Company from 1980 to 1992. In June 1992, Dr. Bogle was appointed Vice President, Exploration for Talisman Energy Inc.

T.N. (Nigel) D. Hares

Vice-President, Frontier and International Operations. BSc Honors in Chemistry from the Polytechnic of North London. Mr. Hares worked for British Petroleum from 1972 to 1994. From 1972 he held various petroleum/drilling engineering positions in the United Kingdom, Abu Dhabi and Europe. From 1980 to 1982, Mr. Hares was Head of Petroleum Engineering for British Petroleum in Norway and from 1982 to 1985 was Operations Manager, Forties Field in the North Sea. In 1985, Mr. Hares became Manager, Reservoir Studies, Europe, Africa, and the Middle East and in 1986 became Manager, Petroleum Engineering Division U.K. In 1988, Mr. Hares attended the Harvard Business School management program and was subsequently appointed Manager, Reservoir Engineering Division U.K. From 1989 to 1992, Mr. Hares was Business Advisor to the Chief Executive of BP Gas where he developed gas strategies for Europe, the Far East and Colombia. In 1992, Mr. Hares was seconded from BP to the Alyeska Pipeline Service Company in Alaska as Director of Planning. In August 1994, Mr. Hares became Vice President, International Operations with Talisman Energy Inc.

Joseph E. Horler

Vice-President, Marketing. Bachelor of Commerce from the University of Calgary; has completed a number of management and executive development programs. Prior to joining Talisman in 1987, Mr. Horler was Manager of Crude Oil Affairs with the Independent Petroleum Association of Canada, Manager of Crude and Product Supply with Husky Oil Operations, managed other assignments within the Supply and Transportation Department of Sun Oil. He was also involved in the formation and establishment of PSR Gas Ventures Inc., a Canadian natural gas marketing company as Vice President, General Manager and Director. Mr. Horler has represented his company and the industry in a variety of regulatory, policy and business ventures before the National Energy Board of Canada, the British Columbia Utilities Commission and the Alberta Energy Resources Conservation Board (now the AEUB). Mr. Horler represents Talisman Energy's shareholding as a member of the Board of Directors of Sultran, Ltd. and Pacific Coast Terminals Co. Ltd.

Michael D. McDonald

Vice-President, Finance and Chief Financial Officer; BA (Honors) in Economics and MA in Economics from the University of Calgary. Mr. McDonald worked on a broad spectrum of fossil fuel-based development projects for the Energy Resources Conservation Board beginning in 1979. He joined BP Canada in 1982 and has held positions of increasing responsibility in economics and corporate planning. In 1985, he was seconded with British Petroleum to the U.K. where he coordinated operating plans, budgets and planning documents, recommending oil and gas strategy, and economic evaluation of engineering projects. On his return to Canada, he worked in operations facility development prior to becoming Manager, Economics and in 1989 was appointed Manager, Corporate Planning where he played a major role in the acquisitions of Encor and Bow Valley. In 1994, Mr. McDonald

---

Exhibit 1   Board of Directors   *(Continued)*

was seconded to Talisman Energy (U.K.) Ltd. in London, England and subsequently Aberdeen, Scotland. In 1995, he was appointed General Manager (U.K.) and was responsible for administration and management of Talisman's activities in the North Sea. In 1998, Mr. McDonald was promoted to Vice President, Business Development and in 2001 he was promoted to Vice President, Finance and Chief Financial Officer.

Robert W. Mitchell

Vice-President, Canadian Operations; BSc Honors in 1969 and PhD from University of Hull. Dr. Mitchell's early career was in teaching and research at Queen's University, Ontario. He entered the oil industry in 1971 and held a variety of petroleum engineering positions in Holland, Africa, the Middle East and the U.S. Dr. Mitchell joined BP International in Aberdeen in 1976 and held various engineering and management positions in the United Kingdom. In 1984, he transferred to BP Canada Inc. as Vice President Oil Sands and in 1990 became Vice President, Operations.

Robert M. Redgate

Vice-President, Human Resources and Corporate Services; BSc (First Class Honors) from the University of Alberta; Masters in Environmental Design Planning and Management from University of Calgary. Mr. Redgate joined BP Canada Inc. in 1977 and held positions of increasing responsibility in Environmental Affairs, Health and Safety from 1977 to 1982. In 1982, he became the Manager, Personnel and Environmental Affairs and in 1985 he was appointed Manager, Staff Planning and Development and in 1987, Manager, Personnel. Mr. Redgate was seconded to Purina Mills Inc., a subsidiary of British Petroleum Company, PLC, at St. Louis, MO, U.S. as Vice President, Corporate Human Resources. In 1992, Mr. Redgate was appointed Vice President, Human Resources and Administration for Talisman Energy Inc. In 1996, he became Vice President Human Resources and Corporate Services.

M. Jacqueline Sheppard

Vice-President, Legal and Corporate Projects, and Corporate Secretary; Honors BA in Political Science from Memorial University, Newfoundland; Honors Jurisprudence BA and MA from Oxford University where she attended as a Rhodes Scholar; LLB (First Class Honors) from McGill University as a faculty scholar. Ms. Sheppard was partner at national law firm Blakes, Cassels & Graydon, based in Calgary, practicing in oil and gas, corporate/commercial and finance areas from 1981 through 1993, concentrating on corporate acquisitions, reorganizations, divestitures and public and private financings of energy companies. Ms. Sheppard joined Talisman in 1993 in her current role.

Exhibit 1   Board of Directors

The senior executive management team at Talisman, under CEO James Buckee included:

- Edward Bogle: vice-president, exploration
- T. Nigel D. Hares: vice-president, frontier and international operations
- Joseph E. Horler: vice-president, marketing
- Michael D. McDonald: vice-president, finance and financial officer
- Robert W. Mitchell: vice-president, Canadian operations
- Robert M. Redgate: vice-president, human resources and corporate services
- M. Jacqueline Sheppard: vice-president, legal and corporate projects and corporate secretary

This senior management team was considered to be very strong. Many had significant tenure with the Talisman Corporation and its precursor and among them they had many years of experience in the oil and gas industry (see Exhibit 1).

TALISMAN IN SUDAN

Talisman Energy (Talisman) owned a 25 per cent interest in the Greater Nile Petroleum Operating Company (GNPOC), covering four blocks in the Muglad Basin. Ownership in the GNPOC was distributed as follows:

Company	Per Cent Share
Talisman	25
Chinese National Petroleum Company	40
Petronas (Malaysian corporation)	30
Sudapet (Sudanese corporation)	5

Talisman also owned a 25 per cent interest in a 1,500 kilometre pipeline from the oil fields to Port Sudan on the Red Sea. Talisman's operations in Sudan accounted for approximately 10 per cent of Talisman's total business operations. Management and the board of directors of Talisman believed that the GNPOC was a good project for Talisman with excellent future exploration potential.

Operationally, the Sudan project continued to perform better than expected for Talisman. Total production reached a record 200,000 barrels/day (bbls/d) during 2000 against original design capacity (also known as nameplate capacity) of 150,000 bbls/day.

Highlights for the year 2000 in Sudan for the Talisman share of the project were:

- Average production of 45,900 bbls/d in 2000 and 49,000 bbls/d in the fourth quarter;
- Spending of $70 million on exploration and development;
- Reserve additions of 26 million barrels, 152 per cent of production;
- Drilling 16 successful oil wells;
- Successful exploration well at Khairat, testing at 1,983 bbls/day;
- Drilling success at Munga and Bamboo, leading to development of these fields.

Talisman's objectives for 2001 in Sudan were:

- Production of 50,000 to 55,000 bbls/day;
- Startup of two new fields, Bamboo and Khairat;
- Development of the Munga area for 2002 startup;
- Capital spending of $120 million, including additional pumping capacity on the pipeline to increase nameplate capacity to 230,000 bbls/day and debottlenecking the central plant facilities at Heglig;

- Participation in 17 explorations and 25 development wells;
- Drilling and testing a number of wells on Block 4 on the unexplored western side of the basin.

Given that approximately five per cent of the GNPOC landholdings in Sudan were developed, Talisman believed there was great upside potential in the area.

Talisman had operated in Sudan for three years and during that time had made a concerted effort to be a good corporate citizen and to enhance the quality of life of the Sudanese people.

SOCIAL CONDITIONS IN SUDAN

The situation in Sudan was complex, and the people of Sudan faced many problems. There were approximately 500 tribes and 300 languages in Sudan and a history of internal conflict for generations. There had been almost continuous fighting between tribes as well as between the north and south since the British had left in the mid-1950s. The almost continuous fighting and famine in Sudan had created a human tragedy in this part of the world.

Despite the problems in Sudan, the United Nations recognized the government of Sudan as a legitimate government. Talisman was one of many companies from United Nations countries operating in Sudan.

The Canadian Department of Foreign Affairs and International Trade described Sudan as follows:

A civil war has raged in Sudan for most of the 43 years since independence in 1956. Although the origins of the conflict are found in the underdevelopment of the south during the colonial period, it is not longer simply north/south in scope. The Sudan Peoples' Liberation Movement (SPLM)—a southern-based movement—has been fighting consecutive, governing regimes. It has been joined by armed northern parties opposed to the current governing regime, led by the National Islamic Front (NIF), which seized power in a 1989 coup. Together they have formed a coalition called the National Democratic Alliance (NDA) that includes all the political parties that existed in the country prior to the 1989 coup, with the exception of the NIF, which retains power. Thus, the war has grown from a southern conflict to a complex crisis that is national in scale. The principal factors now driving the conflict are disparities in the allocations of power, land and resources, the imposition of sectarian laws and the violation of the human rights of Sudan's marginalized people. Interstitial fighting was also widespread and a traditional activity. As is common in contemporary conflicts, civilians—particularly women and children—are the principal casualties. The human toll arising from war-related causes in Sudan, including famine, is horrific. Nearly two million people, according to the United Nations, have died since 1983; in excess of four million people are internally displaced, dispossessed of their homes and separated from their families.[6]

See Exhibit 2 for "Sudan as described by the World Bank" and "Sudan as described by the United States Energy Information Administration (EIA)."

The oil fields in Sudan were located on the 10th parallel; the dividing line between the north and south districts of the Anglo-Egyptian Condominium. Critics have stated that the oil revenue was fuelling the war there and that Talisman's presence lent legitimacy to the government. Rebels have stated that the oilfields were a legitimate target of war.

PUBLIC PRESSURE TO CEASE OPERATIONS IN SUDAN

Throughout the past three years in Sudan, Talisman had come under fire from many social, human rights, religious and government-based entities.

North American and European human rights organizations had accused Talisman of supporting the Sudanese government by providing oil revenues that would then be used to support the government's civil war efforts. Following intense media scrutiny in the fall of 1999, the Canadian Department of Foreign Affairs and International Trade sent an envoy, John Harker, to Sudan on a fact-finding mission. According to Harker's final report on this mission, issued

in February of 2000, the oil project was making the conflict worse.

In initial discussions with the Canadian government, Talisman had been told that its involvement in Sudan was acceptable, but the attitude of government appeared to have recently changed to one of uncertainty.

The United Nations Commission on Human Rights had also censured Sudan for its poor record in human rights protection, particularly with respect to the aerial bombing of civilian targets and the denial of food aid to needy populations. Further, it had been alleged that areas around the oilfields had become increasingly depopulated due to a "scorched earth" policy practiced by the Sudanese government. Several other organizations, including Africa Watch, Human Rights Watch, Doctors Without Borders, the Co-operative for American Relief Everwhere Inc. (CARE) and the Inter-Church Coalition on Africa had repeated these assertions. Talisman executives had, in their possession, satellite photos taken at various times over decades that showed continuous development of communities surrounding the areas in which the GNPOC had its operations, not depopulation as was suggested by these organizations. Given the gravity of these issues, the past two Talisman annual general meetings and church-sponsored "town halls" (or town hall–styled meetings), had become focal points for individuals protesting Talisman's involvement in Sudan.

The Bush/Cheney administration in the United States appeared to be more supportive of oil holdings in the Middle East than the Clinton/Gore administration had been, but neither administration had approved of activities in Sudan. Bush had said he was opposed to capital market sanctions, as was Alan Greenspan, chairman of the U.S. Federal Reserve. Greenspan said that such measures could be "downright harmful" to the United States by pushing trade to other markets.[7]

TALISMAN AND CORPORATE RESPONSIBILITY

Talisman was committed to being a good corporate citizen worldwide and had participated

SUDAN AS DESCRIBED BY THE WORLD BANK

Sudan gained its independence from Britain in 1956. The first episode in what has become an intractable civil war in southern Sudan occurred through a mutiny of southern forces in 1955. Civil strife escalated as southern demands for political expression and economic development were ignored by the ruling elite in the north. Sudan consequently endured a civil war that has spanned more than three decades. Since 1997, the Sudan People's Liberation Army (SPLA) has controlled much of the south. More recently, the southern-based rebels and the government have conducted direct negotiations under the auspices of the Inter-Governmental authority on Development (IGAD).

Economic progress has been constrained by the civil war, military expenditures, social dislocation, deterioration of basic infrastructure and lack of access to aid and foreign investments. Sudan is also vulnerable to external shocks, including floods and drought. As a result, poverty levels have risen despite growth.

Since 1996, GDP growth has averaged 5.5 per cent led mainly by agriculture which accounts for an estimated 45 per cent of GDP. Inflation has slowed from 133 per cent to 16 per cent. The general economic improvement has been helped by reforms supported by the IMF. These reforms emphasise containing fiscal deficits, and limiting monetary growth and inflation.

The key structural reforms aim at enhancing efficiency by liberalising the trade and exchange rate regime, phasing out price controls and privatising public enterprises.

More recently, Sudan has benefited from investment in oil production which is expected to reduce the country's import bill and improve the availability of foreign exchange for development financing.

COUNTRIES; SUDAN, SEPTEMBER 2000

Source: www.worldbank.org, September 2000.

SUDAN AS DESCRIBED BY THE UNITED STATES ENERGY INFORMATION ADMINISTRATION (EIA)

Sudan gained its independence from Egypt and the United Kingdom in 1956. The current government, led by General Omar Hassan Ahmad al-Bashir, came to power in 1989 after overthrowing a transitional coalition government. A new constitution was promulgated on January 1, 1999. Multi-party presidential and parliamentary elections are scheduled for December 2000.

Sudan is among the world's poorest countries. Its economy is primarily agricultural—a mix of subsistence farming and production of cash crops such as cotton and gum arabic. In the past four years, however, Sudan's economic performance has been strong; annual GDP growth has averaged 5.5 per cent, while inflation has slowed from 133 per cent to 16 per cent. Exports have grown by one-quarter to $780 million, while Sudan's current account deficit has dropped from nearly 8 per cent of GDP to 2.4 per cent. Sudan's real GDP growth rate is forecast at 6.5 per cent in 2000, while inflation is predicted to reach the 9 per cent year-end target set by the government. In May 2000, the International Monetary Fund (IMF) expressed its satisfaction with Sudan's implementation of a 1999-2001 structural adjustment program. However, representatives of the IMF advised the Sudanese government to move to full market liberalisation in the petroleum product sector as quickly as possible and to adopt full public disclosure of oil revenue data. In August 2000, the IMF lifted the suspension—in place since 1993—of Sudan's voting rights in the IMF.

Sudan recently has become more engaged in the global economy. In February 2000, Sudan opened its Red Sea Free Trade Zone, designed to encourage foreign direct investment, and in March 2000, Sudan publicly repeated its desire to join the World Trade Organisation. Since the end of 1999, Sudan has signed various trade and investment agreements with Saudi Arabia, Bahrain, Iraq, Kuwait, Ethiopia, and Syria, while simultaneously predicting that Malaysian investment in Sudan, particularly in the oil, gas and petrochemical industries, would exceed $1 billion by the end of 2000.

Despite its economic progress, Sudan still faces developmental obstacles, including a limited infrastructure and an external debt at the end of 1999 of nearly $24 billion, representing a debt-to-GDP ratio of 218.3 per cent. Furthermore, the government remains embroiled in the long-running conflict with rebel movements in the south of the country, inhabited primarily by non-Muslims. The conflict has maintained the scarcity of national development resources, despite the increase in government oil revenues. Over the past two decades, the civil war has claimed 1.5 million Sudanese lives.

SUDAN COUNTRY ANALYSIS BRIEF NOVEMBER 2000

Source: www.eia.doe.gov, November 2000.

Exhibit 2   Sudan as Described by the World Bank

in a number of initiatives to that end. Talisman had a history of being respectful of ethical issues in all of its operations. In light of the Sudan controversy, Talisman had added the International Code of Ethics for Canadian Business to its existing corporate Code of Ethics in December 1999, acting on a suggestion from Canadian Foreign Minister Lloyd Axworthy (see Exhibit 3).

Talisman believed that corporate responsibility should be a mainstream issue for the company and that corporate responsibility was intrinsic to all business. Talisman's CEO had repeatedly asserted that "ethically aware

---

VISION

Canadian business has a global presence that is recognized by all stakeholders[1] as economically rewarding to all parties, acknowledged as being ethically, socially and environmentally responsible, welcomed by the communities in which we operate, and that facilitates economic, human resource and community development within a stable operating environment.

BELIEFS

We believe that:

- we can make a difference within our sphere of influence (our stakeholders);
- business should take a leadership role through establishment of ethical business principles;
- national governments have the prerogative to conduct their own government and legal affairs in accordance with their sovereign rights;
- all governments should comply with international treaties and other agreements that they have committed to, including the areas of human rights and social justice;
- while reflecting cultural diversity and differences, we should do business throughout the world consistent with the way we do business in Canada;
- the business sector should show ethical leadership;
- we can facilitate the achievement of wealth generation and a fair sharing of economic benefits;
- our principles will assist in improving relations between the Canadian and host governments;
- open, honest and transparent relationships are critical to our success;
- local communities need to be involved in decision-making for issues that affect them;
- multistakeholder processes need to be initiated to seek effective solutions;
- confrontation should be tempered by diplomacy;
- wealth maximization for all stakeholders will be enhanced by resolution of outstanding human rights and social justice issues; and
- doing business with other countries is good for Canada and vice versa.

VALUES

We value:

- human rights and social justice;
- wealth maximization for all stakeholders;
- operation of a free market economy;
- a business environment which militates against bribery and corruption;
- public accountability by governments;
- equality of opportunity;
- a defined code of ethics and business practice;
- protection of environmental quality and sound environmental stewardship;
- community benefits;
- good relationships with all stakeholders; and
- stability and continuous improvement within our operating environment.

Exhibit 3   Talisman Energy International Code of Ethics for Canadian Business   *(Continued)*

PRINCIPLES

Concerning Community Participation and Environmental Protection—We will:

- strive within our sphere of influence to ensure a fair share of benefits to stakeholders impacted by our activities;
- ensure meaningful and transparent consultation with all stakeholders and attempt to integrate our corporate activities with local communities as good corporate citizens;
- ensure our activities are consistent with sound environmental management and conservation practices; and
- provide meaningful opportunities for technology, training and capacity building with the host nation.

Concerning Human Rights—We will:

- support and promote the protection of international human rights within our sphere of influence; and
- not be complicit in human rights abuses.

Concerning Business Conduct—We will:

- not make illegal and improper payments and bribes and will refrain from participating in any corrupt business practices;
- comply with all applicable laws and conduct business activities in a transparent fashion; and
- ensure contractors', suppliers' and agents' activities are consistent with these principles.

Concerning Employee Rights and Health and Safety—We will:

- ensure the health and safety of workers is protected;
- strive for social justice and promote freedom of association and expression in the workplace; and
- ensure consistency with universally accepted labor standards, including those related to exploitation of child labor, forced labor and non-discrimination in employment.

Exhibit 3   Talisman Energy International Code of Ethics for Canadian Business

Source: Company files.

Note: The "Code" is a statement of values and principles designed to facilitate and assist individual firms in the development of their policies and practices that are consistent with the vision, beliefs, values and principles contained herein.

1. Stakeholders include: local communities, Canadian and host governments, local governments, shareholders, the media, customers and suppliers, interest groups and international agencies.

---

corporate engagement is the best way to improve the lives of people in the developing world, as opposed to isolation and sanctions." He based this assertion on the following:

- The generation of wealth in any country is a necessary precursor for progress and over time, has the potential to benefit the entire community.
- Corporations can do well in pursuit of their normal activities, such as: local job creation, expansion of infrastructure, building community capacity and creating opportunities for a better future for local people. In addition, it provides the opportunity to promote ethical business practices and advocates respect and tolerance.
- Corporate presence heightens international awareness and knowledge. Certainly, Talisman's presence in Sudan has greatly increased public awareness and debate about issues in Sudan.

- Public company presence leads to analyst coverage, quarterly reports, and press interest—all of which leads to international scrutiny. This produces the "external observer effect," which, like a police car on the highway, induces ethical behavior in the vicinity.
- Investment and trade lead to discussion and trust, exchange of ideas and resolution of differences.[8]

Dr. Buckee was fond of a quote by Kofi Annan, Secretary General of the United Nations and Nobel Peace Prize winner, that stated, "The only developing countries that really are developing are those that have succeeded in attracting significant amounts of direct foreign investment."

Talisman repeatedly made a strong business case for corporate social responsibility. In keeping with its commitment to corporate responsibility, in the year 2000, Talisman had set up a separate Corporate Social Responsibility Unit under the direction of Reg Manhas, previously a member of Talisman's legal staff department.

Talisman's mandate in the area of corporate social responsibility included the following:

- Conducting activities in an economically, socially and environmentally responsible manner.
- Working together with stakeholder groups to identify constructive solutions to problems while bringing direct benefits to the communities in which they operated, including creation of jobs, expansion of infrastructure and support of community projects.
- Maintaining and promoting ethical business practices.
- Advocating respect and tolerance by and for all people.
- Advocating human rights to the Government of Sudan.[9]

Talisman held that the business case related to a number of factors:

- The corporation's ability to attract and retain top quality employees. In the case of Talisman, there was certainty that Canadian and British employees in the field in Sudan would not be party to unethical behavior on the part of Talisman or the GNPOC.
- Most shareholders would also be attracted to corporations that acted in a socially responsible manner.
- Implementation of Corporate Social Responsibility (CSR) initiatives within an operating area would enable a corporation to manage risks to its assets and personnel in operating areas; an unpopular operation in the community could threaten security and financial performance.
- The benefit of a favorable reputation. Making the corporation an attractive business partner for other companies and host nations would increase business opportunities.

In Sudan, despite its commitment to corporate social responsibility, it was difficult for Talisman to operate in a corporately responsible manner to the extent it would want to, as it held only a 25 per cent share of the GNPOC project.

TALISMAN AND CORPORATE RESPONSIBILITY IN SUDAN

One reality of the oil business was the vast majority of known remaining conventional oil reserves were located in developing countries, more than three quarters of them in Muslim countries. As well, most oil investment was capital-intensive, had a 25-year life and couldn't be moved. Economic and operational realities dictated that oil production from a project could not simply be "stopped" as had been suggested of the Sudan project. In addition, oil business was often one of the largest foreign earners for host governments and thus had influence and importance. This influence and importance made the oil companies' relationships with communities and host governments extremely important, in that both must see the presence of the oil company as directly beneficial.

Difficulties, such as those experienced by Talisman with its Sudan operations, arose when projects become the focal point of unrelated social unrest. Despite this negative attention, and despite the fact that there was indeed a civil war ongoing and the oilfield revenues were disbursed to the Government of Sudan, Talisman held fast to the belief that walking away from Sudan was not the proper response to public outcry.

Instead, Talisman, with the support of its shareholders, developed a response in keeping with its business practices and beliefs. At Talisman's annual general meeting in May 2000, a number of shareholders presented a proposal to the shareholders of Talisman whereby they raised concerns about the Company's investment in Sudan. The proposal asked the board of directors to take a number of measures including the preparation of an independently verified report on the Company's compliance with the International Code of Ethics for Canadian Business within 180 days. In a second resolution, proposed by management, the board of directors was asked:

1. To cause the Company, in consultation with an independent third party, to develop and implement procedures for monitoring the Company's compliance with the International Code of Ethics for Canadian Business, including the

human rights provisions thereof, with respect to the operations of the Company and its subsidiary in Sudan; and

2. To cause to be prepared annually an independently verified report on the Company's compliance with the International Code of Ethics for Canadian Business, with respect to such operations and to provide a summary of each such report to the shareholders, in conjunction with the Company's normal annual reporting to shareholders and to make a full report available to shareholders and the public on request.[10]

The shareholders accepted the resolution proposed by management and the Corporate Social Responsibility Report 2000: Sudan Operations was compiled (see Exhibit 4).

Peter Widdrington (chairman of the board of Talisman), in his introductory statement in the Corporate Social Responsibility Report 2000: Sudan Operations, reinforced the Talisman belief that corporate social responsibility must be a mainstream issue and intrinsic to all business. He indicated that Talisman, in response to public concern over the company's investment in Sudan, had enhanced its existing governance procedures to ensure accountability and control regarding corporate social responsibility issues. Talisman had endorsed and approved the Sudan Operating Principles, management structures and participation initiatives as outlined in the report and had endorsed the development of formal policies and procedures to implement codes of conduct and international standards that would define appropriate activities for business. Talisman was committed to providing to the board of directors comprehensive corporate social responsibility reviews and updates on Sudan twice a year, with other reports being made available throughout the year as deemed appropriate. A steering committee, consisting of the CEO, senior executives and senior people responsible for Corporate Responsibility, also met weekly to review issues related to Sudan and the implementation of the International Code of Ethics for Canadian Business.

In September 2000, Talisman had persuaded the GNPOC to adopt a code of ethics and proceeded to develop operating principles.

As outlined in the Corporate Responsibility Report 2000, Talisman's commitment to corporate social responsibility in Sudan encompassed the areas of human rights, community participation, employee rights, business conduct and health, safety and environment.

Specific objectives in each of these areas were:

- HUMAN RIGHTS—a commitment to addressing human rights concerns arising from Talisman and GNPOC operations, supporting the Universal Declaration of Human Rights and advocating the beliefs with their joint venture partners and the Government of Sudan.
- COMMUNITY PARTICIPATION—ensuring that local communities received long-term sustainable benefits from Talisman operations; consulting with local communities, governments and non-governmental organizations and the joint venture business partners to identify suitable projects and initiatives.
- EMPLOYEE RIGHTS—Talisman endeavored to respect individual rights and to provide a safe and healthy working environment with meaningful employment opportunities for local people, competitive pay and a training/development program for staff.
- BUSINESS CONDUCT—Talisman was committed to carrying out all business activities in accordance with its Policy on Business Conduct, the Sudan Operating Principles and the International Code of Ethics for Canadian Business.
- HEALTH, SAFETY and ENVIRONMENT— Talisman was committed to maintaining high standards in occupational health, safety and environment, and saw these standards as being key to achieving efficiency and profitability in the oil and gas business.

Talisman, in keeping with its corporate social responsibility mandate had made significant contributions to the people of Sudan in each area, including:

- HUMAN RIGHTS
  - Extensive dialogue with the Government of Sudan expressing Talisman's support for the protection of human rights and supporting the peace process;

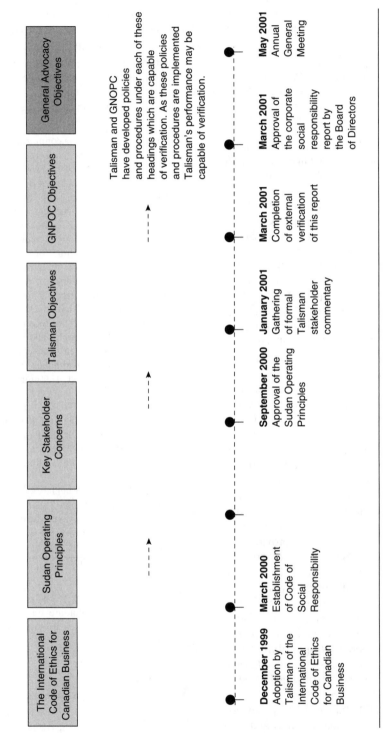

The International Code of Ethics for Canadian Business

Sudan Operating Principles

Key Stakeholder Concerns

Talisman Objectives

GNPOC Objectives

General Advocacy Objectives

December 1999
Adoption by Talisman of the International Code of Ethics for Canadian Business

March 2000
Establishment of Code of Social Responsibility

September 2000
Approval of the Sudan Operating Principles

January 2001
Gathering of formal Talisman stakeholder commentary

March 2001
Completion of external verification of this report

March 2001
Approval of the corporate social responsibility report by the Board of Directors

May 2001
Annual General Meeting

Talisman and GNOPC have developed policies and procedures under each of these headings which are capable of verification. As these policies and procedures are implemented Talisman's performance may be capable of verification.

Exhibit 4   Corporate Social Responsibility Report 2000: Sudan Operations: Timeline and Framework

– Development of a detailed human rights monitoring and investigation program manual to address concerns arising from GNPOC operations;

– Introduction of a human rights awareness program for Talisman employees in Sudan;

– Participation of the four most senior GNPOC security officials and Talisman's human rights Field Co-ordinator in human rights and modern peacekeeping training at the Lester B. Pearson Canadian International Peacekeeping Centre.

• COMMUNITY PARTICIPATION

– Completion of 15 independent community development projects for a total cost of Cdn$1 million;

– Completion of 25 GNPOC community development projects for a total cost of close to Cdn$2 million;

– Attainment of Sudanization targets: at December 31, 2000, Sudanese nationals held 72 per cent of all skilled and unskilled positions at GNPOC;

– In the area of community development, Talisman's focus was on water, health, learning and capacity building. Talisman had constructed a 60-bed hospital in the concession area, had built four schools and provided or renewed 28 water wells in the concession area and along the pipeline. Talisman had also given mechanical and technical support for successful agricultural development in the concession area (see Exhibit 5).

- Construction of a 60-bed hospital in Heglig with a staff of four doctors, who see an average of 260 people per day in the 24-hour emergency department. Minor operations, dental care, x-rays, vaccinations and obstetric services are also provided free of charge to all patients.
- Construction, outfitting and staffing of five medical clinics and Abyei hospital. Environmental health classes are held for local community members from each clinic on a regular basis.
- Funding of medical treatments, including 15,000 vaccinations and an ongoing tuberculosis prevention program.
- Construction of four schools. Educational development and adult literacy programs in Paryang and Karkaria villages.
- Provision of new or restored water supplies in 28 communities. The program included well maintenance and repair training for local residents as well as an inventory of spare parts to keep the wells, usually hand pumps, in good working condition. Provision of six high-capacity water well systems (200-foot deep wells, storage containers and pumps/faucets) in Kummagon, Rubkona (2), Kailak Lake and Paryang (2).
- Provision of emergency relief for displaced people in Bentiu and Mayom including tents, mosquito netting, medication and an emergency medical clinic.
- Funding for an artificial limb camp in Khartoum, which has provided more than 2,000 lower limbs to amputees.
- Funding to support the development of entrepreneurial skills among 720 women in the internally displaced peoples (IDP) camps of Mayo and Shagara in Khartoum. Training in tailoring and pasta making provides opportunities to generate income. Flexible loans to fund business startup costs are also provided.
- Funding, mechanical and technical support for agricultural development in the concession including the tilling and seeding (dhura or sorghum) of 16,000 acres near Kailak Lake.
- A twice-weekly fruit program directed at the inmates of the Kober and Jaref Reformatories. This was the earliest of Project Health Opportunities for People Everywhere's (Project HOPE's) programs and ran for about 10 months.
- Provided beds and bedding to the Mother Theresa Orphanage as well as a cash donation towards food.
- The funding of capital costs for an orthopedic shoe fabrication facility at the Cheshire Home.
- The free distribution of 26 tricycles for disabled adults in Khartoum and 20 to a group of disabled people in Bentiu.
- The construction of two classrooms and the replacement of a roof covering two existing classrooms at the METADEC School.
- The purchase of tables and chairs for the children of the St. Joseph Kindergarten.
- Purchase of school text books for the Episcopal Church of Sudan (ECS) Basic and St. Phillips Basic schools.
- The provision of art supplies and musical instruments to a street boys' program.

Exhibit 5   Major Talisman Community Projects in Sudan

- EMPLOYEE RIGHTS
  - Provided training to 1,159 participants in 67 different programs;
  - Formalized policies regarding: discrimination; screening of contractors; use of child and forced labor; respect for the cultural, spiritual and social needs of National employees; and a grievance and disclosure policy.

- ETHICAL BUSINESS CONDUCT
  - Implementation of an Ethical Business Conduct Management System;
  - Adoption by GNPOC of a Code of Ethics that deals with a wide range of issues including human rights and community participation.

- HEALTH, SAFETY AND ENVIRONMENT
  - Completion of an independent review of the GNPOC health, safety and environmental management system;
  - Provided over 600 person days of safety and loss control training to GNPOC employees.[11]

In addition to these achievements, Talisman had taken on an advocacy role at the highest levels of the Government of Sudan, discussing numerous issues including the protection of human rights, the peace process and the equitable distribution of oil revenues to all people and regions of Sudan. Talisman had also acted as a conduit for external opinion to the Government of Sudan. Talisman had seen positive results on all fronts, though many issues remained.[12]

A major challenge facing Talisman in its efforts to bring CSR standards to the GNPOC project in Sudan was related to ownership. Despite the fact that each of the partners had its own CSR standards, Talisman had been very successful in implementing many of its CSR initiatives.

U.S. HOUSE OF REPRESENTATIVES SUDAN RESOLUTION

On June 13, 2001, the United States House of Representatives voted to prevent Talisman and other foreign companies engaged in the development of oil and gas in Sudan from selling securities in the U.S. market. If approved, the new law would cost Talisman its stock market listing on the New York Stock Exchange.[13]

The United States Senate passed the Sudan Peace Act (without the capital market provisions) on July 19, 2001, via a Unanimous Consent Agreement.

The next step in this process was the staging of a "conference," where representatives from the House and Senate would meet to reach a compromise between the conflicting versions of the Act that had been passed. Talisman had not yet been made aware of the timing of the conference or the names of the conferees (see Exhibit 6).

Bush Admin, Greenspan Oppose Tighter Sudan Sanctions[1]

WASHINGTON—(Dow Jones)—President George W. Bush's administration and Federal Reserve Chairman Alan Greenspan have both voiced opposition to a proposed tightening of sanctions on Sudan that would restrict access to U.S. capital.

Congress is considering preventing oil and gas companies operating in Sudan from listing equity shares or offering debt in U.S. markets. Last month, the House voted 422-to-2 in favor of a bill that would do just that.

Such capital markets sanctions "would significantly damage our relations with European and African countries that are essential to the peace process in Sudan," a Bush administration official familiar with U.S. sanctions policy told Dow Jones Newswires.

The remark suggests Bush would veto any bill that restricts capital markets.

Exhibit 6   Press Releases   *(Continued)*

While the Bush administration official cited diplomatic concerns, Greenspan weighed in with concern about the economy.

The Fed Chairman told the Senate Banking Committee Tuesday that the proposed capital market sanctions would "effectively move a considerable amount of financing out of the United States to London, Frankfurt, and Tokyo." The humanitarian goals of the Sudan bill are laudable but Greenspan said he is "most concerned that if we move in directions which undermine our financial capacity, we are undermining the potential long-term growth of the American economy."

The Senate and House have both passed versions of the Sudan Peace Act, legislation aimed at alleviating suffering in the war-torn African country. But the Senate's version has no capital markets sanctions. The two versions must be reconciled in conference between House and Senate negotiators.

Bush Admin Differs With Religious Freedom Commission[2]

U.S. companies are barred from operating in Sudan. But affiliates of companies listed on U.S. exchanges—including Canada's Talisman Energy Inc. (TLM) and China's Petrochina Co. (PTR)—have major stakes in Sudan's burgeoning oil industry.

Talisman and Petrochina, an affiliate of state-owned China National Petroleum Company, have been targets of human rights activists and religious groups that say their investments support the Sudanese government's military campaign against religious and ethnic minorities.

In March the Congressionally established U.S. Commission on International Religious Freedom recommended tighter sanctions on companies like Talisman and CNPC for their roles in Sudan, as well as a complete prohibition on U.S. import of Sudanese gum Arabic, a food additive in soft drinks and candy. The Bush administration has demurred. The administration official said the House bill's proposal of more stringent disclosure requirements for companies seeking financing in the U.S. "has a lot of potential to damage U.S. capital markets and undermine the authority of the Securities and Exchange Commission."

In May the SEC said it was requiring more-detailed reporting by non-U.S. companies offering securities on U.S. financial markets, a move that largely preempts the disclosure provision in the House's bill.

As for restricting access to U.S. capital markets, the Bush administration official said, "it wouldn't reduce oil revenues to the Sudanese Government and therefore wouldn't affect the ability of that country to fund the war against its own people."

Sanctions Would Affect Subsidiaries, Parents[3]

As proposed in the House bill, companies operating in Sudan would have a hard time avoiding sanctions through "firewalling" techniques such as using affiliates for investments.

A spokesman for Rep. Spencer Bachus, R-Ala., who sponsored the capital markets amendment, said sanctions would apply to parent companies, subsidiaries and affiliates of companies operating in Sudan. "This is similar to how it's worded in the Iran-Libya Sanctions Act: it applies to both subsidiaries and their parent companies," the spokesman said.

Sudan is the scene of one of the world's bloodiest and longest civil wars. The Khartoum-based government has fought non-Muslim separatist groups in the country's southern regions where its major oil fields are. The war has claimed an estimated 2 million lives over two decades.

Since an export pipeline was finished in 1999, Sudan has become a significant oil producer. Output rose to more than 200,000 barrels a day last year, while exports reached 180,000b/d.

The oil exports have raised hopes in some quarters that one of the world's poorest countries will make rapid economic progress. But human rights advocates say oil sales have also funded bombing campaigns by the Khartoum government against southern rebels and civilians.

In February 2000, the U.S. imposed financial sanctions on Greater Nile Petroleum Operating Co., the joint venture producing most of Sudan's oil. But those sanctions don't apply to the individual members of the venture, including Talisman, CNPC and state-owned Malaysian company Petronas (P.PDG).

Exhibit 6   Press Releases

1. Campion Walsh, "Bush Admin, Greenspan Oppose Tighter Sudan Sanctions", *Dow Jones International News*, July 25, 2001.

2. Campion Walsh, "Bush Admin Differs With Religious Freedom Commission," *Dow Jones International News*, July 25, 2001.

3. Campion, Walsh, "Sanctions Would Affect Subsidiaries, Parents," *Dow Jones International News*, July 25, 2001.

FINANCIAL IMPLICATIONS

Talisman was financially sound. In 2000, cash flow reached $2.4 billion ($17.51/share and a 97 per cent increase over 1999) and net income was $906 million ($6.41/share). Both cash flow and net income exceeded the company's previous record set in 1999. Talisman maintained targets for debt to cash flow of two times or less and 40 per cent or less for debt to debt-plus-equity. Talisman was well below these targets at year-end with a debt to cash flow ratio of 0.7 and debt to debt-plus-equity of 32 per cent (see Exhibits 7 and 8).

Talisman's share price had increased 51 per cent over the course of 2000. Talisman had consistently outperformed the oil and gas producers' index, the TSE 35 as well as the Dow Jones Industrial Average from its inception and continued to do so in 2000. Management was convinced that Talisman shares were still undervalued. The adverse publicity over Talisman's holdings in Sudan in 2001 had, however, an adverse effect on share price (see Exhibit 9).

LUNDIN OIL—ACQUISITION WITHOUT SUDAN HOLDINGS

Talisman had announced on June 21, 2001, that a wholly owned Swedish subsidiary would make an offer to acquire all the outstanding shares and warrants of Lundin Oil AB (Lundin Oil). Talisman offered SEK36.5 (approximately US$3.43) for each Class A and Class B share of Lundin Oil. In addition, if the offer was successful, all of Lundin Oil's current interests in Sudan and Russia would be conveyed to a newly formed spinoff company (Newco) and the shares of Newco distributed to holders of Lundin Oil shares on a one-for-one basis. Newco would be managed by the current Lundin Oil management team.

Talisman, as a result of the deal, would retain Lundin's interests in the North Sea, Malaysia, Vietnam and Papua New Guinea at a cost of approximately US$344 million (Cdn$529 million) including debt and working capital. In a separate transaction, Lundin Oil's interests in Libya were to have been sold to a third party (Petro Canada) for US$75 million.

Subject to the satisfaction or waiver of all conditions to the offer, settlement was expected to begin on or about August 28, 2001.

THE DECISION

There had been ongoing frustration on the part of Talisman's management and board; 10 per cent of operations had been receiving a disproportionate amount of attention in the public eye, as well as a disproportionate amount of management time. In addition, the negative publicity surrounding Talisman's holdings in Sudan had been hard on staff morale.

Talisman CEO Jim Buckee had staunchly defended Talisman's position in Sudan and had taken steps to ensure the company continued to act responsibly in this area. In April 2001, Buckee said

> I think we are right . . . We are Canadians, we send Canadian values down into this area that needs it, and we are moving behavior, we are moving opinion by our presence, by our systems on health, safety, environment, human rights, corporate contributions.[14]

Despite its efforts, Talisman was in danger of losing U.S. capitalization if it did not sell off its interest in the GNPOC. One week after the U.S. House passed its version of the Sudan Peace Act, Buckee said, "We want to remain in compliance with laws, and we will. No asset is worth more than that." He indicated that Talisman was "taking prudent steps" that could result in Talisman selling its 25 per cent stake in the GNPOC. Buckee indicated that Talisman had been evaluating opportunities for new country entry in a new core area that was less politically controversial.

Steve Calderwood, an analyst from Salman Partners Inc., was reported to have said, after the U.S. government's decision was made, that Talisman had also considered dividending out to shareholders its Sudan interests as a separate company that would trade in Europe. Calderwood also indicated his belief that should Talisman get out of

(Text continues on page 165)

FINANCIAL STATEMENTS 2000 for Years Ending December 31 (millions of Cdn$ except per share amounts)

(millions of Canadian dollars except per share amount)	2000	1999	1998
Revenue			
Gross sales	4,835.9	2,317.6	1,533.6
Less royalties	945.8	389.0	213.5
Net sales	3,890.1	1,928.6	1,320.1
Other (note 11)	98.8	46.2	50.6
Total revenue	3,988.9	1,974.8	1,370.7
Expenses			
Operating	826.9	603.5	581.0
General and administrative	94.9	70.1	58.9
Depreciation, depletion and amortization	1,152.6	746.6	614.8
Dry hole	77.3	50.6	91.2
Exploration	99.6	79.5	102.4
Interest on long-term debt (note 5)	135.9	119.6	91.0
Other (note 5 and 12)	15.8	(60.6)	143.7
Total expenses	2,403.0	1,609.3	1,683.0
Income (loss) before taxes	1,585.9	365.5	(312.3)
Taxes (note 13)			
Current income tax	333.5	48.8	14.6
Future income tax (recovery)	196.5	109.2	(87.9)
Petroleum Revenue Tax	149.6	30.7	19.8
	679.6	188.7	(53.5)
Net Income (loss)	906.3	176.8	(258.8)
Preferred security charges, net of tax	22.5	13.3	—
Net Income (loss) available to common shareholders	883.8	163.5	(258.8)
Per common share (Canadian dollars) (note 8)			
Net income (loss) available to common shareholders	6.41	1.31	(2.31)
Diluted net income (loss) available to common shareholders	6.32	1.30	(2.31)
Average number of common shares outstanding (millions)	137.8	124.6	111.9

Source: Company files.

Exhibit 7   Financial Statements 2000 for Years Ending December 31 (millions of CDN$ except per share amounts)   *(Continued)*

CONSOLIDATED STATEMENTS OF CASH FLOWS for Years Ending December 31 (millions of Cdn$)

(millions of Canadian dollars)	2000	1999	1998
Operating			
Net income (loss)	906.3	176.8	(258.8)
Items not involving current cash flow (note 14)	1,406.9	854.5	787.5
Exploration	99.6	79.5	102.4
Cash flow	2,412.8	1,110.8	631.1
Changes in non-cash working capital (note 14)	321.5	(179.4)	(64.1)
Cash provided by operating activities	2,734.3	931.4	567.0
Investing			
Corporate acquisitions (note 2)	—	(79.2)	(28.4)
Capital expenditures			
Exploration, development and corporate	(1,194.4)	(1,013.0)	(1,158.7)
Acquisitions	(430.8)	(481.7)	(65.4)
Proceeds of dispositions			
Resource properties	81.0	132.5	157.2
Investments	0.2	3.2	—
Investments	—	—	0.1
Changes in non-cash working capital	(406.9)	379.9	76.4
Cash used in investing activities	(1,950.9)	(1,058.3)	(1,018.8)
Financing			
Long-term debt repaid	(2,880.3)	(1,422.7)	(740.8)
Long term debt issued	2,367.2	1,249.5	1,029.0
Common shares (purchased) issued	(172.8)	19.1	8.7
Preferred securities issued	—	428.0	—
Preferred security charges	(40.1)	(23.7)	—
Deferred credits and other	(35.7)	83.9	(5.0)
Changes in non-cash working capital	0.3	(150.7)	150.3
Cash (used in) provided by financing activities	(761.4)	183.4	442.2
Net increase (decrease) in cash	22.0	56.5	(9.6)
Cash (bank indebtedness), beginning of year	54.0	(2.5)	7.1
Cash (bank indebtedness), end of year	76.0	54.0	(2.5)

Exhibit 7 Financial Statements 2000 for Years Ending December 31 (millions of CDN$ except per share amounts) *(Continued)*

	Canada 2000	Canada 1999	Canada 1998	North Sea 2000	North Sea 1999	North Sea 1998	Indonesia 2000	Indonesia 1999	Indonesia 1998	Sudan 2000	Sudan 1999	Sudan 1998	Other 2000	Other 1999	Other 1998	Total 2000	Total 1999	Total 1998
Revenue																		
Gross sales																		
Oil and liquids	798.9	450.7	307.2	1,513.0	583.0	380.6	288.9	261.3	203.7	588.9	133.7	—	—	—	—	3,189.7	1,428.7	891.5
Natural gas	1,215.6	609.0	466.4	159.4	128.4	148.6	227.1	121.8	8.1	—	—	—	—	—	—	1,602.1	859.2	623.1
Synthetic oil	41.3	28.3	20.0	—	—	—	—	—	—	—	—	—	—	—	—	41.3	28.3	20.0
Sulphur	2.8	1.4	(1.0)	—	—	—	—	—	—	—	—	—	—	—	—	2.8	1.4	(1.0)
Total gross sales	2,058.6	1,089.4	792.6	1,672.4	711.4	529.2	516.0	383.1	211.8	588.9	133.7	—	—	—	—	4,835.9	2,317.6	1,533.6
Royalties	510.8	223.5	131.0	70.4	16.7	6.7	112.7	118.6	75.8	251.9	30.2	—	—	—	—	945.8	389.0	213.5
Net sales	1,547.8	865.9	661.6	1,602.0	694.7	522.5	403.3	264.5	136.0	337.0	103.5	—	(1.6)	0.5	1.8	3,890.1	1,928.6	1,320.1
Other	18.9	18.0	19.5	78.1	26.8	28.6	2.7	—	0.3	0.7	0.9	0.4	—	—	—	98.8	46.2	50.6
Total revenue	1,566.7	883.9	681.1	1,680.1	721.5	551.1	406.0	264.5	136.3	337.7	104.4	0.4	(1.6)	0.5	1.8	3,988.9	1,974.8	1,370.7
Segmented expenses																		
Operating																		
Oil and liquids	97.5	73.4	70.2	374.1	250.4	266.4	39.9	52.5	54.9	63.8	22.4	—	—	—	—	575.3	398.7	391.5
Natural gas	155.4	127.7	115.9	25.3	31.9	39.5	15.7	15.8	3.7	—	—	—	—	—	—	196.4	175.4	159.1
Synthetic oil	16.5	12.5	13.0	—	—	—	—	—	—	—	—	—	—	—	—	16.5	12.5	13.0
Pipeline	3.5	3.1	3.0	35.2	13.8	14.4	—	—	—	—	—	—	—	—	—	38.7	16.9	17.4
Total operating expenses	272.9	216.7	202.1	434.6	296.1	320.3	55.6	68.3	58.6	63.8	22.4	—	0.1	0.2	0.2	826.9	603.5	581.0
DD&A	477.9	368.7	306.7	512.3	282.7	253.0	83.0	71.8	54.9	79.3	23.2	—	12.8	8.2	16.6	1,152.6	746.6	614.8
Dry hole	29.1	12.7	22.5	14.9	26.4	48.2	17.2	1.3	3.9	3.3	2.0	—	18.0	11.5	12.5	77.3	50.6	91.2
Exploration	53.9	39.8	39.9	13.1	8.5	37.5	6.4	8.1	10.0	8.2	11.6	2.5	4.9	0.4	4.1	99.6	79.5	102.4
Other	9.9	(61.0)	(57.8)	(4.1)	(2.4)	190.3	5.6	(0.4)	7.7	(0.5)	2.8	(0.6)				15.8	(60.6)	143.7
Total segmented expenses	843.7	576.9	513.4	970.8	611.3	849.3	167.8	149.1	135.1	154.1	62.0	1.9	35.8	20.3	33.4	2,172.2	1,419.6	1,533.1
Segmented income (loss) before taxes	723.0	307.0	167.7	709.3	110.2	(298.2)	238.2	115.4	1.2	183.6	42.4	(1.5)	(37.4)	(19.8)	(31.6)	1,816.7	555.2	(162.4)
Corporate expenses																		
General and administrative																94.9	70.1	58.9
Interest on long-term debt																135.9	119.6	91.0
Total corporate expenses																230.8	189.7	149.9

Exhibit 7　Financial Statements 2000 for Years Ending December 31 (millions of CDN$ except per share amounts)　*(Continued)*

SEGMENTED INFORMATION

	Canada			North Sea			Indonesia			Sudan			Other			Total		
	2000	*1999*	*1998*	*2000*	*1999*	*1998*	*2000*	*1999*	*1998*	*2000*	*1999*	*1998*	*2000*	*1999*	*1998*	*2000*	*1999*	*1998*
Income (loss) before taxes																**1,585.9**	365.5	(312.3)
Property, plant and equipment	**3,658.0**	3,369.8	2,304.7	**2,483.9**	2,217.6	1,537.1	**516.3**	553.4	579.6	**748.3**	768.4	523.9	**94.1**	73.8	51.5	**7,500.6**	6,983.0	4,996.8
Segmented assets	**4,057.1**	3,497.6	2,393.3	**2,873.1**	2,475.6	1,654.9	**714.4**	808.8	701.6	**824.6**	853.2	553.5	**101.4**	78.8	55.9	**8,570.6**	7,714.0	5,359.2
Add corporate																**105.1**	94.1	88.5
Total assets																**8,675.7**	7,808.1	5,447.7
Capital expenditures																		
Exploration	**252.4**	106.2	126.9	**45.6**	39.2	101.9	**30.1**	18.1	32.9	**33.1**	35.8	4.3	**45.6**	38.4	47.4	**406.8**	237.7	313.4
Development	**434.0**	217.0	276.8	**257.2**	256.3	263.9	**38.7**	36.1	146.7	**36.8**	245.1	144.4	**5.5**	3.8	—	**772.2**	758.3	831.8
Exploration and development	**686.4**	323.2	403.7	**302.8**	295.5	365.8	**68.8**	54.2	179.6	**69.9**	280.9	148.7	**51.1**	42.2	47.4	**1,179.0**	996.0	1,145.2
Acquisitions[1]																**430.8**	481.7	65.4
Proceeds on dispositions																**(81.0)**	(132.5)	(157.2)
Corporate																**15.4**	17.0	13.5
Net capital expenditures																**1,544.2**	1,362.2	1,066.9

Exhibit 7   Financial Statements 2000 for Years Ending December 31 (millions of CDN$ except per share amounts)

1. Excluding corporate acquisitions

Indonesian oil revenues in 2000, 1999 and 1998 consist entirely of sales to Pertamina. North Sea total revenue for the year ended December 31,2000 and property, plant and equipment as at December 31, 2000 were $1,656.9 million (1999–$697.6 million; 1998–$518.6 million) and $2,435.7 million (1999–$2,169.4 million; 1998–$1,500.3 million), respectively, from the U.K. and $23.2 million (1999–$23.9 million; 1998–$32.5 million) and $48.2 million (1999–$48.2 million; 1998–$36.8 million), respectively, from the Netherlands.

FINANCIAL RESULTS Q.2, 2001				
	Three months ended March 31		*Six months ended June 30*	
	2001	*2000*	*2001*	*2000*
Financial (millions of Canadian dollars unless otherwise tated)				
Cash flow[1]	**640.9**	572.7	**1,404.6**	1,144.1
Net income[1]	**237.2**	213.9	**582.7**	420.1
Exploration and development	**474.4**	278.5	**848.3**	517.2
Per common share (dollars)				
Cash flow[1] – Basic	**4.73**	4.14	**10.37**	8.27
– Diluted	**4.64**	4.07	**10.18**	8.17
Net income[2] – Basic	**1.71**	1.51	**4.22**	2.96
– Diluted	**1.68**	1.48	**4.14**	2.92
Production (daily average production)				
Oil and liquids (bbls/d)	**224,085**	252,372	**232,271**	245,452
Natural gas (mmcf/d)	**980**	987	**978**	1,000
Total mboe/d (6mcf = 1boe)	**387**	415	**397**	412

1. Amounts are reported prior to preferred security charges of $10.5 million ($5.9 million, net of tax) for the three months ended June 30, 2001 (2000—$10.0 million; $5.6 million, net of tax).

2. Per common share amounts for net income and diluted net income are reported after preferred security charges. Cash flow for the quarter ended June 30, 2001 increased 12% to $640.9 million ($4.73/share), compared to 2000. Cash flow for the first six months was $1.4 billion ($10.37/share). Significantly higher North American natural gas prices and higher Canadian gas production were offset by reduced North Sea oil and natural gas production. Net income per share increased to $1.71, an increase of 13% over 2000. Revenues for the quarter were $1.3 billion, with crude oil and natural gas accounting for 60% and 40% of the total, respectively.

	Three months ended March 31		*Six months ended June 30*	
	2001	*2001*	*2001*	*2000*
Production (daily average production)				
Oil and liquids (bbls/d)				
Canada	**66,624**	66,177	**66,456**	65,775
North Sea	**85,751**	119,376	**95,533**	114,816
Indonesia	**18,502**	20,874	**18,628**	20,850
Sudan	**53,208**	45,945	**51,654**	44,011
	224,085	252,372	**232,271**	245,452
Natural Gas (mmcf/d)				
Canada	**792**	735	**791**	751
North Sea	**99**	135	**103**	138
Indonesia	**89**	108	**93**	111
	980	978	**987**	1,000
Total mboe/d (6mcf = 1boe)	**387**	415	**397**	412

Exhibit 8   Financial Results Q.2, 2001

Chart for TLM by Stockwatch.com 604-687-1500 http://www.stockwatch.com © 2001
Last 09/07/2001 hi = 63.00 lo = 61.25 cl = 62.40 vol = 467,045 Year hi = 65.77 lo = 43.80

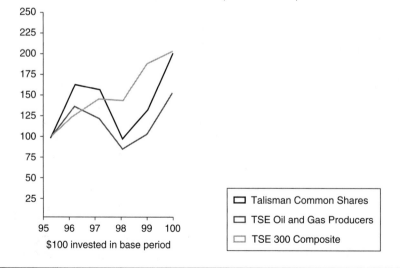

Share Price vs TSE Indices (at December 31)

$100 invested in base period

☐ Talisman Common Shares
☐ TSE Oil and Gas Producers
☐ TSE 300 Composite

Exhibit 9   Share Price History

Source: www.stockwatch.com

Sudan, because of pressure from peace advocates, claiming oil development was fueling the war and displacing people, these peace advocates would have a tougher time getting attention for their cause. He believed the oil operations would become less transparent and likely less relevant to the West. "If there isn't a North American or western company as a target for those interest groups, it's going to be tougher for them to make a case for oil development in Sudan to stop."[15]

A number of Middle East, Asian and Russian companies in need of oil holdings had expressed interest in Talisman's GNPOC interest. Talisman management and board were concerned, however, that selling their interest, while it may take the pressure off Talisman, could ultimately be harmful to the people of Sudan. The governments of the prospective buyers had not been strong advocates of human rights and corporate responsibility in the past, and Talisman had to question whether the sale of the GNPOC interest would be in keeping with its corporate social responsibility policies.

While Talisman had not named the potential buyers, members of the press and other industry followers speculated on which company or companies would be the most likely buyers:

- Talisman's partner in Sudan, China National Petroleum Co., which wanted to boost its production from Sudan;
- The French multinational, Total, which owned a vast concession south of Talisman's operations;
- Lundin Oil Corporation of Sweden's Newco, with current operations in Sudan;
- Petroliam Nasional Berhad of Malaysia, with operations in Sudan;
- ONGC Videsh Ltd. (OVL).

The Talisman board of directors and management team believed that the fundamental issue was that Talisman's investment strategy was driven by a business perspective. From both technical and strategic perspectives, Talisman had gained terrific stature from bringing about achievements in Sudan. It was clear that growth in the North American oil markets was not possible at this time. Only by expanding in international markets could Talisman continue to grow. The challenge of growth for a company the size of Talisman was to ensure that any projects undertaken fit both the technical expertise of Talisman and its financial capabilities.

Talisman's management and board had to make a decision: Should Talisman keep the property in Sudan and continue to try to make a difference through Talisman's corporate social responsibility initiatives? Would this action be sufficient to cause the share price to rebound? Or should Talisman sell its interest in the GNPOC property and maximize shareholder wealth in the short term?

NOTES

1. Company sources.
2. www.opec.org., November 2002.
3. Company annual report.
4. Internal company document.
5. Internal company document.
6. "Canada Announces Support to Sudan Peace Process," No. 232, October 26, 1999. www.dfait.maeci .gc.ca
7. Claudia Cattaneo, "Talisman Hopes to dodge U.S. Sanctions," *Financial Post,* July 31, 2001.
8. Company files.
9. Ibid.
10. Ibid.
11. Corporate Social Responsibility Report 2000.
12. Company files.
13. Claudia Cattaneo, "Talisman Wavers on Sudan," *Financial Post,* June 19, 2001, p. C1.
14. Claudia Cattaneo, "Talisman Wavers on Sudan," *Financial Post,* June 19, 2001, p. C10.
15. *Financial Post*, June 19, 2001.

5

ETHICAL ISSUES IN BUSINESS POLICY AND STRATEGY

This chapter includes a variety of cases that address broad policy issues and acceptable business practices. The issues covered in the cases deal with fundamental rights and obligations of businesses in a capitalist context. For example, the Biovail Corporation (A) case explores the morality of monopoly, as created through patents. A patent is the legally instituted right to a level of profitability above normal competitive levels that society grants to an inventor as the reward for taking the risk of development of the patent. The moral justification for these profits is that, in the long run, they serve society better by promoting innovation. A company has the right to protect its patent from infringement, but does this right give the company unlimited powers to defend it? Eventually a drug's patent expires, after which the good of society is better served by competition. Biovail aggressively protects its monopoly provided by a brand-name drug that is threatened by generic alternatives. The context of the case is an investor who is considering selling her stock of Biovail in response to adverse analyst comments about the company and possible regulatory action that the Securities & Exchange Commission (SEC) is threatening. The case also permits a discussion of the social responsibility of drug companies to sick patients. A subsequent case, Biovail (B) (available separately), discloses some significant questionable practices in the analyst community and raises additional discussion points around ethics in the financial services industry.

Organizational culture is an important determinant of corporate behavior, and the Enron—What Went Wrong case takes a second look at this corporate fraud, this time from the perspective of the role of corporate culture in driving questionable ethics. The paradox is that Enron enjoyed a reputation as one of the best-managed and highest performing companies of the "new economy." In addition to the popular press, a number of leading academics joined in the parade of admirers. Author Gary Hamel (2000) featured Enron as one of the leading revolutionaries in his popular book on radical innovation. Chief Executive Officer Jeffrey Skilling recognized that to support the evolution from asset-heavy energy provider to a knowledge-dependent trading company, they would have to align Enron's human resources management policies and practices with their strategy. The case documents in some detail the company's espoused values and corporate culture.

Entrepreneurs are known to be risk takers and mold breakers, with a healthy disregard for rules. This creativity may serve them well in a start-up business, but it also brings ethical problems. Even if the entrepreneur is a majority (or even the sole) owner of a private business, the manager is still morally, if not always legally, accountable to other stakeholders. The OrangeWerks: A Question of Ethics case documents an employee's discovery of some serious lapses in management's responsibility for ethical conduct. OrangeWerks, which creates software applications, is preparing to make a presentation to venture capital firms for its first major round of funding. However, during routine network maintenance, the network administrator becomes aware that the company may not have purchased the original software used to create the company's product and that government workplace safety insurance was not in place. He must decide how to proceed with the knowledge by assessing available options and judging the stakeholder impact, as well as his career implications.

For many organizations, their Web presence is a core part of their business. A Web site can be a portal though which a client may access information, transact, and make payments—indeed, conduct all aspects of business—whereas for others, is it primarily used by potential customers as a source of information. Unfortunately, Web addresses (domain names) are not provided with as much intellectual and trademark protection as brands and business names are. One questionable, but easily implemented, practice that takes advantage of this lax regulation is for a company to acquire the rights to a range of Web addresses that could easily be mistaken for those of a competitor. The www .centralmba.com case, based on a disguised Central University, has developed a highly successful executive MBA program. Its closest competitor, State University, has aggressively responded, to the point of registering the Internet domain name "www .centralmba.com" and meta-tagging the State University Executive MBA home page with this domain name. The associate dean of programs at Central must decide what course of action to take. The case describes the domain name registration process, explains meta-tagging, and raises a number of ethical, marketing, and information management issues.

The final case in this chapter is an exception to the norm in this book, in that it is a documentation of one company's highly regarded ethics management process. Imperial Oil has enjoyed a generally excellent reputation for sounds management, and the Ethics Management at Imperial Oil case presents the decisions that a communications manager at the company must make as part of his review of the design of the organization in regards to its ethical corporate culture. Various organization design efforts have been made, including a code of business practices, an annual sign-off, training and development, recruitment and selection, and a focus on ethics in the overall framework of management control. Despite the culture, two incidents have recently occurred, which causes the communications manager to wonder whether enough has been done.

REFERENCE

Hamel, G. (2000). *Leading the revolution.* Boston: Harvard Business School Press.

BIOVAIL CORPORATION (A)[1]

*Prepared by Jessica Frisch under the
supervision of Professors David Sharp and Mary Heisz*

Copyright © 2004, Ivey Management Services   Version: (A) 2004-03-12

On April 29, 2002, Ashley Taylor, a professional who invested in the stock market, was distressed by an announcement from Bank of America pharmaceutical analyst Jerry Treppel. Earlier that morning, Treppel had downgraded Biovail stock to a "sell" rating. Biovail, a large Canadian-based pharmaceutical company, had recently been the recipient of widespread scrutiny by financial analysts; Biovail's patent acquisition methods had been labelled as "untruthful"[2] and their accounting practices had been called "frisky."[3] Taylor considered herself to be a morally conscious person, and she wondered whether she wanted to invest in a company that had recently been targeted for its low ethical standards.

THE PHARMACEUTICAL INDUSTRY

The pharmaceutical industry was the fifth largest high knowledge manufacturing industry in Canada. The industry was highly competitive and included brand name corporations, generic drug manufacturers, small and medium-sized biopharmaceutical companies and well-known contract research and clinical trial organizations. Some of the largest players in the industry included Pfizer, GlaxoSmithKline and Merck & Co. In Canada, the big pharmaceutical companies were clustered in metropolitan areas such as Montreal and Toronto. The Canadian pharmaceutical sector employed a large, highly skilled and highly paid work force.

The pharmaceutical industry was one of the most research and development (R&D) intensive sectors; in 2002, the research-based pharmaceutical industry in the United States would invest *$12.6 billion*[4] in R&D. Each new drug required a great deal of R&D before it could be approved. In the United States, it took an average of 12 years for an experimental drug to travel from the lab to someone's medicine cabinet.[5]

The approval process started with preclinical testing. This stage consisted of laboratory and animal tests to show the biological activity of the drug and to ensure the safety of the product. After preclinical testing, a company had to file an investigational new drug application (IND) with the Food and Drug Administration (FDA) before it could begin to test the drug in people. After approval had been granted, three phases of clinical trials were conducted. These experimental phases studied dosage, efficacy and side-effects associated with the drug. The clinical trials included up to 3,000 human volunteers. Lastly, a company had to file a new drug application (NDA) with the FDA. In the United States, only five in 5,000 compounds that entered preclinical testing made it to human testing. Moreover, only one of those five tested on people was approved.[6] A company's profits could suffer drastically if the FDA did not grant drug approval.

COMPANY BACKGROUND

Eugene Melnyk, Biovail's chief executive officer (CEO), started his first company when he was 23 years old. As the son of a Toronto doctor, he formed a company called Trimel, which created crib notes for physicians who did not have time to read the lengthy medical literature available to them. In the late 1980s, Melnyk had shifted Trimel's focus toward the pharmaceutical field, particularly on the area of controlled-release drug delivery technology.[7] Melnyk acquired advanced proprietary technology, and he teamed up with an internationally respected pioneer in the industry; the new company's operations were consolidated under the name Biovail. In 1989, at 29 years old, Melnyk sold Trimel for Cdn$8 million and continued to focus on his new pharmaceutical business.

In the beginning, Biovail licensed its products early in the development cycle to pharmaceutical companies that conducted clinical trials, regulatory process, manufacturing and sale of their products. However, by the mid-1990s, Biovail had become an international full-service pharmaceutical company based in Mississauga, Ontario. The company used advanced drug delivery technologies in the formulation, clinical testing, registration, manufacture, sale and promotion of pharmaceutical products. The company produced over 20 controlled-release products that were under licence in more than 55 countries. The company's full portfolio included more than 25 products, both branded drugs and generic[8] medications.[9]

In 2002, Melnyk, by now a 43-year-old billionaire, was named as the sixth richest individual in Canada. In that year, Biovail reported revenues of $788 million and net income of $87.4 million.[10]

THE TIAZAC CONTROVERSY

Taylor had recently been reading the extensive media coverage regarding one of Biovail's most successful products, Tiazac. Tiazac was a branded prescription drug used to treat high blood pressure and to decrease the occurrence of chronic chest pain. Tiazac's main ingredient was a controlled-release formulation of a chemical called diltiazem hydrochloride. In 2000, Tiazac's sales were nearly $200 million, accounting for 38 per cent of Biovail's gross sales.[11] Taylor

knew that Tiazac provided a strong revenue stream for Biovail. However, recently there seemed to be a great deal of controversy surrounding the drug.

In 1998, Andrx Pharmaceuticals, a Florida-based company that developed generic drugs, submitted an application to the U.S. Food and Drug Administration (FDA) to produce and sell a generic version of Tiazac. In order to have a generic drug approved by the FDA, a company had to file an abbreviated new drug application (ANDA) demonstrating that their product was bioequivalent to the branded version. Furthermore, the company had to prove that it did not infringe on any patents claimed on the branded version of the drug. A list of all FDA-approved drugs and the related patents claimed could be found in an FDA reference called "the Orange Book."

When Andrx applied to market the generic version of Tiazac in 1998, Biovail alleged that the company infringed on Biovail's patent held on the drug. As a result, Biovail filed a patent infringement suit against Andrx, which effectively prevented Andrx from entering the high blood pressure drug market for a 30-month period, expiring February 1, 2001.

On January 8, 2001, one month before the protection period expired, Biovail listed a second patent on Tiazac in the Orange Book. The second patent covered a formulation of the drug that included both immediate-release and slow-release diltiazem. Analysts speculated that Biovail's filing of the second patent was a result of the company's fear that a generic copy of Tiazac, offered at a lower price, would substantially affect Biovail's sales of the drug. When Andrx again applied to produce its generic form of the drug, Biovail filed another patent infringement suit in respect of the second patent, ensuring another 30-month period without generic competition.

On April 23, 2002, the Federal Trade Commission (FTC) announced its first complaint against a pharmaceutical manufacturer for:

allegedly illegally acquiring an exclusive patent licence and wrongfully listing that patent in the U.S.

FDA "Orange Book" for the purpose of blocking generic competition to its branded drug Tiazac.[12]

In order to solicit public comment before they ruled on the issue, the FTC posted a document entitled "Analysis to Aid Public Comment" on the Internet. This document helped to explain the situation to the public, and the site could be used as a forum for public comment.

Taylor read the following excerpts from the document:

> The Commission's complaint alleges that Biovail acquired exclusive rights to the '463 patent[13] for the purpose of listing it in the FDA's Orange Book and thereby blocking Andrx's entry into the Tiazac market.

The document explained that the new patent protected a drug with a specific amount of the immediate-release diltiazem; however, Tiazac did not contain the amount of immediate-release diltiazem for the new patent to be relevant. Analysts speculated that Biovail had not been entirely honest in the process of obtaining the second patent.

> According to the complaint, Biovail was aware that the '463 patent did not claim the formulation of Tiazac that it had been marketing. The product described in the [new] patent contains at least one per cent of uncoated immediate-release diltiazem, in addition to extended-release diltiazem in the form of coated beads. By contrast, the only form of Tiazac that Biovail has ever sold contains only negligible amounts—that is, well below one per cent—of uncoated immediate-release diltiazem. Accordingly, Biovail did not need the '463 patent in order to make or sell its existing FDA-approved formulation of Tiazac, and it could have continued to do so without infringing the [new] patent.

Jerry Treppel, an analyst with Bank of America, accused Biovail of being "untruthful" in its patent dealings. He stated

> We think that if management was willing to mislead the government [in its patent filing], we believe it might have little compunction about misleading investors.[14]

LEGAL ACTION

In the "Analysis to Aid Public Comment," Taylor also found more concerning news about Biovail. It was not only analysts and investors who were questioning the company; Biovail's customers were outraged. In 2002, the state of Pennsylvania filed a class action law suit alleging that Biovail monopolized the market for Tiazac.

> The complaint concludes that as a result of Biovail's conduct, consumers of Tiazac have been deprived of the benefits of lower-priced generic competition that might have been possible had Biovail not acquired exclusive rights to, and then listed, the [new] patent, thereby precluding the FDA from granting final approval to Andrx's generic Tiazac in February 2001.

Taylor also read about the Pennsylvania class action suit in newspapers and magazines.

> Specifically the suit alleges that the unavailability of a generic equivalent caused the class to pay higher prices for Tiazac than they would have if a generic version had been available.[15]

In Biovail's 2002 annual report, Taylor found the Pennsylvania lawsuit disclosed in the Notes to Consolidated Financial Statements. The disclosure defended Biovail's position and did not discuss any potential monetary losses as a result of the suit. However, Taylor found analyst reports that said a generic version of Tiazac could have saved high blood pressure drug consumers $60 million in 2001. These analysts argued that Biovail could be held liable for this potential cost savings.

TAYLOR'S DECISION

Taylor did not know whether she should keep her stock in Biovail. She had owned stock in the company for three years and had achieved good return on her investment, but she wondered how the "sell" rating would affect the value of her shares. Furthermore, Taylor was concerned with the non-financial issues related to the situation. She considered herself to be a moral and ethical person, and she was uneasy about supporting a company with questionable ethical standards.

NOTES

1. This case been written on the basis of published sources only. Consequently, the interpretation and perspectives presented in this case are not necessarily those of Biovail Corporation or any of its employees.

2. *The Globe and Mail,* June 22, 2002.

3. *Forbes,* March 18, 2002.

4. All amounts in US$ unless otherwise specified.

5. www.allp.com/drug_dev. June 23, 2003.

6. Ibid.

7. Rather than an individual taking several doses of the same pill in one day, controlled-release technology allows people to take only one dosage of medication, and the technology releases the drug at a controlled pace.

8. A generic drug is proven to be bioequivalent to its branded counterpart. Generic drugs are offered at a lower price.

9. www.biovail.com. June 26, 2003.

10. *Triangle Business Journal,* April 21, 2003.

11. Analysis to Aid Public Comment. www.ftc.gov/os/2002/04/biovailanalysis.

12. [Ip-health] FTC on Biovail illegal orange book listing. Thursday, April 25, 2002. www.lists.essential.org/pipermail/ip-health/2002-April/002946.

13. The second patent acquired by Biovail.

14. *The Globe and Mail,* June 22, 2002.

15. *BNA's Health Law Reporter,* Volume 11, Number 12, March 21, 2002.

ENRON—WHAT WENT WRONG[1]

Prepared by Professor Bert Spector

Version: (A) 2004-02-23

On December 14, 2000, Houston-based Enron Corporation seemed to stand at the peak of its meteoric rise to prominence. Chief Executive Officer (CEO) Kenneth Lay announced that he would soon turn over the reins to Jeffrey Skilling. Lay and Skilling exuded both pride in the past achievements of the company and confidence in their future. Most observers agreed. At the time of the transition from Lay to Skilling, the company reported $15 billion in assets, $100 billion in revenues and 20,000 employees.

Such impressive achievements told only part of the story. Enron had done more than just succeed within the parameters of the energy industry; it had virtually redefined that industry. Embracing deregulation and free markets, adopting new technology with remarkable quickness and radically reinventing its own business model several times over, Enron seemed to stand as a paradigm of successful innovation. In 2000, *Fortune* named Enron as the "Most Innovative Company" for the fifth year in a row, and the magazine's praise did not stop there. Enron was also rated 24th on its list of "Best Companies to Work For," 29th on "America's Fastest Growing Companies," second on "Reputation of Employee Talent," and first—just ahead of General Electric—on "Reputation of Quality of Management."[2]

Almost precisely one year later, on December 2, 2001, Enron declared bankruptcy. The stunning swiftness with which Enron tumbled from one of the New Economy's most admired companies to the largest bankruptcy ever in U.S. history up to that point, led to debates as to what had caused the collapse. Multiple theories abounded, and they all had one core idea in common: the roots of the collapse spread both deep and wide through the company's history.

ENRON CORPORATION

Enron Reshapes the Energy Industry and Itself

Kenneth Lay headed Enron since its creation from a 1985 merger between InterNorth, Inc. and Houston Natural Gas Corporation. "Spend long enough around top Enron people and you feel you are in the midst of some sort of evangelical culture," observed *The Economist*. "In a sense, you are. Mr. Lay, with his 'passions for markets,' is the cult's guru." Enron employees came to view Lay as a father figure in whom they could place complete trust. Said one executive, "The employees loved him. He walked the floors. . . . He was this warm, fatherly figure. . . . They trusted him."[3]

As Lay worked to build the biggest pipeline system in the country, he focused his time and company resources on lobbying governments, especially state governments, to deregulate the energy industry.

> Early on when other natural gas companies were attempting to hold onto a regulated market, we were pushing hard to move our business upstream into unregulated businesses. We thought there'd be more opportunity here to differentiate ourselves on products and services and make a profit at it.

To achieve that goal, Enron needed deregulated energy markets, so Lay became heavily involved in state-level political campaigns, spending more than $1.9 million of Enron's money on 700 candidates in 28 states. Between 1997 and 2000, 24 states moved toward greater energy market deregulation. Up-ending the industry was an accomplishment that Lay himself viewed with pride:

> In this new world, the public utility industry will fade into memory. Competition and technological change is turning the gas and electric industry into yet another mass-marketing segment of the U.S. and global economy.[4]

Lay also focused his energies on the promulgation of four core Enron values: communication, respect, integrity and excellence (a statement of those values can be found in Exhibit 1). He had banners hung in the company's corporate lobby proclaiming those values. "I was always in the forefront of trying to make sure that our people

---

Communication

We have an obligation to communicate. Here, we take the time to talk with one another . . . and to listen. We believe that information is meant to move and that information moves people.

Respect

We treat others as we would like to be treated ourselves. We do not tolerate abusive or disrespectful treatment.

Integrity

We work with customers and prospects openly, honestly and sincerely. When we say we will do something, we will do it; when we say we cannot or will not do something, then we won't do it.

Excellence

We are satisfied with nothing less than the very best in everything we do. We will continue to raise the bar for everyone. The great fun here will be for all of us to discover just how good we can really be.

Exhibit 1   Enron Corporate Values

Source: Company files.

did in fact live and honor those values. . . ." recalled Lay. "Integrity and character are incredibly important to me."[5]

Becoming a Trader

A free market for natural gas allowed Enron the opportunity for its first major innovation: a "gas bank." In the late 1980s, gas prices entered a period of instability, and Enron found itself with a vast inventory of natural gas and uncertain future prices. To turn this apparent disadvantage into an opportunity, Jeffrey Skilling, who, at that time, was a McKinsey & Co. consultant working with Enron, proposed the idea of selling gas futures to customers at agreed-upon prices or price ranges. Natural gas customers, seeking a hedge against the future fluctuation of prices, could enter into a contract with Enron. They would be able to withdraw gas from the bank in the future according to the provisions set forth in a current contract. *Fortune* magazine described the trading process:

> A utility wanted gas for 30 days at a fixed price? Floating prices, but with a maximum and minimum price? A guaranteed supply of gas whenever the temperature went over 95 degrees? No problem: Enron could slice and dice the gas to a customer's specifications—and, in return, of course, could charge a little extra.

It was this notion of a gas bank that would, according to Skilling, provide Enron with the "huge breakthrough" that would allow the company to "conquer the world because we had a better idea."[6]

When Skilling left McKinsey to join Enron in 1990 as CEO of the company's gas bank division, he moved the company more decisively into trading gas futures, seeking contracts of 15 years and longer. Given the volatility of gas prices, such long-term arrangements were not without risks, so the company needed to create an ability to manage that uncertainty. Enron's risk management centered on "two simple rules: all trades must be balanced with an offsetting trade to minimize unhedged risks and each trader must report a daily profit-and-loss statement."[7]

When wholesale electricity was deregulated in 1992, Enron leaped into the market. By 1994, it was selling $10 million worth of electricity, very little of which Enron generated itself. Instead, it relied on "the arts of swaps, collars, caps, floors, and hybrids." Three years later, Enron reported revenues in electricity sales to be $4 billion, and by 2000, 95 per cent of its revenues came from wholesaling energy and services.[8]

"WALL STREET IN HOUSTON"

Jeffery Skilling saw the gas bank as a model for ever-greater growth. Why not enter other non-energy markets that had never been traded before as commodities? If Enron had made money from gas and electricity futures, why could it not do the same for fiber-optic bandwidth, pollution-emission credits, even weather derivatives? Enron could move even farther afield with its trading and risk management competency, trading wood pulp, steel and television advertising. "The application [of the trading model] is almost limitless because every single business has, at its heart, markets," Skilling explained. "Enron is an incumbent player's worst nightmare."[9]

As Enron moved more decisively into the trading business, it could shed physical assets and become highly flexible and adaptive. "Jeff's theory," said a senior Enron executive, "was assets were bad, intellectual capital was good." Skilling himself disdained what he called "old economy" companies that were burdened with assets. "These big companies will topple over from their own weight," he warned.[10]

Enron's transition to pure trader was widely noted by business analysts, typically with admiration for Enron's ability to, once again, reinvent itself. *CIO Magazine* called the transformation "Enron's boldest move to date," which involved "its own version of Wall Street in Houston. . . ." *The Economist* agreed: "Enron, in effect, was abandoning its roots as an energy provider in favor of becoming a Wall Street trader that just happened to be based in Houston, Texas." A stock analyst suggested that Enron had become "a company that traded for trading's sake."[11]

Jeffrey Skilling and Andrew Fastow

Skilling, the man behind Enron's transformation, had joined McKinsey in 1979 after receiving an undergraduate degree from Southern Methodist University and an MBA from the Harvard Business School. At Harvard he was a Baker Scholar and, according to one professor, "may have been the single best student I ever had, and he did not suffer fools." Another professor found him to be passionate and relentless, adding that all the professors who had dealings with Skilling remembered him and "I don't think anybody remembered an unpleasant thing about him."[12]

When Skilling began working with Enron in 1988—this was the point at which he introduced the gas bank idea—he was a senior partner in McKinsey's Houston-based North American Energy and Chemical Practices division. Within two years, he was CEO of the Enron Finance Corporation. "I've never not been successful in business or work," Skilling told a reporter, "Ever." Ken Lay recognized and rewarded Skilling's success by naming him president and chief operating officer (COO) (Lay retained the positions of chairman and CEO) in 1996.[13] Over the next three-and-a-half years, Enron's stock soared 350 per cent to a high of $90 a share.

Skilling himself claimed General Electric's transformational leader Jack Welch as his personal role model and extolled the organizational virtues of flexibility and innovation. "You should always value the ability to move and change, because that creates options." In order to create an appropriate environment for innovation, he said, "You wanted to have an environment that weird people liked operating in. It's the weird ideas that create new businesses."[14]

Skilling took pride in surrounding himself with talented, tough-minded individuals, and none played a more important role in determining the way Enron reported its financial performance than Andrew Fastow. A graduate of Tufts University and the Kellogg School of Management at Northwestern University, Fastow joined Enron in 1990 at age 29. Eight years later, he was chief financial officer (CFO). Said

a colleague of Fastow's: "What the guy knew was numbers and finance. He knew how to close a deal. No one did that better than Andy." *USA Today* noted the similarity between Fastow and Skilling: "Skilling could be cold and impersonal, but Fastow took it further—when he wasn't secluded in his office, he was arrogant and abrasive, capable of pounding his fist on the table and dressing down colleagues in front of their peers." Others talked about a kind of split personality. Said a former executive, "He was very smart and very good at what he did. He could be nice, but he could also be quite volatile and short-tempered. He didn't have a lot of patience with people who weren't as smart as him."

Skilling and Fastow helped drive Enron's performance in the 1990s, and in December 2000, Ken Lay recognized Skilling's contribution by naming him president and CEO, effective the following February. Said Lay:

> The best time for succession is when the successor is ready and when the company is well-positioned for the future. Jeff is a big part of Enron's success and is clearly ready to lead the company. With Jeff's promotion, succession is clear, our deep pool of management talent remains intact, and no other organizational changes need to be made to take the company to new levels of growth.

Ken Lay had hung a banner in Enron's corporate lobby proclaiming "The world's leading energy company." Skilling replaced that with a new banner: "The world's leading company."[15]

During his tenure as CEO, Skilling's brash style often rubbed people the wrong way, including a number of Wall Street analysts. Said one, Skilling "was famously boastful . . . and thin-skinned, declaring on a conference call that a money manager who dared ask for a balance sheet was an 'asshole.'" A colleague of Skilling offered this view: "He was always saying people don't get it."[16]

Building Businesses

"To get ahead here," said Skilling, "you have to be a business builder." Human resource executive

Cindy Olson agreed. "Entrepreneurs can build something of their own . . . with the luxury of a stable organization." Enron supported the idea of "cellular division" wherein entrepreneurial new businesses, especially ones that challenged established business models, would become separate divisions. Executive Lou Pai explained the reasons for this differentiation:

> A lot of times you're off running an existing business and are responsible for new business as well, you're not really as accountable for the success of the new business as long as your old business continues to do well. We want everyone building the new business to be involved 100 per cent.

To enhance that sense of involvement, Enron offered "phantom equity" to the start-up teams of these new businesses. At the point where the business began to show a profit, that phantom equity could be swapped for real Enron shares. Once businesses were up and running, they became highly autonomous, selecting their own infrastructure and often raiding other units for employees.[17]

Company executives could point to a number of examples of bottom-up generators of new business ideas, including the 1999 genesis of Enron Online. "We didn't start it because the chairman said we need an e-commerce strategy," said Executive Vice-president Steve Kean. Louise Kitchen drove the initiative while heading Enron's gas trading operation in Europe. Based on previous experience with Internet trading (while she was working in Enron's Scandinavian office), she began to work on an ad hoc basis, pulling together an informal coalition of commercial, legal and technical people. She informed her immediate supervisor, John Sheriff. Chief Operating Officer Skilling remained out of the loop until the ad hoc group, which grew to 250 people, were ready to launch the online business. Sheriff finally approached Skilling in November 1999, and the COO was unenthusiastic but willing to explore the idea. Recalled Skilling:

> So John says to me, "Actually, we're almost done." I was never asked for any capital. I was never asked for any people. They had already purchased the servers. They had already started ripping apart the building. They had already started legal reviews in 22 countries by the time I heard about it.

Skilling approved, and Enron Online was up and running in less than a year. Enron's head of information technology (IT), Michael McConnell, said that online trading was revolutionary for the company, not so much because of the technology, but because of the impact it had on Enron traders: "Since Enron Online has reduced our transaction time to less than a second, our guys have to manage their businesses by the second—not just by the day as in the past."[18]

Building a Trading Culture

An Enron executive said a key to the company's culture was "an overweening pride, which led people to believe they could handle increasingly exotic risks without danger." The apparent success Enron enjoyed led to increasing pressure for ever-improving performance. "The driver was this unbelievable pressure to keep portraying Enron as something very, very different," said another executive, "and keep the track record going and going." The deal makers at Enron, said a former deal maker, "thought they were so brilliant they could overcome any obstacle." Added an employee, "We were doing deals that no one had done before. We were taking risks that no one else had taken before."[19]

Lay and Skilling recognized that in order to fuel this trading culture, they would have to attract to Enron a different breed of employee from those who might otherwise find their way to Texas-based energy firms.

> We not only had to attract talent from investment banking houses, commercial banks and elsewhere, but we also had to compete against them. We also had to go up against the big consulting firms for some of the new MBAs coming out of graduate schools.

The head of an executive search firm that worked for Enron talked about this "new" type of recruit: "Enron was a real pioneer in bringing a new type of executive to the energy business.

They started a trend in the energy business of attracting executives who otherwise would have gone into investment and commercial banking." What attracted these new recruits, in part, was their view of Enron "as a hip, dynamic, New Age, blue-chip company that you could join and have a good time of it."[20]

Following the vision of Lay and Skilling, these new recruits recreated the Enron culture. In Enron's world, the engineers have been replaced by theoretical physicists trained in portfolio analysis; the reliability is engineered on the trading floor, where young traders price and strike deals with customers in something like 90 seconds.

These new traders, according to Gary Hamel, "were bold, hungry, and creative. They were assigned to a territory and/or a specialty, but their real assignment was simply to find ways to make money." There were occasional examples of traders overstepping the boundaries: between 1985 and 1987, two Enron oil traders defrauded the company out of $136 million. These two employees, viewed by the company as "rogue traders" and "expensive embarrassments" to the otherwise positive culture, were promptly fired.[21]

Global Expansion

As a counter-trend to Skilling's preference for pure trading, in the early 1990s, Enron began buying energy-related assets overseas. "We have created a new model based on an at-risk, entrepreneurial culture; we look for opportunity in chaos," said an Enron executive explaining the company's approach to global expansion.[22] Under the leadership of Rebecca Mark, Enron aimed first at Europe, South America and Russia, and later focused on China and India. *Newsweek* wrote of Mark:

> When she entered the utility business in the early '80s, it was populated with frumpy males in baggy suits and short-sleeved shirts with pocket protectors. Mark was a builder. . . . By the mid-'90s, she had constructed or acquired five plants in the United States and was on her way to buying or building well in excess of 15 in Europe, Asia, South America and the Middle East.[23]

Like Skilling, Mark had graduated from the Harvard Business School. Unlike Skilling, however, Mark believed in building hard assets.

In the late 1990s, Enron engaged in two large-scale overseas ventures. Azurix, Enron's subsidiary, which held its water-related assets, purchased the U.K.'s Wessex Water for $1.9 billion. Mark brought what she referred to herself as a "missionary zeal" to her overseas expansion:

> . . . we are bringing a market mentality and spreading the privatization gospel in countries that desperately need this kind of thinking. We are in the business of doing deals. This deal mentality is central to what we do. It's never a question of finding deals but of finding the kind of deals we like to do. We like to be pioneers.

Enron also moved to build a power plant in Dabhol, in the state of Maharashtra, India. Despite a World Bank warning that such an investment in India was not viable, Enron partnered with General Electric and Bechtel to contribute $1.2 billion of the total $2.9 billion project. ("We make our own rules," said an Enron executive explaining this decision. "Most people look at the world and think too small; when we went to India, the majors said we were crazy.") The effort generated little revenue, however. A major shift in local political alignments accompanied by accusations of corruption and illegality on the part of Enron officials led the plant's sole customer, the Maharashtra State Electricity Board, to stop purchasing power. They also declined to pay past bills. Enron and its partners shut down the project in June 2001.[24]

By that time, Skilling was moving to unload Enron's international assets. In August 2000, Rebecca Mark left Enron. Skilling placed virtually the entire global holdings on the market, hoping to recover as much as possible of the $7.5 billion Enron had invested. No buyers, however, were found.[25]

Employee Development

"I prefer a smart person to an asset," said Jeffrey Skilling, referring to his belief that intelligent, flexible, performance-oriented employees would provide Enron with a competitive advantage, especially when compared to asset-heavy traditional companies. Enron's human resources department sought to take advantage of that flexibility and knowledge by creating an open market for internal labor. "We have so many business units," said Executive Vice-president Cindy Olson, that "the opportunities are limitless."[26]

To maximize mobility, Enron sought to allow seamless movement across businesses and units. Common compensation and evaluation systems removed potential barriers, as did policies that allowed employees to transfer their titles as they moved. An emphasis on stock options was meant, at least in part, to keep employees focused on the overall performance of the company.[27]

In Skilling's view, knowledge had to be balanced with an emphasis on individual performance. To ensure such an emphasis, Enron employed a fixed-curve rating system. Employees were evaluated not by supervisors alone, but by a group of employees called a Performance Review Committee. Each year, units were required to identify the bottom 15 per cent of their performers, and, in a system nicknamed "rank-and-yank," fire those on the bottom.[28]

Observers found both plusses and minuses in Enron's employee development system. A *Fortune* survey found Enron to be one of the most successful companies at attracting and retaining top talent in a highly competitive labor market:

> Employees are encouraged to be risk-taking career builders. College recruits spend time in several business units to see which is the best fit. As employees progress, they are pushed to manage their careers by moving around within the firm and acquiring new skills. In fact, 85 per cent of the people in Enron's core business units have held at least two positions within the company. Enron also keeps a database of online résumés—updated regularly by employees—so that managers can recruit from within. As result, the company's annual turnover is a minuscule three per cent, even though it hired nearly 5,000 people last year [1999].

Much internal criticism, however, was aimed at the ranking-by-committee approach. "Everyone was in it for themselves," said an executive. "People stabbed you in the back." Another complained that the review process focused entirely on the amount of revenue generated by the employee: "I never once heard a discussion about a person's teamwork or integrity or respect." Aware of such concerns, Skilling expressed support for changing the committee aspect of the ranking system.[29]

Compensation

Lay and Skilling recognized that if they were going to compete with investment houses and consulting firms for talent, they would have to offer competitive compensation packages. "Young traders just out of school were tantalized with promises of $500,000 within a year," said one observer. High salaries were matched by lavish perks: $1.5 million company parties (at one, Rebecca Mark rode in on the back of an elephant); $100 bills left on each employee's desk when the stock price reached $50. Employees felt they earned such lavishness because of their long hours and frequently gruelling travel schedules. The environment, said one executive, was, "Get it done. Get it done now. Reap the rewards." The extravagance, said another, "is what made it great to work" for Enron. Lay himself maintained that corporate spending could have a desirable motivational impact. "All these planes," he said, referring to Enron's fleet of corporate jets, "give my CEOs something to aspire to."[30]

Skilling was keen on moving Enron's compensation plan to be more rewarding of entrepreneurial behavior. "If we've broken a paradigm," an executive said, "it's the compensation paradigm. We pay people like entrepreneurs." High bonuses were paid, based on deals completed and revenue booked. Said one employee:

> The bonuses led employees to focus on pushing deals through the system, even if the deal was a bad deal. The people working on Dabhol power plant in India did very well in bonus time because they worked on a deal and got it done. Two years later, the deal went into the tank, but the system was not good at differentiating between temporary value and long-term value.

Top executives could receive sizable bonuses based on a calculated combination of dividends paid to shareholders plus improvements in the stock price. On January 11, 2001, for example, CFO Andrew Fastow received a bonus check of $350,000; on February 5, he received a check for $1.3 million and then on February 7, he received a bonus payment of $1.4 million. Sizable bonuses were not the exclusive domain of corporate officers, though. In 2001, a 27-year-old energy trader earned an $8 million bonus on reported profits of $750 million in natural gas contracts.[31]

Increasingly, as Enron's stock price rose, the company came to rely on stock options—granting employees the right to buy shares in the future at a fixed price, typically the price of the share at the time the option is granted—as a way of rewarding executives. Skilling pointed to the reliance on stock options as a practice "used by every corporation in the world." In addition to basing rewards on company performance, stock options allowed companies to look more profitable than if they had paid executives with a salary. Granting stock options is the only form of compensation that is not reported as an expense.[32] Skilling made clear that top Enron executives were quite conscious of that advantage. "Essentially what you do is you issue stock options to reduce compensation expense," he explained, "and therefore increase your profitability." In 2000, Skilling exercised options that netted him $62.5 million.[33]

Culture of Confidence

A sense of confidence and pride infused Enron's culture in a way that could be, and often was, experienced as arrogance. "The Enron way was to be brash," said an executive, "and there was an arrogance about it." Said another, "Anyone who criticized Enron—internally or externally—was taken out and flogged." If you were an Enron employee, "you thought you were better. You were smarter than everyone else."[34]

Ken Lay dismissed charges of corporate or even personal arrogance. In a June 2000 interview with *The Economist,* he compared himself and his company to Michael Milikin and Drexel

Burnham Lambert. Milikin and Lambert had likewise been accused of arrogance. (Milikin had also been accused and convicted of securities fraud.) Like Enron, Lay insisted to the reporter, they were really being "very innovative and very aggressive."[35]

Aggressive Accounting

Enron followed the "mark to market" rule for recognizing revenues. The fully legal practice allowed the company to book as revenue the entire projected downstream value of a deal at the time the deal was made. Thus, a deal to provide $500,000 a year in natural gas to a customer for five years would be recognized as $2.5 million at the inception of the deal.

Of course, most of Enron's trading deals were far more uncertain and ambiguous that that example. Prices and needs varied in the complex agreements struck with customers. Additionally, many of the agreements stretched out for 10 to 15 years; or, in the case of the New York State Power Authority, 33 years.[36] Would a customer exist in 10 to 15 years, let alone be willing and able to pay? Enron had just such an example of that uncertainty when the Maharashtra State Electricity Board, the sole customer of Enron's multibillion-dollar investment in India, canceled all future contracts with the Dabhol power plant and refused to pay past bills.

Rather than projecting revenue streams cautiously, Enron tended to be aggressively optimistic. For instance, in a state where power had not yet been deregulated, Enron based its projections on the assumption that power would soon be deregulated, allowing the company to raise the price. It was this aggressiveness that, while approved by Arthur Andersen, Enron's accounting firm, led to the designation of "cutting edge." Enron executive Gary Foster said that even at the time it was reporting these revenues, "we knew that we pushed the limit in our accounting practices, and that people would come in with their numbers whether we really did [achieve them] or not."[37]

Many analysts, both critics and supporters, acknowledged that openness concerning performance numbers was never Enron's strong suit. Writing in *Fortune,* Bethany McLean noted:

> ... the company remains largely impenetrable to outsiders, as even some of its admirers are quick to admit. Start with a pretty straightforward question: how does Enron makes its money? Details are hard to come by because Enron keeps many of the specifics confidential for what it terms "competitive reasons."[38]

When Azurix, an Enron subsidiary, was trying to win a contract from the Houston Area Water Corporation to build a purification plan, the negotiations fell through because the Water Corporation's board was uneasy about Azurix's financial status. "We could never flush out of Azurix the financial documents we wanted," explained the board's chairman. "The first tell-tale sign of something being amiss is the refusal to turn over documents."[39]

When doubts were expressed about the validity of Enron's high-performance claims, company executives responded aggressively. On August 21, 2001, for example, broker Chung Wu of PaineWebber's Houston office sent a pre-dawn e-mail to clients warning about the performance of Enron's stock. Clients, Wu suggested, should "take some money off the table." Aaron Brown, Enron's manager of employee stock option plans, fired off his own e-mail to PaineWebber executives saying that he found Wu's advisory to be "extremely disturbing" and asking them to "Please handle the situation." By that evening, PaineWebber executives had fired Wu and issued a retraction, assuring clients that Enron's stock was "likely heading higher than lower from here on out." All this occurred on the same day that Ken Lay sold $4 million worth of his own personal Enron holdings.[40]

In 2000, Carl Bass, a partner at the Houston office of Enron's accounting firm, Arthur Andersen, sent an e-mail to partners in the accounting firm's Chicago headquarters expressing concern over various accounting practices— how the company recognized revenues, its dealings with various off-balance sheet partnerships—and the fact that these practices had been "sustained" by the local Andersen office. Executives within Enron got wind of these concerns and lobbied, unsuccessfully on this occasion, for Andersen to "replace Carl."

The Collapse

It was possible to trace the collapse of Enron—at least the public manifestation of that collapse—to a Tuesday afternoon in the summer of 2001. At the close of the markets on August 14, Jeffrey Skilling who had served as Enron CEO since the previous February, unexpectedly announced his resignation. Chairman Kenneth Lay offered reassuring words: "The company is probably in the strongest and best shape it has ever been in."[41] Lay would assume the day-to-day leadership of Enron. The financial markets, however, were not reassured. The stock price, which had been as high as 90 a year earlier, now tumbled through the 30s.

Troubled by Skilling's sudden resignation and the investor scrutiny that the bombshell announcement was sure to attract, an Enron vice-president, Sherron Watkins, wrote a memo to Ken Lay expressing her concern that Enron would "implode in a wave of accounting scandals."[42] At the heart of Watkins' expressed concern was her belief that the many complex deals that Enron had constructed with off-balance sheet entities had obfuscated the true financial picture of the company. From 1999 to 2000, a period of explosive growth in Enron's stock price, CFO Andrew Fastow created hundreds of off-balance sheet partnerships. Known collectively as LJM2 and run by Fastow and fellow executive Michael Kopper, these partnerships could be used to hide debt and inflate revenues. But they rested on stock issuance, cross-collateralization and stock "trigger points." As Enron's stock price plunged, Enron faced losses in the hundreds of millions of dollars.[43]

The following week, Watkins met face-to-face with Lay. The CEO assured Watkins that he would investigate the matter, and he did in fact contact both the company's law firm as well as David B. Duncan, the senior partner of Enron's accounting firm, Arthur Andersen, in charge of the Enron account. The law firm conducted a month-long investigation and concluded there was nothing to be concerned about. Duncan pulled together an unofficial committee within Andersen to review past practices.[44]

On October 16, Enron released its third-quarter results, showing a loss of $1 billion in bad investments. And the bad news was just beginning. In a conference call with analysts the following day, Lay mentioned, in a fleeting way, an additional $1.2 billion in capital reduction stemming from unspecified problems arising from off-book partnerships run by CFO Andrew Fastow. This write-down resulted from the review conducted by Duncan, although none of these specifics was enunciated in the call. Lay was so off-handed in his handling of the announcement, in fact, that participants in the call were not sure until days later that this charge was *in addition* to the $1 billion loss announced in the quarterly report. "They were trying to sneak it by," recalled one participant.[45]

To calm investors, Lay removed Fastow as CFO, but the stock price took another hit on October 22 with an announcement by the Securities and Exchange Commission (SEC) that it had opened an investigation into certain accounting practices relating to the off-balance sheet partnerships. The stock fell to $21. On October 30, Moody's downgraded Enron's bonds to "junk" status, and the stock price plunged again. Enron employees who might have wanted to sell stock from their retirement package were prevented from doing so; the company was shifting plan administrators, and retirement accounts were temporarily frozen.

The news went from bad to worse. In the first week in November, with the stock price now in the single digits, Enron announced that it was reducing its earnings over the past four years by almost $600 million, due to the manner in which three "unconsolidated entities" had been accounted for in past financial statements (more fallout from Duncan's review of past practices) and warned that additional reductions might be forthcoming. Although Enron had

borrowed $6 billion in the six weeks after the October announcement of third-quarter results, it still faced more than $31 billion in combined debt. With the stock price now below a dollar a share, with debt spiraling out of control and with no further access to capital markets, Enron filed for Chapter 11 bankruptcy on December 2, 2001.

NOTES

1. This case has been written on the basis of published sources only. Consequently, the interpretation and perspectives presented in this case are not necessarily those of Enron Corporation or any of its employees.

2. See *Fortune,* Jan. 10, 2000, p. 88; Feb. 21, 2000, p. 110; Sept. 4, 2000, p. 146.

3. *The Economist.com,* June 1, 2000, p. 2; Laura Goldberg and Mary Flood, "The Rise of Ken Lay As Dramatic As His Fall," HoustonChronicle.com, Feb. 3, 2002, p. 1, John Schwartz, "As Enron Purged Its Ranks, Dissent Was Swept Away," *New York Times,* Feb. 3, 2002, p. C1.

4. Lay is quoted in *Fortune,* June 23, 1997, p. 87; and Kenneth L. Lay, "Coming Soon To Your Home and Business: The New Energy Majors," in G. William Dauphinais and Colin Price, eds., *Straight From the CEO: The World's Top Business Leaders Reveal Ideas That Every Manager Can Use* (New York: Simon & Schuster, 2000), p. 255. See also *New York Times,* March 27, 2002, p. A20; Kurt Eichenwald, "Audacious Climb to Success Ended in a Dizzying Plunge," *New York Times On the Web,* Jan. 13, 2002, p. 7; Greg Farrell and Chris Woodyard, "Three Powerful Men Forged Enron's Path," p. 2B.

5. Gruley and Smith, "Keys to Success Left Kenneth Lay Open to Disaster," p. A5.

6. Brian O'Reilly, "The Power Merchant," *Fortune* (April 2000), p. 154. Skilling is quoted in *USA Today,* Jan. 28, 2002, p. 3B and Gary Hamel, *Leading the Revolution,* (Boston: Harvard Business School Press, 2000), p. 221.

7. Kathleen M. Eisenhardt and Donald N. Sull, "Strategy As Simple Rules," *Harvard Business Review* (January 2001), p. 114.

8. Economist.com, Feb. 26, 1998, pp. 1–2; *Fortune,* April 17, 2000, p. 156; Fortune.com, March 5, 2001, p. 2.

9. Skilling is quoted in TheIndustryStandard.com, Aug. 14, 2001, p. 2.

10. The Enron executive is quoted in *Business Week Online,* Dec. 17, 2001, p. 1. Skilling is quoted in Bethany McLean, "Why Enron Went Bust," *Fortune.com,* Dec. 24, 2001, p. 2.

11. Koch, "Reinvent Now: 100 Leaders For the Next Millennium," p. 2. The analyst is quoted in McLean, "Why Enron Went Bust," p. 3. See also the Economist.com, Nov. 29, 2001, p. 2.

12. Quoted in Marie Brenner, "The Enron Wars," *Vanity Fair,* April 2002, p. 190 and John Schwartz, "As Enron Purged Its Ranks, Dissent Was Swept Away," *New York Times,* Feb. 3, 2002, p. C1.

13. Skilling is quoted in John Schwartz, "Darth Vader. Machiavelli. Skilling Set Intense Pace," *New York Times On the Web,* Feb. 7, 2002, pp. 2–3.

14. Farrell and Woodyard, "Three Powerful Men Forged Enron's Path," p. 3B; Thomas A. Stewart, "Taking Risk to the Marketplace," *Fortune.com,* March 6, 2000, p. 1; Schwartz, "As Enron Purged Its Ranks, Dissent Was Swept Away," p. C1.

15. Ken Lay is quoted in "Skilling Named Enron CEO," FinancialTimes.com, Dec. 14, 2000, p. 1. The banner change is reported in the Economist.com, June 28, 2001, p. 2.

16. Bethany McLean, "Enron's Power Crisis," Fortune.com, Sept. 17, 2001, p. 1; John Schwartz, "Darth Vader. Machiavelli. Skilling Set the Pace," *New York Times On the Web,* Feb. 7, 2002, p. 2.

17. Skilling and Olson quoted in Nicholas Stein, "Winning the War To Keep Top Talent," Fortune.com, May 29, 2000, p. 4. Pai quoted in *Hamel, Leading the Revolution,* p. 271.

18. Skilling is quoted in *Hamel, Leading the Revolution,* p. 216. McConnell is quoted in Economist.com, June 28, 2001, p. 4. On Enron Online, see also Economist.com, June 28, 2001, p. 2 and Nicholas Stein, "The World's Most Admired Companies," Fortune.com, Oct. 2, 2000, p. 2.

19. Economist.com, June 1, 2000, p. 1; McLean, "Why Enron Went Bust," p. 2; *Washington Post,* Jan. 27, 2002, p. A1; "Enron's Aggressive Risk-Taking Culture That Eventually Led to Its Demise, *National Public Radio's All Things Considered,* Feb. 6, 2002.

20. Lay is quoted in *Fortune,* June 23, 1997, p. 87. Ron Lumbra of Russell Reynolds Associates is quoted in *Houston Chronicle,* Dec. 9, 2001, p. A1.

21. Economist.com, Feb. 26, 1998, p. 1; *Hamel, Leading the Revolution,* p. 213; Corey Kilgannon, "Coincidences From a Case 15 Years Old," *New York Times On the Web,* March 5, 2002, pp. 2–3.

22. Quoted in Andrew Inkpen, Enron and the Dabhol Power Company (American Graduate School of International Management/Thunderbird, 2002), p. 2.

23. Johnnie L. Roberts and Evan Thomas, "Enron's Dirty Laundry," *Newsweek,* March 11, 2002, p. 25.

24. *New York Times,* March 7, 2002, p. C7. Mark is quoted in V. Kasturi and Krishna G. Palepu, Enron Development Corporation: The Dabhol Power Project in Maharashtra, India (A). (Boston: Harvard Business School Publishing, 1997), p. 1. The Enron executive is quoted in Inkpen, Enron and the Dabhol Power Company, p. 2.

25. Laura Goldberg and Tom Fowler, "The Myth of Enron," HoustonChronicle.com, Jan. 26, 2002, p. 2; *New York Times,* March 9, 2002, p. B3.

26. Skilling is quoted in Thomas A. Stewart, "Taking Risk to the Marketplace," Fortune.com, March 6, 2000, p. 1; Olson is quoted in Nicholas Stein, "Winning the War To Keep Talent," Fortune.com, May 29, 2000, p. 2.

27. Stewart, "Taking Risk to the Marketplace," p. 2.

28. Matthew Boyle, "Performance Reviews: Perilous Curves Ahead," Fortune.com, May 28, 2001, p. 1.

29. Stein, "Winning the War To Keep Talent," p. 4; *Houston Chronicle,* Dec. 9, 2001, p. A1; Joshua Chaffin and Stephen Fidler, "The Enron Collapse," *Financial Times,* April 9, 2002, p. 30.

30. Brenner, "The Enron Wars," p. 196; Schwartz, "As Enron Purged Its Ranks, Dissent Was Swept Away," p. C1; Neela Banerjee, "At Enron, Lavish excess Often Came Before Success," *New York Times,* Feb. 26, 2002, p. C1. Lay is quoted in Brenner, "The Enron Wars," p. 195.

31. The executive is quoted in Hamel, *Leading the Revolution,* p. 271; *Houston Chronicle,* Dec. 9, 2001, p. A1. Information on Fastow's bonuses as documented by company records, is reported in Kurt Eichenwald, "Enron Paid Huge Bonuses in '01; Experts See a Motive for Cheating," *New York Times on the Web,* March 1, 2002, p. 2. On John Arnold's bonus, see David Barboza, "Enron Trader Had a Year to Boast of, Even If . . ." *New York Times,* July 9, 2002, p. C1.

32. If stock options were counted as an expense, profitability of many large corporations would be reduced substantially. A study by the Federal Reserve estimated that between 1995 and 2000, the average earnings growth rate for S&P 500 companies would have been reduced by 25 percent if stock options had been reported as expenses. When the option is exercised, the issuing company declares a tax deduction based on the difference between the option price and the exercise price. The exercise of stock options by all Enron executives in 2000 accounted for a $390 million tax break for the company.

33. Skilling is quoted in "Transcript of Senate Commerce Committee Hearing on Enron," p. 41. On his 2000 stock option income, see "Stock Option Excess," *New York Times,* March 31, 2002, Section 4, p. 8.

34. All quotes are from the *Houston Chronicle,* Dec. 9, 2001, p. A1.

35. Lay is quoted in Economist.com, June 1, 2000, p. 2.

36. Hamel, *Leading the Revolution,* p. 214.

37. Gruley and Smith, "Keys to Success Left Kenneth Lay Open to Disaster," p. A5.

38. Bethany McLean, "Is Enron Overpriced?" Fortune.com, March 5, 2001, p. 1.

39. Quoted in *Houston Chronicle,* Dec. 9, 2001, p. A1.

40. Quotes from Richard A. Oppel, Jr., "The Man Who Paid the Price For Sizing Up Enron," *New York Times,* March 27, 2002, pp. C1, C4.

41. "Enron CEO Jeffrey Skilling Unexpectedly Resigns," FinancialTimes.com, Aug. 14, 2001, p. 1.

42. The full text of this memo is provided in Fortune.com, Jan. 16, 2001, pp. 1–6.

43. In August 2002 Michael Kopper pleaded guilty to charges of conspiring to commit fraud and money laundering in connection to these partnerships. Federal investigators made clear that the Kopper plea bargain was only the beginning in the prosecution of other Enron executives.

44. It is this committee that, on October 23—a day after the S.E.C. announced that they had opened an investigation into "certain related party transactions"—commenced the destruction of thousands of Enron-related documents. That destruction led, eight months later, to the conviction of Andersen on federal charges of obstruction of justice.

45. "Analysts Vent Anger at 'Hidden' Enron Charge," FinancialTimes.com, Oct. 18, 2001, p. 1.

ORANGEWERKS: A QUESTION OF ETHICS

*Prepared by Ken Mark under the
supervision of Professor Christina Cavanagh*

Copyright © 2001, Ivey Management Services

Version: (A) 2001-03-23

INTRODUCTION

David Samarin, network administrator for OrangeWerks, laced his skates as he prepared to head out for his lunch break on Ottawa's now-frozen Rideau Canal. It was December 28, 2000, and Samarin needed to decide what to do with the information he had uncovered while performing a routine file-clean of his company's servers.

Located in Ottawa's trendy Glebe neighborhood, software developer OrangeWerks was preparing to present to venture capital firms for its first major round of funding. It was also fielding media interview requests the following week from the *Ottawa Citizen* and *The National Post,* both interested in writing news stories about OrangeWerk's phenomenal increase in business-to-business software licenses for its Content-In-Color (CIC) product.

ORANGEWERKS

OrangeWerks was founded in March 2000 by two successful entrepreneurs to create software applications for the Palm OS Platform. The founders had noticed the growing popularity of Palm hand-held organizers since the device's launch in 1996. Furthermore, independent research by firms as diverse as Merrill Lynch, Forrester and Jupiter MediaMetrix suggested that the consumer market would continue to demand these and other hand-held products designed to wirelessly access the Internet.

Fueling the popularity of Palm OS-based organizers was the proliferation of Web sites serving stripped-down content designed for these relatively low-powered machines (Palm processors operated at an average 30 megahertz [Mhz] versus 900 Mhz for the newest desktop computers).

OrangeWerks proposed a "Content-In-Color" software tool (CIC) that enabled development of color-rich Web sites specifically for access by Palm OS handhelds.

To attract media attention, OrangeWerks had been targeting business customers for CIC, reporting on December 15, 2000, that the number of business software licences awarded for both its rough and beta versions had jumped from 1,500 to 20,000 in the last two months.

STAFFING ORANGEWERKS

The founders had assembled their team largely from personal connections, and Samarin was employee number five and their first engineer hired. Although hired as chief product developer, Samarin was initially tasked with everything from setting up desktop computers for the public relations consultants and marketing personnel to fixing broken light bulbs. His projects also included configuring OrangeWerk's hardware and software to run its Web site and internal operations.

SAMARIN'S FIRST PROJECTS

Starting with personal funds of less than Cdn$20,000, the two founders had intended to seek angel funding immediately. To do that, they needed to show that they were on track to building a viable business. First, they needed a Web site, and a staff of developers to create a working model of their software program.

For OrangeWerk's software platform, the company asked Samarin to create a functioning Oracle database on top of a UNIX-based operating system. Samarin realized that the five-year-old server and packet switching hardware that they had recently purchased to run the software was outdated and inadequate. He convinced the

founders that they would have to acquire newer server boxes and Web switches to achieve the desired functionality. Reluctantly, Samarin's request was met after a week of indecision.

When the new hardware arrived in April 2000, Samarin offered to telephone the major software companies to purchase the requisite Oracle and Sun Solaris (UNIX) software licenses. Thus, Samarin was surprised when the founders decided to take the discussion out of the office by inviting him to a lunch meeting. OrangeWerks had been in operation for four weeks at this point, and had only five employees.

THE REQUEST

Over lunch at the "Market" (as the Byward Market was known in Ottawa), Samarin was informed that no more funds existed for the purchase of software. Samarin was told that it was his responsibility to load software onto the machines.

Samarin had several other projects that were awaiting his attention, but he did not want to disappoint his friends and new employers. Relying on several industry contacts, Samarin acquired new, cracked[1] versions of software required to run OrangeWerk's operations.

Known in the software industry as "warez,"[2] these were fully functional software programs made available to the public by software engineers who had cracked the software's security and validation codes. Legitimate users typically purchased a software license from the supplier, who included a code to validate the software, making it available for use. Samarin knew that it was not legal to condone the use of warez. He explained:

> Of course I know it's an ethical dilemma. But which side of the line do I stand on? The white line, the black line, or do I thread the fine line in the middle?

THE ANGEL ROUND OF FUNDING

One month later, in May 2000, OrangeWerks secured Cdn$3 million in funding from various angel investors in Canada and the United States.

The founders were extremely proud of having secured the amount, in spite of the fact that the technology-heavy NASDAQ stock index's devaluation was destroying investor confidence. Euphoric, they embarked on an office expansion, hired another 45 people, and prepared a fall marketing campaign.

Samarin was rewarded with a bonus of Cdn$5,000, payable upon completion of a year's work, but was reassigned as a network administrator.

Samarin did not notice any attempt by the founders to acquire software licence agreements.

RAPID GROWTH AT ORANGEWERKS

With the infusion, a newly hired team of 35 engineers began coding the first beta release of CIC. The team of marketers were given cellular phones and unlimited travel budgets to fly to seminars and conferences (often business class) to promote CIC. Booths were purchased at COMDEX in Las Vegas and OrangeWerks representatives were sent to PalmSource 2000 to drum up interest in CIC. The Canadian media, hungry for stories in the slow August to September period, pounced on the chance to tout OrangeWerks as the most promising start-up in the new wireless hand-held market, generating thousands of media impressions in the process.

PROGRESS IS SLOWED

But the internal climate at OrangeWerks was different. The team of 35 engineers had split into three factions, bickering over creative control of the project. In the process, engineering work for CIC stalled, and key engineers tendered their resignations in frustration. By November 2000, OrangeWerks had only a rough working model of CIC. However, plans were still in place to approach venture capitalists in December for Cdn$15 million, and interested parties were still being promised a December beta release.

THE FOUNDERS TAKE ACTION

The two founders began taking control of the situation in late November, firing 20 of the software engineers and giving the remaining team new goals to meet. Within two weeks, the situation stabilized and a climate of productivity returned. It seemed that a sense of urgency at OrangeWerks had re-emerged, and on the 12th of December, the founders announced to employees that the beta version was ready.

A press release was issued on the 15th of December, announcing that OrangeWerks' CIC was being rapidly adopted by the developer community, reaching 20,000 licences awarded. The licences had been awarded at no cost to developers in order to rapidly gain market share.[3] OrangeWerks, paraphrasing a company press release, explained that it intended to charge developers for its 1.0 release.

THE DISCOVERY

As part of his monthly duties, Samarin performed a file-clean-up of OrangeWerk's internal LAN file folders.

One of the founders had purchased a new computer and had asked Samarin to load new software and transfer old files for him.

While manually transferring the files on the morning of December 28, Samarin recovered a deleted e-mail. In the e-mail fragment, the founder outlined that 15,000 fake accounts had been created by him to download the CIC program. The e-mail had apparently been written to the other founder in order to inform him of this occurrence.

Scrolling further, he chanced upon a more recent e-mail fragment from the Canadian Workers' Safety and Insurance Board (WSIB):

> ... You have not filled out the necessary forms to register your company with the WSIB ... the employees of OrangeWerks are not covered and cannot claim benefits if they are involved in a workplace accident ... you are in direct violation of workplace safety standards.

Perplexed, Samarin shut down the computers and headed out for his break.

SAMARIN'S DILEMMA

Finishing his skate, Samarin decided to take an extended lunch to stroll around Ottawa's Parliament buildings. Even though it was 15 degrees below zero, Samarin did not notice the biting cold. He had other things on his mind.

> Has OrangeWerks paid for the software we use to create CIC? What do these e-mail fragments mean?

> We're not covered under the WSIB. If I had fallen and broken my neck while changing light bulbs or electrocuted myself while wiring computers, I would have been finished.

Calming himself, Samarin headed back to his desk at OrangeWerks. He had a lot to think about.

NOTES

1. "Cracked" refers to the fact that the security code has been cracked, enabling use of the program without purchase.

2. Pronounced "wares."

3. It was common practice in the software industry to award free licences to developers willing to test a new software tool. At the company's discretion, a fee could be charged for subsequent software upgrades.

WWW.CENTRALMBA.COM

Prepared by Professors Michael Parent and Robert J. Fisher

Copyright © 1999, Ivey Management Services   Version: (A) 2004-11-23

Dave Newman, Associate Dean—Programs at the School of Business at Central University, stared at his computer screen in disbelief. Acting on an e-mail message from an Executive MBA student, he'd typed the Uniform Resource Locator (URL) "www.centralmba.com" into the address line of his Web browser, and watched in amazement as the home page for Central's closest competitor, State University's Executive MBA Program, loaded onto his monitor.

While competition between the two schools for Executive Education students had been particularly fierce over the past few months, he refused to believe that State or its agents might resort to such action. He wondered what Central should do about it, if anything at all.

THE GROWING COMPETITION IN EXECUTIVE EDUCATION

Executive Education programs were intensive, part-time educational programs that lasted from one to three weeks and did not award a university degree for completion. Program participants tended to be middle- or upper-level managers in large organizations who did not hold a graduate degree. In 1999, the cost for top-tier non-degree programs was approximately $6,000 per week, including meals and accommodation, and a variety of recreational and social activities. In contrast, full-time MBA degree programs typically lasted two years and cost between $12,000 and $15,000 per year. Participants of both degree and non-degree programs selected a school on the basis of a number of factors such as cost, educational benefits, program prestige, and networking potential.

The competition between Central and State began in the early 1980s, when State entered the two-week executive education market with non-degree programs in human resources management and industrial relations. State had got up and running by hiring several Central faculty (including Newman) to teach on a part-time basis. Strong demand led State to expand its non-degree product line to the general management, marketing, operations, finance, and strategy areas. In addition, State, like Central, also offered a full-time MBA program, albeit on a smaller scale.

While State programs now differed from Central's in several significant ways, perhaps the most obvious distinction was program faculty. Whereas Central used only faculty from its own school, State used faculty from other academic institutions, as well as management consulting firms, and private companies. Program content also differed. Central was known for the case method which required the application of broad skills, concepts and approaches on core issues to real managerial problems. Its executive education classes used this method of learning almost exclusively. State, on the other hand, placed a much greater emphasis on lecture-discussions that claimed to deal with current managerial concepts and frameworks. A final major difference was in the marketing area. Although both institutions offered an internet presence, provided a full range of glossy brochures, and advertised frequently in leading business publications, State was seen to be much more aggressive by Newman. State routinely claimed to offer the "number one" MBA, and compared itself to leading international business schools in its advertising.

Newman recognized that State now threatened Central's market leadership in executive education, and recent actions made him uneasy. In particular, State was now offering a video executive MBA program in Central's hometown. This relatively new technology, which Central had pioneered in the region, enabled State to "produce" executive education in one location and "distribute" it to students across the country in a flexible and efficient manner. They were supporting the launch with information sessions at a local hotel and a series of provocative half-page ads in the region's major newspapers.

Newman was convinced that competition between State and Central would remain fierce and probably intensify over the next few years. According to his estimates, approximately $350 million was being spent in their market each year on university-based executive education (as opposed to executive education supplied by consultants or in-house personnel), and the industry was highly profitable. Nevertheless, overall growth was flat and so a market share increase by State would almost certainly come partly at Central's expense. He was determined not to let this happen.

METATAGGING, IP ADDRESSING AND CYBERSTUFFING

Hypertext Markup Language (HTML) was developed to publish information on the Internet using Web browsers like Internet Explorer and Netscape. Unlike more traditional languages, HTML allowed for easy embedding of images into a document, and supported a wide range of typefaces. A key component of HTML was insertion of special codes, or "tags," that instructed Web browsers on where to insert page breaks, new paragraphs, images and the like. HTML tags were hidden from normal view, though they might be seen using a browser's "View Source" function.

One special type of HTML tag was the "meta-tag." As its name implies, the meta-tag contained information about the HTML document such as its author, its expiration date, its version date, a description of its contents and a list of keywords describing the page. Users did not directly see these tags, even though they were used by browsers to load pages onto their computer screens.

When users typed in a text-based address (such as www.centralmba.com) their server, or computer connecting them to the Internet, translated that address into a numerical one. This numeric address was called the "IP Address." The global standard form of an IP address was *protocol://machine:port number/ filename.* "HTTP," the most common prefix on the World Wide Web (WWW), referred to the "hypertext transfer protocol" used by public pages on the WWW. Thus, the English-language Internet address http://myhomepage.com was actually interpreted by the computer as a 12-digit number like 111.111.111.22.3. Coding a page then involved cross-referencing the alphabetical name to the numeric one so that every time someone typed in a given address, they were sent to the same location.

Meta-tags were also used extensively by Web Search Engines—programs which "found" pages for users based on keywords they typed in. Search Engines, like Yahoo, Alta Vista, and Lycos, created indexes of Web pages. For example, in Yahoo's case, the engine presented a number of links to pages based on broad categories selected by users. Some Web sites, anxious to promote their pages to as wide an audience as possible, tried to fool search engines by including as many keywords as possible on their pages. This practice, known as "cyberstuffing," attempted to ensure that a given Web page came up in the first five or ten listed by a search engine in order to encourage users to "click on." For example, five years ago, when the Web was still in its infancy, adding the word "sex" to a page's meta-tags was an almost surefire way to generate "hits"—at least until every other developer caught on! Today, most search engines either disregarded meta-tags altogether (Excite, for example), or use them in conjunction with their own rules for categorizing Web pages.

It remained possible, though, for Web page developers to take advantage of meta-tags by including and registering alphabetic addresses, or "domain names," that were permutations of their company names in order to ensure that users reached their pages. For example, General Motors might include in its home page's meta-tags the names "GM," "GMC," "Chevrolet," "Chevy" or any of its other brands in order to ensure as broad coverage of its trademarked names as possible.

REGISTERING DOMAIN NAMES

The Domain Name System (DNS) was created by the Internet Society (ISOC), a joint government-industry governing body regulating the assignment of domain names on the Internet. As of 1999, the most popular naming authority was the Internet Network Information Centre (InterNIC) run by Network Solutions company at www.network solutions.com. Network Solutions held an exclusive licence over all site names ending in the ".com," ".net," ".org" and ".edu" suffixes.

In order to register a domain name, applicants filled in an application online at Network Solutions' site, and paid a registration fee of about $100. Ongoing yearly renewal fees also amounted to about $100. Network Solutions was a registration service, and acted as a clearing-house for domain names. It did not have the resources, nor was it willing, to monitor registrations, although it would cancel illegitimate or inappropriate registrations. Network Solutions' Web site included its own search engine, allowing prospective registrants to see if the name they were interested in had already been registered, or conversely, to obtain a list of all names that had been registered.

The ability to see what had and had not been registered led to speculation on the part of some investors. Perhaps the most famous case of domain name speculation involved Joshua Quittner, who, writing in *Wired Magazine's* October 1994 issue, registered the domain name www.McDonalds.com. Quittner and McDonald's eventually settled out-of-court for a $3,500 donation to a New York City school, and the practice of speculating on domain names had since been disallowed. However, domain name speculation remained unavoidable, and Network Solutions only reacted by rescinding unauthorized registrations.

CENTRAL'S REACTION

A search of Network Solutions' registry by Central's Marketing and Communications department chief revealed that the domain name www.centralmba.com had been registered on February 17, 1999 by WebAd, Incorporated, State School of Business' advertising agency-of-record. The Network Solutions' record listed Jake Web, the agency's principal, as the main contact.

To Newman, this removed the possibility of a malicious hack or student prank. The question was, what should the Central School of Business do?

Newman saw two main options. The first was to simply do nothing. If prospective Executive MBA students wanting information on Central's programs typed in what they thought might be Central's address and obtained information on State's programs, they'd likely be annoyed, and feel ill-will towards State for doing this. State's strategy might, in fact, backfire, and work to Central's advantage. On the other hand, doing nothing might tacitly condone this behavior. Prospective students who weren't familiar with Central might think that Central was part of State University. Newman was particularly concerned about this issue because the business school name had been changed to "Central" in 1996. Further, prospective students who had sought information on Central might examine State programs as well, "since they were already at the site."

The second option involved varying degrees of remedial action. A number of similar precedent-setting cases had already been adjudicated. Newman felt confident that Central could at the very least compel State to remove this meta-tag from their page and rescind their registration. On the far end of this spectrum, Central could sue State for copyright infringement, or even generate negative publicity of its own against State programs. Newman realized, though, that this would be time-consuming, expensive, and might even work against Central.

Newman also wondered about the marketing implications of any follow-up action. The two schools had been competing fiercely for students in their programs. Newman wondered if drawing attention to this situation might not affect the overall market for executive education.

Finally, Newman was concerned about Central's own internal processes, infrastructure and procedures. Who should be responsible for monitoring the Web, and competitors' actions? Should it be the school's Webmaster? Program directors? Marketing or some other central function? Should the school have registered all possible permutations and combinations of its name, programs, and degrees? What actions should be taken, by whom, to ensure this didn't happen again?

ETHICS MANAGEMENT AT IMPERIAL OIL LTD.

*Prepared by Nadine Hayes under
the supervision of Professor Jeffrey Gandz*

    Version: (A) 2003-05-05

As Ron Willoughby, communications manager in Esso Petroleum Canada, looked back on his many years with Imperial Oil Limited (IOL), he wondered what useful recommendations he could leave with the company in view of his approaching retirement. Specifically, he was concerned about several incidents that had taken place that were in conflict with the company's code of ethics. He wondered what the company could do to minimize the occurrence of these incidents and whether IOL was doing something wrong, not doing enough, or doing all it could reasonably be expected to do.

BACKGROUND

Imperial Oil Limited and its family of companies was one of Canada's largest energy companies, with 1985 earnings from operations at $684 million. It consisted of three major operating segments:

- Esso Resources Canada Limited, a wholly-owned subsidiary involved in the production of crude oil, natural gas and coal, contributed $542 million to 1985 earnings from operations;

- Esso Petroleum Canada, a division of Imperial, with 1985 earnings from operations at $93 million, operated five refineries and marketed petroleum products; and
- Esso Chemical Canada, another division, produced and marketed a wide variety of fertilizers and petrochemicals and had earnings from operations of $5 million in 1985.

In addition to these major operating segments, Imperial was involved in several other areas: Building Products of Canada Limited, a wholly-owned subsidiary, produced construction materials; Esso Minerals Canada, a division of Esso Resources, explored for profitable investment opportunities in minerals unrelated to energy; and a property development group provided a variety of real-estate services to the company.

Although Imperial was 69.6 per cent owned by Exxon Corporation of the United States, approximately one-fourth of its outstanding shares were held by some 31,000 Canadian residents. Most of the directors were Canadians, and Imperial was well-known for its pursuit of policies and practices that supported the Canadian economy, such as its "buy Canadian" policy.

CORPORATE CULTURE

Incorporated in 1880 by 16 London, Ontario businessmen, IOL had a reputation as a socially conscious and responsible organization. Frederick Fitzgerald, the first president of IOL and described as "a man of unbending honor and incorruptible honesty," was the first in a long line of patriarchal figures who established a strong corporate culture oriented towards high ethical standards. Imperial earned this reputation for fair and ethical business practices through progressive policies in the areas of internal organizational effectiveness and human resources management. It was the first Canadian company to adopt a system of joint industrial councils in 1918; one of the first to permit four- and three-day compressed work weeks and flexible hours in 1932; one of the first Canadian business corporations to offer major support to Canadian

culture with the purchase of the Canadian-made film classic "The Loon's Necklace"; the largest Canadian corporate contributor to the arts, amateur sports, education and community service; and one of the first to support employee health centres that offered company medicals, with the frequency of visits correlated to the age of the employees. As part of this commitment, Imperial believed that it provided excellent pay levels closely linked to performance, and administered comprehensive benefit plans with items such as physical fitness refunds or the payment of higher education tuition costs for children of both current employees and retirees.

The extent and strength of Imperial's ethical culture was difficult to describe. It was spoken of by employees, not as something that they were continually aware of, but merely as "a way of life." This way of life was sustained by both control mechanisms and "a tremendous amount of trust" between the company and its employees.

In fact, Imperial's ethical standards were often emulated by other companies attempting to upgrade their own standards. One Royal Bank employee commented:

> As we begin the job of reviewing and refining our code of ethics and how to apply it, Imperial's code and the way it implements it are invaluable models.

ETHICS POLICY

The ethics policy at IOL was not administered from one functional area, but had bases of responsibility in several departments. The range of tools used to ensure employee participation in ethical business practices was best described in the form of two action phases: the proactive phase and the reactive phase.

The proactive phase of Imperial's ethics policy sought, through communication tools, to raise employees' awareness of potentially difficult situations, and to educate them in IOL's definition of appropriate business practice. Richard Michaelides, vice-president public affairs and general secretary, described IOL's communication process as a central element in the company's ethical culture because, as he stated, "there is no point in enforcing something people know nothing about." The tools considered to be proactive consisted of:

- a corporate ethics booklet;
- an annual sign-off procedure;
- the integration of ethics into training and orientation material;
- an annual review process conducted at the individual department/division level;
- the integration of ethics into company policies and procedures through the Framework of Management Control; and
- the Business Practice workshops that presented material contained in the Framework of Management Control to IOL employees.

Corporate Ethics Booklet

The 20-page corporate ethics booklet outlining IOL's expectations of behaviour with respect to business dealings was the core tool of the ethics policy. It was prepared, coordinated and updated through the general secretary's department and therefore focussed at the corporate level. However, it was applied, implemented and tested within all IOL's operating arms and subsidiaries. The content was purposely designed to be general and understandable, and to prevent any impediment in its application to the unique business units.

The booklet stressed the need for integrity in relationships (both within the company itself and in its external dealings) and made reference to a series of stakeholders that should be given due consideration during the decision-making process: employees; shareholders, including Exxon; customers; sales associates; suppliers; and the communities within which IOL operated.

The booklet was firm in its requirement for employees to follow the letter of the law in areas such as combines and conflict of interest. However, it was also explicit in its requirement for them to follow the "spirit" of the law. The concern for both the letter and spirit of the law stemmed from a desire to have both the perception of fairness, as well as the reality, open to public opinion. This was considered an "absolute

must" due to IOL's size and level of foreign ownership and was well summarized in the booklet:

> It has always been the policy of Imperial Oil and the Esso family of companies to maintain the highest standard of ethics in its relations with whomever it does business or is associated with— its employees, shareholders, customers, sales associates, suppliers, governments, and the public. No director or employee, from the chief executive officer to the newest staff member, is ever expected to commit an illegal or unethical act. Not in the name of business efficiency. Not to get results. Not for any other reason.

> In addition to strict compliance with all laws applicable to company business, the highest standards of integrity must be observed throughout the organization. The company's reputation for ethical practices is one of its most valued assets. This reputation was achieved through the efforts of its employees and their avoidance of any activity or interest that might reflect unfavourably upon their own or the company's integrity or good name.

Since its inception approximately 10 years ago, the corporate ethics booklet was given to each new employee, and distributed to all employees whenever it was updated, approximately every two years. Several very specific and explicit addenda were included for individuals in especially sensitive areas (Exhibit 1). To ensure that the addenda were understood and followed, an annual sign-off process was in place.

Annual Sign-Off

Each year, approximately one-half of all IOL's 14,000 employees were required to sign an assent document stating that they had read or re-read the corporate ethics booklet, that it was understandable to them, and that they had been in compliance with it over the previous year. This sign-off procedure, administered by the general secretary's department, was designed for supervisors who had responsibility for sensitive areas, but it was not uncommon for those supervisors to require their staff to sign the document. As well as being a tool that communicated the company's ethical orientation, the actual signing-off was intended to induce

Addendum 2
Gifts and entertainment

Statement of basic principles

It is company policy to discourage the receiving of gifts or entertainment by employees from persons outside the company, and to discourage the giving of gifts or entertainment by employees on behalf of the company to persons outside the company. Such practices are permissible only where they involve moderate values and conform to the following basic principles:

- they are infrequent
- they legitimately serve a definite business purpose
- they are appropriate to the business responsibilities of the individuals
- they are within limits of reciprocation as a normal business expense

Gifts

Employees should neither give nor receive cash gifts or commissions, loans, shares in profit, securities or the equivalent of any of these things.

Employees should neither give nor receive gifts with more than a nominal value without the knowledge and consent of their department head, or functional vice-president, or where appropriate, an executive vice-president of the company. The current level deemed to be of nominal value is $25 or less.

Entertainment and business meetings

The company discourages giving or receiving entertainment (dining or an amusement, sporting or recreational event); however, it is recognized that entertainment within the basic principles in the policy may be appropriate from time to time.

Full statement of policy

A full statement of the company's policy on gifts and entertainment is available from division or department management.

Exhibit 1

personal commitment from those employees who actively put their name on that document.

Integration Into Training and Orientation

The corporate human resources department took an active part in communicating Imperial's high ethical standards, beginning with the recruitment stage, through orientation and into management development.

While recruiters for Imperial Oil did not explicitly search out individuals they felt were "relatively more ethical," the interview process did incorporate an implicit "ethical" criterion. It tried to attract individuals with an initial mental set that would be compatible with IOL's high standards. The interviewer maintained an awareness for what people said was important to them and how they spoke about what they had done, and when a suitable individual was found, the prospective employee was made well aware of IOL's expectations of behaviour with respect to relations with both co-workers and business associates before an employment contract was confirmed.

New management-level hires at IOL would spend their first two years at Imperial becoming familiar with the culture, the accepted methods of business practice and the general atmosphere of such a large corporation. They would then be taken through a two-to-three-day orientation session as part of IOL's planning and development training. The ethics component would be discussed in the context of where the concern for ethical activity originally stemmed from, and what it did **for** IOL rather than **to** it. The tools used in these sessions included simulated ethical situations on videotapes, as well as group discussions over actual cases. A similar format was used in the annual review process.

Annual Review Process

Each department or division was responsible for conducting an annual business practices, ethics and control review. These were not consistently applied throughout IOL or its family of companies, in order to allow managers in these companies to mold the process to their specific departmental requirements. This flexibility allowed managers to discuss specifics with their staff, as well as retaining the autonomy in decision-making that was very much a part of IOL's management philosophy.

Examples from two departments illustrate both the diversity and the common threads that ran through the reviews. The general secretary's department, which handled confidential information and corporate security, used a "Business Ethics Compliance Checklist" for its annual review process (Exhibit 2). The list addressed sensitive activities or situations commonly encountered in that area. Once a year, the 60-member department would be divided into groups of 20 or 30, which would then analyze the previous year's activities against the checklist. Each situation on the checklist was discussed to ensure that everyone had complete understanding of its implications, and to determine if re-definition was necessary. In addition to the situations specified on the annual list, situations were presented that had not been covered. One of the requisite items asked if the individual had re-read the booklet, and if they had understood it. This systematic process acted as a catalyst to ensure that the policies outlined at the corporate level were both understandable and applicable to the day-to-day jobs.

Hilda Mackow, communications manager in the Retail Department of Esso Petroleum Canada, used a less formal, more specific annual review process. As her department had responsibility for dealing with suppliers for printed communication needs and promotion ideas, she felt that her department was in a highly sensitive area that could be vulnerable to unethical temptations. For this reason, she chose to run a seminar-type workshop with her 15 managers where they discussed specific situations that had occurred, or that they felt could possibly be encountered. These were used, not to pass judgment on whether the decision taken had been the appropriate one, but to determine how similar situations could best be handled. This format allowed

(Text continues on page 199)

| | EHB 030-003 |
| | |

| EMPLOYEE HANDBOOK | SECTION:
CORPORATE ETHICS/CONFLICT OF INTEREST |
| | SUBJECT:
BUSINESS ETHICS CHECKLIST |

September 4, 1986

PUBLIC AFFAIRS AND SECRETARY'S DEPARTMENT EMPLOYEES

BUSINESS ETHICS COMPLIANCE CHECKLIST

The business ethics checklist has been reviewed at secretary's division meetings to ensure everyone understands the requirements and that possible areas of concern are identified.

Changes to the checklist this year are minor, but you should note section (I) that requires each of us to be knowledgable and adhere to the department's microcomputer security and control guidelines. (Copies of the guidelines and instructions are available through business services)

If at any time you have any questions on any of the items on the checklist, or if you are aware of anything we are doing which is contrary to them, please talk to me or any one of our senior managers.

RJMichaelides/cac

| DATE: | | PAGE: |
| September 1986 | | 1 |

Exhibit 2   *(Continued)*

EHB 030-003

SECTION:	SUBJECT:
CORPORATE ETHICS/CONFLICT OF INTEREST	BUSINESS ETHICS CHECKLIST

<u>PUBLIC AFFAIRS AND SECRETARY'S DEPARTMENT</u>

The following list supports the company's policies and guidelines given in "Our Corporate Ethics" providing a checklist of items of particular significance to public affairs and secretary's department.

A) <u>ETHICS</u>

<u>Corporate ethics booklet:</u>
- employees aware of the standards set down in the booklet. Copies are given to new employees.

<u>Conflicts of interest policy and combines law statement:</u>
- all appropriate employees read and sign the form contained in this booklet, including new employees to the department. Employees sign-off for compliance on an annual basis.

B) <u>INFORMATION HANDLING AND REPORTING</u>

<u>Safeguarding company information:</u>
- all public affairs and secretary's personnel recognize the responsibility to maintain the confidentiality of sensitive information. This would include items such as board and management committee matters, shareholder ownership records, earnings and other financial data, employee records, etc. Personnel must be concerned about verbal communication, security of paper documents, and security of documents in the electronic media, e.g. word processing.

<u>Disclosure guidelines - investor relations:</u>
- awareness of and understanding of up-to-date guidelines for discretionary disclosure; press releases, speeches and informal remarks to be checked against guidelines; questionable items to be cleared with law department and/or investor relations manager.

<u>Reporting to government:</u>
- copies of regulations on reporting are up-to-date and employees are familiar with the reporting requirements, e.g. corporate business acts filings, insider trading reporting.

- all accidents requiring the attention of a physician outside 111 St. Clair are <u>immediately</u> reported to Workmen's Compensation by the supervisor through the business services manager. Employees report any first aid incidents or injury concerns to their supervisor. Supervisors maintain a record of these incidents or suspected injuries.

DATE:		PAGE:
September 1986		2

Exhibit 2   *(Continued)*

```
                                        | EHB 030-003
                                        |
```

SECTION:	SUBJECT:
CORPORATE ETHICS/CONFLICT OF INTEREST	BUSINESS ETHICS COMPLIANCE CHECKLIST

INFORMATION HANDLING AND REPORTING (cont'd)

<u>Applications to government departments and agencies for permits, etc.:</u>
- proper channels, using prescribed forms; no undue pressure or unusual communications, e.g. changes to articles, Access to Information Act, etc.

C) <u>CONTRIBUTION TO OUTSIDE ORGANIZATIONS</u>

<u>Contributions to political organizations:</u>
- no direct or indirect donations permitted; employees attending events where part of the ticket price is considered a donation must buy the tickets personally; no reimbursement by company.

<u>Employees requested by supervisors to become involved in outside organizations, professional bodies, charities, and to do personal work:</u>
- differentiate between attendance as employee or in personal capacity; safeguard confidentiality of proprietary information and procedures; speeches and presentations to be cleared with superiors; sensitivity to combines requirements recompetition

- review for instances where undue influence is exerted by the supervisor on employees to participate in outside activities not essential to carrying out their jobs

- check to ensure that it is totally voluntary on part of individual and degree to which activity is to Imperial's benefit.

<u>Use of company in-house facilities and services for personal purposes:</u>
- clearly defined limits; clearance with supervisor.

D) <u>ENTERTAINMENT AND GIFTS</u>

<u>Contact with and entertainment of government officials and other outsiders:</u>
- legitimate business purposes; reasonable value; in line with industry norms; reciprocal relationships.

<u>Entertainment of company associates and subordinates:</u>
- legitimate expense if guest from another geographic area; generally no reimbursement if same area, unless special purpose (e.g. sensitive or confidential topic best handled in an outside setting, anniversaries, termination, or transfers).

<u>Granting and receiving transportation:</u>
- proper permission to invite outsiders to use company planes; legitimate reason to accept ticket or transportation from outsiders: travel by spouse only when attendance required by custom; proper approval.

DATE:		PAGE:
September 1986		3

Exhibit 2 *(Continued)*

	EHB 030-003

SECTION: CORPORATE ETHICS/CONFLICT OF INTEREST	SUBJECT: BUSINESS ETHICS COMPLIANCE CHECKLIST

D) ENTERTAINMENT AND GIFTS (cont'd.)

Acceptance of unsolicited goods or services:
- determine whether gift or sample; if over nominal value, return/decline it or pay for it.

Acceptance of gifts or entertainment from outside businesses:
- nominal value only ($25); anything above to be cleared by a manager; above $100 to be cleared by a senior vice-president.

E) TRAVEL

Choice of hotels and carriers:

- employees are required to use approved hotels and carriers through air transport and reservations, or accomodation at similar cost.

F) CONTRACTORS AND CONSULTANTS

Use of company-engaged contractors, company employees, caterers, etc., for personal use:
- avoid appearance of the unethical; proper documentation of legitimate use; clearance with supervisor if necessary; no acceptance without full payment.

Contracts with consultants and "independent contractors":
- terms are to be fair and ethical and outlined in a letter of agreement or contract.

Ethical obligations of consultants and independent contractors:
- assurance that they subscribe to the same standards as the corporation; managers to decide whether to formalize.

G) PURCHASING

Use of tenders and competitive purchasing:
- all purchasing will be handled by materials and services department who will ensure adherence to the necessary guidelines.

Use of Canadian suppliers:
- purchase decisions to be tested against the company's "buy Canadian" policy.

DATE: September 1986		PAGE: 4

Exhibit 2 *(Continued)*

	EHB 030-003

SECTION:	SUBJECT:
CORPORATE ETHICS/CONFLICT OF INTEREST	BUSINESS ETHICS COMPLIANCE CHECKLIST

H) <u>ACCOUNTING PROCEDURES</u>

<u>Accounting and coding procedures for purchases of goods and services:</u>
- observance of established procedures; care taken not to hide or misrepresent an item

- payment of expenses for staff social external functions should be by the senior person at the function, e.g. department manager or division manager. A subordinate should not pay the bill in order that the expense can be approved within the division. All such expenses are to be recorded on a travelling expense statement form, not reimbursed through a cheque requisition, and approved by the department manager or executive manager, as appropriate.

<u>Documentation of cash transactions to individuals:</u>
- full documentation, including names; while not in themselves illegal, cash transactions should be fully documented for our protection.

<u>Unusual payment procedures:</u>
- payments to third parties, discount arrangements to be used only if standard to the industry and ethical; to be fully documented.

I) <u>COMPUTER SOFTWARE</u>

<u>Microcomputer software:</u>
- the microcomputer security and control guidelines are to be adhered to (copy is available from Business Services). No software program is to be copied without written permission from the Business Services Manager.

J) <u>RIGHTS OF AN EMPLOYEE</u>

<u>Human rights statement:</u>
- if employees are aware of any violations of the company's human rights policy as identified in the corporate ethics booklet, they should report the violation as provided for in the policy.

<u>Harassment guidelines:</u>
- a copy of the corporate harassment guidelines, dealing with harassment in the workplace, has been circulated to employees and is available from business services. (It will be circulated for all detailed business ethics reviews.)

DATE:			PAGE:
September 1986			5

Exhibit 2

open discussion where individuals could speak candidly about experiences they had encountered, and areas they were particularly concerned with.

Framework of Management Control

The internal control system at IOL consisted of numerous policies and procedures. Permeating this system was the orientation toward ethics. The IOL comptroller's office developed a framework of management control that established fundamental principles for ethical and responsible business and administrative practices. It gave a clear indication of IOL's expectations of management behaviour by explicitly stating objectives, and offering examples of the characteristics of appropriate business conduct. Managers then measured their performance against these examples. The alliance of controls and ethics is illustrated by contract clauses.

All contracts entered into by IOL and its family of companies contained three customary clauses that outlined IOL's standards of business practice: an Ethics clause stating that no gifts would be accepted; a Standard of Conduct clause stating that no false billing would be consented to; and an Audit clause stating that IOL retained authority to perform an audit on contractors and suppliers with contracts and major purchase orders.

Another form of integration of ethics and the management control system was exemplified in the Communications department. Mackow felt that contraventions of ethical codes tended to occur as the result of a misrepresentation or misperception. In order to prevent this from occurring, she was careful to ensure that her employees were knowledgeable about what could be verbally misinterpreted, and was able to rely on IOL's internal control measures to present guidelines for verifiable situations such as those involved in bidding procedures, "idea" gathering for promotions, and supplier presentations.

These procedures delineated information flows, documentation and reporting requirements, and were used as the base for the monitoring process.

Mackow stated that although the systems and procedures sounded "bureaucratic," their consistency gave the perception of "fairness" in the marketplace. Bill Beacom, vice-president and comptroller, saw the controls as minimal, due to the strength of the company culture, and he was explicit in stating that "the strong ethical orientation allows for less controls because people are very aware of expectations of business practices."

The controls not only established methods to monitor work flows and communication flows; they were also set up as guidelines for ethical business practices and measured with both actual compliance and the "spirit" of compliance in mind. On a periodic basis, internal company auditors entered the business units and analyzed these control procedures in the business practices, ethics and controls audit.

Business Practice Workshops

At Esso Petroleum Canada, the framework of management control was reinforced through business practice workshops. The half-day sessions were attended by all management personnel, as well as the administrative and clerical employees with high customer involvement, and focussed on four major areas: contracting, sales, moral dilemmas, and gifts and entertainment. The participants were placed in groups, where each group prepared an analysis of a case study. The results of the group work were then presented and discussed. Since the workshops had been implemented approximately two and one-half years earlier, Jim Dunlap, business control manager at EPC, was pleased. He frequently received calls from former participants regarding a decision they were in the process of making, and saw that as a sign of the program's success: higher awareness was leading employees to consider their actions beforehand, rather than having to correct decisions that were made out of carelessness.

Monitoring and Appeal Processes

All business practices, ethics and controls were subject to review by an internal audit group.

Consisting of approximately 45 auditors reporting at the corporate level, the audit group looked at the internal controls, efficiency, and business practices of each business unit in IOL and its family of companies. The audits occurred every two to four years, and had a mandate to assess the overall state of control. They were followed up with auditors' reports offering an overall opinion (good, satisfactory, not satisfactory, unacceptable) and outlining some possible recommendations for improvement. The internal auditors also met on a quarterly basis with the presidents of the three operating companies in Audit Committee Meetings to discuss ethics and control issues. They checked for compliance with corporate ethics as well as the other, more traditional, performance measures and operating procedures.

Also occurring quarterly were stewardship meetings where the presidents of the three major operating segments would speak with their respective internal management groups concerning line-management accountability issues. The presidents would then speak with IOL management in the upward-reporting stewardship format.

These reporting mechanisms culminated in an annual representation letter from each company's president to the IOL comptroller confirming their company's compliance with business practices, ethics and conduct. The letter explained any deviations, the recommendations developed to deal with them, and any action that had been taken.

The corporation emphasized the responsibility of every employee to engage in a continual monitoring process in all areas they were in contact with. Although it was not inconceivable for concerns to be received and actioned from the office of the CEO, there were four well-communicated channels for reporting ethical concerns: the comptrollers of IOL and its operating companies; internal auditors; the general secretary; and the legal department.

While each incident was handled according to its type and seriousness, the investigative process followed a fairly predictable pattern upon receipt of a concern:

- the concern was passed to the internal auditors;
- an attempt was made to clarify and verify the information;
- an investigation would begin;
- the auditors would determine the type of contravention:
  - if the individual involved was acting in their own self-interest, the incident was treated as fraud under the criminal code and the appropriate authorities were contacted;
  - if the individual involved was acting in the interest of the company, the incident was considered to be a conflict of ethics, and dealt with internally;
- the auditors would report in writing to the president of IOL on the incident and its consequences.

The final steps were situation-specific depending on the nature and severity of the incident—some were considered grounds for dismissal, others were infractions of the law and subject to judicial consequences, while others were discussed and set aside.

FURTHER ACTIONS?

As Ron Willoughby analyzed IOL's process of disseminating its code of ethics, he wondered what else could be done. Having recently seen two incidents arise—one a conflict of ethics, the other a conflict of interest—he wondered how they could have happened and how they might have been prevented. Was there a hole somewhere in the process? Was the communication lacking directness? Or was the process thorough and all-encompassing, and the cause was on the part of the individual? He wanted to answer these questions and make some recommendations to his successor.

6

CORPORATE SOCIAL RESPONSIBILITY

As noted in an earlier chapter, in the view of many people, shareholders are only one of many stakeholders with legitimate claims on a company's resources. Corporate social responsibility (CSR) is a recognition that companies are social entities, with explicit commitments beyond short-term—and even long-term—shareholder profit maximization. One focus of corporate social responsibility is a concern for the environment. Traditional economic analysis essentially ignores the cost imposed by firms on the environment, treating it as an "externality"—in effect, beyond analysis. Financial reporting, which takes a shareholder/owner perspective, is equally flawed, in that the only costs that it includes in the calculation of profit are those incurred by the firm. Costs that the firm imposes on others (such as the cost of pollution) are excluded (as is the value of inputs that the environment provides without cost, such as clean air and water).

Implementing measures to reduce pollution is costly to shareholders in the short run but results in a net benefit to society as a whole. However, some authors have argued that the impetus provided by the environmental movement—to redesign working conditions to increase efficiency, for example—often results in a net benefit to shareholders as well as lower levels of pollution. Nevertheless, for most firms, reducing the level of pollution is costly. In AWC Inc.: The Ventilation Dilemma, Alex MacDonald, president and owner of AWC, a southwestern Ontario aluminum fabrication operation, has to decide whether to install ventilation equipment that will adversely affect the financial performance of the company, possibly forcing the company out of business. His alternative is to ignore environmental regulations and risk being charged by government authorities for contravening the law. This case provides the opportunity to discuss several environmental forces that affect business decision making and to recognize the rights of various stakeholders in the decision.

No doubt because of increasing public interest in the role of business in preserving the environment, the legitimacy of corporate social responsibility is now a fact of corporate life. Managers often take the initiative in disclosing in their firms' annual reports their efforts to minimize the harm their companies impose on the environment, as well as their contributions to philanthropic causes. Some are probably merely self-serving, whereas others indicate a genuine interest in balancing shareholder interests against society's interests. An ethical utilitarian might argue that as long as the result is better for society, management motivation is secondary.

An ongoing debate is whether corporate social responsibility really is good for shareholders—that is, that there is no conflict between corporate social responsibility and shareholder returns. A range of investment funds is now available to investors who are unwilling to invest in companies with poor records of accomplishment in corporate social responsibility. The Ethical Funds—The Stevensons' Debate case explores a couple's choices. They think that they should direct some of their investment savings into ethical (or socially responsible) mutual funds. The case provides a historical review of the development of such funds and describes and compares the investment performance of a number of specific U.S. and Canadian ethical mutual funds.

Societies in the developed world generally accept a responsibility to transfer some wealth from their richest members to the poorer. Nevertheless, poorer members of society have needs, and business should serve them. However, serving this market poses ethical challenges because consumers are likely to be less educated, less informed about alternative products available to them, more easily misled by advertising, and less likely to make the best choice for themselves. Therefore, a business that targets low-income individuals and families is likely to be under unusual scrutiny not to make "excessive" profits. The Rent-to-Own Industry is such a $4 billion industry in the United States, which rents appliances, furniture, and electronic goods to customers. There is a potential threat to the rent-to-own industry because an article in a national newspaper accuses the industry of taking advantage of poor consumers. Lawmakers and politicians were becoming active on the issue, and the industry must formulate a response. Would the public really care enough about the rent-to-own industry for new laws to be passed that would change their operations? This case deals with the relationship between business, government, and society and implications of public perception.

Perception and the management of communications to key stakeholders are important issues in the Pembina Pipeline Corporation case. Pembina Pipeline Corporation transports light crude oil and natural gas liquids in western Canada. The president of the company is abruptly awakened one night by a phone call from his operations manager. He informs him that one of Pembina's pipelines has burst and is spilling thousands of barrels of crude oil into a nearby river. Emergency crews have responded to the disaster, but more help is needed. The president has to decide the best way to handle this situation with the media and plan a strategy for the company to contain the spill.

AWC Inc.: The Ventilation Dilemma

Prepared by Wayne MacLeod, David Ager and Alan Andron under the supervision of Professor Donald J. Lecraw

In July 1991, Alex MacDonald, President and owner of AWC Inc., returned to his office more frustrated and confused than ever. He had just met his 64-year-old father, the company's founder, for lunch to seek his advice. AWC's pollution control systems were not in compliance with Ontario's Environmental Emissions and Health and Safety regulations. To comply with the Health and Safety regulations, the company would have to install new ventilation equipment in the welding shop. The cost of this ventilation equipment was estimated at somewhere between $240,000 and $400,000, and would require a Certificate of Approval under environmental regulations. The costs of such an investment would have a major effect on the company's profits and cash flow.

AWC Inc., founded in 1950 by Jim MacDonald, was a Southwestern Ontario aluminum fabrication plant specializing in the production of commercial aluminum windows, doors, storefronts, and curtain wall products. Sales and shipments varied from as small as a single door and window to contracts to supply aluminum framing and glass curtain walls for entire buildings.[1] AWC was well known for the quality and design of its products as well as its competitive prices.

According to Alex's father, there was no issue:

Son, in all my years running this company, never once has anyone from Toronto come poking around my business. As long as the politicians in Toronto knew that I was providing honest work to the local community, no one ever bothered me. I don't see how anything has changed. Work translates into votes, and, given the government's poor economic performance, the last thing they want to do is to shut us down. They'd be hanging themselves, especially with the number of businesses that have shut down in our area over the past year.

Those regulations will only be applied to the big companies like General Electric and General Motors, not to small operations like ours. They know you don't have the money to buy all that fancy air cleaning stuff, and furthermore, they don't expect you to buy it. They know that compared to the large companies, the amount of stuff you pump out into the air doesn't have much effect on the environment. Case in point, Alex: Do you ever read in the newspaper about a small company being fined for polluting the environment? Never, it's always the "big guys."

How could Alex argue with that logic? His father had run the company successfully for 40 years, before retiring due to health problems, and handing over day-to-day management to Alex the previous year. Still, there was something that made Alex feel uneasy about ignoring the issue altogether.

AWC Inc.

Since its founding in 1950, AWC Inc. had grown and prospered. Many of the people working in the company in 1992 were the children of the first employees Alex's father had hired back in 1950. AWC was more than a company, it was a family. As Shirley Jenkins, Director, Design Engineering, explained:

I came to work here in 1962 as an engineer. Over the years AWC has helped me to provide a comfortable life for my family. When my children were going to university, AWC always made sure there was work for them over the summer months. AWC treats all its employees this way. It's not uncommon to see the workforce increase by 10 to 15 people between May and August. This may not be unusual for Northern Telecom, but for a company of 100 employees it's quite something.

Sandeep Sharma, a production line manager, added:

I've been working in the plant since 1952. The company has always sponsored one or two teams in the local hockey and basketball leagues. Recently, they've started sponsoring a local soccer team as well. And, anytime anyone has a problem—you know, financially—AWC is there to help them out, and the company doesn't make you feel embarrassed or ashamed about it. It's no wonder people take such pride in their work. I've seen people rework entire orders without being told to do so, just because they aren't satisfied with the quality of the final product. We just don't want to see the company name going on anything that isn't perfect. I might add that what we consider less than acceptable quality, our competitors sell as "top" quality.

Of the 100 people employed by the company, 45 were production workers and 55 were office staff. The office staff consisted of 25 engineers who worked closely with customers from the design-proposal stage through quoting and on to the final installation. The company found that design and product performance were critical to success in this market, and that the best way of achieving this was through a force of competent and capable engineers supported by committed, skilled and quality-conscious production workers.

ALUMINUM FABRICATION INDUSTRY

Aluminum is a relatively easy product to work with and is suitable for numerous applications. Aluminum fabrication does not require heavy machinery and production is often handled on a one-shift basis. (There is no need to run the equipment 24 hours a day to maximize use of expensive equipment, as is the case with steel fabrication.) AWC purchased aluminum of various alloys and with various finishes in 20 and 24-foot lengths, cut the lengths to size, and machined and assembled them. AWC employed different assembly methods including: corner bracket, tie-rod, and welding. Finished products were shipped completely assembled or as pre-machined, ready-to-assemble components.

As a result of the minimal costs required to set up an aluminum fabrication operation, AWC had 37 competitors in southwestern Ontario alone. This number did not include the 15 suppliers of extruded[2] aluminum, some of whom also manufactured door and window products.

Most of the contracts received by AWC were awarded through a competitive bidding process. Very often these contracts were for standard products, although configuration and usage differed. Price, and sometimes distance from the supplier, were the only factors distinguishing one operation from another. Yet, even for these contracts, it was essential for AWC's engineers to work closely with a customer in order to determine the specifics of a particular project to ensure that the product met performance standards including air and water infiltration and structural requirements. The quotation also needed to be competitive, and at the same time profitable, for AWC. Because of the number of projects the company was involved with at any one time at the bidding, design or installation phase, the company required its large engineering force and its large office staff. Competition for these contracts was fierce, and had become even more so as a result of the construction slow-down in southwestern Ontario over the 1989–1991 period. Alex explained:

Since the late 1980s, competition for contracts has become incredibly fierce. Whereas before you could expect to earn five to seven per cent profit on a contract, today we're lucky to get three per cent. And the recession, at least in the construction industry, shows no signs of recovery for at least the next three years.

There were also some "custom" contracts. These were rare and occurred only when an architect's drawings called for a specific product that was available exclusively through a particular fabricator. To secure such a "specification" was a time-consuming, costly process and rarely occurred unsolicited, although the rewards could be significant. AWC had earned profits of up to 20 per cent on such contracts.

The industry had seen many other recent changes. Alex commented:

> Over the past five years I have witnessed many changes in the industry. One third of my competitors have gone out of business, while others have joined together to spread their overhead costs over a larger volume. Profits in the industry are minimal. On average, they are approximately three per cent. To survive, I've had to reduce my workforce through attrition, although I may soon be forced to lay off employees. This is not something that I've done easily, nor did I do it without a lot of deliberation and heartache. When any of my employees leave, even if it is through attrition, I feel like I'm firing my own mother.

> The construction industry, the major client for our product, has been devastated by the recent recession. Although there has been a shake-out in the aluminum fabricating industry, we have survived, but only by drastically cutting our prices, margins and profits and increasing our efficiency.

> The bulk of our fabrication costs are labour costs and engineering overhead. We cannot at this time afford any increase in these costs, unless we wish to jeopardize the business. But if we're to remain competitive in the industry, we can't lay off engineers. They are our future.

> The Canada-U.S. Free Trade Agreement has threatened to increase the competitiveness in the aluminum fabrication industry. The reduction in tariffs will allow large U.S. fabricators with lower cost structures to enter the Canadian market and offer lower priced products of equal quality. I see this as the beginning of the end of Canadian aluminum fabricators.

AWC and Aluminum Fabrication

Recently, AWC had introduced a superior door design for general purpose use. This had resulted

in a significant increase in the company's sales of commercial aluminum doors and the need for high volume production. Not only was the new product more attractive in terms of price and ease of assembly, but it also offered equal or superior performance to comparable products. The door was designed and fabricated using a tie-rod assembly.

When the door was intended for heavy use areas, for example, the entrance way to a shopping mall, the door assembly would need to be reinforced by a stronger welded-corner design that required a greater time in the production process, specifically on the welding line. This design enhancement was a requirement in many orders.

The AWC welding line was used for existing products, but not on a full-time basis. To meet the production demands for the new door product, the welding line was now being used full-time, and, depending on the volume of product flowing through the plant, very often required a second shift.

The problem with a second shift on the welding line was twofold. Alex commented:

> If we move to a second shift on the welding line, we need to find someone who is capable of supervising it on the second shift. Not only does this cost extra money, but also, finding someone qualified to supervise the line will be difficult. I know this because it took us six months to find the supervisor we have at present. And even then, she required additional training. The second problem with a second shift is that AWC will be required to pay a shift premium to the six people who operate the line. This will increase costs. As well, the output of the night shift will have to be stacked all over the floor of the plant. We have no easily accessible storage area.

> One option is to install a second welding line. We could then have the existing supervisor assume responsibility for both welding lines. This would save a shift premium and reduce work in progress inventory. On the other hand, the equipment for a second line would cost $75,000.

The Toronto Trade Show

At a recent trade show that he had attended in Toronto, Alex had visited a booth set up by the

Ontario Ministry of the Environment. The booth was staffed by various government representatives. Among other information, they provided an overview of various aluminum fabrication processes and the harmful by-products of each. In addition, the government representatives outlined the various regulations concerning the emissions of various substances into the air, and they outlined the penalties for failing to comply with the regulations.

Of particular interest to Alex was the discussion that centred around welding. The welding process for aluminum produced various fumes composed of toxic and environmentally harmful metal particles and metal oxides. The law was quite specific: releasing high concentrations of these particles into the internal work environment or outside the plant was forbidden, and was punishable by fines of up to $400,000 per day. According to Ministry of the Environment and Ministry of Labour studies, even in small concentrations, these particles had been proven to be responsible for serious respiratory damage and, in some cases, cancer after long-term exposure.

As one government representative put it, "Inhaling these particles is more harmful than smoking a package of cigarettes a day."

Alex was puzzled by this last comment:

We've been welding for years and have never vented the fumes from the plant. To date we've received no complaints. I wonder how sound these studies really are. After all, if the stuff really is harmful, Dad would never have let us work in the plant as kids. In fact, I've been in and out of that plant for almost 40 years, and look at me, no problems.

Sure, the welding line has never been used as much as we are using it to meet the demand for our new product, but then maybe all we need to do is cut a hole in the ceiling of the plant and let more fresh air than usual in to mix and dilute that other stuff.

While at the trade show, Alex had also visited a booth set up by a company that specialized in ventilation emission control systems. He had taken advantage of this opportunity to do some research on systems that, if installed, would ensure that AWC did not contravene existing environmental legislation.

EMISSION CONTROL SYSTEMS

If AWC were to install an emissions control system, it had a choice of two different types of emission control. The first was an exhaust system that would vent fumes outside the plant. While an exhaust system that vented the fumes to the outside was by far the cheaper of the two options, Alex had determined that the system would cost approximately $240,000. Although it satisfied Ministry of Labour occupational health and safety regulations, this system merely moved the problem from inside the plant to outside the plant. If AWC simply used the ventilation system, it would be subject to Ministry of the Environment regulations concerning external emissions of by-products. According to the regulations, AWC would be required to obtain a Certificate of Approval from the Ministry of the Environment for its industrial exhaust system. The Ministry of the Environment would require an air quality impact study be conducted on neighbouring property owners, and based on the results, would decide whether to approve AWC's exhaust system.

Alex continued:

I couldn't believe it when I first heard about that requirement. I mean, my neighbour out here in the industrial park is a ready-mix concrete plant. They throw more dust and gunk into the air in one week than we could produce in a lifetime.

The second, and more expensive alternative, was to install a recirculating filtration system. Alex had determined the cost of the system AWC required would be $400,000. This system would take the air from the welding station, run it through a set of electrostatic filters, and expel it back into the plant. While these filters would not require approval from the Ministry of the Environment to operate, as they were not releasing the air to the outside of the building, the system would have to be approved by the Ministry of Labour, Department of Occupational Health and Safety.

There was an additional requirement for this system. The filters in a recirculating system had to be cleaned once a month to function effectively. The cleaner was a proprietary substance which had no acceptable substitutes. The cleaner was also corrosive and caustic, and would require special employee training and protection from health and safety hazards. In addition, the cleaning process generated about two litres of toxic sludge that had to be disposed of as a hazardous material under Ministry of Environment waste disposal regulations.

AWC could not legally store this sludge on its plant site unless it was first licensed as a hazardous materials storage site, which would require expensive facilities and safety precautions. Neither could AWC legally haul the materials to an authorized storage or disposal site as AWC was not licensed to haul hazardous materials. Again, seeking such a license would require an investment in specialized equipment and training. Under the law, the only option open to AWC was to use the services of a licensed hazardous waste disposal company who would pick up and dispose of this material at a cost of $500 per trip. The fee was fixed; whether the shipment was one litre of sludge or 101 litres of sludge, AWC would be charged the same price. The hazardous waste disposal companies also insisted on testing the substance each time, at a charge of $200, before they would collect and dispose of it.

Alex concluded:

I can't believe that the government creates all of these obstacles for us. They won't let us vent directly into the plant, and they won't let us vent directly outside the plant. They expect us to somehow "clean" the air entirely. So, first they require us to put in equipment that creates the sludge, then they make it nearly impossible to dispose of it.

ENVIRONMENTAL REGULATIONS

Over the previous few years, the provincial government in Ontario had raised the profile of environmental issues in response to demands from various stakeholder groups and as part of their underlying belief that the government must regulate business to preserve the environment. The province had reviewed its environmental legislation and had increased the legal and economic deterrents for polluting. In particular, fines were substantially increased and new penalties, such as incarceration, were introduced. Under the new rules, company directors, managers, and employees could be held personally liable for regulatory infractions.

A furniture manufacturer in Cambridge had recently been charged for exhausting paint fumes and other harmful vapours, a by-product of their finishing process, into the air. In response to complaints from neighbours, the provincial government approached the firm to eliminate the problem. The recommendation of the province was that the company install a two-process system that consisted of an air scrubber and a filter that would capture by-products. The price tag for this new system was $1.25 million. The company responded by stating that they would rather relocate to the United States than incur the cost of compliance. Because the company refused to comply, the province took it to court. The company was subsequently fined $100,000 and the company's general manager was personally fined $25,000. The case was still in appeal.

Alex MacDonald had done some checking and had discovered that of the 1,000 companies who had been charged for emitting harmful substances into the external environment, only 250 had actually been prosecuted, of which only 100 were fined an average of $30,000 each. As well, of the 1,000 charges, only one person had been incarcerated. Alex estimated that all in all, over 50,000 companies were affected by the law and 70 to 80 per cent were probably in violation of it.

Alex knew that in his situation, the maximum penalty for the firm was a fine of $500,000. At the same time, he was also aware that he could personally be fined $25,000, and that any of his employees could be fined up to $25,000 for violating the health and safety legislation.

In all the years that AWC has been in business, I can't remember having been visited by an environmental inspector, nor can I remember any of my competitors having been visited by an inspector, except perhaps for one or two of the larger operations like World Aluminum Industries.

This explains why my large competitors have installed expensive air quality control equipment in their plants. This doesn't seem all that unusual though. After all, their plants are usually very prominent in the community, have multiple locations, and are unionized. As well, they are large, and by virtue of this fact, create a large amount of pollution that is highly visible.

The government guys are always breathing down their backs; hell, if one of the guys gets a paper cut from his pay cheque, the union calls the health and safety guys in. I can also tell you that those big guys have been struggling lately; their costs are so high, and they are having a hard time getting profitable contracts in this recession.

Alex figured that if there was a problem, someone would have said something by now.

One employee described the work environment:

Sure, it's noisy and smelly in here, but hey, this is a factory after all. I work next to the welding line. Yes, sometimes I go home with a headache, but then so does my wife who works in an office. Who

says the world is perfect? At least we have a job when many don't. And it's a good job at that.

Another employee commented about his experience at AWC:

My dad worked here, I spent my university summers here, and Mr. MacDonald's dad even helped me get my engineering degree. I'm proud to work for this company and have a hand in designing what I think are the best damn aluminum doors and windows in the country.

THE DECISION

As Alex mulled over the estimates before him and his projected financial statements (Exhibits 1, 2 and 3), he began to become annoyed. AWC had been in business for more than 40 years and no one had complained. Furthermore, as his father had said: "We're running a factory, not a hospital operating room!" Alex added some additional thoughts about the firm:

Income Statement	Actual 1990	1991	1992	1993	1994
Sales	$3,535,118	3,623,496	3,732,201	3,844,167	3,959,492
Cost of Goods Sold	2,386,205	2,445,860	2,556,558	2,633,254	2,712,252
Gross Profit	1,148,913	1,177,636	1,175,643	1,210,913	1,247,240
Wages and Benefits	768,000	791,040	791,040	806,861	822,998
Advertising	40,000	42,860	42,860	42,860	42,860
Utilities	46,700	48,500	49,015	49,100	49,700
Insurance	10,000	10,000	10,000	10,000	10,000
Depreciation	28,945	28,945	28,945	28,945	28,945
Travel	77,000	80,000	82,700	83,400	84,400
Trade Shows	25,000	27,000	27,000	27,000	27,000
Executive Salary	100,000	100,000	100,000	100,000	100,000
Interest Expense	46,200	42,540	42,540	42,540	42,540
Total Expenses	1,141,845	1,170,885	1,174,100	1,190,706	1,208,443
Earnings Before Tax	7,068	6,751	1,543	20,207	38,797
Taxes	2,333	2,228	509	6,668	12,803
Net Income (Loss)	$4,736	4,523	1,034	13,539	25,994

Exhibit 1   Projected Income Statement 1991–1994 (no purchase of ventilation equipment)

Note: AWC charges engineering salaries to cost of goods sold.

Income Statement	Actual 1990	1991	1992	1993	1994
Sales	$3,535,118	3,623,496	3,732,201	3,844,167	3,959,492
Cost of Goods Sold	2,386,205	2,445,860	2,556,558	2,633,254	2,712,252
Gross Profit	1,148,913	1,177,636	1,175,643	1,210,913	1,247,240
Wages and Benefits	768,000	791,040	791,040	806,861	822,998
Advertising	40,000	42,860	42,860	42,860	42,860
Utilities	46,700	48,500	49,015	49,100	49,700
Insurance	10,000	10,000	10,000	10,000	10,000
Depreciation	28,945	28,945	58,945	58,945	58,945
Travel	77,000	80,000	82,700	83,400	84,400
Trade Shows	25,000	27,000	27,000	27,000	27,000
Executive Salary	100,000	100,000	100,000	100,000	100,000
Interest Expense	46,200	42,540	76,140	74,403	72,422
Total Expenses	1,141,845	1,170,885	1,237,700	1,252,569	1,268,325
Earnings Before Tax	7,068	6,751	(62,057)	(41,656)	(21,085)
Taxes	2,333	2,228	—	—	—
Net Income (Loss)	$4,736	4,523	(62,057)	(41,656)	(21,085)

Exhibit 2   Projected Income Statement 1991–1994 (purchase of $240,000 exhaust equipment)

Note: AWC charges engineering salaries to cost of goods sold.

Projections assume that equipment is installed for 1992.

Income Statement	Actual 1990	1991	1992	1993	1994
Sales	$3,535,118	3,623,496	3,732,201	3,844,167	3,959,492
Cost of Goods Sold	2,386,205	2,445,860	2,556,558	2,633,254	2,712,252
Gross Profit	1,148,913	1,177,636	1,175,643	1,210,913	1,247,240
Wages and Benefits	768,000	791,040	791,040	806,861	822,998
Advertising	40,000	42,860	42,860	42,860	42,860
Utilities	46,700	48,500	49,015	49,100	49,700
Insurance	10,000	10,000	10,000	10,000	10,000
Depreciation	28,945	28,945	78,945	78,945	78,945
Travel	77,000	80,000	82,700	83,400	84,400
Trade Shows	25,000	27,000	27,000	27,000	27,000
Executive Salary	100,000	100,000	100,000	100,000	100,000
Waste Disposal	—	—	8,400	8,400	8,400
Interest Expense	46,200	42,540	98,540	95,642	92,338
Total Expenses	1,141,845	1,170,885	1,288,500	1,302,208	1,316,641
Earnings Before Tax	7,068	6,751	(112,857)	(91,295)	(69,401)
Taxes	2,333	2,228	—	—	—
Net Income (Loss)	$4,736	4,523	(112,857)	(91,295)	(69,401)

Exhibit 3   Projected Income Statement 1991–1994 (purchase of $400,000 air recirculation equipment)

Note: AWC charges engineering salaries to cost of goods sold.

Projections assume that equipment is installed for 1992.

My dad, mom, sister, and brother have all worked in the company. We started out as kids coming in on the weekends and helping to clean things up, or watch Dad draw up estimates for customers. I still have some of Dad's original staff here, and some of their children work here. Just like my Dad did, I help my employees send their kids to college when they need help.

I went to school and studied business administration, but you know, I hated shuffling paper. This is where my heart is; this is where I'm happiest making things. When Dad was forced to retire early, I was glad to jump in. We build things here—if the boys on Bay Street are so smart, how come so many firms are in trouble? Just look at the real estate developers. How come we keep reading about all of these large businesses that keep screwing up because they tried to become so-called financial conglomerates? All they do is shuffle paper and push buttons on computers, but without people like us who actually create things, those guys would have zip!

Before people go to work for the government, they should spend some time in the real world! They complain about our lack of competitiveness, about the job drain and the brain drain. Then they slam the working person and their employer with taxes, taxes, and more taxes, and with more and more of the same damned regulations that tie me in red tape anytime I want to do something. And then they wonder why firms are moving out of this province and setting up shop in Mexico!

Alex reviewed the figures in front of him. To comply with the provincial environmental regulations would be financially devastating for AWC and would lead to 100 people becoming unemployed. Alex reasoned that such an argument would suffice in explaining to the provincial environment officials why AWC might decide not to comply with the regulations. And after all, what were the chances of being caught? Alex leaned back in his chair, realizing that resolving his dilemma would not be easy.

NOTES

1. A curtain wall is the visible exterior glass envelope of a high-rise building, commonly consisting of glass windows and panels in an aluminum frame. The frames are generally suspended from mounting brackets built onto the structure of the building.

2. Aluminum extrusion is the process whereby aluminum ingots are heated and shaped into various sizes and lengths. The resulting extruded products are sold to fabricators who use them in making various products including doors and window frames.

ETHICAL FUNDS—THE STEVENSONS' DEBATE

Prepared by Craig Gilchrist and Dana Gruber under the supervision of Professor Ron Wirick

Version: (A) 1998-10-07

People make compromises every time they choose a mutual fund. Investors are always making a choice as to what their special needs are. If ethical investing is important,

you can do it and still achieve above-average returns.

—Larry Lunn, Co-Manager
of the Ethical Growth Fund[1]

By providing the tools to put money at the service of local communities, disadvantaged people and the environment, ethical investment can help to build a new economy based on human needs without rejecting investors' personal goals of security and happiness.

—Eugene Ellman, The 1998
Canadian Ethical Money Guide[2]

If you could make an investment that would yield 50 per cent or more return for less risk, would you take it? . . . What if you found out that, while technically legal, it involved child pornography?

—John Montgomery,
President of Bridgeway
Social Responsibility Portfolio[3]

Ian, I agree that it would be nice to feel like we're "doing good" with our money, but I'm just not sure that I'm willing to sacrifice the returns that we could make if we were open to investing in all possible funds.

Ian Stevenson understood that his wife, Beth, was concerned that they might be forgoing a better return by investing their money in a socially responsible mutual fund; however, he felt very strongly that ethical investing was the right thing for them to do. He was convinced by his own research that they would not be jeopardizing any potential returns. In their late twenties, and after their first few years of marriage, the Stevensons were fortunate enough to have no substantial debt, and had managed to save approximately C$20,000 that they were interested in investing in the equity portion of their portfolio.

Ian pressed his position,

I just don't feel right about making money from companies whose policies I disapprove of. I'm concerned about supporting companies that are involved in producing arms, nuclear power or unsafe products. Aren't you uneasy at all about investing in companies that use child labor or operate sweat shops? How about companies that test their products on animals?

All of these issues concern me, too, Ian! But we've worked hard for our savings and we have to be practical. I want our investment to provide us with some extra money for something down the road. I know that you've told me that these funds can perform as well as other, "more conventional" funds, but I'm worried that some industries might be avoided. Wouldn't that hurt our diversification? And another thing, if the managers of these funds are spending all their time monitoring these ethical corporations, when do they have time to worry about the companies' financial performance and prospects for the future?

PRINCIPLES OF ETHICAL INVESTING

Socially responsible investing, or ethical investing, described the placement of money in mutual funds, stocks, bonds or other securities and investments, that were screened to reflect moral, environmental, social, and political values. Many supporters suggested that a better way of articulating the ethical investing concept was to say that socially responsible investors accepted the responsibility for the impact of their investments and their financial decisions.

Ethical investors wanted to have their money build a future that was congruent with their beliefs and values. Each person had their own individual concerns and ideas about what constituted "ethical behaviour"; however, there were some concerns that were widespread and were common to many. By examining investments based on specified issues of concern, fund managers determined which corporations were acceptable and desirable to invest in. This screening process could be administered in two different ways: positive and negative screening. Positive screening involved choosing those companies that focused on "doing good," while negative screening involved eliminating those companies that were deemed in some way to be harmful to society. Fund managers focused on either type of screening to varying degrees, but each fund would be based on some identified selection criteria. Exhibit 1 outlines common criteria that were used by a majority of ethical funds to determine whether an investment was ethical or not. Nearly 90 per cent of socially responsible investment funds were managed with at least three or more screens.[4]

THE EMERGENCE OF ETHICAL INVESTING

Shareholders became increasingly aware of their potential for influence, as well as their ability to hold companies responsible for their activities. As a result, some investors became more discerning with their investments and more actively involved in communicating their positions in regard to company developments, management and operating practices.

In the United States, as of 1998, there were over 160 mutual funds based on particular social or environmental criteria, amounting to assets greater than US$1 trillion. Ethical funds accounted for approximately nine per cent of the US$13.7 trillion of assets invested under professional management in the U.S., at the end of 1997.[5]

In Canada, 15 ethical mutual funds were offered by five different mutual fund companies: Ethical Funds Inc., Clean Environment Mutual Funds, Fiducie Desjardins, Investors Group and Working Opportunity Fund.[6]

Criteria	Identify	Avoid
Environment	Positive programs, such as pollution prevention	Major polluters, nuclear power operators
Employer Relations	Positive labor relations and benefits, strong equal employment opportunity	Companies with records of discrimination or aggressive anti-union activity
Product	Safe, beneficial products	Tobacco, alcohol, gambling, unsafe products
Weapons/Military		Companies with significant weapons production, or arms trade
Human Rights	Companies that surpass international and local standards	Companies that fail to meet international conventions, or practise child labor
Community	Responsible corporate citizens	Financial institutions that discriminate in lending
Animal Welfare	Companies reducing animal testing	Companies lacking standards for humane treatment of animals
Equality	Companies that support all races, religions, sexes, and sexual orientation	Companies that discriminate against any individual sexual orientation

Exhibit 1   Common Investment Screens

Available funds represented the full range of mutual fund categories; including Canadian, International, North American, and Pacific Rim equities, as well as Canadian balanced funds, Canadian and International bond funds, Canadian money market, and Canadian small capitalization companies. Although ethical funds were becoming increasingly popular in Canada, representing close to C$3 billion[7] they only represented less than one per cent of the C$300 billion in total investment.[8] For example, Investors Group had more than C$33 billion in assets and less than one per cent of it, or C$300 million, was invested in their ethical fund, the Investors Summa Fund.[9]

There were at least two U.S. indices that existed that were based on socially responsible securities; the Good Dow and the Domini 400 Social Index. The Good Dow was the longest-running socially responsible index, created in the late 1970s by Good Money, Inc. Between 1976 and 1994, the Good Dow had an average annual return of 12.4 per cent versus 7.7 per cent for the Dow Jones Industrial Average.[10]

Kinder, Lyndenberg, Domini & Co. created the Domini 400 Social Index (DSI) for the purpose of studying how social criteria affected investment performance. Since May 1990, it had been the benchmark for measuring the performance of socially screened portfolios. Modelled on the S&P 500, the DSI was a market capitalization-weighted common stock index. Since its inception, it had outperformed the S&P 500 on a total return basis and on a risk-adjusted basis. Exhibit 2 illustrates the performance of the DSI

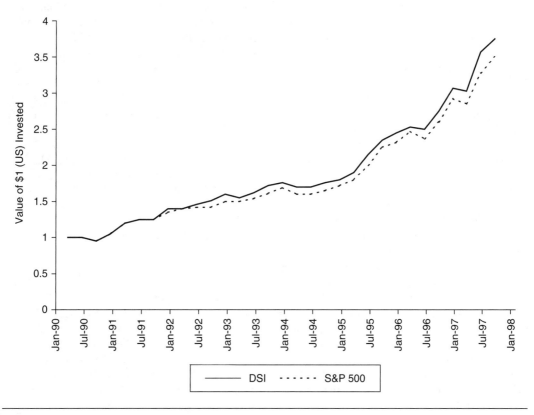

Exhibit 2　　Domini 400 Social Index Performance

Source: Graph is approximated from http://www.kld.com

against the S&P 500 since May 1990. About half of the stocks on the S&P 500 passed the ethical screen and were chosen for the DSI, and 150 other stocks were selected to round out the 400 that made up the index. The DSI had a very low turnover of about six to eight per cent, roughly in line with the S&P 500.[11]

PERFORMANCE OF ETHICAL FUNDS

Reviews about ethical fund performance in Canada and the U.S. have been mixed. Proponents maintained that ethical investments could perform as well as conventional investments and in some cases better. While the stocks listed in the Domini 400 Index had grown by more than 302 per cent in terms of their stock prices, for the year ended December 31, 1997, the S&P 500 had increased by only 262 per cent for the same period.[12] Exhibit 3 outlines the investment performance of 23 popular U.S.-owned and eight Canadian-owned ethical equity funds. These 31 funds can be benchmarked against the Median Canadian Diversified Equity Fund, Domini 400, MSCI World, TSE 300 and S&P 500.

One major concern with ethical funds was the fear of higher management expense ratios to cover the additional effort spent selecting and monitoring "ethical companies." High management expense ratios reduced the amount of return to an investor. Exhibit 3 displays the management expense ratios and sales fees (loads) for the 31 popular funds mentioned earlier.

The diversity among funds, in relation to their composition and screening criteria, often made it difficult to compare the financial performance of certain funds. Funds with limited screening might have been considered with other traditional mutual funds, making the distinction between ethical funds and conventional funds vague. Exhibit 4 illustrates the variety of criteria different ethical funds used to screen their investment selections.

CANADIAN ETHICAL FUNDS

Ethical Funds Inc.

Ethical Funds Inc. was Canada's largest group of socially responsible mutual funds. The group offered eight different funds, and included screens for industrial relations, racial equality, tobacco, military production, nuclear energy and environmental practices.

All funds were based upon their "Ethical Principles," which were created through a consultative process involving the public, unitholders and a special advisory council on ethics. Their selection process involved first selecting investments with excellent growth potential, and then applying a "best-of-sector" approach. This involved picking the best companies in a sector based on predetermined criteria. It was owned and controlled by the Canadian credit union system and was available to Canadian residents only. The distributor of Ethical Funds Inc. was Credential Asset Management Inc., a subsidiary of Credit Union Central of Canada. Credit Union Central of Canada (Canadian Central) was the national trade association and central finance facility for credit unions in Canada.

Ethical Funds Inc. offered Canada's largest ethical fund, the Ethical Growth Fund (Exhibit 5). This fund had over C$818 million in assets, as of April 30, 1998. It was launched in 1986 by its administrator, Vancouver City Savings Credit Union (VanCity), and was Canada's first fund of its kind.[13] It invested in the common stock of Canadian corporations with medium-to-large market capitalization.

The Ethical North American Equity Fund (Exhibit 6), had over C$181 million of assets, as of April 30, 1998. Fund manager, Cynthia Frick argued that she, "can easily find well-performing proxies for the firms that are off limits."[14] She used a bottom-up strategy for her stock selection, and constantly rebalanced the fund, turning over its value by 125 per cent each year.

Fund Name*	Assets ($M)	Annual Average Return				Load	Exp. Ratio
		1 Year	3 Year	5 Year	10 Year		
Canadian-Owned Equity Funds (CAN$)							
Ethical Growth	$818.96	26.88%	23.38%	16.86%	12.57%	—	2.10%
Ethical Special Equity	$96.70	21.12%	18.26%	N/A	N/A	—	2.71%
Ethical North American Equity	$181.18	55.14%	37.33%	24.45%	14.78%	—	2.47%
Investors Summa	$465.30	39.53%	27.53%	18.44%	12.21%	Both	2.48%
Clean Environment Equity	$283.53	45.89%	30.98%	22.11%	N/A	Optional	2.88%
Clean Environment International Equity	$32.38	53.05%	28.53%	N/A	N/A	Optional	2.77%
Desjardins Environment	$141.88	30.40%	22.04%	16.18%	N/A	—	2.08%
Working Opportunity	$196.07	6.56%	7.31%	5.22%	N/A	—	3.30%
Canadian Average	$277.00	34.82%	24.42%	17.21%	13.19%	—	2.60%
US-Owned Equity Funds (US$)							
Ariel Appreciation Fund	$236.10	48.23%	29.71%	19.75%	N/A	—	1.33%
Ariel Growth Fund	$194.90	47.19%	28.81%	18.92%	14.75%	—	1.25%
Bridgeway Fund Social Responsibility Portfolio	$1.10	41.33%	26.99%	N/A	N/A	—	1.50%
Calvert Capital Accumulation Fund	$70.50	48.73%	25.69%	N/A	N/A	4.75%	1.96%
Calvert Social Investment Fund Equity Portfolio	$166.70	30.53%	23.33%	12.65%	11.39%	4.75%	1.21%
Citizens Emerging Growth Portfolio	$87.00	49.51%	27.97%	N/A	N/A	—	2.01%
Citizens Index Fund—Retail	$318.00	45.31%	32.56%	N/A	N/A	—	1.59%
Delaware Quantum Fund	$41.50	46.04%	N/A	N/A	N/A	4.75%	1.50%
DEVCAP Shared Return Fund	$7.20	39.22%	30.24%	21.15%	N/A	—	1.75%
Domini Social Equity Fund	$397.50	40.59%	31.79%	22.49%	N/A	—	0.98%
Dreyfus Third Century Fund	$899.70	40.48%	31.79%	20.03%	16.55%	—	1.03%
Green Century Equity Fund	$12.80	40.28%	31.46%	21.94%	N/A	—	1.50%
Meyers Pride Value Fund	$3.10	32.46%	N/A	N/A	N/A	—	1.95%
MMA Praxis-Growth Fund	$132.00	37.70%	26.16%	N/A	N/A	—	1.75%
Neuberger & Berman Socially Responsive Fund	$93.90	39.47%	28.46%	N/A	N/A	—	1.48%
New Alternatives Fund	$41.00	25.40%	15.10%	10.00%	N/A	4.75%	1.15%
Noah Fund	$1.80	37.40%	N/A	N/A	N/A	—	1.42%
Parnassus Fund	$366.90	34.92%	14.88%	15.32%	14.58%	3.50%	1.11%
Pax World Growth Fund	$7.30	5.80%	N/A	N/A	N/A	2.50%	1.49%
Rightime Social Awareness Fund	$13.70	22.99%	19.74%	12.70%	N/A	4.75%	2.35%
Security Social Awareness Fund	$12.90	37.33%	N/A	N/A	N/A	5.75%	0.67%
Total Return Utilities Fund	$11.20	42.00%	N/A	N/A	N/A	—	1.80%
Women's Pro-Conscious Equity Mutual Fund	$7.00	43.09%	25.13%	N/A	N/A	—	1.50%
US Average	$135.82	38.09%	26.46%	17.50%	14.32%	1.54%	1.49%
Benchmarks							
Median Can Diversified Equity Fund (CAN$)	$54.20	22.90%	20.00%	14.50%	10.30%	N/A	2.33%
Domini Social Index 400 (US$)		43.07%	34.05%	24.30%	N/A		
MSCI World (CAN$)		32.55%	21.77%	19.02%	13.06%		
TSE 300 (CAN$)		30.35%	23.85%	17.65%	11.82%		
S&P 500 (CAN$)		44.36%	34.20%	26.09%	20.66%		
S&P 500 (US$)		41.06%	31.96%	23.23%	18.91%		

Exhibit 3   Historical Ethical Fund Equity Performance

Source: Canadian funds found at http://www.globefund.com (May 29, 1998)

U.S. funds found at http://www.socialinvest.org/sriguide/mfpc.htm (May 29, 1998)

*All information is for the period ending April 30, 1998.

Fund Name*	Environment	Labour/Employment	Products/Service	Defense/Weapons	Alc./Tob./Gambling	Animal Testing	Human Rights/Equality	Other
Canadian-Owned Equity Funds								
Ethical Growth	X	X	X	X	X		X	
Ethical Special Equity	X	X	X	X	X		X	
Ethical North American Equity	X	X	X	X	X		X	
Investors Summa	X		X	X	X		X	
Clean Environment Equity	X		X					X
Clean Environment International Equity	X		X					X
Desjardins Environment	X		X					X
U.S.-Owned Equity Funds								
Ariel Appreciation Fund	X			X	X			
Ariel Growth Fund	X			X	X			
Bridgeway Fund Social Responsibility Portfolio	X	X	X	X	X	X	X	
Calvert Capital Accumulation Fund	X	X		X	X			
Calvert Social Investment Fund Equity Portfolio	X	X	X	X	X	X	X	
Citizens Emerging Growth Portfolio	X	X	X	X	X	X	X	
Citizens Index Fund—Retail	X	X	X	X	X	X	X	
DEVCAP Shared Return Fund	X	X	X	X	X			
Domini Social Equity Fund	X	X	X	X	X		X	
Dreyfus Third Century Fund	X	X	X	X	X		X	X
Green Century Equity Fund	X	X	X	X	X		X	
Meyers Pride Value Fund		X						X
MMA Praxis-Growth Fund	X	X	X	X	X		X	
Neuberger & Berman Socially Responsive Fund	X	X	X	X	X		X	X
New Alternatives Fund	X	X	X	X	X	X		
Parnassus Fund	X	X	X	X	X		X	
Pax World Growth Fund	X	X	X	X	X			
Rightime Social Awareness Fund	X	X	X	X	X			
Security Social Awareness Fund	X	X	X	X	X		X	
Total Return Utilities Fund	X		X	X	X	X		
Women's Pro-Conscious Equity Mutual Fund	X	X	X	X	X	X	X	X

Exhibit 4   Investment Screening Criteria

Source: All information on Canadian-owned funds was complied from the case writers' research.

All information on U.S.-owned funds was found at http://www.coopamerica.org/mfsc.htm

*All information was last updated on September 30, 1996.

Fund Profile—Ethical Growth Fund			

		Top Holdings (as of March 31, 1998):	
Fund Sponsor:	Ethical Funds Inc.		
Portfolio Manager:	Ethical Funds Inc.		
Inception Date:	Jan-86	Bank of Nova Scotia	4.80%
Total Assets:	$818.96 Million	Magna International Inc	4.60%
Sales Fee Type:	No Load	Royal Bank of Canada	4.40%
Mgmt Expense Ratio:	2.10%	Canadian National Railway Co	4.10%
Fund Type:	Canadian Equity	Suncor Energy Inc	3.80%
Globe 5 Year Rating:	A+	Abitibi-Consolidated Inc	2.80%
RRSP Eligibility:	Yes	Bank of Montreal	2.80%
Min. Initial Investment:	$500.00	Geac Computer Ltd	2.80%
		Laidlaw Inc	2.80%
		Nova Corp	2.70%

Returns (as of April 30, 1998):

	Fund	Index*	Sector Weightings (as of March 31, 1998):	
1 Year	26.88%	30.35%	Financial Services	14.50%
3 Year	23.38%	23.85%	Oil and Gas	12.80%
5 Year	16.86%	17.65%	Industrial Products	11.50%
10 Year	12.57%	11.82%	Transport and Environment	7.40%
3 Year Risk	12.41	12.16	Others	5.50%
3 Year Beta	0.99	1.00	Gold and Precious Metals	4.30%
			Paper and Forest	3.80%
*Index refers to TSE 300 Total Return			Metals and Minerals	3.70%
			Communication and Media	2.30%
			Utilities	2.30%

Investment Objective:

The investment objective of this Fund is to maximize long-term capital return by investing in a diversified portfolio consisting primarily of shares of Canadian corporations. The assets of the Fund may from time to time, however, be placed in different classes of assets such as short-term investments, bonds, and debentures.

Exhibit 5   Ethical Growth Fund

Source: http://www.globefund.com (May 29, 1998)

*All figures are in Canadian dollars (C$).

Clean Environment Mutual Funds

This was a Toronto based mutual fund company offering four funds that invested in companies reflecting the concept of sustainable development. These funds included: Clean Environment Equity, Clean Environment International Equity, Clean Environment Balanced and Clean Environment Income. Exhibits 7 and 8 profile the two equity funds in complete detail. President and lead portfolio manager, Ian Ihnatowycz, did not use negative screening, but rather, looked for companies offering unique solutions to today's problems: "We focus on the science underlying the products or service and only buy companies that meet our financial and sustainability criteria."[15] Many of these companies were involved with waste cleanup and were environmental leaders. Ironically, Ihnatowycz also stated, "We don't really consider ourselves ethical funds,"[16] explaining that their primary concern was simply to invest in companies committed to a strong ecological future.

Fund Profile—Ethical North American Equity Fund

Fund Sponsor:	Ethical Funds Inc.	**Top Holdings (as of March 31, 1998):**	
Portfolio Manager:	Ethical Funds Inc.		5.00%
Inception Date:	Sep-68	Merck & Company Inc	5.00%
Total Assets:	$181.18 Million	Lucent Technologies Inc	4.60%
Sales Fee Type:	No Load	Bristol-Myers Squibb Common	4.50%
Mgmt Expense Ratio:	2.47%	Airtouch Communications	4.30%
Fund Type:	U.S. Equity	Dell Computer Corp	4.20%
Globe 5 Year Rating:	A+	MBNA Corp	4.20%
RRSP Eligibility:	Foreign	Colgate Palmolive Co	4.00%
Min. Initial Investment:	$500.00	Campbell Soup Co	3.80%
		Walt Disney Company	3.80%
		Home Depot Inc	3.60%

Returns (as of April 30, 1998):

	Fund	Index*	Sector Weightings (as of March 31, 1998):	
1 Year	55.14%	44.36%	Others	63.00%
3 Year	37.33%	34.20%	Financial Services	20.50%
5 Year	24.45%	26.09%	Consumer Products	9.20%
10 Year	14.78%	20.66%	Transport and Environment	5.40%
3 Year Risk	15.42	11.15		
3 Year Beta	1.24	1.00		

*Index refers to S&P 500 Composite (CAN$)

Investment Objective:

The investment objective of this Fund is to maximize long-term capital return by investing in a diversified portfolio consisting primarily of North American stocks. The assets of the Fund may from time to time, however, be placed in different classes of assets such as bonds, money market securities and debentures.

Exhibit 6   Ethical North American Equity Fund

Source: http://www.globefund.com (May 29, 1998)

*All figures are in Canadian dollars (C$).

Investors Group

Investors Group, the largest mutual fund company in Canada, operated the Investors Summa Fund, profiled in Exhibit 9. The company's only social fund began in 1987 and in 1998 had over $465 million in assets. Fund manager, Allan Brown, also used a "best-of-sector" approach to picking stocks.[17] After he selected his picks, they were screened for things such as alcohol, tobacco, gambling, military weapons, pornography, environmental issues and repressive regimes. Brown explained that his management team was open to all potential investment opportunities: "We do not exclude any sectors when picking stocks. We want to reward companies for being responsible and trying to improve their ethical standards."[18]

U.S. ETHICAL FUNDS

The concept of socially responsible investing has been around for quite awhile in the U.S.[19] The founder of The Pioneer Group, a religious man, used a "sin" test to screen out companies when he started his fund in 1928. There were 24 funds

---

Fund Profile

Fund Sponsor:	Clean Environment Mutual Funds	**Top Holdings (as of March 31, 1998):**	
Portfolio Manager:	Acuity Investment Management		
Inception Date:	Jan-92	Ati Technologies Inc	8.80%
Total Assets:	$283.53 Million	Fairfax Financial Holdings Ltd	6.60%
Sales Fee Type:	Optional	Yogen Fruz World-Wide Inc	6.40%
Mgmt Expense Ratio:	2.88%	Geac Computer Ltd	5.20%
Fund Type:	Canadian Equity	Philip Services Corp	4.40%
Globe 5 Year Rating:	A+	American Eco Corp	4.00%
RRSP Eligibility:	Yes	CFM Majestic Inc	3.70%
Min. Initial Investment:	$500.00	Zenon Environmental Inc	3.60%
		Optus Natural Gas Dist Income Fund	3.10%
		Cinram International Inc	2.80%

Returns (as of April 30, 1998):

	Fund	Index*	**Sector Weightings (as of March 31, 1998):**	
1 Year	45.89%	30.35%	Industrial Products	37.00%
3 Year	30.98%	23.85%	Transport and Environment	22.00%
5 Year	22.11%	17.65%	Others	14.00%
10 Year	N/A	11.82%	Financial Services	11.00%
3 Year Risk	11.70	12.16	Consumer Products	10.00%
3 Year Beta	0.75	1.00	Communication and Media	3.00%
			Metals and Minerals	3.00%

*Index refers to TSE 300 Total Return

Investment Objective:

The investment objective of this Fund is to maximize long-term capital appreciation. The Fund will seek to generate strong, reasonably reliable growth of capital over the long-term by investing in equity securities of companies that have outstanding potential for growth. To reduce risk the Fund will invest primarily in a broad selection of equity securities, convertibles and warrants. It is intended that under normal circumstances the Fund will be almost fully invested in these securities. In periods of unusual market conditions, a significant portion of the Fund's assets may be held in cash and cash equivalents.

Exhibit 7　　Clean Environment Equity Fund

Source: http://www.globefund.com (May 29, 1998)

*All figures are in Canadian dollars (C$).

---

in this group, and in 1980, Pioneer added a South African screen. Methodists and Quakers started the Pax World Fund in the 1970s to avoid investments supporting the Vietnam War. The Dreyfus Corporation became the first traditional money-management house to add a socially screened fund in 1972, by developing the Dreyfus Third Century Fund. In addition to avoiding companies that did business in South Africa, the fund also chose to invest in companies that had records of good safety, health and environmental standards, as well as those that supported equal opportunity initiatives. In 1982, the Calvert Group offered both a mutual and a money market fund with a number of thorough social screens. The next few to follow were; the New Alternatives Fund, an energy fund; the Working Assets Money Fund;

Fund Profile

Fund Sponsor:	Clean Environment Mutual Funds	**Top Holdings (as of March 31, 1998):**	
Portfolio Manager:	Acuity Investment Management		
Inception Date:	Nov-93	Ati Technologies Inc	9.20%
Total Assets:	$32.38 Million	Yogen Fruz World-Wide Inc	7.40%
Sales Fee Type:	Optional	Scaffold Connection Corp	7.20%
Mgmt Expense Ratio:	2.77%	Fairfax Financial Holdings Ltd	6.00%
Fund Type:	International Equity	Dalsa Corp	5.40%
Globe 5 Year Rating:	N/A	Geac Computer Ltd	5.00%
RRSP Eligibility:	Foreign	Open Text Corp	5.00%
Min. Initial Investment:	$500.00	Philip Services Corp	4.00%
		Laidlaw Environmental Svcs Inc	3.90%
		Thermo Electron Corp	2.20%

Returns (as of April 30, 1998):

	Fund	Index*	**Sector Weightings (as of March 31, 1998):**	
1 Year	53.05%	32.55%	Industrial Products	42.00%
3 Year	28.53%	21.77%	Transport and Environment	18.00%
5 Year	N/A	19.02%	Others	14.00%
10 Year	N/A	13.06%	Financial Services	9.00%
3 Year Risk	13.71	10.47	Consumer Products	9.00%
3 Year Beta	0.54	1.00	Metals and Minerals	5.00%
			Communication and Media	2.00%
*Index refers to MSCI World (CAN$)			Utilities	1.00%

Investment Objective:

The investment objective of this Fund is to maximize long-term capital appreciation. The Fund will seek to generate strong, reasonably reliable growth of capital over the long-term by investing in equity securities of companies that have outstanding potential for growth and are located primarily outside of Canada. To reduce risk the Fund will invest primarily in a broad selection of equity securities, convertibles and warrants. It is intended that under normal circumstances the Fund will be almost fully invested in these securities. In periods of unusual market conditions, a significant portion of the Fund's assets may be held in cash and cash equivalents.

Exhibit 8   Clean Environment International Equity Fund

Source: http://www.globefund.com (May 29, 1998)

*All figures are in Canadian dollars (C$).

the Amana Mutual Funds Trust, offering a Muslim screen; and the Ariel Growth Fund, designed by an African-American financial firm. After the mid-1980s, the development of these funds took off, particularly, a trend toward environmentally friendly investment vehicles, and those supporting workers' rights. In 1998, the number of socially responsible funds was growing at a steady pace as investors continued to demand more options within the ethical investing category. Exhibit 10 displays the growth of ethical funds within the U.S. from 1982 to 1997.

The Calvert Group

The Calvert Group provided a large family of funds, which included seven equity funds. Two of these funds, the Calvert Capital Accumulation Fund A, and the Calvert Social Investment Fund Equity Portfolio A, are detailed in Exhibits 11

Fund Profile			
Fund Sponsor:	Investors Group	**Top Holdings (as of March 31, 1998):**	
Portfolio Manager:	I.G. Investment		
	Management Ltd.	Bank of Montreal	6.70%
Inception Date:	Jan-87	Royal Bank of Canada	3.80%
Total Assets:	$465.30 Million	Toronto Dominion Bank	3.80%
Sales Fee Type:	Both	CIBC Common	3.70%
Mgmt Expense Ratio:	2.48%	Yogen Fruz World-Wide Inc	3.00%
Fund Type:	Canadian Equity	Nokia Corp	2.90%
Globe 5 Year Rating:	A+	Petro-Canada	2.50%
RRSP Eligibility:	Yes	Aflac Inc	2.10%
Min. Initial Investment:	$1,000.00	Edperbrascan Corp	2.10%
		Boardwalk Equities Inc	2.00%

Returns (as of April 30, 1998):

	Fund	Index*	**Sector Weightings (as of March 31, 1998):**	
1 Year	39.53%	30.35%	Financial Services	24.30%
3 Year	27.53%	23.85%	Industrial Products	14.40%
5 Year	18.44%	17.65%	Consumer Products	9.50%
10 Year	12.21%	11.82%	Real Estate and Construction	7.00%
3 Year Risk	10.09	12.16	Oil and Gas	6.50%
3 Year Beta	0.75	1.00	Merchandising	4.90%
			Utilities	4.80%
*Index refers to TSE 300 Total Return			Communication and Media	4.10%
			Transport and Environment	4.00%
			Gold and Precious Metals	3.30%

Investment Objective:

The Fund's principal objective is long-term capital growth with moderate income generation. The Fund intends to invest primarily in common shares of Canadian corporations. In addition, investments other than common shares and securities convertible into common shares like rights and warrants will be included in the Fund's portfolio where such investments provide a valuable supplement to the Fund's holdings. These investments may include, but are not limited to, preferred shares and interest bearing investments such as bonds and money market instruments like commercial paper issued by corporations and government issued treasury bills. The Fund may invest in companies which are socially responsible and have adopted progressive standards and practices illustrative of an awareness towards economic, social and environmental issues.

Exhibit 9   Investors Summa Fund

Source: http://www.globefund.com (May 29, 1998)

*All figures are in Canadian dollars (C$).

and 12, respectively. Created in 1982, The Calvert Social Investment Funds employed a group of social researchers to conduct a "social audit" to determine the impact of a prospective investment. Using many of the same criteria as other similar funds, this fund focused on choosing stocks that supported the "quality of life."

Investments in these funds included household names like; Microsoft, Hewlett-Packard, Disney, Kellogg, Polaroid, BankAmerica and Whirlpool. Financially attractive investment opportunities were identified first, and then examined to determine the suitability of their inclusion in these funds.

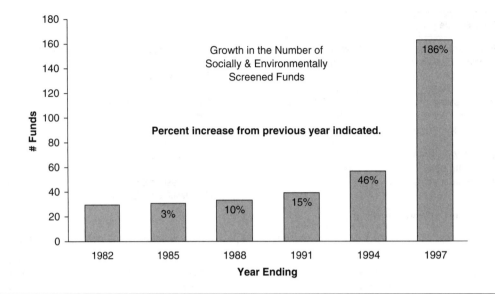

Exhibit 10   Growth of U.S. Ethical Funds

Source: http://www.goodmoney.com/fundsgrow.htm

Fund Profile

Fund Sponsor:	Calvert Group	**Top Holdings:**	
Portfolio Manager:	Eddie Brown		
Inception Date:	Oct-94	Home Depot Inc	4.47%
Total Assets:	$70.50 Million	Cisco Sys Inc	4.25%
Max. Sales Fee:	4.75%	Cardinal Health Inc	3.95%
Mgmt Expense Ratio:	1.96%	Carnival Corp	3.88%
Fund Type:	U.S. Equity	Chase Manhattan Corp	3.65%
RRSP Eligibility:	Foreign	Autozone Inc	3.43%
Min. Initial Investment:	$2,000.00	T Rowe Price & Associates	3.20%
Category:	Mid Cap (MID)	Networks Assocs Inc	3.06%
		Alza Corp Del	2.95%
		MCN Energy Group Inc	2.95%

Returns (as of April 30, 1998):

1 Year	48.73%	**Sector Weightings:**	
3 Year	25.69%		
5 Year	N/A	Utilities	24.53%
10 Year	N/A	Cap. Goods & Tech.	21.81%
Beta	1.35	Consumer Non-Cyclicals	16.23%
		Finance	16.10%
		Consumer Cyclicals	10.05%
		Basic Industries	4.91%
		Miscellaneous	3.43%
		Transportation	2.95%

Exhibit 11   Calvert Capital Accumulation Fund A

Source: http://www.findafund.com (May 30, 1998)

http://www.socialinvest.org/sriguide/mfpc.htm (May 29, 1998)

*All figures are in U.S. dollars (US$).

Fund Profile			
Fund Sponsor:	Calvert Group	**Top Holdings:**	
Portfolio Manager:	Loomis Sayles & Co.		
Inception Date:	Aug-87	SBC Communications Inc	5.02%
Total Assets:	$166.70 Million	Albertsons Inc	3.78%
Max. Sales Fee:	4.75%	Computer Assoc Intl Inc	3.73%
Mgmt Expense Ratio:	1.21%	Federated Dept Stores	3.72%
Fund Type:	U.S. Equity	General Nutrition Cos	3.56%
RRSP Eligibility:	Foreign	American Greetings Corp	3.42%
Min. Initial Investment:	$1,000.00	Dover Corp	3.20%
Category:	Growth—Domestic (GRD)	Symantec Corp	2.98%
		Ameritech Corp	2.95%
		Black & Decker Corp	2.93%
Returns (as of April 30, 1998):			
1 Year	30.53%	**Sector Weightings:**	
3 Year	23.33%		
5 Year	12.65%	Cap. Goods & Tech.	17.99%
10 Year	11.39%	Utilities	13.81%
Beta	0.93	Consumer Non-Cyclicals	13.67%
		Consumer Cyclicals	12.85%
		Basic Industries	12.41%
		Finance	10.01%
		Transportation	9.27%
		Miscellaneous	8.37%
		Energy	1.63%

Exhibit 12   Calvert Social Investment Fund Equity Portfolio A

Source: http://www.findafund.com (May 30, 1998)

http://www.socialinvest.org/sriguide/mfpc.htm (May 29, 1998)

*All figures are in U.S. dollars (US$).

Management stayed actively involved with the companies it had selected. Company management was engaged in dialogue with each corporation, sending numerous letters and holding meetings. When necessary, resolutions were voted on at annual shareholder meetings, at which time participants could elect to divest. In this way, Calvert representatives acted as advocates for higher social and environmental practices.

The Dreyfus Corporation

The Dreyfus Corporation was one of the oldest and largest mutual fund companies in the U.S. It was primarily an investment adviser or administrator for more than 150 mutual fund portfolios. The Dreyfus Third Century Fund (Exhibit 13) was a capital growth oriented fund concerned with the enhancement of the quality of life in America. As of April 30, 1998, net assets were nearly US$900 million and the one-year return was 40.48 per cent. The fund screened for investments that did not involve weapons, alcohol, tobacco, gambling or unsafe products. The fund also looked for companies with good environmental practices and labor relations.

Domini Social Investments

Domini Social Investments offered two socially responsible investment products; the

Fund Profile

Fund Sponsor:	The Dreyfus Corporation	**Top Holdings:**	
Portfolio Manager:	Maceo K. Sloan		
Inception Date:	Mar-72	Federal Natl Mtg Assn	3.56%
Total Assets:	$899.70 Million	Colgate Palmolive Co	3.33%
Max. Sales Fee:	No Load	Cisco Sys Inc	3.31%
Mgmt Expense Ratio:	1.03%	Merck & Co Inc	3.25%
Fund Type:	U.S. Equity	BMC Software Inc	3.20%
RRSP Eligibility:	Foreign	Medtronic Inc	3.13%
Min. Initial Investment:	$2,500.00	Bristol Myers Squibb Co	2.96%
Category:	Growth—Domestic (GRD)	Guidant Corp	2.92%
		Allstate Corp	2.69%
		Sunamerica Inc	2.66%

Returns (as of April 30, 1998):

		Sector Weightings:	
1 Year	40.48%		
3 Year	31.79%		
5 Year	20.03%	Finance	23.06%
10 Year	16.55%	Consumer Non-Cyclicals	20.29%
Beta	1.11	Cap. Goods & Tech.	20.21%
		Basic Industries	13.00%
		Utilities	11.30%
		Transportation	5.09%
		Energy	3.60%
		Consumer Cyclicals	3.46%

Exhibit 13   Dreyfus Third Century Fund

Source: http://www.findafund.com (May 30, 1998)

http://www.socialinvest.org/sriguide/mfpc.htm (May 29, 1998)

*All figures are in U.S. dollars (US$).

Domini Social Equity Fund (Exhibit 14), and the Domini Money Market Account. The Domini Social Equity Fund sought to provide long-term capital appreciation from a diversified equity portfolio of socially screened companies. The fund was an index fund, which held the 400 stocks that make up the Domini Social Index. Although the fund sought to match the index, its performance typically fell short by a small percentage due to operating costs. The fund included companies with records of good community involvement, the environment, employee relations and hiring practices. It also avoided those companies involved with alcohol, tobacco, gambling, nuclear power and weapons contracting. The social objectives of the fund were advanced by proxy voting, by filing shareholder resolutions and by maintaining constant communication with the chosen corporations.

Praxis Funds

Ranked in the top one-third of U.S. mutual funds in 1997, the four-year-old Praxis Funds was considering moving north to become Canada's first religiously based mutual fund. This group included three funds; an international fund, a growth fund and an income fund. These funds used a variety of Mennonite screens to sort out nondesirables, and looked for corporations involved in health care, housing, food and education.[20] As of April 30, 1998, the MMA

Fund Profile—Domini Social Equity Fund			
Fund Sponsor:	Kinder, Lyndenberg, Domini & Co.	**Top Holdings:**	
Portfolio Manager:	Team Managed		
Inception Date:	Jun-91		
Total Assets:	$397.50 Million		
Max. Sales Fee:	No Load	Not available	
Mgmt Expense Ratio:	0.98%		
Fund Type:	U.S. Equity		
RRSP Eligibility:	Foreign		
Min. Initial Investment:	$1,000.00		
Category:	Growth—Domestic (GRD)		
Returns (as of April 30, 1998):			
1 Year	40.59%	**Sector Weightings:**	
3 Year	31.79%		
5 Year	22.49%		
10 Year	N/A		
Beta	1.04	Not available	

Exhibit 14   Domini Social Equity Fund

Source: http://www.findafund.com (May 30, 1998)

http://www.socialinvest.org/sriguide/mfpc.htm (May 29, 1998)

*All figures are in U.S. dollars (US$).

Praxis-Growth Fund (Exhibit 15) had assets totalling US$132 million.

ETHICAL FUNDS—THE DEBATE

As a fairly new investment practice, ethical investing was still undergoing a great deal of research and debate regarding its ultimate impact, as well as the level of returns and relative performance.

It was argued that an obvious benefit for a company with a public image of being environmentally friendly, or "ethical," was the resulting public goodwill, which had the potential to boost profits. Another argument in favor of ethical screening was that ethical companies might be more efficient. These companies could be expected to produce less waste, to have a more motivated and productive workforce, and to avoid law suits and bad publicity. Ethical firms also had established new industries or technologies that redesigned processes, used alternative techniques, preserved, reduced and recycled materials, and reduced pollution.

Ethical investments were sometimes based on smaller sized companies for two reasons. First, many large companies were eliminated because of their poor social records or unacceptable practices. Second, many small and emerging companies were those identified for their conscientious developments and re-engineered processes. Smaller companies often provided more room for potential growth, as well as adaptability to political and social changes. On the other hand, smaller firms were often more sensitive to economic swings.

The most common argument against ethical investing was that by applying screens to stock selection, fund managers were constrained in picking securities and could not choose stocks that would yield the highest returns. Diversification objectives could be impaired if a manager was limited to certain stocks and not others.

Fund Profile—MMA Praxis-Growth Fund

Fund Sponsor:	Mennonite Mutual Aid	Top Holdings:	
Portfolio Manager:	Keith Yoder		
Inception Date:	Jan-94	Thomas & Betts Corp	3.75%
Total Assets:	$132 Million	SBC Communications Inc	3.68%
Max. Sales Fee:	No Load	Alza Corp Del	3.64%
Mgmt Expense Ratio:	1.75%	Boston Scientific Inc	3.59%
Fund Type:	U.S. Equity	Williams Cos Inc Del	3.46%
RRSP Eligibility:	Foreign	Albertsons Inc	3.33%
Min. Initial Investment:	$500.00	First Data Corp	2.93%
Category:	Growth—Domestic (GRD)	Johnson & Johnson	2.91%
		Deere & Co	2.90%
		Lowes Cos Inc	2.85%

Returns (as of April 30, 1998):

1 Year	37.70%	Sector Weightings:	
3 Year	26.16%		
5 Year	N/A	Consumer Non-Cyclicals	25.10%
10 Year	N/A	Utilities	17.08%
Beta	0.79	Finance	17.07%
		Transportation	10.82%
		Basic Industries	8.48%
		Energy	7.22%
		Consumer Cyclicals	4.38%
		Miscellaneous	4.05%
		Cap. Goods & Tech.	3.86%
		Non U.S.	1.93%

Exhibit 15   MMA Praxis-Growth Fund

Source: http://www.findafund.com (May 30, 1998)

http://www.socialinvest.org/sriguide/mfpc.htm (May 29, 1998)

*All figures are in U.S. dollars (US$)

Another common concern of suspicious investors related to the level of research and monitoring required to select and manage an ethical fund. This additional effort could come with a price tag attached in the form of higher management expense ratios. Given the extra work required of ethical fund managers, there was also concern that they might lose sight of the financial outlook for each company, while finding themselves wrapped up in ethical debates and controversial discussion.

Some critics were particularly worried about the additional risk created by potential ethical crises. Top-rated ethical companies could be downgraded in anticipation of bad publicity relating to an accident, debatable practice, or destructive product. Investors could lose money, if an "ethical" company came under heavy investigation. Most ethical funds would sell off the same company under such circumstances, accentuating the drop in share price.

Investors that chose socially responsible funds wanted their money to form part of a solution and to be a catalyst for social change. Critics complained that these funds did not actually advance the causes they supported because mutual funds themselves did not affect the value of a company. The transfer of shares of stock in the open market, it has been argued, did not help or hinder a company's ability to raise additional capital. There was no question, however, that when investors worked together with other concerned parties, such as socially-aware consumers, unions, religious organizations and social activists, change could happen. The South African experience of the end of apartheid was used as an example of what could be accomplished. By refusing to support the South African economy, social groups, political groups and investors were able to instigate substantial change.

THE STEVENSONS—THE DEBATE CONTINUES

We know in our complex economic system it's impossible to be absolutely pure. We do our best, but we recognize there are always grey areas.

—John Liechy,
President of Praxis Funds[21]

If they were to go ahead with making an ethical equity investment, the next decision for Ian and Beth Stevenson would be to determine which companies to invest with, and which fund would best meet their objectives. Ian had already gathered some information to help them with their decisions. Exhibits 5 to 9 outline the Canadian-owned funds, and Exhibits 10 to 15 outline the U.S.-owned funds that they could select from. Exhibits 16 and 17 break down the top 15 holdings of the S&P 500 and TSE 300, respectively.

Beth looked confused and turned to Ian,

It does sound as though these funds offer comparable returns, but I still have a number of questions. What about RRSP eligibility? And what if we determine that a U.S. fund is the best choice? If we are going to call ourselves ethical investors, is it ethical for us to invest in another country's companies rather than our own?

Besides, I am not even sure what I consider to be ethical. It's true that a company like Walt Disney Co. has an excellent reputation as an employer, but what about some of the violence in the movies they produce?[22] Or what about nuclear power plants? A significant portion of our electricity is nuclear power generated, but it is extremely destructive to

Top 15 Company Weights (as of April 30, 1998)	
General Electric Common	3.2%
Microsoft Corp Common	2.5%
Coca Cola Co Common	2.2%
Exxon Corp Common	2.1%
Pfizer Inc Common Cum Rts	1.7%
Merck & Co Inc Common	1.6%
Intel Corp Common	1.5%
Royal Dutch Pete Nlg1.25 (NY Regd)	1.4%
Wal-Mart Stores Inc Common	1.3%
IBM Common	1.3%
Procter & Gamble Co Common	1.3%
Bristol Myers Squibb Common	1.2%
Lucent Technologies Common	1.1%
AT&T Corp Common	1.1%
Johnson & Johnson Common	1.1%

Exhibit 16   S&P 500

Source: 1998 Portfolio Analytics Limited (Pal Trak).

Top 15 Company Weights (as of April 30, 1998)	
BCE Inc Common	6.3%
Royal Bk Cda Common	4.3%
Northern Telecom Ltd Common	3.6%
CIBC Common	3.4%
Bank of Montreal Common	3.3%
Toronto Dominion Bk Common	3.1%
Bank of Nova Scotia Common	3.1%
Cdn Pacific Ltd Common	2.3%
Seagram Common	2.2%
Barrick Gold Corp Common	1.9%
Alcan Aluminium Common	1.7%
Newcourt Credit Grp Common	1.6%
Bombardier Inc Class B Sub Vtg	1.6%
Canadian Natl Ry Co Common	1.3%
Magna Intl Inc Class A Sv	1.2%

Exhibit 17   TSE 300

Source: 1998 Portfolio Analytics Limited (Pal Trak).

the environment, not to mention dangerous. Or what about Microsoft? They're a great company and many funds carry the company in their portfolio, but what about all the anti-competition law suits that are pending? Should we avoid these things, or are some things a necessary evil?

Ian nodded in agreement with his wife; there were still a number of things to consider before they made an investment. He couldn't ignore the feeling, however, that they should be using their money to help create a future that they could be comfortable with, both financially and socially.

NOTES

1. Mary Hagerman. "The Values of Rowing in the Ethical Pond," *The Financial Post.* February 19, 1998.

2. http://www.web.net/ethmoney/intro.htm, May 28, 1998

3. http://www.mfmag.com - John Montgomery. "Speaking Out: The Case for Socially Responsible Investing." September, 1995.

4. http://www.socialinvest.org/invsritrends.htm, May 25, 1998.

5. Ibid.

6. Mary Hagerman. "The Values of Rowing in the Ethical Pond," *The Financial Post.* February 19, 1998.

7. Ibid.

8. http://www.socialinvest.org/invsritrends.htm

9. Mary Hagerman. "The Values of Rowing in the Ethical Pond," *The Financial Post.* February 19, 1998.

10. http://www.mfmag.com - John Montgomery. "Speaking Out: The Case for Socially Responsible Investing." September, 1995.

11. http://www.kld.com, May 25, 1998.

12. http://www.web.net/ethmoney/what.htm - "The Ethical Money Guide," May 25, 1998.

13. http://www.vancity.com - "Wise Choices, Great Performance."

14. Andrew Allentuck. "Report on Mutual Funds," *The Globe and Mail.* August 21, 1997.

15. Mary Hagerman. "The Values of Rowing in the Ethical Pond," *The Financial Post.* February 19, 1998.

16. Mary Hagerman. "The Values of Rowing in the Ethical Pond," *The Financial Post.* February 19, 1998.

17. Ibid.

18. Ibid.

19. http://www.goodmoney.com. "How the Social Funds Have Grown Through the Years," May 30, 1998.

20. http://www.globefund.com - Lila Sarick. "Letting Conscience be Their Guide," *The Globe and Mail.* April 6, 1998.

21. http://www.globefund.com - Lila Sarick. "Letting Conscience be Their Guide," *The Globe and Mail.* April 6, 1998.

22. http://www.globefund.com - Lila Sarick. "Letting Conscience be Their Guide," *The Globe and Mail.* April 6, 1998.

THE RENT-TO-OWN INDUSTRY

Prepared by Professors Doug Schuler and Gerry Keim

Version: (A) 2004-11-23

Rhonda Ward[1] was devastated as she read her morning paper on September 22, 1993. As director of public and governmental affairs for the Association of Progressive Rental Organizations, the main trade association for the rent-to-own (RTO) industry, she was in charge of monitoring events concerning the industry, providing information to the public, following the regulatory events and planning governmental lobbying strategies. Ward knew, sipping her coffee, that today's article in the *Wall Street Journal* would pose challenges for her in the days and months to come.

THE RENT-TO-OWN INDUSTRY

RTO was a $4 billion-dollar industry in 1993. There were about 7,500 stores across the United States that rented furniture, appliances, electronic goods and similar products to over 3.5 million households. The industry experienced rapid growth in the early and mid-1980s, but this rate had slowed over the past five years.

About 70 per cent of the firms in the RTO industry were small, either being single shops or part of a group of five or fewer shops. But there were also large companies involved in the RTO business; approximately 20 firms were responsible for about 60 per cent of the industry sales.[2] Rent-A-Center was the largest company, with over 1,000 stores and about $600 million in revenues in 1992. Exhibit 1 lists the principal RTO companies in the United States.

The service that RTO firms offered is the rental of a consumer good, with some option of ownership. This arrangement is similar to the

Company	Annual Sales	Employees
Rent-A-Center	$600 M	5,000
RTO, Inc.	160 M	800
Aaron's Rentals, Inc.	145 M	1,400
REMCO American, Inc.	70 M	500
Colortyme	60 M	37
DEF Investments, Inc.	43 M	560
UCR, Inc.	36 M	540
WBC Holding, Inc.	30 M	295
Action TV & Appliance Rental	21 M	225
Racord, Inc.	12 M	160

Exhibit 1   Principal Rent-to-Own Companies in the United States, 1993

Source: David L. Ramp. Report on Dominant National and Regional Rent-to-Own Dealers in the United States. Submitted to the U.S. House of Representatives, Committee on Banking, Finance & Urban Affairs. April 6, 1993.

Note: This list does not include Magic Rentals, a subsidiary of Transamerica, which has about 300 stores nationwide, and had assets valued by Transamerica of $141.2 million at 1991.

British hire-purchase agreement, traditionally used as a way for lower middle class individuals to finance purchases of consumer goods. Typically, rentals were weekly, bimonthly and monthly, with weekly being the most popular. Customers did not incur debt upon renting the product, they simply "pay as they go." If consumers do not desire the product, they can return it to the RTO firm with no obligation. For people who desired the use of, for example, a large screen television for a week or a month, a RTO transaction may be more convenient than buying. Industry surveys indicated that 75 per cent of customers did not pursue ownership (although industry critics state that this figure is misleading because of rewritten rental contracts. The critics estimate that about 60 per cent of RTO customers pursue ownership.[3]), returning the rented item in less than four months.[4] Additionally, the RTO companies would deliver and install the product, repair it if necessary, and provided a loaner or replace the product if a repair cannot be made.[5]

But customers paid a price for these options. If the total amount of the payments required for ownership was summed, the annual effective interest rates typically exceeded 100 per cent and could be as high as 200 per cent to 300 per cent. For example, at Rent-A-Center, a television that had a suggested retail price of $299 had a rental price of $11.70 per week for 78 weeks and totalled $920.10 to own, an effective annual interest rate of 200 per cent.[6] See Exhibit 2 for a sample of rental rates. The promise of ownership could be costly. Says industry critic Congressman Henry Gonzalez (Democrat-Texas), "Through rent-to-own, a poor woman pays $1,200 for a $400 television set that a rich man can buy on credit for $450."[7] Furthermore, many of these customers are often educationally disadvantaged and may not fully understand the terms of the rental.[8]

An RTO store calculated a monthly balance on rent (BOR). The BOR was the monthly average of the number of units rented. A typical RTO store would have 500 to 600 units rented, with a range of 50 to over 3,000 units in a few stores in large cities. The average income per unit was between

$55 and $60 per unit per month. This was slightly lower than the figure in the mid-1980s, when $60 to $62 was the average income per unit. Theft of inventory was a problem for RTO stores; about 12 per cent of a rental dealer's inventory could be expected to be stolen each year.[9]

The most typical goods rented are: 1) furniture (30 per cent of total units on rent); 2) appliances (24 per cent); 3) TVs (19 per cent); 4) VCRs (11 per cent); and stereos (nine per cent). Other items rented include jewelry, pagers, home entertainment centres, exercise equipment and air conditioners, among others.

The industry claimed that it does not prey on the poor.[10] According to the industry, a typical customer of a RTO firm is an unmarried, single mother of two earning $20,000, or a newly married couple under the age of 35 with one or no children, and a median income of $30,000.[11] Critics state that these figures are highly inflated and that the poor and nearly-poor make up the vast majority of RTO customers.[12] Furthermore, according to Walter Gates, chairman and CEO of Thorn EMI Rental Americas, the real family income for the rental-purchase segment's core customers has and would continue to shrink in the foreseeable future.[13] The average renter would spend $1,075 annually for rental products.[14] Most of the customers lived near the RTO store; the industry's trade association estimated that 80 per cent of a store's business would be done with customers who live within a three- to five-mile radius of the store.[15]

At most RTO operations there was a limited, if any, credit check. Rent-A-Center simply verified the residence given, the source of income and contacted one or two of the six references a customer is required to provide.[16] See Exhibit 3 for a typical RTO application.

THE WALL STREET JOURNAL ARTICLE[17]

The *Journal's* article was a sweeping indictment of the RTO industry, through the investigation of the industry's largest player, Rent-A-Center, a subsidiary of Thorn-EMI PLC. Rent-A-Center is the largest player in the RTO industry and is Thorn's most profitable subsidiary and its largest contributor to operating profit.

Much of Rent-A-Center's growth comes from high pressure sales. "Upselling," which involves talking customers into more than they had originally wanted to rent, and aggressive closing tactics are commonplace. Scrambling to meet ambitious sales targets, employees routinely encourage unsophisticated buyers to rent more goods than they can afford. Says a former store manager, "Even if a customer can't afford it and you know it and they know it, we'll rent to them anyway." Sales pressures are particularly intense during holidays and around welfare-cheque day.

Despite the healthy profits made in renters fulfiling contracts (see the section above and Exhibit 2), this is not where Rent-A-Center

	New/Used	Cash Price	Pmt/Period	No. Pmts.	Total Pmts.	Est. APR
Product						
Washing Machine	Used	$150	$40.00	18	$720.00	315%
Refrigerator	New	$862	$22.99	78	$1,793.22	185%
TV	New	$550	$42.99	18	$773.82	46%
TV	Used	$200	$12.99	52	$675.48	323%
Refrigerator	Used	$700	$20.00	78	$1,560.00	125%

Exhibit 2   Sample Rates of Rent-to-Own

Source: U.S. Public Interest Research Group, Rent-to-Own Survey, 1993.

REMCO
The Goaheadandgetit Store.

Date _____ Time _____ am

Del. Date _____ pm

Del. Time _____

Taken By _____

Verified By # 1: _____ Verified By # 2: _____

Cust. Code _____

Prod. Code _____

Rates Quoted Mo. _____ Wk. _____

Terms _____

Unit # _____

CHECK ALL THAT APPLY

☐ NEW ☐ MONTHLY ☐ PHONE-IN

☐ RENTAL RETURN ☐ WEEKLY ☐ WALK-IN

DELIVERY/INSTALLATION INSTRUCTIONS

Rent _____

Del. & Proc. _____

Waiver _____

Total C.O.D. _____

Next Due Date _____

Key Map # _____

DELIVERY INSTRUCTIONS

Employment Code: ☐ Blue Collar ☐ White Collar ☐ Medical ☐ Domestic ☐ Sales ☐ Clerical ☐ Unemployment

Residence: ☐ Renting ☐ Own Home

Marital Status: ☐ Married ☐ Single

Race: ☐ White ☐ Black ☐ Hispanic ☐ Other

Sex: ☐ Male ☐ Female

Age: _____

Monthly Income: ☐ 1 = less than $700 ☐ 2 = $701-1,000 ☐ 3 = $1,001-1,250 ☐ 4 = $1,251-1,666

☐ 5 = $1,667-2,000 ☐ 6 = $2,001-2,500 ☐ 7 = $2,501 +

How Ordered: ☐ 1 = TV ☐ 2 = Radio ☐ 3 = Yellow Pages ☐ 4 = Flyers ☐ 5 = Other

Customer Type: ☐ 1 = New ☐ 2 = Repeat Customer ☐ 3 = Referral

Waiver: ☐ Yes ☐ No

Promo Code: AC = Advo Coupon CN = Store Coupon DM = Direct Mail FL = Flyer GV = Grapevine

MA = Mailer NP = Newspaper RF = Referral Freetime RA = Radio TV = Television

---

My name is _____ I'd like to ask you a few questions about the services Remco has provided you so far:

Product:

Did we . . .

Deliver your product?	☐ YES	☐ NO
Do it on time?	☐ YES	☐ NO
Have it clean and in good working order?	☐ YES	☐ NO
Give you the Owner's Manual?	☐ YES	☐ NO
Give you the Accessories?	☐ YES	☐ NO
Demonstrate the product?	☐ YES	☐ NO

Other:

Did we . . .

Explain the Agreement?	☐ YES ☐ NO
Satisfy you with our services?	☐ YES ☐ NO
Do you have any questions?	☐ YES ☐ NO

_____

_____

_____

Again, my name is _____, and I really appreciate you doing business with us. Should you have any questions, or need anything else, please call me at _____. We'll be happy to help you in any way that we can.

Actions Needed: _____

Actions Taken: _____

Date: _____ Call made by: _____

Exhibit 3 Sample Rent-to-Own Application

makes most of its profits. The big money is made in repossession: items that are rented, repossessed and then re-rented, can really make a lot of money for Rent-A-Center: in California, a $179 VCR brought in over $5,000 in a five year period. It is estimated that three out of four Rent-A-Center customers have items repossessed.

Given the tremendous profit potential, the "repo-man" is a regular part of Rent-A-Center's strategy: they will use phone calls, door knocking and intimidation to repossess items. Allegations of physical and psychological abuse are rampant. One Rent-A-Center employee dressed up in a Cookie Monster outfit on Halloween night, knocked on the door of a customer, and when they opened the door, barged into the house to repossess the rented merchandise. Reports were made of "couch payments," illicit sexual favors solicited by Rent-A-Center employees in exchange for a rental obligation. Rent-A-Center also fully employs the legal system to get liens on its delinquent customers' pay cheques, alimony or welfare cheques.

For low-income customers, however, Rent-A-Center has tremendous appeal. The chain gives them immediate use of brand name merchandise with no future obligations and the weekly payments are usually less than $20. Many of the customers are unemployed and on governmental assistance and are usually denied more traditional credit sources. As one store-owner put it, "They can't get a Sears card."

A similar industry tale comes from *Forbes*[18] in 1987: Many of Rent-A-Center's poor customers understand they're getting poorer. But given their financial standing, the point is academic. "Sure, you can get stuff for a lot cheaper if you've got the money outright," said customer Vernon Smith, a 26-year-old garbage truck driver in Wichita. But the father of three doesn't have the money. Why not just save $9.95 a week for 25 weeks and then go pay cash for a television set? With a sigh of resignation, Smith explained that he wanted the merchandise immediately and he didn't want anybody hassling him about creditworthiness.

ENTER HENRY GONZALEZ

While the sensationalized stories from the *Journal* brought tremendous public attention on the industry, the RTO industry had been under the watchful eye of House Banking Committee Chairman Henry Gonzalez for some time (see Exhibit 4). In March of 1993, Gonzalez called for hearings on the RTO industry, which were attended by industry representatives, state governments and consumer advocates.

Gonzalez introduced H.R. 3136, the "Rent-to-own Protection Act," into the House Committee on Banking on September 27, 1993, only five days after the *Journal's* article. This legislation would classify rent-to-own transactions as credit sales. The bill started with the findings of the March hearings on the industry, in which Gonzalez noted that RTO firms targeted low income and minority neighborhoods, that the majority of customers who entered RTO contracts did so as a means of financing their purchase, and that there existed a lack of disclosure on payment and collection practices and no protection for consumers similar to retail installment sales laws at the state and federal levels.

The most important aspect of the Gonzalez bill was its specification of a limit on the interest rate which an RTO firm could charge (Section 1004). Credit sales were regulated by the federal and state governments, and most states had capped interest rates at about 20 per cent maximum per year. In general, the limit on interest depended upon the maximum allowed by state usury laws on installment sales plus a reasonable markup for some of the services that the RTO firms performed for their customers. Furthermore, the bill made RTO transactions comply with federal credit laws, including the Truth in Lending Act, the Equal Credit Opportunity Act, the Fair Debt Collection Practices Act, and the Fair Credit Reporting Act.

The Gonzalez bill also put a prohibition upon aggressive repossession techniques and made violations subject to fine. Additionally, the bill

Democrats	Republicans	Independent
Kennedy (Chair-Subcommittee)	McCandless	Sanders
Gonzalez (Chair-Committee)	Castle	
LaRocco	King	
Gutierrez	Pryce	
Rush	Linder	
Roybal-Allard	Knollenberg	
Barrett	Bereuter	
Furse	Thomas	
Velazquez	Lazio	
Wynn	Grams	
Fields	Bachus	
Watt	Huffington	
Hinchey		
Kanjorski		
Flake		
Waters		
Maloney		
Deutsch		

Exhibit 4   Membership of the U.S. House of Representatives Committee on Banking, Finance & Urban Affairs, Subcommittee on Consumer Credit and Insurance (1993)

Source: Commerce Clearing House, Inc. September, 24, 1993.

required full disclosure of terms such as the cash price, the total amount of payments required for ownership and all additional costs and fees.

Parallel legislation was introduced by Senators Metzenbaum (Democrat-Ohio) and Durenberger (Republican-Minnesota) in the Senate (as Section 1566) on October 19, 1993.

THE CONSUMER CREDIT SYSTEM AND GOVERNMENT REGULATION

Consumer Credit

Banks, finance companies, credit unions, savings institutions, and retailers provide the majority of consumer credit. Almost 50 per cent of consumer loans are provided through banks and about 20 per cent through credit companies.[19]

A bank makes money by making loans to "good" customers. Of course, choosing good customers is not easy. Therefore, a priori, banks will screen potential borrowers with a number of criteria. Typically, banks will ask about employment, residence, and credit history. Exhibit 5 contains a consumer credit application from a major bank. The bank will "score" the applicant; enough satisfactory responses and the bank will judge that the applicant has the probability of making good on the loan. Applicants below the benchmark are denied loans.

Theoretically, a bank will make a loan to any individual if it correctly knows the risk profile of the applicant. A low risk individual will pay a relatively low interest rate, while a higher risk individual will pay a higher interest rate. If the bank can judge the situation correctly, it can make profits. However, banks generally will not make high-interest loans because they expect that it encourages very risky applicants.

Empirically, this seems to be the case. While the banking system provides credit to millions of customers, many individuals cannot qualify for credit through these channels. Manufacturer estimates indicate that about one third of the adult American population does not have

Consumer Loan Application

PLEASE TELL US ABOUT YOUR LOAN REQUEST

☐ AUTO ☐ NEW   PURCHASE PRICE$ _____
☐ BOAT ☐ USED   DOWN PAYMENTS$ _____
☐ OTHER _____
☐ SECURED ☐ UNSECURED

☐ INDIVIDUAL APPLICATION
☐ JOINT APPLICATION

SPECIFIC PURPOSE

DAY OF MONTH PREFERRED FOR PAYMENT (Circle One)
1   6   11   16   21   26

REPAYMENT TERM PREFERRED

COLLATERAL (IF SECURED)

AMOUNT REQUESTED $	ONEPLUS ☐ YES ☐ NO	WHERE DID YOU HEAR ABOUT US?	☐ TV ☐ BILLBOARD ☐ DIRECT MAIL ☐ NEWSPAPER/MAGAZINE ☐ RADIO ☐ FRIEND/RELATIVE ☐ OTHER SPECIFY_____

YOURSELF

NAME (FIRST, MIDDLE, LAST)   BIRTHDATE   SOCIAL SECURITY NO.
U.S. CITIZEN OR ☐ YES   ☐ UNMARRIED*
RESIDENT ALIEN ☐ NO   ☐ MARRIED ☐ SEPARATED

ADDRESS (STREET, APT. #)   CITY   STATE   ZIP
☐ OWN   ☐ LIVE W/RELATIVES
☐ RENT   ☐ OTHER SPECIFY _____

HOME PHONE NO.   YEARS/MONTHS AT PRESENT ADDRESS   MONTHLY RENT OR PAYMENT   PREVIOUS ADDRESS (IF CURRENT IS LESS THAN 2 YRS.)

NAME AND ADDRESS OF NEAREST RELATIVE NOT AT YOUR ADDRESS   RELATION TO YOU   RELATIVE'S PHONE NO.

NAME AND ADDRESS OF YOUR EMPLOYER (IF APPLICABLE, INDICATE: STUDENT, RETIRED, HOMEMAKER, ETC.)   TYPE OF BUSINESS   BUSINESS PHONE NO.

POSITION/TITLE   LENGTH OF EMPLOYMENT   GROSS SALARY   ☐ ANNUALLY ☐ MONTHLY ☐ WEEKLY

NAME & ADDRESS OF PREVIOUS EMPLOYER (IF CURRENT IS LESS THAN 2 YRS.)   POSITION/TITLE   LENGTH OF EMPLOYMENT

SOURCES OF OTHER INCOME AND MONTHLY AMOUNTS**

*Includes single, divorced and widowed.
**OPTIONAL: Alimony, child support, or separate maintenance income need not be revealed if you do not wish to have it considered as a basis for repaying this obligation. If revealed, indicate if received under: ☐ Court Order ☐ Written Agreement ☐ Oral Understanding

YOUR BANKING RELATIONSHIPS (CHECK ALL THAT APPLY)

DO YOU HAVE A BANK ACCOUNT?
☐ CHECKING ☐ SAVINGS ☐ OTHER SPECIFY: _____

OTHER FINANCIAL INSTITUTIONS? SPECIFY: _____
☐ CHECKING   ☐ SAVINGS   ☐ OTHER SPECIFY: _____

YOUR CREDIT REFERENCES (CHECK ALL THAT APPLY)

☐ MAJOR CREDIT CARDS (MASTERCARD, VISA, AMEX, DINER'S DISCOVER, ETC.)
☐ RETAIL STORES (SEARS, MONTGOMERY, ETC.)

☐ GAS & OTHER CARDS
☐ MANUFACTURER'S FINANCE COMPANY LOANS (GMAC, FORD, ETC.)

☐ OTHER FINANCE COMPANY LOANS (BENEFICIAL, TRANSAMERICA, ETC.)
☐ LOANS & OTHER INDEBTEDNESS* (PLEASE PROVIDE DETAILS BELOW)

*DETAILS FOR LOANS & OTHER INDEBTEDNESS (INCLUDE ALIMONY/CHILD SUPPORT)

BANK/CREDITOR	TYPE OF LOAN	MONTHLY AMOUNT	BALANCE

ALL APPLICANTS

☐ YES, I AUTHORIZE BANK NA TO AUTOMATICALLY DEBIT THE LISTED DEPOSIT ACCOUNT EACH MONTH IN THE AMOUNT OF THE PAYMENT DUE.
DEPOSIT ACCT. NO. _____

HAVE YOU DECLARED BANKRUPTCY, OR HAS AN INVOLUNTARY PETITION BEEN FILED AGAINST YOU IN THE LAST 10 YEARS?
☐ YES ☐ NO

DO YOU HAVE ANY OUTSTANDING JUDGMENTS OR PENDING LAW SUITS AGAINST YOU?
☐ YES ☐ NO

WOULD YOU LIKE CREDIT LIFE INSURANCE ON YOUR LOAN?
☐ NO ☐ YES IF YES, WOULD YOU LIKE ACCIDENT AND HEALTH INSURANCE ON YOUR LOAN?
☐ YES ☐ NO

DO YOU GUARANTEE/CO-SIGN ANY DEBT NOT SHOWN ABOVE?
☐ NO ☐ YES IF YES, DESCRIBE.

ARE YOU AN OFFICER, DIRECTOR, OR PRINCIPAL SHAREHOLDER OF ANY BANK?
☐ NO ☐ YES IF YES, WHAT BANK?

In applying for this loan, I/we certify that the statements contained herein are true and that I/we have filled out this loan application in sufficient detail that it will not be misleading. The Bank is authorized to obtain any information it deems necessary for the review of my/our application. I agree that if anything occurs before the Bank makes this loan which changes any of my statements, I will promptly tell the Bank. The Bank may request a credit report on me. If the Bank reviews, renews or extends my loan, the Bank may request a new credit report without telling me. I agree to pay any filing, lien search, appraisal, or survey fees incurred by the bank on my behalf in furtherance of this appilication request.

APPLICANT SIGNATURE	DATE	CO-APPLICANT SIGNATURE (IF APPLICABLE)	DATE

Exhibit 5   Sample Bank Application for a Consumer Credit Loan

credit.[20] Some are new in the market or have used up all available credit, while others are deemed too risky for any credit.

Credit Sales and Governmental Regulations

The Truth-in-Lending Act[21] was a federal law that covered credit sales, including certain leases (although not RTO contracts). Passed in 1968, the statute was Congress' most comprehensive effort to guarantee the accurate and meaningful disclosure of the costs of consumer credit and thereby to enable consumers to make informed choices in the credit market.[22] The Act generally required disclosures of the costs and terms of the loan, including such things as interest rates, grace periods for collections and repossession rights. It was administered and enforced by the Federal Trade Commission.

The Consumer Leasing Act required disclosures to consumers in certain lease transactions involving personal property and a lease term that exceeded four months. It also fell under the governance of the Federal Trade Commission.

Most credit sales are governed by state laws, which are generally more substantive and restrictive on leases than federal laws.[23] States have usury laws, disclosure laws, credit insurance laws, and default, repossession and resale laws. States also provide limited protections to consumers through Articles 9 and 2A of the Uniform Commercial Code.[24] The state usury laws set a maximum rate which a financial institution may charge annually for a consumer credit loan. These interest rates differ across states and through time, but generally do not exceed 25 per cent. States generally have installment sales laws or consumer credit codes that parallel the "contracts to pay" language of the federal Truth-in-Lending Law.[25]

Consumer groups have challenged the classification of RTO as non-consumer credit in state and federal courts. The RTO industry has prevailed in the vast majority of these cases. In one of the most recent rulings, a Federal District Court jury in St. Paul, Minnesota, decided in March of 1992 that these contracts were not credit sales, and thus are not covered by credit laws.[26]

STATE REGULATION OF THE RTO INDUSTRY

Currently, the RTO industry is regulated in 34 states. Michigan enacted the first RTO statute in 1984. In every state except Pennsylvania, the RTO transaction has been defined not to constitute a consumer credit sale under state retail instalment statutes or consumer credit codes.[27] The state regulations merely require certain disclosures and do not put a ceiling on interest rates (except in Pennsylvania). Typical state legislation includes disclosure of the weekly cost of an item, the number of payments required for ownership, the total cost to the consumer at the end of an agreement and a description of the goods. Most of these state regulations were supported by the RTO industry. Such state legislation has forced some of the sleaziest firms out of the industry for non-compliance.[28]

In Pennsylvania, RTO transactions are included under the state's installment sale law, which requires the merchant to state a cash price for the item and limits interest charges to 18 per cent. However, an investigation by the state's Attorney General found that this law has not been fully effective; RTO firms have evaded the state law by changing the "nominal" payment for ownership at the end of the lease or using a system of "disappearing payments," in which an individual pays a small rental amount, i.e., $1 per month, ad infinitum.[29] Thus, even in "regulated" Pennsylvania, effective annual interest rates from 82 per cent to 265 per cent can be found.[30]

THE LaROCCO BILL

In spite of imposed legislations, the RTO industry was not shunning Congressional politics completely. After an unsuccessful attempt at federal regulation in 1992,[31] Congressman Larry LaRocco (Democrat-Idaho) introduced H.R. 2803, the "Rental-Purchase Reform Act of 1993" (LaRocco Bill), to the Committee on Banking, Finance and Urban Affairs in the summer of 1993. The LaRocco Bill basically spread the pro-RTO industry state disclosure requirements to the Federal level.

The stated purposes of the bill were: 1) To assure meaningful disclosure of the terms of rental-purchase agreements, including the disclosure of all costs to consumers under those agreements; 2) to regulate collection practices; and 3) to provide certain substantive rights to consumers under rental purchase agreements (Section 1002). Commercial rentals were exempt.

The LaRocco Bill distinguished between rental-purchase and credit sales. Rental-purchase agreements provide the use of personal property for an initial period of four months or less, are automatically renewable with each payment, and permit but do not obligate the consumer to become owner of the property (Section 1002. Definitions 8A).

The types of disclosures which the RTO firm must make to the consumer, in writing and at the time of rental, involved: 1) the amount of the initial rental payment, including any fees or taxes at the inception, 2) the amount and timing of each payment; 3) the total number and total dollar amount of rental payments and other charges necessary to acquire ownership of the property; 4) a statement that the owner would not own the property until the consumer had made the total dollar amount necessary to acquire ownership; 5) a statement as to whether the rental item was new or used; 6) a statement of the manufacturer's suggested retail price of the item and the cash price for which the property was available from the RTO firm for sale; 7) a clear statement of the terms of the option to purchase contract (Section 1006).

Additionally, the LaRocco Bill specified certain consumer rights with late payments (a seven-day grace period), with returned rental goods and with substantial payment (60 per cent) of the total dollar amount necessary to acquire ownership of the rental good. The conduct for collection practices of RTO firms was also covered in the bill. Certain advertising disclosures were also mandated by this bill.

A POLITICAL DECISION

At January 31, 1994, Rhonda Ward had to assess the situation. The Gonzalez/Metzenbaum bills were well under way in the House and the Senate. The LaRocco Bill was sitting in the Banking Committee's Subcommittee on Consumer Credit and Insurance since August, 1993. The furor over the *Journal's* article had subsided, but had not gone away. Furthermore, for some consumer advocates, disclosures were not enough. Margot Saunders, managing attorney for the Washington office of the National Consumer Law Center stated: "This problem is about an industry targeting a segment of the population from whom they can charge outrageous prices."[32]

Ward had a number of issues to consider: 1) Did the public really know about the RTO industry? 2) Did the public really care about the RTO industry? 3) Did voters know about the RTO industry? 4) Were politicians focusing on this industry to protect the public interest? 5) Or was the self-interest of politicians the driving force for the Congressional hearings?

Ward also had to decide if the industry should mount a political campaign. If so, how should it be done? Her Association of Progressive Rental Organizations had political capabilities, but how should their resources be deployed most effectively? What possible alliances could be made? Should they use a Washington "hired gun" strategy or a grassroots approach? Should the battleground be in Congress or at the state level or in the courts?

None of these answers seemed evident. Still, the answers to these questions would help her understand the next steps that her Association of Progressive Rental Organizations should take.

NOTES

1. This name has been disguised.

2. David L. Ramp. Report on Dominant National and Regional Rent-to-Own Dealers in the United States. Submitted to the U.S. House of Representatives, Committee on Banking, Finance & Urban Affairs. March 31, 1993.

3. See written testimony of David L. Ramp. U.S. House of Representatives, Committee on Banking, Finance & Urban Development. March 31, 1993. pp. 253–254.

4. *Furniture/TODAY,* August 23, 1993: p. 31. In the hearings by the U.S. House, Committee on Banking, Finance & Urban Affairs, the industry trade association stated that the average rental agreement is terminated in about 100 days.

5. Association of Progressive Rental Organizations. Various publications. 1993.

6. *Wall Street Journal,* September 22, 1993. p. A1(6).

7. *Washington Post,* April 4, 1993.

8. *Washington Post,* November 23, 1992: p. B5.

9. Written testimony of the Association of Progressive Rental Organizations, U.S. House Committee on Banking, Finance & Urban Affairs, March 24, 1993, p. 2.

10. *Washington Monthly,* October 1993, v. 25. p. 12 (4).

11. *Washington Post,* November 23, 1992, p. B5.

12. See Testimony of Ernest D. Preate, Jr., Attorney General of Pennsylvania, U.S. House of Representatives, Committee on Banking, Finance & Urban Affairs, March 31, 1993, pp. 99–113.

13. *Furniture/TODAY*, August 23, 1993: p. 2.

14. Association of Progressive Rental Organizations, 1993.

15. Association of Progressive Rental Organizations, November 1993, p. 3.

16. Critics state that the industry's claim of no credit check is false. For examples of credit checks, see testimony of David L. Ramp, before the U.S. House of Representatives, Committee on Banking, Finance & Urban Affairs, March 31, 1993, p. 249.

17. Alix M. Freedman. Peddling Dreams: A Marketing Giant Uses Its Sales Prowess To Profit From Poverty, Thorn EMI's Rental Centers Push Sofas, Rings, VCRs To the Poor at High Rates, Repos and 'Couch Payments,' *Wall Street Journal,* September 22, 1993, p. A1(6).

18. This paragraph was taken in full, from *Forbes,* May 19, 1987, p. 73.

19. Mona J. Gardner and Dixie L. Mills. *Managing Financial Institutions: An Asset/Liability Approach.* Second Edition, 1991, Chicago: Dryden Press, p. 404.

20. Association of Progressive Rental Organizations, Fact Sheet, November, 1993, p. 2

21. The Truth-in-Lending Act is found at 15 U.S.C. Sec. 1601 et seq.

22. James P. Nehf. Effective Regulation of Rent-to-Own Contracts, *Ohio State Law Journal,* Summer, 1991, Vol. 52.

23. See prepared statement of the Federal Trade Commission on RTO, before the House Banking, Finance & Urban Affairs Committee, March 31, 1993.

24. See James P. Nehf, *ob. cit.,* for a detailed explanation.

25. Association of Progressive Rental Organizations. RTO Legal Reference Index: Understanding the Rent-to-Own Industry, 1993.

26. John Hendren. State News Services, March 31, 1993.

27. Written testimony of the Association of Progressive Rental Organizations, U.S. House Committee on Banking, Finance & Urban Affairs, March 26, 1993.

28. Mike Hudson. *Washington Monthly,* October 1993, v. 24 p. 12 (4).

29. See testimony of Ernest D. Preate, Jr. Attorney General of Pennsylvania. Before the U.S. House Committee on Banking, Finance & Urban Affairs, March 31, 1993, pp. 112–113.

30. *Washington Post,* April 4, 1993.

31. Larry LaRocco (Democrat-Idaho) introduced the Lease Purchase Agreement Act, H.R. 4497, into the House in 1992. It was heard in the Consumer Affairs Subcommittee in June 1992, but did not make it out of committee. The bill mirrored the state level RTO regulations fairly closely.

32. Paul Kirby, State News Service, March 25, 1993.

PEMBINA PIPELINE CORPORATION

Prepared by Ken Mark under the supervision
of Professor Alexandra Hurst

Version: (A) 2001-07-06

INTRODUCTION[1]

Patrick Walsh, president of Pembina Pipeline Corporation, was abruptly awakened by a telephone call from Jim Thomas, his operations manager. It was 4:30 a.m. on August 2, 2000, in downtown Calgary, Alberta, and Thomas had no time for pleasantries:

> Walsh, I just heard from one of our pipeline operators that our new Taylor-Prince George pipeline burst open this morning! Get up! We're leaking thousands of barrels of crude into a pristine salmon river. Our emergency response crews have started containment efforts but we're going to need much more help. What are we going to do next?

A wave of panic shook Walsh awake. Grabbing his car keys and the cellular phone, he scrambled into his Ford Explorer and began driving to Pembina's Calgary head office. Negotiating corners with one hand on the steering wheel, Walsh kept Thomas on the line:

> I want to know all the details of the spill now! Our first concern will be to contain the oil! I'll join you in a few minutes at the office and we'd better come up with something. Damn it, Thomas, we don't even have media relations people, much less a PR agency!

PEMBINA PIPELINE CORPORATION

Involved in the transportation of light crude oil, condensate and natural gas liquids in western Canada, Pembina Pipeline Corporation owned the Pembina Pipeline Income Fund (the Fund), a publicly traded Canadian income fund. This fund was established in 1997 to give the investing public the opportunity to participate in a stable, well-managed pipeline transportation entity that had provided high quality, reliable service to the Canadian oil and gas industry since the mid-1950s. The Fund was intended to provide unitholders with attractive long-term returns through its investment in Pembina, which had a mandate to efficiently operate its pipeline systems and actively seek expansion opportunities. The Fund paid cash distributions to unitholders on a monthly basis. The trust units traded on the Toronto Stock Exchange under the symbol PIF.UN.

Pembina's pipeline systems served a large geographic area with 7,500 kilometres of pipeline and related pumping and storage facilities. The systems were well positioned in the heart of western Canada's oil and natural gas production areas. There were four systems in total:

- Peace Pipeline System—Central Northwest Alberta
- Pembina Pipeline System—Central Southwest Alberta
- Bonnie Glen Pipeline System—Central South Alberta
- Wabasca Pipeline System—Northern Alberta

Collectively, Pembina's pipeline systems transported over 40 per cent of conventional light crude oil production in Western Canada.

OPERATIONS

Pembina's pipeline systems were maintained and operated by a dedicated group of field employees located in 10 field offices. Pembina's corporate head office was located in Calgary, Alberta where technical and administrative staff supported the pipeline operations. Through its pipeline, Pembina transported light crude oil, condensate and natural gas liquids. Virtually no heavy oil was transported on any of the Pembina systems, nor was Pembina a natural gas carrier. The company did not own the product it transported but, similar to a trucking company, it took custody of the product from when it entered the pipeline until it was delivered to the owners.

Pipelines and the materials used in them were designed, built and tested to high standards. When pipelines were properly maintained failures due to pipe breakdown were rare. Pembina had several maintenance programs in place to ensure line integrity. These were:

Internal Inspection Program

Internal inspection tools were designed to allow pipeline operators to measure the wall thickness along the pipe so that areas of metal loss could be located and repaired. These tools had been incorporated into Pembina's monitoring program, and pipeline systems were inspected on a rotating seven- to eight-year cycle. Pembina's pipeline systems, with the exception of the recently purchased Federated system, were last checked in 1998.

Hydrostatic Testing

Government regulations required new pipelines be filled with water and pressure tested to 125 per cent of their licensed maximum operating pressure before the lines could be put into service. The hydrotest was designed to reveal any structural weakness in the pipe or welds. Although not a regulatory requirement, all of the major pipelines in the Peace and Pembina System (built prior to 1970) had been hydrostatically retested. The first two phases of hydrostatic testing of the 16-inch mainline had been completed and confirmed the strength and quality of the pipe tested.

Bacterial Monitoring and Treatment

Pembina's pipeline systems employed programs of regular product sampling and testing for bacteria. Producers with excessive bacteria were required to treat their tanks with a biocide to kill the bacteria. Similarly, biocide was periodically shipped through pipelines to control and kill bacteria.

Cathodic Protection

Cathodic protection systems were used on steel pipelines to impress a small voltage on the pipe to help protect it from external corrosion. Every month, readings were taken on Pembina's pipelines to ensure that these systems were operating at effective levels. A complete cathodic protection survey was done annually in compliance with regulatory requirements and any necessary repairs or adjustments to the systems were made. Evaluation of the survey results provided important information on the condition of the pipeline coatings.

EXPANSION

Pembina intended to continue to expand its service through new battery and facilities connections, tie-ins to third-party pipelines, and expansion of Pembina's existing systems to service new oil- and gas-producing areas. Ongoing exploration and development activity by the producer community was expected to continue to fuel demand for pipeline service in the regions served by Pembina's pipeline systems, particularly on the Continental System operating in northwestern Oregon and northeastern Washington.

The most significant increase in throughputs on the Pembina System could potentially come from technology developments to improve the recovery of crude oil in the oil fields. It was estimated that only 21 per cent of initial crude oil in place was recoverable using present technology.

Pembina's management was actively reviewing potential acquisitions and believed that Pembina was very well positioned to take advantage of any favorable opportunities to acquire or otherwise expand Pembina's business.

INCIDENT CONTROL MECHANISMS

While environmental incidents had never occurred on Pembina's pipeline systems, Pembina maintained insurance to provide coverage in relation to the ownership and operation of its pipeline assets. Property insurance coverage provided coverage on the property and equipment that was above-ground or that facilitated river crossings, with recovery based upon replacement costs. Business interruption insurance covered loss of income arising from specific property damage. The comprehensive general liability coverage provided coverage in actions by third parties. The latter coverage included Pembina's sudden and accidental pollution coverage, which specifically insured against certain claims for damage from pipeline leaks or spills.

THE PIPELINE BREAK

Thomas continued to feed more information to Walsh:

> At about 1:20 this morning, the pipeline break and subsequent spill of crude oil occurred at mile post 102.5 of the Federated Western Pipeline—the same pipeline company that we bought 12 hours ago.[2] The break released crude oil into the Pine River just upstream of Chetwynd, B.C.
>
> Our emergency response field team set up a control site half a mile downstream from the spill. A second control site was set further downstream at the creek's entry into the Pine as a precautionary measure, and a third control site beyond the town of Chetwynd is to be set up today.

When he heard that the spill had occurred near a small town and could threaten its water supply, Walsh knew that there was no stopping immediate media coverage. He let Thomas continue uninterrupted.

> We've set up vacuum facilities at each control site which are being manned right now, removing oil from the river. My guys are telling me that we'll lose as much as 6,300 barrels.[3] In the next hour, I'm going to set up a mobile lab to continuously test the water upstream from Chetwynd. I'll also contact district officials to inform residents along the Pine River of the situation and to put in guidelines to restrict their water usage.

AT PEMBINA'S HEAD OFFICE

Walsh parked his car and ran up two flights of stairs to the office. Thomas and the crew of pipeline monitors were hovering over a computer screen detailing Pembina's network of pipelines. Walsh knew that he would need help in dealing with the media. Even if he were able to contact and retain a media relations firm, he realized that the initial press release would be his responsibility. Thomas exclaimed:

> We still do not know what caused the pipeline break, but I can tell you that we have between 70 to 80 people already onsite, beginning clean-up activities. They're using oil booms to stop the flow of oil and sponges to soak up what they can.

A map of the area was laid out on the table. Walsh could now clearly see the proximity of the town of Chetwynd to the spill. He knew that the health of the town and surrounding area would have to be his first priority. First, Pembina had to contain the oil spill.

It was 5 a.m. and daylight would break within the next two hours.

NOTES

1. This case was written with public sources and the permission of Pembina Pipeline Corporation. Some facts have been altered.

2. The deal to purchase Federated was completed on July 31, 2000—see Exhibit 1.

3. This amount (6,300 barrels) was equivalent to one million cubic metres of oil.

NEWS RELEASE

Attention Business Editors:

Pembina Pipeline Corporation Completes Purchase of Federated Pipe Lines Ltd.

Not for distribution to United States Newswire Services or dissemination in the United States.

CALGARY, July 31 /CNW/—Pembina Pipeline Income Fund (TSE-PIF.UN) announced today that its wholly-owned subsidiary Pembina Pipeline Corporation has successfully completed its purchase of 100% of the shares of Federated Pipe Lines Ltd. from Anderson Exploration Ltd.'s subsidiary, Home Oil Company Limited, and Imperial Oil Limited. In a related transaction, Pembina closed the purchase of the Cynthia Pipeline from Imperial on the same date.

Following the completion of this transaction, Pembina's combined pipeline network comprises roughly 7,000 kilometres of pipeline and related pumping and storage facilities and in 1999 transported 548,400 barrels per day of crude oil, condensate and natural gas liquids. The Federated acquisition entrenches Pembina's position as Canada's leading feeder pipeline transportation business. Total consideration paid by Pembina for the Federated shares was $340-million, including the assumption of Federated debt. A further $9-million was paid for the Cynthia pipeline. The transactions were financed utilizing a new $420-million syndicated credit facility arranged with a Canadian chartered bank.

Pembina is working toward the timely and orderly integration of the Pembina and Federated pipeline networks, and expects a seamless transition during the consolidation process. The combination of these considerable pipeline operations is expected to produce significant synergies and operating efficiencies which will provide substantial value for Pembina's customers and Unitholders of the Fund. Incremental cash flow generated by the acquired assets is expected to be sufficient to service the acquisition debt as well as fund an increase in the distribution payments to Unitholders of the Fund once the pipelines have been successfully integrated.

Pembina's purchase of the pipeline assets of the Western Facilities Fund for $40.3-million is scheduled to close in late August 2000 following approval by the Unitholders of Western.

The Pembina Pipeline Income Fund is a Canadian income fund engaged, through its wholly-owned subsidiary Pembina Pipeline Corporation, in the transportation of crude oil, condensate and natural gas liquids in Western Canada. Trust Units of the Fund trade on the Toronto Stock Exchange under the symbol PIF.UN.

This news release contains forward-looking statements that involve risks and uncertainties. Such information, although considered reasonable by Pembina at the time of preparation, may prove to be incorrect and actual results may differ materially from those anticipated in the statements made. For this purpose, any statements that are contained herein that are not statements of historical fact may be deemed to be forward-looking statements.

Such risks and uncertainties include, but are not limited to risks associated with operations, such as loss of market, regulatory matters, environmental risks, industry competition, and ability to access sufficient capital from internal and external sources.

This news release shall not constitute an offer to sell or the solicitation of an offer to buy securities in any jurisdiction. No securities of Pembina Pipeline Income Fund have been registered under the United States Securities Act of 1933, as amended, and such securities may not be offered or sold in the United States absent registration, or an applicable exemption from the registration requirements of such Act.

Exhibit 1   The Purchase of Federated Western Pipelines

Source: www.pembina.com, December 29, 2000.

7

INDIVIDUAL ETHICS
IN THE CORPORATION

One of the most challenging dilemmas facing an employee at any level of an organization is to know what to do when she finds herself an unwilling bystander to questionable organizational ethics. The employee is not directly responsible for a situation, but she may observe a questionable action and may find herself in a position where she can either ignore it or take a proactive stance. The classic choices in this situation are "exit, voice, or loyalty"—leave the organization, blow the whistle, or simple carry on in the job, taking no action.

Leaving the organization or ignoring the problem and carrying on (the exit and loyalty options) beg interesting questions: To what extent does an individual have a moral obligation proactively to prevent unethical activity at his or her workplace? Clearly, one is under a moral obligation not to take part, even when instructed to (this was a central discussion in trials of lower-level military officers as war criminals at Nuremburg after World War II, when they claimed that they were following orders, a defense that was not accepted). But is it morally acceptable to walk away from a problem? Do we have a *duty* to try to prevent questionable acts? What do you do if you are not sure that what you see is illegal or unethical? Does it make any difference if you were in a position to exert some influence but did not do so? What are your obligations when you honestly think that any action that you could take would be completely ineffective?

If you believe that you are morally bound to do something, just how far are you obliged to go? There is plenty of evidence that blowing the whistle often carries an enormous personal cost—loss of job, a reputation as a troublemaker, and so on. You may be at the receiving end of a sophisticated corporate communications effort to discredit you, and an individual is far less powerful than a large corporation is, and few individuals have the communications and public relations expertise to match a well-oiled corporate press campaign. You need look no farther than the movie *The Insider,* which documents Dr. Jeffrey Wigand's experiences with the tobacco industry. Blowing the whistle may be the right thing for *you* to do, even if it causes you personal loss. But do you have the right to impose that cost on others, such as your family? And if you do, how big a cost? What duty do you have to involve them in your decision?

If, after careful consideration, you decide to blow the whistle, what is the best way to do it? You have a responsibility to yourself (and invariably your family) to minimize the cost to yourself, and it makes sense to ensure that you disseminate your message to the most effective political constituencies—those in a position to take effective corrective action—and that the message is not ignored. In the Jane Lennox case, an administrative assistant at the Edmonton, Alberta, branch of Vandelay Securities was faced with a dilemma. Her superior had requested a purchase of shares in a firm whose securities were restricted to residents of Alberta for one of her clients who resided in British Columbia. On the purchase request form, the client's province of residence was listed as Alberta, and a post office box address was given. This transaction was the latest in a series that made her feel uncomfortable. The primary teaching objective of this case is to explore when and how one should blow the whistle. The case allows debate on the individual's responsibility to herself, the firm, the clients, and other stakeholders in exposing the unethical acts of a colleague. Secondary ethical issues include insider trading, high-pressure sales tactics, conflict of interest, and misrepresentation to a regulator. In the Simon Donato case, the vice president at a large insurance company (Northeastern Mutual Life, included in Chapter 1) has been terminated along with several hundred colleagues. He believes that his former employer has misrepresented the magnitude of the terminations to the government to avoid incurring the cost of meeting pension obligations to other employees. He himself does not stand to benefit from any settlement but has to decide whether to incur significant personal costs to pursue his crusade. Does he have any moral obligation to do so, or is his pursuit of justice for his colleagues virtuous beyond expectations?

A second challenging situation, which was alluded to in Chapter 1, arises when a superior or corporate norms and incentive systems expect (or require) someone to do something questionable—nothing illegal, but something that nevertheless raises concerns. Many management bonus schemes are flawed, for example, in that individuals receive rewards for doing something that increases profitability in the short run that the manager knows will be harmful to the shareholders (or other stakeholders) in the long run. Aggressive sales quotas cause salespeople to persuade customers to buy a product now that they would have preferred to buy later (or not at all). Imposing dysfunctional rewards systems on employees places unreasonable burdens on their integrity. Employees are human and should not be expected to display superhuman virtue to do their jobs right.

In TALFI-Sudbury Canada, an assistant manager of a branch has been asked by his superior to hide documents relating to a lawsuit outside of the office until the trial is over. He does not have the best of relationships with this superior, and so he must decide what to do. The Winston Liu, Bookman case provides a situation in which a new sales representative for an educational book and software company faces a request from a prospect for a "deal." The request goes against company norms but not against any firm corporate policy. He is caught on the horns of a dilemma, which is heightened by the fact that he has not sold a lot recently and needs the commission to survive. In the WestWood Securities (A) case, a junior broker at a securities firm has mixed emotions. He enjoys the success his sales have brought him; however, he is concerned about misleading clients to obtain those sales. He has been offered a promotion to senior broker and must decide whether to accept the promotion, continue in his current position, leave the firm, or do something else. A supplementary case, WestWood Securities (B), discusses his decision.

Humans are not perfect—their ethical reasoning is flawed, they are prone to temptation, they make ethical errors, and sometimes they are caught. This always places their supervisor in a difficult position—although some collective agreements leave little room for discretion, many workplaces are not unionized, with the result that the manager discovering the violation has to deal with the situation fairly. In the Harrison-Lockington (A) case, a partner at a leading Canadian law firm discovers that one of the firm's employees has been stealing from the business. After a discussion with the employee, he must decide immediately how to handle the crisis: How did this happen? What steps are needed to prevent this from happening again? How should he deal with the employee? A supplement, Harrison-Lockington (B), which is available separately, highlights how the partner addressed the issue with staff at the office. In the Graham Stewart—General Manager (A) case, Graham Stewart, a general manager and partner in a chain of restaurants, is faced with a serious problem. His restaurants have been struggling to stay afloat for some time, and he has been concerned about the reasons for cash flow problems. An innocuous question from the company bookkeeper sets off an alarm bell in Stewart's head, and an investigation reveals several problems in his partner's financial activities, both personally and professionally. At the time of this discovery, Stewart's partner is on vacation. The general manager must concern himself with the ethical and legal implications of his discovery, trying to assess what he might do and how and when he should do it. The A case outlines the history of the restaurant chain and the details of its current issues. The Graham Stewart—General Manger (B) and Graham Stewart—General Manager (C) supplements discuss Stewart's investigation of the problems and the meeting between the partners.

Following Aristotle, the cases in this chapter provide an opportunity for students to learn more about their personal approach to ethics and, in so doing, to enhance their virtue. The final cases cover a range of dilemmas in which an individual has to make a decision in response to a difficult work situation. The John McCulloch—United Beef Packers case presents a harrowing description of the meat packing industry. John McCulloch takes a job as an assistant general manager at a meat packing plant. After a short time in the job, he discovers that it was nothing like he expected, worker safety is constantly compromised, the safety of the public from consuming tainted food is compromised, and everything is subordinated to the production line's constant movement. The primary focus of the case is McCulloch's decision—he must decide whether to stay with the company. However, it also provides an opportunity to review the trade-off between shareholder and employee rights.

In the case of Stephen Zhang's Opportunity, a university graduate working as a project manager for a small Chinese consulting firm is in the middle of a very important project when he receives a call from a former colleague offering him an attractive package to move to a new company. His decision would affect many stakeholders, and he wonders what might happen to the project he is working on. He has only three days to decide whether to stay with the firm or accept the offer. The Tanya Silk case is set in the intersection of the financial services and information industries. Publicly available information is vital for well-functioning capital markets, and rules prohibit insider trading (on the ethical grounds of fairness to investors and the utility of market effectiveness). But who is an insider from an ethical point of view? An investment adviser has received an order to buy 1,000 coffee contracts for her client. The client, a senior weather analyst at Environmex, a private weather forecasting service, told her that he had just seen the latest long-range satellite weather data for Brazil that indicated a strong likelihood of frost in the coffee-producing regions. Frost would kill the coffee plants, seriously reducing the supply of coffee, which in turn would lead to an increase in price of the contracts. The information would be made public in a day or so. She thought to herself, "This client has been pretty accurate with these forecasts; maybe it's time I started telling my other clients and put in some of my own capital." The main pedagogical objective of this case is to explore the definition of, and responsibility for, insider trading. The question "When is it appropriate to use information not widely available to the market?" should be the main focus of student debate. Other ethical issues include confidentiality and using corporate information for personal use when it does not harm the company.

JANE LENNOX

*Prepared by Niels Billou under the
supervision of Professor David J. Sharp*

Version: (A) 1999-08-20

"This one's really pushing the limit," Jane Lennox, administrative assistant at the Edmonton, Alberta, branch of Vandelay Securities (Vandelay), thought to herself. It was late Friday afternoon, in June 1997, and her superior, Martha Richards, had requested a purchase of shares of a firm whose securities were restricted to residents of Alberta for one her clients who resided in British Columbia. On the purchase request form, the client's province of residence was listed as Alberta and a post office box address was given. This transaction was the latest in a series that made Jane feel uncomfortable. "What am I supposed to do now?" Jane wondered.

MARTHA RICHARDS

Martha Richards was 37 years old, single and had been in the securities industry for the past 15 years. She had been with Vandelay, a medium-sized regional brokerage house, for the past five years. Before that she had been employed by five other securities firms, changing firms, on average, once every two years. She was a good performer, consistently placing in the top quartile in terms of trading volume and assets under management. Her blunt and direct style garnered the respect of her co-workers for "telling it like it is." At the same time, some felt a little intimidated by her forceful manner. A colleague commented:

> Martha is a very focused and driven person. She doesn't have the time for those who don't catch on to her way of thinking and aren't prepared to get down to business. She has no problem telling you what she thinks of you either—usually in no uncertain terms. I think she loses some clients due to her style, but she's a street smart pro who's been in the

business for a long time and clients come to appreciate her expertise.

JANE LENNOX

Jane Lennox was 23 years old, single and had been working for Vandelay for the past year. She had recently graduated from an office administration program at the local community college and had been fortunate to find an opportunity to work at a securities firm. Having decided that she wanted to establish a career in the industry, she was working towards completing the Canadian Securities Course. Initially, she was pleased that she had been assigned to work with Martha, given her impressive track record. However, it was not before long that she began to regret her assignment.

PRIOR EVENTS

Within a few months of working for Martha, Jane noticed several things that disturbed her. For example, Jane noted that Martha had a tendency to browbeat her clients, especially those who were novice investors, into accepting trades with which they were not comfortable. Jane explained:

> Martha tends to get very intense when talking about a deal. She makes it seem like you would be stupid not to take a deal that she is recommending. At times, she practically forces clients into something they aren't altogether comfortable with. Take Mrs. Monmore, for example. She's retired, unmarried, disabled and relies on income from her portfolio to support her. Martha recommended that she redeem $100,000 of her Canada Savings Bonds and put them into an oil and gas company that was

trading on the Alberta Stock Exchange for $7.75 a share and an industrial income fund. Mrs. Monmore didn't really understand these investments and didn't want to make the trades, but Martha told her that they had virtually no downside risk and that she would be making a stupid mistake if she let the opportunity slip by her. She went so far as to say that the oil and gas stock is "almost guaranteed" to hit $15 by the end of the year and the income fund has never produced less that 10.5 per cent return per year. Well, the oil stock was at its high at the time, and the low for the year was about $2 per share—it was highly speculative. The income fund had been producing fairly good returns but it had only been running for two years.

Jane gave another example of what she considered unsettling behavior:

In February, Martha started promoting debentures for a small manufacturing company called Tri-Star International. At the time, the Tri-Star debentures had not yet qualified for distribution, although they did qualify a month or so after Martha started selling them. In April, she started to promote shares of another small manufacturing company, Tropez International, which recently announced they were going to merge with Tri-Star. She was promoting these companies rather heavily to pretty well all her clients, which I found odd, as both firms were unknown. As I was mailing some documentation confirming a client's purchase of Tri-Star debentures, I noticed that the documents were signed by its secretary-treasurer, a James Kaczmarski, who happens to be Martha's boyfriend.

CURRENT EVENTS

It was now June 1997 and Jane was faced with yet another example of what she considered to be questionable behavior. Martha had requested a purchase of shares of a firm whose securities were restricted to residents of Alberta for one of her clients who resided in British Columbia. On the purchase request form, the client's province of residence was listed as Alberta and a post office box address was given. The client, an elderly doctor who had lived in Edmonton previously but had retired to British Columbia two years earlier, had continued to maintain an account with Martha.

Given what she thought of as Martha's increasingly questionable acts, Jane wondered what to do now.

SIMON DONATO: DECIDING ON A COURSE OF ACTION

Prepared by Ken Mark under the supervision of Professor David Sharp

Copyright © 2001, Ivey Management Services   Version: (A) 2002-04-10

INTRODUCTION

On the 7th of June, 2000, Simon Donato had to decide whether to fight the Northeastern Mutual Life appeal of the Alberta Pension Commission's ruling that the firm's pension scheme be partially wound up. His position had been terminated three years ago, after 15 years of employment as vice-president of corporate lending with Northeastern Mutual Life. Since then, he had been on a personal mission to correct what he perceived as some of the wrongs in the management of Northeastern Mutual Life. The major issue was that Northeastern Mutual Life had decided not to volunteer to do a partial wind up of its pension fund when it had terminated what Donato thought was a significant number of positions.

Now his dealings with the Pension Commission had progressed beyond letter writing into legal preparation. The hiring a lawyer to act on the employees' behalf in the tribunal against the company's appeal of the commission order could cost upwards of $80,000 over the next few years. In addition, what effect would his involvement have on his future employment prospects?

SIMON DONATO

Donato had been vice-president of corporate lending during his 15-year tenure with Northeastern Mutual Life. He managed a department of three people who handled approximately 20 per cent of Northeastern Mutual Life's cash flow. He had received his MBA from the Richard Ivey School of Business in 1971. What Donato saw was, in his opinion, a recent gross imbalance of profit-sharing among shareholders, employees and customers. He also believed that a few senior employees received an excessive amount of gain from timely allocated stock options—just prior to a brutal cost-cutting program. In his view, as the company had only provided terminated employees with the value of the pension contributions (plus nominal interest) and had not volunteered a partial pension windup, between $25 million and $50 million had been arbitrarily transferred from long-term employees to shareholders.

NORTHEASTERN MUTUAL LIFE

From its beginnings in northern Alberta selling small life insurance policies, Northeastern Mutual Life now marketed a full range of financial service products across the country and in many parts of the world. Headquartered in Calgary, Northeastern Mutual Life was the major subsidiary of the Alberta Insurance Group, which operated life insurance, reinsurance, general insurance and investment and other activities in North America and internationally. Calgary Insurance Group was a publicly-held Canadian corporation which owned 98 per cent of the shares of Northeastern Mutual Life.

In 2000, Northeastern Mutual Life's investments totaled more than $15 billion, and included mortgages for tens of thousands of Canadians. The company's investments also provided financial support for a wide variety of Canadian industries and governments. Significant investment subsidiaries included the National Care Corporation, which developed and operated retirement homes, Doran Properties Limited, which owned commercial properties and Edmonton Park Limited, an office, residential and hotel complex.

Almost 3,000 people were members of Northeastern Mutual Life's Canadian sales organization, the largest among insurance companies in Canada. In addition, Northeastern Mutual Life had about 2,600 administrative staff.

Since 1996, Northeastern Mutual Life's return on equity had declined steadily from 11.5 per cent to seven per cent. In early 2000, a meeting of Senior Management Partnerships (SMP), the management body of Northeastern Mutual Life, decided that administrative costs had to be cut by 20 per cent and that an acquisition of a U.S.-based rival would permit additional increased efficiencies.

The layoffs began in the fall of 1995, with the closing of three mortgage offices and terminations in the information systems department. In early spring 1996, the president of Northeastern Mutual Life announced a major restructuring that involved layoffs of over 400 administration staff. Later that year, Northeastern Mutual Life acquired the Canadian operations of Central Insurance, a U.S.-based insurer, and announced further layoffs of 500 to 700.

EX-STAFF INVOLVEMENT WITH THE ALBERTA PENSION COMMISSION

Under Alberta law, if a company with a pension fund restructures and there is a substantial staff reduction, then it may be required to do a partial windup of the pension for all terminated staff. A partial windup involved the payment at age 65 of a full pension to any ex-employee whose age plus service on the date of termination was 55 or over (known as qualified employees) and payment to all terminated employees of a portion of the pension surplus. In 1996, on the basis of reports sent to the Alberta Pension Commission by Northeastern Mutual Life that indicated 371 staff out of a complement of 5,000 had been terminated, the Commission reported to Northeastern Mutual Life that no partial windup would be required.

However, in early 1997, former staff, including Donato, began to question the administrative staffing numbers that Northeastern Mutual Life had provided to the Commission in 1996. Staff managed to obtain an internal company report indicating that the gross administrative staff reductions in 1996 were in the 650 to 700 range. Reporting their findings to the Pension Commission triggered a Commission request for clarification from Northeastern Mutual Life. Donato commented:

> We knew that their number of 371 terminated was not right. I deduced the number in three different ways and figured out that it's got to be in the 600 to 900 range. The counter-argument of the company was that the rest of the people left voluntarily, but the legislation does not distinguish between voluntary or forced leave—a partial windup is appropriate either way.

> About the principle of fairness: Does the employment contract that stipulates that when you leave, you get only the cumulative nominal contributions back, constitute a fair contract? Does it cause managers to fire people near retirement if the present value of future obligations to such is very high versus the pension contribution amounts? Who does this surplus belong to?

In its reply, Northeastern Mutual Life claimed that only 371 administrative staff had been terminated and that another 125 had left voluntarily. Clarification requests by the Commission continued until December 24, 1999, when an extensive list of questions was sent to the company by the superintendent of the Pension Commission. Northeastern Mutual Life responded that they had already answered all the questions. The superintendent, not satisfied with their answer, ordered a partial windup of the pension fund in February 2000. This applied to employees terminated in 1996, and possibly 1995 and 1997, in

addition to those terminated in 1998 and 1999. This was estimated to cost Northeastern Mutual Life up to $100 million.

Northeastern Mutual Life appealed the superintendent's ruling to an independent tribunal. The hearings would commence in August 2000.

THE NORTHEASTERN MUTUAL LIFE MEMBERS COMMITTEE

Since initiating the Northeastern Mutual Life Members Committee in 1997, Donato had been engrossed in his quest for a partial windup of the pension fund. He commented:

> My eight-person committee did not even know me before working on this project—I was in a different department. Some of our committee members have spent days doing lists, e-mails, letters—an unbelievable amount of work. I estimate that of the 600 to 800 people let go, there are probably 200 people who have contributed hard cash—roughly $200 each.

> At first Northeastern Mutual Life did not know who was behind the committee. Once the appeal is launched, they will know my identity. It's funny that I'm involved in this: even if the employees win and there is a partial pension windup, I will not get anything from the partial windup—I'm in this to correct an injustice. This is not right.

DECISION TIME

Donato sat down and did some rough calculations: he knew that if he were to pursue this further, it may cost upwards of $80,000. Furthermore, his employment opportunities would be limited if prospective employers did not wish to hire a "whistle-blower." Already, Northeastern Mutual Life had blocked his access to Calgary lawyers—he knew that the corporation's reach was nationwide. Without his involvement, however, he was certain that the Northeastern Mutual Life Members Committee would not have the drive to continue. He had to make a decision.

TALFI-Sudbury Canada

Prepared by Peter McCann under the
supervision of Professor James A. Erskine

     Version: (A) 1999-07-12

Joe Hills, assistant manager of the Sudbury branch of Term and Lease Financing, Inc. walked into his office at 8:10 a.m., Thursday, September 17, 1998. He was preoccupied with thoughts about the company's annual management conference starting on Sunday. He read quickly a facsimile on top of a pile of documents on the corner of his desk. It was a message to the regional vice-president from Hills' boss relating to a pending $8,000,000 lawsuit. There was a handwritten message to the branch secretary in the distinctive red ink scrawl of Hills' boss: "Give these documents to Joe to hide somewhere out of the office until the trial is over." It was not signed.

Term and Lease Financing Inc. Background

Term and Lease Financing Inc. (TALFI) was incorporated in 1974 as a Toronto-based, wholly owned subsidiary of a European manufacturer to facilitate the sale of its open pit excavation equipment in the resource and commodity sectors of the Canadian economy. In 1984, TALFI increased its services to include commercial and industrial real estate financing. By the mid-1990s, TALFI had grown to assets of $3.5 billion, with regional offices in Vancouver, Edmonton, Ottawa, Toronto, Montreal and Halifax, and a staff of 327. The chairman of its board of directors was European, but all other officers and employees were Canadian. TALFI branches were "lending and sales" branches only, as TALFI was not a deposit-taking institution.

TALFI had enough branches and people to write three times its volume of new business. Its client base was largely composed of small companies

that had been prepared to pay a higher interest rate in exchange for the higher ratio financing that TALFI extended. During the current recession in the resource and commodity sectors, these companies suffered from decreased sales, often high fixed costs, and high interest rates on their operating lines of credit and variable rate term debts. TALFI's expenses, due to borrower defaults, tripled while net income continued to suffer due to substantial losses on its loans to companies.

Over a three-day period in February 1998, the company announced the closure of 11 of its 38 branches. Two regional offices were closed: one vice-president and one assistant vice-president were fired along with 133 people, or about 40 per cent of TALFI's staff. Some of the people had been with TALFI since the late 1970s. The aura of corporate care and concern was shattered and the surviving staff wondered if a second wave of cuts would follow. The release in mid-August of the June 30, 1998, financial statements increased the fear in the organization. (See Exhibit 1 for a partial organization chart.)

Annual Management Conference

TALFI's 1998 annual management conference was scheduled for September 20 to 23, 1998, at Monte Ste. Marie, a major conference centre about 60 miles north of Ottawa. All management and executive officers, from branch assistant managers up to and including the chairman, were required to attend. In all, there would be about 75 at the conference. Hills had attended every conference since 1993 and he expected that this conference would be considerably more sombre than previous conferences.

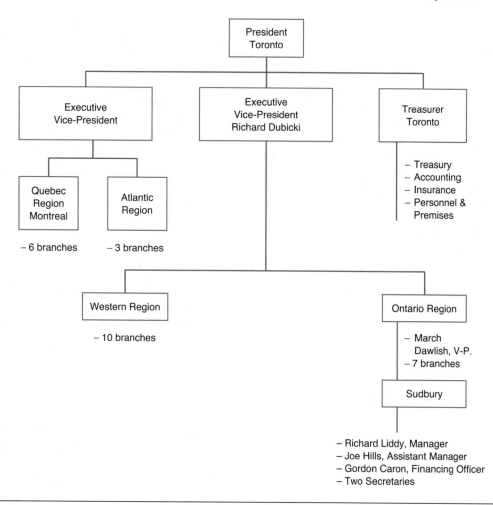

Exhibit 1   Partial Organization Chart February 1995

Source: Casewriter's summary.

JOE HILLS

Joe Hills was born and raised in a small Manitoba town. Hills was the eldest of six children, and he worked part-time from the age of 13 in his parents' feed mill. When he was 18, he left home and worked in a variety of unskilled jobs in and around Winnipeg. After two years, he married a young woman from his home town and, a year later, he started a three-year community college business program. Hills worked nights and weekends and during the summers as a laborer and car-wash attendant to supplement his wife's income.

Upon graduation, Hills talked the regional office of a well-known Crown corporation into hiring him.

I told them that their policy of hiring only university graduates was stupid. If they never hired community college graduates, they didn't have any basis of judgment and, therefore, they didn't know what they were talking about. I told them to hire me and, if I didn't work out in the first six months, to fire me. I learned a lot, but the bureaucratic rules and old fogeys drove me to distraction, and before two years were up, I started to look for another job.

Hills applied to TALFI and was accepted in April 1990. He started in TALFI's Winnipeg office as a junior financing officer reporting to the branch manager. Joe Hills brought the staff total to four. After a few months, he was promoted to "financing officer," and when the senior financing officer was transferred in late 1991, he was promoted to senior financing officer. In early 1992, Hills wrote a five-page memo to Richard Dubicki, the executive vice-president, recommending that TALFI investigate new systems technology in its branches to speed up financial statement analysis and lighten the branch administration burden. In September 1992, he was invited to the head office to discuss his recommendations. A week after the head office discussions, he was offered a head office position as a policy and procedures manager. The position was new, and it paid 25 per cent more than he was making. He accepted the job, and he and his wife and their new infant moved to Toronto in January 1993.

Joe recalled his short tenure in Toronto:

Taking that promotion was a big mistake. I was a small-town boy and I did not like Toronto. I had been successful in field operations because I was street smart and aggressive and never took no from a client whom I was trying to sell a lease or loan to. I liked the informality of the Winnipeg branch and the flexibility in my hours. I liked the adrenaline rush of trying to sign up deals. I liked the hustle. Head Office did not run like the Winnipeg office, and after a year or so, I had made so many stupid political mistakes that my boss fired me in April 1994. In retrospect, some of my mistakes were simple things like being frequently late, and although I worked late and sometimes on weekends, my boss's schedule was tied to the commuter train and so he never noticed.

Other mistakes were political—like threatening to boycott the head office golf day because it was for men only and trying to fire the first person hired by TALFI, a 78-year-old gentleman.

A suicidal mistake was an argument (in front of the president, the two executive vice-presidents, the senior vice-president, and the treasurer) with the vice-president of corporate planning about a new

subsidiary that was his pet project. I claimed that the underlying cost data were faulty and that more valid data would show that we would lose a huge amount. I won the argument insofar as TALFI did not proceed, but I alienated some key people.

After I was fired, I sat down and counted about 20 major fiascoes, and I guess that the root cause was that I was too opinionated and too quick to express my opinions without due regard for my own status or power base and without any regard for other people's sensitivities. In retrospect, I was right on every major issue, but being right isn't enough. You have to line up your allies and wait until the timing is right. Timing and allies are everything. Getting fired made me stop and think.

Fortunately, I had not made an enemy of Richard Dubicki, the executive vice-president, and he told me to work away during my six-month notice period. I sent out 254 one-page letters, with two-page résumés to every possible employer that I could think of. I was very aware that I didn't have a university education and that employers could pick from a big pool of well-educated professional credit people. I started to drink heavily, and I gave up working out and trying to get my black belt in Karate.

In July, my wife told me that she was pregnant with our second child; that snapped me out of my depression. In late August, the executive vice-president called me in and told me that someone had left Sudbury and that he wanted me to go there. He said that TALFI would pay all moving expenses and even absorb the real estate drop on our house. I was desperate and said yes right away. He told me that I might not be so pleased after I had been in the branch for awhile, but he didn't say anything else.

Before leaving the head office, Hills decided to investigate Dubicki's comments by calling Ed Zarkov, a former vice-president of TALFI who had supervised Sudbury until he left to assume the presidency of an unrelated company in 1993. Hills had gotten to know and admire Zarkov when Hills had done some analysis of branch and regional administration functions and had used Zarkov's region as a model of efficiency. Zarkov told Hills that Sudbury was a difficult branch to work in, that the manager was a heavy drinker who had a constant staff turnover, and that Zarkov had always felt that he had to double-check Sudbury loan submissions.

SUDBURY

Hills and his wife bought a large house and took a big mortgage. They discovered that Sudbury was a much nicer community than its reputation indicated. They hoped to stay a long time and to raise their two children in one community. A long stay in Sudbury would enable them to get on their feet financially. He was making $85,500, including the taxable benefits of a company car and a nominal-rate company mortgage, but they were struggling on the one income with total debts of over $168,000, and soon, two children to feed and clothe.

The first week in the Sudbury branch was busy. The branch had a level of loans in arrears that was above the national average and indicators of branch administrative efficiency were below the national average. Hills worked about 55 hours the first week to scan the files of his portfolio of accounts. At night, he would try to help his pregnant wife finish the unpacking and look after their child to give his wife a rest. On Monday of the second week, Richard Liddy, the branch manager, made some pointed remarks to the effect that the branch was busy and that the job of an assistant manager was not a "cushy head office job." Later in the week, when Hills made a passing reference to the high level of arrears in the branch, Liddy became extremely upset and told Hills that he did not need "some head office refugee to tell me how to run my branch." Liddy also made another reference to the brevity of Hills' 11-hour days. Hills had met Liddy at the management conferences and Liddy seemed like a highly social person, quick with a smile and a handshake. The sharpness of Liddy's remarks and his imperial attitude to the staff came as a shock to Hills. Hills was also surprised at the hours that Liddy worked. Liddy was often in the office before 6:30 in the morning and rarely left before 7:00 at night. Hills resolved to make a concerted effort to placate Liddy and to work at least as many hours as Liddy. Hills was convinced that the commodities recession could continue to force a shakeout at TALFI and he was morbidly afraid of losing his job for a second time.

The other staff members seemed to be pleasant. The secretary and the part-time secretary had been with TALFI for seven and four years, respectively. They were both diligent, and the secretary was especially competent in her normal secretarial duties plus in certain administrative functions that TALFI secretaries did not usually handle.

GORDON CARON

Gordon Caron, the financing officer when Joe arrived, had joined the branch a year earlier, and he seemed to be pleasant and anxious to please. Caron was 29 years old, and he and his wife had two small daughters. Caron was studying at night for his certified general accountant's designation. Hills had been impressed at Caron's restraint in the face of a tirade from Liddy about a late client financial statement review. Hills assumed that Caron was also concerned about job security, but he avoided discussing job security or personalities with Caron.

On the Monday of the week before he was to leave on holidays in mid-September 1995, Caron wrote up two small loans in draft form and with handwritten notes. He gave the two drafts to Liddy. Liddy, who was very busy with some chamber of commerce business, authorized both loans after a cursory review of Caron's work. Caron delivered typed finance contracts to both companies on Tuesday and both companies accepted the deals immediately. Caron finished a proper write-up of the deals, had them typed, and put them on Liddy's desk on Thursday afternoon. On Friday morning, when Liddy carefully reviewed the analysis of the two deals, he found that Caron had made fundamental and inexcusable errors in the analysis and that the two deals were, in fact, bad risks.

Unfortunately, TALFI was now under a contractual commitment to provide funding. Liddy phoned regional office and received authorization to fire Caron. At 4:30 Friday afternoon, just before Caron left for two weeks' holidays, Liddy called Caron into his office and shouted at him about his errors, his parentage and his intelligence. Then he told Caron that he was fired, but that TALFI would give him three months' severance pay and the references for another employer that he deserved.

Hills never forgave Liddy for the brutality of how he fired Caron.

RICHARD LIDDY

Richard Liddy was 46 years old, about five feet ten inches tall, still with a trace of the body of a competitive diver, which he had been in his university days. He had worked for TALFI for 14 years, and he had been named assistant vice-president the year before when the Sudbury branch had achieved a portfolio of outstanding accounts in the upper third of TALFI's branches. He was known as a steady marketer ("a cocktail party marketer" in the acid words of a senior head office executive). A common joke at regional conferences was that when he died, his body would have to be donated to science: no one could figure out how he could drink such massive amounts of scotch in an evening and still function the next day.

Liddy was married, and he and his wife had four children. Occasionally, the Liddys' youngest boy would come over to play with the Hills' children, as the two couples lived only a block and a half apart. Liddy played golf a few times a year, and he was an avid gun enthusiast, going skeet shooting and duck hunting whenever possible. Liddy was active in Kiwanis and in the Sudbury Chamber of Commerce.

Hills had heard Liddy lie to clients and then laugh about it. Hills had seen Liddy yell at one secretary until she broke down in tears. Hills had seen Liddy browbeat Caron before other staff members. Hills and Liddy had had some shouting matches in the office, especially since June 1998, when Liddy returned from his first annual appraisal meeting with the new regional office people who had taken over when Liddy's old friend, Arthur Seals, had been fired as regional vice-president.

The atmosphere in the office was so poisoned that Hills had thought that Liddy, during a shouting match in July 1998, was about to take a swing at him: Hills had been appalled to realize that he was hoping that Liddy would swing at him.

THE LOAN

In mid-October 1994, Gordon Caron received head office authorization for a $3,500,000 loan to finance the construction of a plaza. The borrower was a small Sudbury contractor who already owned the land and three derelict buildings on it. The plan was to gut the interior of the buildings and then to link them in a "Z" formation, with a bowling alley in the centre strip, a donut shop and bingo hall in the north strip, and a retail shop and restaurant in the south strip. The project was to be done in three stages: first the diagonal section, then the north section and lastly the south section. TALFI was to disburse in the normal institutional manner: progress draws against costs incurred up to 60 per cent of costs budgeted for that section, and the balance upon the signing of leases sufficient to pay the total TALFI disbursements. Loan payments were scheduled to start only after the total loan was disbursed, although accrued interest could be deducted from each disbursement.

Richard Liddy assigned Hills the responsibility of supervising Gordon Caron's disbursement of the loan. When Hills read the loan submission file, he was appalled. The project did not make sense insofar as the mix of tenants, the orientation of the building, and the managerial, technical and financial capacity of the borrower were concerned. Hills also wondered if the security values were unreasonably inflated. Nonetheless, he said nothing as the loan had been approved by head office, and as he did not want to start any arguments with Liddy, especially so soon after arriving.

The first two disbursements totalling $950,000 were fairly straightforward; the third disbursement of $475,000 was the start of every credit professional's worst nightmare. Gordon Caron reported that the borrower had found unexpected structural problems and that he had had to work on both section one and three at the same time. Caron insisted that there would be no overruns and that "we just have to bend the rules a little to help this guy." Reluctantly, Hills recommended the disbursement to head office which, in turn, approved it. There was now $1,425,000 disbursed.

In January 1995, Caron came in with another disbursement request, this time for $325,000. There were not sufficient confirmed expenditures to justify more than a $100,000 disbursement and Hills insisted that Caron change the request to the lower figure.

In March 1995, Caron gave Hills a request for an additional $650,000. After reviewing Caron's notes and discussing the disbursement for six hours over two days, Hills refused to recommend any further disbursements of any amount unless there were confirmed leases as outlined in the loan agreement. Hills also demanded that Caron have the borrower sign an agreement to add more conditions that would have to be satisfied before each disbursement: confirmation of all expenditures by an auditor, an updated and detailed budget for the remaining expenditures, and a firm commitment from the borrower that he would stop work on the third section and complete section one or two so that it could be rented and generate some cash flow. Caron insisted that there was nothing really wrong, that he had a good handle on the project, and that TALFI had an obligation to help the borrower to pay urgent invoices due the sub-trades. Hills refused again and Caron appealed to Liddy. Liddy agreed to a disbursement of $495,000 provided that future disbursements met the requirements that Hills had outlined. Hills was not involved in the file from that point onwards. Head office approved the disbursement. At the end of March 1995, there was $2,020,000 disbursed.

In June 1995, Caron brought Liddy a request for disbursement of $800,000. Few of the conditions that the borrower had agreed to in September and March were completely satisfied. Before Liddy could decide on Caron's request, the building inspector of the City of Sudbury closed the construction site for a long list of building code violations.

At this point, Liddy had no choice but to brief regional office and, from this point forward, regional office and, to a much lesser extent, head office were responsible for all significant decisions on the file. Liddy became the implementer of regional office decisions and a conveyor of local conditions to regional office. Liddy hired an independent consulting engineer. The consulting engineer submitted his report in mid-July. He stated that inferior cement had been used, that there was inadequate structural steel in the centre section, that there was a sanitary sewer leaking into the basement below the bingo hall, that live electrical wires were lying on the floor of section one, that the firewalls between the bodyshop and the rest of the building had a 15-minute rating instead of a four-hour rating, etc. At the end of July, there was $2,020,000 disbursed, plus there was accrued interest of $64,000.

The borrower was given until October 15, 1995, to raise the $500,000 that the consulting engineer estimated would be required to rectify the construction defaults. The borrower had invested everything that he had in the project, and he was unable to raise the funding.

On November 7, 1995, TALFI, in the person of Liddy, but based on approval by regional office and head office, demanded its funds within seven days. The borrower was unable to raise $2,100,000 and TALFI seized the building under the terms of its debenture[1] with the borrower.

In late November 1995, after consultation among Liddy, regional office and head office, TALFI appointed a local property management company to maintain the property and to solicit a purchaser. After more than a year and after internal consultation, TALFI discharged the property management firm due to alleged dereliction of duty. TALFI then appointed a nationally known real estate firm, which arranged a sale within 45 days. The deal was for $2,890,000 and the actual sale closed July 10, 1997.

THE LAWSUIT

In August 1997, the borrower launched a lawsuit of $8,000,000, representing the total of his estimated original equity of $1,800,000 plus his estimated potential gain on the project, if he had been allowed to complete it, of $3,500,000 plus punitive damages of $2,300,000. He stated in his statement of claim that TALFI had acted in a "manner inconsistent with TALFI's obligation to make an equitable and sincere effort to assist the borrower in the completion of the said project." The borrower also claimed that Liddy and Caron had verbally agreed to each change in the program and each cost increase. Finally, the borrower claimed that the property was sold for an unreasonably low amount due to incompetence by the first property management firm and by Liddy. Exhibit 2 is a brief description of the legal process.

TALFI and Liddy were named as co-defendants of the $8,000,000 lawsuit. TALFI carried $4,000,000 of insurance to cover itself and its employees against lawsuits arising from the performance of their normal duties.

Liddy had expressed the hope that the borrower would run out of money to pay his lawyer and, thus, be forced to drop the lawsuit. Somehow the borrower had kept his lawyer motivated with cash or promises and after a long time, Liddy on his own behalf, and Liddy and Mark Dawlish, vice-president, on behalf of TALFI, had signed the affidavit of documents. The affidavit had been delivered to the court and to the borrower's lawyer on August 29, 1998. Hills had noticed the affidavit the following day in the intra-office circulating file. The examination of discovery was set for October. Hills did not expect to be called as his involvement was limited to part of the disbursement period. Liddy, on the other hand, was expecting to testify for several days, as he was the only person who was really familiar with the account and who was still with TALFI.

In Ontario the settlement of lawsuits can take several years, or more, and involve considerable judicial time; accordingly, a process of exchange of views and information is required of both plaintiff and defendant.

A detailed statement of claim is filed by the plaintiff with the court empowered to handle a particular lawsuit, and it is delivered to the defendant.

The defendant must then file a statement of defence with the court and with the plaintiff's lawyer; otherwise, the defendant may be found liable if the plaintiff asks the court for judgment.

After the filing of the two statements, each party will normally prepare for the examination of discovery by preparing an affidavit of documents.

The affidavit of documents must be filed with the court and the opposing lawyer. The affidavit of documents has four parts. Part one lists by name and date all documents pertaining to the lawsuit and in the possession of the plaintiff or defendant, as the case may be. Part two lists all documents pertaining to the lawsuit that the plaintiff/defendant knows of but does not have for reasons such as prior seizure by police or federal income tax officials. Part three lists documents that cannot be produced for reasons such as unknown location or client/lawyer confidentiality. Part four is an oath sworn to the court that the affidavit is true.

After the affidavits have been filed, the lawyers schedule an examination of discovery.

In an examination of discovery each lawyer may examine documents listed in the opposing side's affidavit and question each person who is named in the suit or who is the knowledgeable representative of a corporation named in the suit.

The examination is held before a court-appointed stenographer. The witnesses speak under oath.

The examination is intended to disclose all information that the two parties expect to rely upon in court, and, thus, to encourage an agreement or settlement without a court appearance. Many lawsuits in Ontario are settled after the discovery phase, i.e., without an actual trial. If not settled, lawsuits then proceed to a pre-trial hearing, and then to trial.

Exhibit 2   The Ontario Legal Process (a highly simplified, partial description)

Source: Casewriter's summary.

Exhibit 3 provides a chronology of events.

Now, a month before his 34th birthday, three weeks before the examination of discovery, and three days before the annual management conference, Joe Hills sat down to read the facsimile one more time (see Exhibit 4).

NOTE

1. A debenture is a combination mortgage on real estate and a charge on non-real estate assets and it often confers on the lender the right and power to seize, administer and sell encumbered assets.

	1964	Hills born
	1974	TALFI incorporated
	1984	TALFI expands its services
	1984	Hills married
	1988	Hills starts at Crown corporation
	1990	Hills starts in Winnipeg with TALFI
	1990	Hills promoted to financing officer
	1992	Hills promoted to senior financing officer
Apr	1992	Hills writes systems memo
Jan	1993	Hills starts in head office, Toronto
	1994	TALFI assets at $3.5 billion; its last year of strong financial performance
Apr	1994	Hills fired
Aug	1994	Hills offered Sudbury posting
Sept	1994	The loan authorized
Oct-Dec	1994	$1,425,000 disbursed
Jan	1995	$100,000 additional disbursed
Mar	1995	$495,000 additional disbursed
June	1995	Building inspector closes construction site
July	1995	Hills recommends Caron be placed on probation
July	1995	TALFI demands that borrower raise $500,000
Sept	1995	Caron fired
Oct	1995	Borrower unable to raise $500,000
Nov	1995	TALFI demands that borrower repay all disbursements
Nov	1995	TALFI seizes property
Nov	1995	TALFI appoints local property manager
Dec	1996	(one year later) TALFI fires local property manager for dereliction of duty; appoints national firm of property managers
Feb	1997	Sale arranged
July	1997	Sale completed
Aug	1997	Borrower sues
Feb	1998	TALFI closes 11 of 38 branches and fires 40 per cent of the staff
Aug	1998	(one year later) Affidavits completed
Sept 17	1998	Hills reads fax
Sept 20	1998	Annual management conference to start
Oct 5	1998	Examination of discovery scheduled

Exhibit 3   Chronology of Events

SUDBURY TALFI

TORONTO TALFI

SEPT. 13-98

ATT: DAWLISH

Have Removed Following From Branch Files:

1-MEMO-LIDDY/SEALS-JULY6,95
2-MEMO-SEALS/LIDDY-JULY10,95
3-MEMO-LIDDY/SEALS-NOV3,95
4-MEMO-SEALS/LIDDY-NOV6,95
5-REPORT-LIDDY/SEALS-NOV20,95
6-MEMO-SEALS/LIDDY-NOV29,95
7-MEMO-LIDDY/SEALS-NOV8,96
8-MEMO-SEALS/LIDDY-NOV15,96
9-REPORT-LIDDY/SEALS-FEB10,97
10-MEMO-SEALS /LIDDY-FEB11,97
11-MEMO-LIDDY/SEALS-FEB17,97
12-REPORT-LIDDY/SEALS-SEPT29,97

RICHARD LIDDY

Exhibit 4   A Note for Joe Hills

WINSTON LIU, BOOKMAN

*Prepared by Sean Barnhart under the
supervision of Professor Donald W. Barclay*

Copyright © 1999, Ivey Management Services   Version: (A) 1999-10-25

Every day, in every way, I get better and better. I feel happy, I feel healthy, I feel terrific!

Winston (Winnie) Liu repeated the mantra to himself as a young woman wearing a salwar suit answered the door he had just knocked on. Almost three months after starting his own business selling children's books door-to-door, Winnie was working through a wealthy neighborhood in Edmonton, Alberta. Surrounded by enormous houses and manicured lawns, he reflected for a moment about the promising summer that now found him hungry, lonely, and desperate for a sale.

Anita Howard, a sales manager with the Southwestern Company, recruited Winnie during his first year at The University of Western Ontario (Western). He filled out a card he had received in a chemistry class indicating he was interested in running his own business during the summer. After meeting with Winnie, Anita believed his work ethic, persistence, and friendly personality combined with his passion for education would make him an excellent salesperson. She asked Winnie to consider starting his own business selling books, and Winnie agreed, excited about the possibility of being his own boss and making a lot of money. Between January and April, Winnie memorized the prepared sales talks and attended sales training meetings given by students who had sold books before. His enthusiasm for a rewarding summer grew.

THE SOUTHWESTERN COMPANY

The Southwestern Company, located in Nashville, Tennessee, was founded in 1855. The American Civil War exhausted the fortunes of many Southwestern-American families, and in 1868 the company began helping students finance their school expenses through selling books door-to-door. Over the years the company realized that educational materials were more profitable than Bibles and more consistent with the image of college students.

At present the educational books and software were sold to families in their homes by students during their summer breaks. Students were independent contractors and had the opportunity to run their own businesses by purchasing products from Southwestern at wholesale and selling them at retail. Students relocated away from home to a different part of the country for the summer, away from distractions that might drain attention and profits from their business.

In 1998 Southwestern recruited 3000 students from over 300 universities across Canada, the United States, and Europe. The average 1998 summer profits of Southwestern Student Dealers who sold for three months (US$) were:

First summer students:	$6,994
Second summer students:	$12,891
Third summer students:	$17,189
Fourth summer students:	$23,364

After the first summer, students could be selected for student management. Many students worked four, five, six or more summers, gaining invaluable experience by developing their own sales organizations throughout their university careers.

THE BOOKS

The two main products sold by the students were the *Student Handbook* (a four-book set, USA) and the *Volume Library* (a three-book set, Canada). These books were study guides designed to complement, not replace, encyclopedias and CD-ROMs. The *Student Handbook* and the *Volume Library* contained practical "how to" information for subjects ranging from math and chemistry to grammar and geography, from the grade one to grade 12 level. Students in Canada sold the *Volume Library* set for $320 retail, taking a 40 per cent commission from the sales price. Though the prices were only a suggestion from the Southwestern Company, students followed the guidelines for consistency across consumers. Since several students would be selling in every city, it was very likely that friends and relatives might buy the books from different students. Consistency also helped maintain the image of Southwestern, which was critical in this door-to-door sales context.

SUCCESS

The first of two keys to students' success in selling children's books was establishing themselves as legitimate education consultants in the community. Students sought to understand the strengths and weaknesses of the schools and teachers in the community, and the attitudes of parents towards the teachers, schools, and school board. This allowed them to better understand customer needs and to connect quickly during a sales call.

The second key to success was financial planning. Students submitted a high portion of their earnings to the Southwestern Company to secure delivery at the end of the summer (time and experience had demonstrated that students were not good credit risks), so planning was essential to ensure cash flow to cover expenses during the summer.

WINNIE'S SUMMER

After a week of sales training at company headquarters in Nashville, Winnie drove to Edmonton, Alberta with seven students. He found a place to live with Holden McArthur, who had also just completed his first year at Western, and Seymour Burke, a student from British Columbia, who had sold books during the previous two summers. Winnie and Holden competed against each other daily, not just for sales, but for what they called "feel gooders." These included positive attitude, random acts of kindness, and the number of people they had cheered up during the day.

Winnie had been successful in all ways until the third week of June. He began working in a much wealthier area than he had been in before. His knowledge of local schools, teachers, and students was unusable because these schools and people were unfamiliar and unrecognized. The children in this neighborhood went to private schools. On Wednesday morning Winnie looked over his sales stats for the past two days: 94 calls, 41 demonstrations, and no sales. Every day without a sale meant stretching his meagre food budget a little further. He had been eating peanut butter and jelly for a week straight. For the first time Winnie allowed himself to think about quitting and going home.

Now Winnie was sitting in the home of Ravish and Kavita Patel, successful stockbrokers and parents of three children. Halfway through the demonstration Ravish asked his wife to bring in the friends they were entertaining in the backyard. These four couples, all wealthy descendants of hardworking immigrants, lived in the immediate neighborhood, and all had children ranging in age from seven to 13. All of their children attended Temple, the private school of choice for parents in this neighborhood.

Each of the parents liked the study guides. More importantly, their children were enthusiastic about the books too. Ravish moved to face Winnie and said, "Okay, you've sold us, so no fancy close, Winnie. How much for the set?" Prepared for the no-close close that a fellow salesperson usually called upon, Winnie replied confidently, "It's not the hundreds or even thousands that these study guides would cost if you bought them by subject individually. All three books for $320. With tax (7% GST) and shipping, the total is only $343. That's pretty good, isn't it?"

Ravish turned to the other four couples and spoke briefly in a language Winnie did not entirely understand but recognized as Hindi. After a brief exchange, Ravish turned to Winnie and said, "Here's the deal. Winnie, what do you make from these, 20 per cent? That's about $65 per couple here, $325 for you. We'll pay you cash, up front, and cover shipping. Don't charge us tax, we'll pay $310 each. We want just a 10 per cent discount. If you don't pay tax, you only give up $50 and you get five sales now. Boom."

Winnie did the math in his head. Ravish had underestimated his margin by one-half (Winnie normally received 40 per cent of the retail price) and he would actually be giving up about $140 for the sale. But the potential profit was about $500, not the $325 Ravish had calculated.

Winnie responded, less confident now, but sure that Ravish was not objecting to the price. "Everyone pays the same price. There are other students in the city running their businesses and they charge the same price. I've charged the same price to everyone so far and I'm going to charge the same price for the rest of the summer. Besides, wouldn't you feel cheated if you found out your neighbor got 20 per cent off? That's why I charge the same price to everybody."

Ravish spoke slower now, "No one has to know, Winnie. Think about $1,550 in your pocket right now. For overlooking a silly tax and giving us a small break. You can call it a 'Volume Discount for *Volume Libraries.*'" His guests chuckled at Ravish's pun. Ravish continued, "Come on, Winnie. We're salespeople too. This is no big deal." He sat back in his plush chair and sighed softly, "If you don't like the deal, you should leave now."

Winnie considered the offer. The names of these families and their children would open doors in this neighborhood. He desperately needed information about Temple, which these people could give him. Next summer, the Southwestern company would send students out to work in this area again, just as he was now working in a territory where someone had sold books in the previous summer. The information he collected would benefit them tremendously, as would the testimonials they would be able to obtain from five families of book owners.

Ravish was right, no one had to find out about this discount. It was only a small discount. Winnie also felt that the GST was a silly tax. And $500 would end his peanut butter and jelly marathon immediately. He could almost taste a steak dinner and chocolate milkshake. Winnie took a slow, deep breath, and spoke to Ravish.

WestWood Securities (A)

Prepared by Joanna Shostack under the supervision of Professor James A. Erskine

                    Version: (A) 2003-04-11

On a Friday morning in early October, Phil Diamond, a junior broker with WestWood Securities, had mixed emotions. In the past hour, he had sold another 5,000 shares at a dollar each to a new client, and his boss, Brian Wood, had just offered him a promotion to senior broker. Diamond had until Monday to decide.

WestWood Securities

WestWood Securities (WestWood) was a young, small broker/dealer (see Exhibit 1) founded in Vancouver, British Columbia, by Brian Wood. The firm consisted of two partners, four senior brokers, 20 junior brokers, five telemarketers and five office staff. Although WestWood bought and sold securities on exchanges like the Toronto Stock Exchange (TSE) and the New York Stock Exchange (NYSE), this kind of activity was not encouraged. The firm's main line of business was in bought deals. Typically, small, privately owned companies would go to WestWood with the hopes of financing an initial public offering (IPO). WestWood would buy all the shares of the company for between $0.03 and $0.10 per share, and the company would then be listed as an over-the-counter (OTC) stock. In turn, WestWood brokers would call their clients and sell them the respective shares for $0.90 to a $1 per share.

Training and Recruitment

Most new hires at WestWood had very limited experience and were assigned to do telemarketing for $10 an hour while completing the Canadian Securities Course (CSC). Telemarketers randomly called potential new clients to tell them about WestWood and about what the company did and to ask if they could send them

Brokers who have a seat on the Toronto Stock Exchange (TSE) or the Vancouver Stock Exchange (VSE) and are governed federally by the Investment Dealers Association (IDA) and provincially by the British Columbia Securities Commission (BCSC). The importance of having a seat on the TSE or the VSE is that a firm can participate in the exchange of shares on the market, and its brokers can publicly trade securities. The IDA monitors brokers' actions closely, especially when it comes to a bought deal. Brokers must disclose their margins to the IDA so as to determine whether it is at fair market value.

Broker/dealers who do not have a seat on the TSE or the VSE, but are governed by the BCSC are still highly regulated, although since they are not governed by the IDA, they do not have to disclose their margins to them. Because Broker/dealers do not have a seat on either the TSE or the VSE, they cannot directly buy stocks listed on these exchanges. Instead, they have to go through a brokerage firm (i.e., Scotia McLeod, TD Waterhouse, etc.) to make the transaction on their behalf. They are licensed to trade over-the-counter (OTC) stock only.

The hierarchy of listing requirements for the exchanges with respect to reporting and stock value is as follows:

*TSE—high listing requirements

**VSE—medium listing requirements

***OTC—low listing requirements

*TSE Buys VSE in 2002

**Listing requirements updated 2000

***Closed in 2000

Exhibit 1   Difference Between Brokers and Broker/Dealers

Source: 1999 I.D.A. Securities Regulations.

---

a brochure (see Exhibit 2). If the client agreed to receive the brochure, the telemarketer would confirm the mailing address and mail the client a brochure. The potential client was also asked if they would like to receive a call from a broker if an opportunity came up. If the answer was yes, the firm would send another brochure to the potential client, telling them about a company that WestWood was taking public and the opportunities for investment. After this mailing, the telemarketer would forward the client contact information to a junior broker.

About a month later, when the client would have received both brochures, a junior broker would call to tell them more about the high-risk investment opportunity and try to sell them up to $5,000 in shares (see Exhibit 2). If the broker was lucky, about one in every 25 phone calls would result in shares purchased. The junior broker would set up an account and get all the required information, including the client's net assets, to determine their net worth. The junior

broker would then forward the client folder to a senior broker.

Within the next four weeks, a senior broker would call this client to sell them more of the same stock (see Exhibit 2). All senior brokers had worked as junior brokers for at least a year and were promoted based on their exceptional sales skills. Because a senior broker was calling existing clients who had already purchased shares in a particular company, nine out of 10 clients contacted would buy more shares. One of the most important things the senior broker told clients was not to sell the stock until told to do so. However, once all the initial stock of the new company was sold, the senior brokers never told the clients to sell. In the event that a client did want to sell their shares, there was no market for the company's stock. In this instance, WestWood would buy the shares back from its clients only if they felt the client was inclined to file a complaint with the British Columbia Securities Commission (BCSC).

Telemarketer to Potential Client

"Hi. My name is _____ and I'm from WestWood Securities. We are a young broker/dealer firm and I was wondering if I could send you some information about our company? [OK] Great! Could you verify your preferred mailing address, please? [Get address]. Thank you. Would it also be OK if one of our brokers contacted you if they came across an opportunity to make some money in the stock market? [yes] Excellent! You should receive our brochure within the week."

Junior Brokers to Potential Client

"Hi. My name is _____ from WestWood Securities. You spoke with *(telemarketer's name)* last week, have you received the brochure? [Yes.] Great! I'm calling you because I'm a new junior broker, and I'm trying to make my way in the company. We just took *(XYZ Co.)* public and we think it has a lot of potential. The stock is now worth 90 cents. I think you should buy 5,000 shares and take a small percentage of the company now. And when the stock is doing well, you can tell your friends to call me to get them in as well."

Senior Broker to Existing Client

"Hi, my name is _____. I'm a senior broker with WestWood Securities. You bought 5,000 shares with (*junior broker's name*), our junior broker, last week. We feel this company has a lot more potential than we initially thought; the stock has already gone up to $0.97. I think you should buy more, at least another $20,000. But don't sell until I tell you to sell, OK? I will call you when I think you should sell."

Exhibit 2   Typical Telephone Conversations

Source: Company files.

Note: Conversations are not verbatim; they are an example only.

COMPENSATION STRUCTURE

For sales of TSE listed stocks, WestWood charged the client a commission of $125 per trade, whereas bought deals were cheaper at $50 per transaction. Both senior and junior brokers received 25 per cent of these trading commissions. However, WestWood made enormous margins on bought deals and therefore could afford to pay its brokers huge commissions for selling these types of stock; these were called "ripps" by brokers. Junior brokers made a commission of 20 per cent of total sales, plus a bonus of 10 per cent of commission per pay check. While junior brokers had a selling ceiling of $5,000 per stock per client, senior brokers had the authority to sell up to 10 per cent of the client's net worth, which typically was in the $500,000 range. Senior brokers made 10 per

cent of their total sales, and the junior broker who opened that account would also make 10 per cent. The senior broker also received a bonus of 20 per cent on total commissions. All brokers were treated very well and received many company perks. For instance, lunch was provided every day, brokers were taken for dinners at fancy steak houses a few times a week as well as other outings, and senior brokers also received a car allowance.

PHIL DIAMOND

At 25 years old, Phil Diamond was an entrepreneur at heart and was driven to make money. In high school, he had a car washing and detailing business. While completing his economics degree, he ran a profitable window washing business. In his last year of university, Diamond and a partner opened a café that broke even within three months. On the evening they realized this great news, Diamond's partner stole all the hard movable assets and disappeared. Diamond had trouble recovering the losses.

When Diamond graduated from university, he still had "dollar signs in his eyes" and started his own online candy business with a college friend. The business proved to be successful, and it expanded into vending machines in local pubs. Once again, he ran into some bad luck when all the candy vending machines were stolen. Although reports were filed, the culprit was never found, and Diamond had no choice but to accept the loss and regain focus on the online aspect.

While managing the online business, Diamond started to get into buying and selling stocks for himself. He loved watching his paper profits accumulate. Friends started coming to him for advice about investments, and he enjoyed talking about it. When he could not answer some of their questions, he decided to enrol in the CSC. He wanted to become a financial advisor and asked his partner of the online company to buy him out.

As Diamond was looking through the paper for financial advisory training courses, he came across an ad for WestWood Securities (see Exhibit 3). He called the number listed and went for an interview. Although he had not completed the CSC, which turned out to be a requirement, Diamond was offered a job. He accepted immediately and was excited about the job's potential for money-making.

Stock Brokers Wanted!

Beginners preferred.

No experience necessary.

Please call John 555-1212

Exhibit 3 WestWood Securities Ad in the Paper

Source: Reconstructed by Phil Diamond.

Life at WestWood

After a year as a junior broker, Diamond was a star seller. On a good month he would sell $5,000 of stock a day, making $20,000 in commission plus $2,000 in bonuses. There was only one month when he made less than $10,000, but the commissions from the senior broker sales made up for it. Diamond got along exceptionally well with Wood and was envied by the other junior brokers. When Diamond first started, he was more excited about making the sales than he was about caring for his clients' needs. Yet over time, he built close relationships with a few clients and started feeling badly when they lost money, which happened almost all the time; it was the other TSE listed stocks that kept them coming back. Wood would keep his brokers motivated by reminding them of Ballard Power's success story. Ballard Power was a broker/dealer-bought deal that managed a successful IPO and graduated to the TSE. Diamond knew that this occurrence was rare.

Early October

There was talk in the office about brokers from other broker/dealer firms possibly losing their securities licences. The British Columbia Securities Commission (BCSC) was revoking senior brokers' licences for high-pressure sales tactics, which were illegal according to the securities commission. Senior brokers would be somewhat pushy to make the sale, so if enough clients got together, they could gather enough evidence for the BCSC to revoke a broker's licence, taking away that individual's privilege to sell stock for life.

It was Friday morning, and Diamond was reading another article about a broker losing his licence (see Exhibit 4). Before he could finish

---

Re: Commission Issues Proceeding Against David Singh and Paul Tindall

The Ontario Securities Commission (the "Commission") has issued a Notice of Hearing and Statement of Allegations against David Singh ("Singh"), the former president of Fortune Financial Corporation ("Fortune") and Paul Tindall ("Tindall"), a former salesperson employed by Fortune.
Staff of the Commission allege that:

- Tindall sold securities to his clients without disclosing his personal interest in the issuer of the securities and on the basis of misrepresentations made to induce clients to invest.
- The investment was wholly unsuitable for the clients who invested.
- In addition, the securities that Tindall sold contravened the prospectus requirements of the Securities Act.
- When Tindall became aware of this and other illegalities, he attempted to conceal the problems in order to deceive his clients, Fortune and the regulatory authorities.
- Tindall eventually discovered that the investment was a fraud, and he made further misrepresentations to his clients to prevent them from speaking to the regulatory authorities.

Staff also made other allegations against Tindall in relation to his conduct while a salesperson at Fortune, including selling shares on the same day that he purchased those securities for his clients' accounts and failing to keep the required documentation in respect of his clients.
Against Singh, Staff allege that he was aware of Tindall's activities but took no steps to discipline, control or monitor Tindall. It is alleged that Singh knowingly permitted Tindall to sell investments that were not approved by Fortune, and he acquiesced in Tindall's scheme to falsify documents to attempt to conceal the illegalities of the investment referred to above.
Allegations are also made that Singh permitted mutual fund representatives to trade securities for which they were not registered by allowing them to use his representative code. It is also alleged that Singh sold securities subject to a hold period imposed by securities law when Singh knew that the hold period existed and prohibited his sales.

Exhibit 4   Article

Source: Ontario Securities Commission; http://www.osc.gov.on.ca

---

reading the article, Wood came into Diamond's cubicle and offered him a promotion to become a senior broker.

Wood: "You're my star junior, and I want to make you a senior broker."

Diamond: "Thanks, Brian. But I'm not sure I want to be a senior broker. I have an issue with the ethical nature of the activities that come with being a senior broker."

Wood: "Just think about it, Phil. You love the sell. You'll be making at least three times more money than the juniors. I'll give you a corner office, and you'll get your own secretary."

Diamond: "I don't mind selling clients up to $5,000 of high-risk stock because that's not going to affect their lifestyle. But I do have a problem selling $50,000 of stock because that would make a difference in some of these clients' lives."

Wood: "Well, let me know on Monday."

DILEMMA

As Wood walked away, Diamond knew Wood was right. "A bad recommendation is just that, whether they buy $5,000 or $50,000," he thought to himself. Diamond loved the stocks and he loved selling, but he felt badly that his clients were constantly losing their money. It was hanging on his conscience so much that he had had trouble sleeping the last few weeks. However, he loved working for Wood, and he knew he would triple his salary as a senior broker, which meant he could pay cash for that condo he wanted. He had until Monday to give Wood his answer.

HARRISON-LOCKINGTON (A)

*Prepared by Sylvia Smellie under the
supervision of Professor James A. Erskine*

       Version: (A) 2003-04-10

At 8:05 a.m. on Monday, January 13, 2003, Jack Gordon, managing partner at Harrison-Lockington, barristers and solicitors in Vancouver, British Columbia, listened in stunned silence. Steven Ross, office manager, was recounting some of the details on how he had stolen several hundred thousand dollars from the firm during the past few years. Gordon was not sure what to say or do.

BACKGROUND

Harrison-Lockington was one of Canada's leading law firms, with more than 250 lawyers located in offices in Toronto, Ottawa, Vancouver and New York. Harrison-Lockington, Vancouver had a reputation in many areas, including—mergers and acquisitions, corporate finance, tax, pension, intellectual property and commercial litigation.

In 2001, Harrison-Lockington acquired the Martin & Turner, LLP law firm in Vancouver in an effort to expand the firm's capabilities and coverage. The acquisition was, for the most part, seamless. The Vancouver lawyers and their support staff continued to operate in the same fashion they had prior to the acquisition. The one minor change was that office managers now reported directly to the principal office, located in Toronto.

The Vancouver office was responsible for achieving billable hour targets, covering a portion of the entire firm's overhead costs and reporting monthly to the Toronto office, on these and other budget items.

JACK GORDON

Jack Gordon was the managing partner of the Vancouver office. Gordon's practice was focused

in the area of administrative law: litigation and dispute resolution. He was the senior partner in the firm's Energy Regulatory Practice. Gordon obtained his LLB degree from the University of Victoria, and was called to the bar in 1988. In 1989 he joined Martin & Turner, LLP as an associate and had been with the firm ever since.

Gordon had extensive experience acting as regulatory counsel before energy boards and tribunals such as the West Coast Energy and Utilities Board. His administrative law focus extended to the transportation field, and his litigation experience had brought him before the Federal Court of Canada on numerous occasions. In addition to his legal practice, Gordon had served as the Senior Instructor in Public Law for the Law Society since 1991.

As managing partner, Gordon was responsible for 90 people, including 15 partners, 20 associates, 30 legal assistants and 25 administrative support staff. Gordon was accountable for the operating budget, performance against the budget, client and the principal office relations and all media relations for the Vancouver office.

Gordon would typically spend approximately 25 per cent of his time on his managing partner activities. He scheduled regular weekly meetings with the office manager, attended the bi-monthly staff meetings, maintained contact with the principal office through conference calls or personal visits and participated in regular monthly meetings with the partners.

STEVEN ROSS

Jack Gordon hired Steven Ross in 1996 to replace the office manager who had chosen to pursue other opportunities. Ross had previous experience as an office manager in an accounting firm in Vancouver. He was a Certified General Accountant and came highly recommended.

Steven Ross was responsible for all non-legal professional matters including facilities, payroll, marketing, social activities, charitable donations and events, and human resources. Prior to the merger, Ross had reported to Gordon. The weekly meetings between the two of them had always been informal and good-natured. They typically discussed outstanding accounts, expenses, staff issues, upcoming events, charitable donations and relationships with other Harrison-Lockington offices. It was a common feeling in the office that Ross was an extremely trusted employee, and he was well respected among the legal professionals and members of the staff.

Following the merger, and as a result of synergies in financial systems, Ross's direct reporting relationship changed, and he began reporting to the chief operating officer of the firm, Tom Welch, in the Toronto office. Ross submitted budget performance statements and office activity reports to Welch on a monthly basis. Occasionally, Ross and Welch talked on the phone, and on a couple of occasions Welch had visited the Vancouver office. For day-to-day operations, Ross continued to work with Gordon.

THE CONFESSION

Just before 8:00 a.m. Monday morning, Gordon walked passed Ross's office and noticed that it was impeccably neat, which he found highly unusual. He went to his office, dropped his jacket, picked up a pad of paper, which included notes on what he wanted to discuss with Ross in their weekly meeting. Gordon walked into Ross's office and began to exchange pleasantries when Ross interrupted him:

"Jack, I have a confession to make. I have been a dishonest employee."

"What do you mean?" Gordon responded.

"Over the past three years or so, I have been taking money from the firm, probably around $300,000," Ross answered.

"You what? I can't believe this. How did you do it?" Gordon asked.

"Through the payroll system. It started with expenses," Ross said.

Ross explained how he had begun by putting personal expenses through the firm. Claims for Visa bills, DVDs and meals were the primary items. In Ross's position, he had authority to put through any expense that was less than $1,000 with his signature alone. Anything above this limit required Ross to have a partner co-sign with him.

"Once expenses were getting through, I began tampering with the payroll," Ross continued.

Among Ross's responsibilities were issuing and signing all payroll cheques. Once his signatures were on the cheques, he would give the pile to Gordon (or another partner in his absence) to countersign. Ross explained:

On some occasions, I would create two cheques for one associate and then endorse one of the cheques and deposit it into my account. On other occasions where the associate had chosen direct deposit, I would complete the direct deposit but also write a duplicate cheque and deposit that in my account.

"What I don't understand," Gordon asked, "Did the bank not notice these double entries?"

Ross responded "I have sole authority to instruct the bank about deposits and payroll. It is also my sole responsibility to do a bank reconciliation at the end of each month, I was the only one noticing the entries."

Gordon could not believe the intricacies of Ross's efforts and how flawless this process seemed to be. Ross described how, on one occasion, he wrote an associate's cheque for double the amount she earned, a mistake that could have led to his being discovered. The associate, upon noticing the double amount, came to see him to have it corrected. Once he gave her a corrected cheque he was arrogant enough to keep the cheque with the mistake, endorse it and deposit it in his own account.

"Steven if this has been going on for almost three years, why did you decide to come clean now?" Gordon asked.

Emotionally, Ross went on to explain that he had bought himself a new laptop for personal use and had charged it through the firm. When the bill arrived he had it charged to his personal account, which was an allowed procedure, as long as all personal accounts were rectified at month's end.

"I remember that. One of the office staff talked to me about how your personal account was overdue," Gordon said. "I just assumed it had been dealt with. I heard nothing more. Why didn't you just pay the bill?"

"I have no money, I have spent everything that I have taken," said Ross.

The overdue account had not been paid over several months and Ross received numerous warnings from a staff member with the Toronto office. Given that there had been no budget set aside for this expense and Ross was not in need of a new computer, Tom Welch began to investigate.

As Welch was already making a trip to Vancouver, he had made an appointment to talk with Ross.

"That's why I am telling you, Jack. I was going to get caught one way or another," Ross concluded.

CONCLUSION

As Gordon listened for 45 minutes to all of the details, numerous thoughts raced through his head. How did this happen? What should he do next? Would this affect client relations? How should he tell the principal office? Besides, Gordon had the regular bi-monthly staff meeting at 9:15 a.m. this morning. What should he say, if anything?

GRAHAM STEWART—GENERAL MANAGER (A)

Prepared by Grant Simons under the supervision of Professor James A. Erskine

     Version: (A) 2002-05-29

> Graham, walk with me . . . Watch your butt! Barry is out to get you.

The words from Jeff Henderson, mall manager, a week ago were still vivid to Graham Stewart, general manager and partner with Barry Steinman in the Steinman & Lee restaurant in Southview Mall, Windsor, Ontario. Now in early July 2001, Diana Calhoun, bookkeeper, had just informed Stewart that a cheque payable to Steinman & Lee could not be deposited to Steinman's personal account. The accounting inconsistencies were beginning to make a lot more sense to Stewart. But were they legal?

THE EARLY YEARS

The Steinman & Lee restaurant chain was designed to combine the continuing Canadian appetite for Chinese cuisine with deli and road-house foods. The menu featured an extensive selection of creatively prepared and presented items priced at a premium to other licensed full-service mall eateries. The first Steinman & Lee restaurant opened in River Road Mall (an upscale regional shopping centre) in Windsor, Ontario, in August 1994. Prior to the development of this concept, Steinman had operated a major brand-name restaurant franchise and had several years' experience in senior level management positions with the franchising company.

The initial response to the Steinman & Lee concept was strong and line-ups were common. Start-up costs were minimized by purchasing used equipment, and utilizing lease financing wherever possible. Occupancy costs were high for this premium mall location and would increase over the term of the lease. The company pursued a rapid growth strategy and funded the expansion by using the cash flow from operations and incurring an increasingly larger debt load. Each unit was situated in leased premises with a minimum commitment for five years.

New store openings occurred at approximately one-year intervals: River Road Mall in Windsor (1994), Kitchener (1995), Waterloo (1996), Southview Mall in Windsor (1997), Etobicoke (a franchised unit in 1998), and Steinman's Café, a spin-off concept, in Windsor (1991). The Steinman's Café concept was a "no-frills" version of Steinman & Lee featuring smaller portions, lesser quality food products, and menu prices on average 30 per cent to 40 per cent lower than those at a traditional Steinman & Lee. The site chosen by Steinman for this concept was a small strip plaza in an upper middle class residential area. This location was previously home to an unsuccessful pizza place.

Graham Stewart

Graham Stewart graduated from The University of Western Ontario in 1993 with a degree in biology and human neurophysiology. He had financed this education by working as a waiter at The Keg restaurant, a very successful full-service dining house with numerous units spread across Canada. During this time, he was involved in new store openings and in the training of new employees. After graduation, Stewart accepted a full-time position as assistant general manager with a Keg restaurant unit in Windsor and worked in this capacity for one and a half years.

In August 1995, Stewart was hired by a local developer to help in the design and operation of an 11,000-square foot dining and entertainment facility. Stewart was hired as the general manager and managed the start-up and operation of this concept for two years until meeting Steinman (see Exhibit 1). Stewart who was married and had two daughters, commented,

When I first met Barry Steinman, I was very impressed with his understanding of the operation of a restaurant. He had worked his way up and was largely responsible for the creative development of Steinman & Lee. I had been recruited by several "chain" restaurants, but I wanted to get involved in a company with rapid growth potential and one where I could make a cash investment. Barry and I negotiated at great length and formulated an agreement in August 1997, allowing me to purchase a 20 per cent partnership in the new Steinman & Lee Southview Mall. Southview Mall was to be Steinman & Lee's flagship store and would require an experienced operator. I knew the operations side of the business and had begun to utilize micro-computer technology to assist in planning and cost control. Barry and I had complimentary strengths; I was driven by day-to-day general management issues and Barry was the designer of decor, menus and plate presentations. I joined Steinman & Lee in August 1997, three months prior to the Southview Mall grand opening.

Steinman & Lee Southview Mall

Steinman & Lee Southview Mall opened in November 1997, just in time for the Christmas season. The opening went smoothly. Company-wide sales records were set in the first week of operation. Cost of goods and labor costs were lower, and profits were higher than in any unit in the organization. Steinman and Stephen Potts (director of operations) were around a lot during the first few weeks of operation.

Barry and Stephen realized early on that I did not need their help in running Southview Mall. Stephen spent most of his time on the road and he was very busy. I believe that Stephen was quite content not to take on any more responsibility and adopted a "hands off" approach with Southview Mall. I was happy with this situation because Stephen and I didn't really get along. I had a lot more experience than he did, and he did not hold a great deal of respect among the other GM's and their employees. I had developed some very strong relationships with the other managers and my own employees. I knew that I held more power in this regard than Stephen, and I felt comfortable that he knew this and would leave me alone.

270

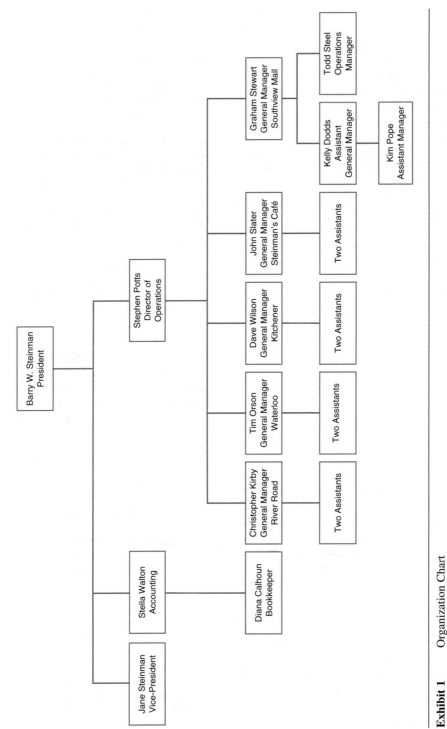

Exhibit 1   Organization Chart

Barry and I got along quite well, although I began to wonder about his commitment to the business. He would show up Monday to Friday at 9 a.m. and sit in his office trying to appear busy. He wore a suit every day but very rarely ever met with anybody. It seemed like he was just putting in time. Sales and profits continued to be strong throughout 1998 and 1999 in Southview Mall, and I was happy not to have anyone looking over my shoulder.

TROUBLED TIMES

In the summer of 2000, the Canadian economy was beginning to show signs of slowing down and there was developing concern in the retail sector with respect to the precipitous drop of the high-tech market segment in North America. Some industry analysts were beginning to predict a fall-off in consumer spending as people tightened their spending, especially in patronizing full-service restaurants. In fact, by the fall of 2000, sales volumes and profits in the Kitchener, Waterloo and Etobicoke locations were well below those achieved in the Windsor market. The River Road Mall and Southview Mall unit contributions were used to offset substantial losses in Kitchener, Steinman's Café and the ever-weakening cash flows in Waterloo. All sales and operating information from each unit was sent to Steinman & Lee head office located within Southview Mall. From this office, an accounting staff of two prepared financial statements and administered payroll and trade payables. Steinman signed all cheques and maintained an office in this facility. Stewart had access to this office and prepared consolidated income statements and cash flow projections for Steinman's consideration.

By November 2000, the company's cash position was becoming a serious concern to senior management. Steinman & Lee senior management including Stewart, Steinman, Potts, Christopher Kirby, Tim Orson, John Slater, and Dave Wilson (see Exhibit 1) met to develop a plan of action to save the company. Several cost-cutting measures were initiated including suspension of all wage increases, elimination of the management bonus plan, reduction in the

number of management shifts allowed in each unit, and negotiation of payment extensions with trade creditors. Where possible, leases were renegotiated and capital projects were eliminated. The meeting focused Stewart and Kirby on the reality that the success of Steinman & Lee rested on their ability to continue to generate cash flow sufficient to float the rest of the company. Stewart used this information to motivate his employees to work harder and smarter.

Shortly after the meeting, the Kitchener location closed and, although this improved the company's overall profitability, it further stretched cash flow, as employee severance packages were paid directly and all the Kitchener 90-day trade payables remained outstanding at closing.

The Confederation Bank was a strong supporter of the Steinman & Lee concept and continued to lend money through 2000. It had added a $1 million line of credit against several corporate cross guarantees. All banking needs were serviced through the regional corporate banking centre in downtown Windsor.

Steinman & Lee's companywide sales deteriorated in 2000. The cost saving measures introduced were effective but were not large enough to produce a positive cash flow.

THE CATERING, TAKE-OUT AND DELIVERY BUSINESS

Steinman's Café began its catering, take-out and delivery business in September 2000 in an effort to increase sales. Steinman became very involved in this process and was instrumental in setting up the operating systems for this new venture. Steinman's involvement included using his expertise to create menu design, making pricing decisions, and establishing cash handling and reporting procedures.

The cash crisis worsened, and early in 2001, the bank began to exercise more control over the disbursement of funds. Stewart recalls:

It was apparent from the consolidated income statements (see Exhibit 2) that the company was not

	River Road (Windsor)	Kitchener	Waterloo	Southview Mall (Windsor)	Steinman's Café	Consolidated
Revenue						
Food Sales	$1,414	$971	$1,238	$1,591	$936	$6,150
Bar Sales	249	172	218	281	104	1,024
Total Sales	1,663	1,143	1,456	1,872	1,040	7,174
Cost of Sales						
Food	491	376	471	541	412	2,291
Bar	70	50	62	76	33	291
Total Cost of Sales	561	426	533	617	445	2,582
Gross Margin	1,102	717	923	1,255	595	4,592
Expenses						
Labor	570	467	524	628	426	2,615
Operating Expenses	161	152	137	135	122	707
Advertising	50	50	40	70	55	265
Research and Marketing	50	50	40	50	30	220
Rent	100	130	104	114	79	527
Fixed & Administration	24	20	27	40	24	135
Corporate Expenses	39	39	39	39	39	195
Total Expenses	994	908	911	1,076	775	4,664
Operating Income Before Interest & Taxes	108	(191)	12	179	(180)	(72)
Interest (Estimate)	25	60	30	60	40	215
Operating Income Before Income Tax	$83	$(251)	$(18)	$119	$(220)	$(287)

Exhibit 2   Consolidated Income Statements ($000s)

Income statements are estimates:

- based on discussions with management.
- of last full year of operation for Kitchener, Waterloo and Steinman's Café.
- of last full year of operation up to May 2001 for Southview Mall and River Road Mall.

generating enough cash to meet its obligations. Little response was heard from Barry. He had become a "phantom" owner. He very rarely visited the restaurants and had lost touch with unit managers. During the time I spent at Steinman & Lee, I saw Barry in the restaurant only twice after Friday at 5 p.m. He had withdrawn himself from the business and from the people running it. Barry would occasionally refer to his role in "running the company"; the truth was he no longer had the support of his management team. We continued to operate as independents with the only formal communication

system being the very informal grapevine developed by Christopher, Tim and myself. Christopher and I talked daily about the challenges we were facing and solutions we had found in our own operations. In many ways we had really formed our own company within Steinman & Lee.

We often discussed our belief that the bank would soon move in and take control of the companies. For those of us at Southview Mall and River Road Mall this seemed like the best thing that could happen. Declaring the parent company bankrupt or allowing us to be severed from it would allow the two profitable restaurants to remain open.

Steinman & Lee restaurant group was able to maintain all existing operations until December 2000, when the assets of Steinman's Café were distrained by the landlord for arrears of rent. This restaurant was closed five days before Christmas, and where possible, senior staff were absorbed into the two other Windsor locations. The closing had been anticipated by Stewart and the other senior managers.

Closing the café was the best thing the landlord could have done for Steinman & Lee. Steinman's Café had been a losing concept from day one. It had drained several hundred thousand dollars out of the company. It seemed that Barry was determined to make this location successful where another franchised operation could not. The closing forced us to rationalize our human resources and operations in the Windsor area. Southview Mall and River Road hired on top quality café employees, and Barry decided to move the successful take-out, delivery, and catering business which he had established at the café, to Southview Mall.

It was an easy transition for Southview Mall. We had excess capacity in our kitchen and the closing of the café application provided us with people trained in this service. Barry had already designed the operating systems and had personally trained my bookkeeper in handling take-out proceeds. I was not very involved in the implementation of this system. The manual had already been written and this was an easy way for Southview Mall to increase revenues.

A designated point of sale (POS) system was installed for this service, and sales receipts and accounting records were handled in the same manner as (but kept distinct from) the eat-in restaurant. A new bank account was established by Steinman at the local Bank of Montreal branch, and all daily receipts were deposited there. Food inventories were common to both the take-out and eat-in businesses. On their own accord, Southview Mall management prepared internal records of the inventory consumed by the take-out operation and the direct labor costs associated with it. This allowed for accurate cost analysis of each operation and the information was passed on to Steinman.

The first five months for the take-out business at Southview Mall were successful. Total restaurant sales at Southview Mall increased by 10 per cent. Management and staff were excited about the opportunity, and in light of the financial crisis facing the company, the amalgamation appeared as a possible channel for long-term sales and profit growth.

However, rumor of overall company insolvency was rampant among employees and suppliers. Creditors were phoning daily demanding payment and threatening additional action. Working from head office, Stewart dealt with several upset callers:

I remember one vendor who supplied us with fruit and vegetables. Steinman & Lee owed him over $25,000, and he was looking to me for payment. This represented a significant amount of his working capital, and he was understandably concerned. Unfortunately, I could not make commitments to pay a supplier without Steinman's approval. I often left a stack of unsigned cheques on his desk. All I could do was tell suppliers that the cheque was made out but not yet signed. I had worked with these suppliers since my days with The Keg, and I wanted to help them.

THE TIP-OFF

In late June 2001, Stewart was walking through Southview Mall on his way home from work when he was approached by Jeff Henderson, the mall's general manager. Stewart recalls Henderson's comments.

Graham, walk with me ... Watch your butt! Barry is out to get you. I had dinner with him last night, and he expressed a lot of concern about your ability to manage the business. Barry says your production costs are far too high. He says he has talked to the Confederation Bank and they are waiting for him to do something about it. Barry leaves in three days for a six-week vacation in Alaska. The bank isn't very happy about the delay, but I think Barry will wait until his return before doing anything. Be careful!

Stewart and Henderson had established a relationship of mutual respect. Even though they were often at odds over issues of common concern to their respective organizations, both men dealt with these issues in a direct manner and compromise was always reached. Stewart did not doubt the validity of the comments Henderson had made to him.

Stewart did not see Steinman after his conversation with Henderson. Steinman had not been in his office for several days. Stewart drove past his house that weekend and was shocked to see that it was vacant and for sale. Furthermore, Stewart did not understand Steinman's comments to Henderson. Steinman had never discussed a cost concern with him, and Southview Mall continued to produce the lowest cost product in the company.

A week after Steinman left for Alaska, Stewart had a conversation with Diana Calhoun, the bookkeeper.

Calhoun: I just got a call from the Bank of Montreal.

Stewart: Is there a problem?

Calhoun: Well, I'm not sure. The teller said that there was a problem with the deposit I took to the bank today.

Stewart: What was wrong?

Calhoun: I received a cheque from one of our catering customers. This is the first time I have ever dealt with a cheque because, as you know, we normally receive only cash and credit cards. Barry never told me what to do with a cheque. So I used my best judgment and I took it to the Bank of Montreal with the rest of the take-out receipts.

Stewart: That seems reasonable. What is the concern?

Calhoun: The cheque is made payable to Steinman & Lee.

Stewart: Yes?

Calhoun: The teller said that she cannot deposit a corporate cheque into Barry's personal bank account!

Stewart: Thanks for coming to talk to me. Please take the cheque to the Confederation Bank with our regular deposit.

After Stewart's conversation with Calhoun, it all began to make sense.

JOHN MCCULLOCH—UNITED BEEF PACKERS

Prepared by Eric Dolansky under the supervision of Professor James A. Erskine

Copyright © 2003, Ivey Management Services   Version: (A) 2003-06-12

In August 2003, three months after John McCulloch had started working as assistant general manager at the United Beef Packers Blue River processing plant in Nebraska, he already felt trapped. He reread the latest memo from his boss ordering him to terminate the employment of a line worker. McCulloch was not sure he could go through with it. McCulloch began wondering why he had taken this job in the first place and how he was going to get out of this mess.

THE MEAT PACKING INDUSTRY[1]

By the turn of the 21st century, the American meat packing industry had gone through many changes since the early 1900s. First dominated by independent ranchers, corporations took control and created the Beef Trust, a council whereby the major beef packers could control prices, wages and supplies and therefore maximize profits. Inspired by Upton Sinclair's book *The Jungle,* an exposé of the industry from the point of view of a laborer, President Teddy Roosevelt ordered the Beef Trust dismantled and anti-competitive actions ended.

Regional competition and small players kept competition in the industry active until the 1970s, when large food processors began consolidating the industry again. In 1980, the top four meat packers processed 20 per cent of the beef in the United States; by the year 2000, the top four companies processed 82 per cent of the beef available for sale in the United States.

A trade association, the American Meat Institute (AMI), represented meat packing companies. According to the AMI, major meat packing companies were at the cutting edge on technology, worker safety, hygiene, and environmental responsibility. Recent attacks on the industry were explained by jealousy of the success of these companies. The AMI pointed to advances in ergonomic tool design (to reduce repetitive stress disorders) as an example of the companies putting the well-being of the employees first. Furthermore, complaints of tainted meat and food poisoning (by salmonella, E. coli, or other pathogens) were deemed frivolous and inappropriate by AMI. According to the AMI, the highest standards of cleanliness were being observed and if there were cases of food poisoning, they were the fault of improper preparation of the meat (by the restaurant or the chef) and not the meat itself.

UNITED BEEF PACKERS

United Beef Packers (UBP) was one of the "big four" meat producers in the United States, and was owned by Wholly Pure Foods, Inc. UBP operated several plants across the Great Plains, primarily in states such as Nebraska, Texas, Iowa, Colorado and Kansas. Founded in the late 1960s, UBP represented the pinnacle of what could be achieved when management and employees worked together with common goals and ideals. The founder of the company, Ken Hill, was a great believer in communication and teamwork, and he treated his employees well. The workers at Hill's Blue River plant enjoyed high wages, a clean work environment, and a general sense that the company was looking out for them. The relationship between the union and the company was amicable, and each tried to help the other out when necessary.

Then towards the end of the 1970s and in the early 1980s, the recession hit, and it hit the meat packing industry hard. Consolidation of the industry began. Hill found he could no longer enjoy profits and still treat his employees well, so he opted for the former and cut wages. Conditions in the various plants deteriorated. Hill bought a new slaughterhouse a few miles down the highway and fired the unionized workers there upon purchase of the plant. He reopened it shortly thereafter without a union, staffing it primarily with recent immigrants and poorly educated locals. The union at the Blue River plant decided to hold a strike in protest. Hill hired "scabs" as retaliation, and soon received numerous death threats. Unionized workers who were let back into the plant posing as scabs committed acts of sabotage. In frustration, Hill closed the Blue River plant and fired the entire unionized workforce. After six months, he reopened the plant with immigrants and new employees. The days of cordial relationships were gone.

In the mid-80s, amidst the consolidation boom, Wholly Pure Foods, Inc. (WPF) bought UBP in a friendly takeover. Hill retired from active duty and accepted a seat on WPF's board. Consultants, industry experts and top managers from other divisions of WPF were brought in to study and direct UBP. By 1994, no upper management from the early days of the company remained.

PLANT OPERATIONS

Despite technological advances, cattle slaughter and processing in 2000 was done in much the same way it had been done 100 years before. Because cows were not grown to uniform size (unlike chickens), automation of meat processing was not possible. It was still a very labor-intensive process. Cattle were led into the plant and struck on the head with a mallet, rendering them unconscious. After this "knocking," a worker wrapped a chain around the hind legs of the cow and the live cow was hoisted far up into the air. There the cow encounters the "sticker," an employee whose job it was to kill the cow with one lance of a long, thin blade, severing the animal's carotid artery and causing death as quickly as possible. From there the carcass had its hide removed, was decapitated, disemboweled and the body split in two by a worker with a large chainsaw. After this, workers began their individual tasks of removing meat and organs from the cattle, grinding the bones (for fertilizer and animal feed), and disposing of the useless and possibly infectious parts of the animal, such as the brain, spine and lower intestines.

In the 20 years leading up to 2000, line speeds in cattle plants increased from approximately 175 cattle an hour to 400 cattle per hour. Because of this, safety and sanitation in the plants had declined. For example, there was a team of workers whose job it was to remove the bowel of the carcass. This was a job that must be done carefully, because if the intestine or bowel was pierced, manure would spray the area and raise the chance of infecting the meat. Even the most competent people on this job still pierced the intestines of one out of every 200 cattle. This meant that, at best, pathogens were released into the plant twice an hour. There were cleaning techniques for the meat, but these were typically reserved for whole cuts of meat (steaks, roasts, etc.). For ground beef, there was no way to ensure that meat sold was clean. Because some plants could produce 400,000 pounds of ground beef per eight-hour shift, one or two accidents could have serious health consequences.

Per-capita beef consumption in the United States had remained flat with little growth in the 12 years leading up to 2000 (see Exhibit 1). The high line speeds, according to the AMI, were necessary to meet demand for beef. New techniques of ensuring safety were under review, such as irradiation of meat (or, as the meat producers prefer to call it, "cold pasteurization"). The concern of the United States Department of Agriculture (USDA), which regulates beef, was that better end-of-line safety mechanisms would cause health standards throughout the line to decline because of the failsafe at the end. As one journalist, commenting on irradiation, put it, "Irradiation is fine; I just don't want irradiated [manure] with my meat."

PLANT EMPLOYEES

By 2000, most meat processing plant employees were immigrants, legal and otherwise. The big four companies used Mexican radio to advertise job openings. Many workers who had earned $7 a day in Mexico jumped at the chance to earn more than that per hour at the U.S. meat plants. The migrant immigrant worker had changed from going from farm to farm to pick seasonal fruits and vegetables into an individual who went from meat plant to meat plant to work until they were injured, fired or otherwise forced off the job. Annual industry turnover was extremely high. On average, an employee remained at a meat packing plant for six months.

Until the industry consolidated, meat processing plant employees were some of the most highly paid workers in the country. In 1983, however, the national average hourly wage for someone working in industry passed the average meat packer's wage. Since then, the industry average wage was typically 25 per cent to 40 per cent higher than the meat industry's average wage (see Exhibit 2), which was due to a number of factors, not least of which was the lack of unions in the sector. Today, less than one-third of all meat packers are unionized. Because of high industry turnover, it was difficult to maintain a union; twice a year, a whole new group of employees must be sold on the idea.

The area where the meat companies had really taken power was in the field of employee

Year	Turkey Pounds	Beef Pounds	Pork Pounds	Chicken Pounds	Total Red Meat & Poultry
1990	13.9	64.1	46.7	42.7	169.3
1991	14.2	63.3	47.3	44.4	171.2
1992	14.2	63.0	49.9	46.4	175.3
1993	14.1	61.6	49.2	46.6	174.5
1994	14.1	63.7	49.8	47.1	177.5
1995	14.1	64.2	49.2	46.7	177.1
1996	14.6	64.4	46.1	48.1	175.5
1997	13.9	63.6	45.7	49.2	174.4
1998	14.0	64.8	51.0	51.2	182.7
1999	14.1	65.8	51.1	53.2	186.0
2000	14.1	66.1	50.5	55.8	188.0
2001	14.1	63.4	50.8	57.1	187.8

Exhibit 1   U.S. per Capita Meat Consumption

Source: Research Education Advocacy People (REAP) 2001 Annual Report.

safety. All the major meat companies were self-insured, which meant that every dime paid out in worker's compensation claims came from the company's bottom line. As a result, the meat producers did everything they could to avoid paying for employees' medical costs. The powerful AMI lobby had rendered the U.S. government's regulatory body, the Occupational Health and Safety Administration (OSHA), virtually powerless. OSHA had to announce all plant visits at least 48 hours prior to the inspection. It was even legal for plant managers to keep two sets of worker accident records; one log for OSHA, and one that listed all the accidents.

Worker injuries remained very common in this industry. On-the-job injuries such as lacerations, repetitive stress disorder, infections, amputations and chemical burns occur frequently (see Exhibit 3). The level of repetitive stress disorders in meat packing plants was 75 times the national average. Despite all this, the AMI and the meat producing companies claimed they met all necessary standards for worker safety.

JOHN McCULLOCH

John McCulloch was born in Chicago, Illinois, in 1972. Because both of his parents were Canadian (his father was studying at university), McCulloch was given dual citizenship so, when the time came, he could decide where he wished to live and work. With his undergraduate degree in engineering, McCulloch found a job in an auto parts plant in Albuquerque, New Mexico. He truly enjoyed working there; the people were friendly, the management/union relations were cordial and he enjoyed living in a culture and community so different from his Welland, Ontario, upbringing. McCulloch even learned Spanish from some of the employees he supervised. He married a local Albuquerque girl, Selena, and they had a son, Theodore.

A reduction in the workload at the plant gave McCulloch the opportunity to continue his education. Using his "golden parachute" from the plant as funding, he enrolled in an MBA program. Though it was nice to be close to his family again, McCulloch was anxious to get out into the workforce. He loved working in operations, and he made that the focus of his studies and job search. McCulloch found UBP through an independent job search on the Web. The pictures on the site and the description of the job sounded great: he would supervise a large number of employees, work for a large multinational with lots of room for advancement, receive good pay (especially relative to the cost of living

Year	Meat Packing Processing	Meat Packing Slaughter	U.S. Manufacturing
1975	$5.36	$5.67	$4.83
1976	$5.87	$6.06	$5.22
1977	$6.28	$6.57	$5.68
1978	$6.73	$7.09	$6.17
1979	$7.40	$7.73	$6.70
1980	$8.06	$8.49	$7.27
1981	$8.73	$8.97	$7.99
1982	$9.08	$9.00	$8.49
1983	$8.83	$8.58	$8.83
1984	$8.89	$8.17	$9.19
1985	$8.74	$8.10	$9.54
1986	$8.76	$8.24	$9.73
1987	$8.85	$8.41	$9.91
1988	$9.04	$8.48	$10.19
1989	$9.22	$8.64	$10.48
1990	$9.37	$8.74	$10.83
1991	$9.43	$8.92	$11.18
1992	$9.62	$9.16	$11.46
1993	$9.89	$9.26	$11.74
1994	$10.06	$9.44	$12.07
1995	$10.41	$9.61	$12.37
1996	$10.47	$9.82	$12.77
1997	$10.74	$10.03	$13.17
1998	$11.03	$10.34	$13.49
1999	$11.17	$10.81	$13.91
2000	$11.80	$10.94	$14.38
2001	$12.27	$11.38	$14.84

Exhibit 2   Average Hourly Wage Comparison: Meat Packing Compared to U.S. Manufacturing According to the U.S. Bureau of Labor Statistics

Source: REAP 2001 Annual Report.

Year	Poultry	Slaughter	Processing	All Private Industry
1996	17.8	30.3	16.3	7.4
1997	16.6	32.1	16.7	7.1
1998	16.8	29.3	13.4	6.7
1999	14.3	26.7	13.5	6.3
2000	14.2	24.7	14.7	6.1

Exhibit 3   Occupational Injuries and Illness per 100 Full-Time Workers, U.S. Bureau of Labor Statistics

Source: REAP 2001 Annual Report.

where the plants were located), and there were many process/control challenges to tackle.

Through e-mail, McCulloch applied for the position of assistant general plant manager and he followed up with a phone call. He met with a contingent from UBP's human resource department following a successful phone interview, and he had the opportunity to ask about the plants, the employees and the day-to-day mechanics of the job. A few weeks later, McCulloch was flown to UBP headquarters in Omaha, Nebraska, where he met with the vice-president of plant operations. Following a short conversation, McCulloch was presented with an offer sheet. After discussing the matter with Selena, he accepted the position.

THE FIRST DAY

When McCulloch reported to the plant for his first day of work and orientation, he did not know how he would possibly be able to work there. The place stank of blood and meat. It was hot and humid. There were hundreds of workers, mostly Mexican, walking around in bloody aprons that looked like chain-mail armor, and carrying knives, lots of knives; long, short, thin, it seemed like everyone had at least one. The plant general manager, Greg Kramer, was waiting for him. Kramer was the only one dressed normally. He had been with UBP for four years, having taken the job after earning his business degree.

The two retired to Kramer's office to discuss McCulloch's role at the plant. Even in Kramer's clean office, McCulloch could still smell the plant and hear the shouting, the grinding of the machinery and general sounds of a slaughterhouse. According to Kramer, the Blue River plant was the best-functioning beef plant in the state. The processing line moved at an average of 350 cattle per hour, and that average was maintained no matter what. Any shutdowns would be made up for by speeding up the line later. The line, however, was Kramer's responsibility; as he put it, he got paid to ensure that the right amount of meat came out of the plant every day.

McCulloch's responsibility was to be much more operational. He was to work closely with the floor supervisors to make sure that all worker issues were taken care of quickly. He would report directly to Kramer. The message was received loud and clear: no problems that could shut down the line would be allowed. Kramer then showed McCulloch to his office and suggested they tour the plant.

Both men suited up in what looked like space-suits. They ventured out into the plant. The floor was covered in blood, inches deep in some places. The line, or chain as it was called, moved above, carrying beef carcasses in various stages of dismemberment. And everywhere, the workers cut and hacked at the pieces of meat in front of them, in a constant, repetitive motion. McCulloch noticed that he and Kramer were the only people wearing protective garb. Other than the aprons, the workers had only metal gloves and chest-plates to protect them from the many knives in motion.

THE FIRST THREE MONTHS

Over the next four weeks, McCulloch met with the floor supervisors and tried to learn from them. These meetings, unfortunately, made him depressed. It seemed that his direct reports would feel more at home as slave drivers than as a plant supervisors. They had no respect for the workers and were trained to care only about keeping the line moving and keeping workers working. McCulloch decided to try to get a different view by talking to others in the plant.

Concerned with the high incidence of workplace accidents, McCulloch went to see the plant nurse. She was a friendly woman who responded to McCulloch's naïveté by letting him know that this was just how the industry worked. They were interrupted by a pair of workers coming in with deep lacerations. The nurse said, "I guess they're making up for lost time today. I can always tell how fast the chain is moving by how many injuries there are."

Just then, one of the supervisors came in. He shoved a piece of paper in front of one of the injured workers and ordered him, in Spanish, to sign it. When McCulloch asked what it was, the supervisor explained in English that all injured workers had to sign a waiver that allowed UBP to administer medical treatment and disallowed the worker from getting an outside medical opinion, seeing a non-company doctor, or suing the company. Signing waivers was standard operating procedure, according to the supervisor. The supervisor then demanded that the other worker sign a copy of the waiver. Because this worker's lacerations were to his hands, he had to sign it by writing with a pen in his mouth.

McCulloch then went to see Kramer and asked about the waiver procedure. Kramer told him that because the company was self-insured, it had a right to insist that all medical treatment come from company personnel. When McCulloch asked what happened when a worker did not sign the waiver, he was told that the worker was then fired. Because an employee could not collect benefits if fired, almost everyone signed the waiver. Kramer assured McCulloch that everything was legal and that he had better get on board with the policy if he was going to last at the plant. Although McCulloch had tried to talk to individual workers on the line, no one would give him the kind of low-down, nitty-gritty information he wanted. McCulloch felt it was all well and good to know how the plant was supposed to operate and how it was suppose to look to the outside world, but if he was going to be an effective manager, he had to know what really went on.

On his way into his office one day, McCulloch saw a large, muscular man in a wheelchair sorting files. He had never seen this man before. After introducing himself, McCulloch asked this man (Bobby Vasquez) if he would be willing to tell McCulloch what went on in the plant. Vasquez seemed more than happy to oblige.

Vasquez started working at the plant in the late 1970s at the age of 24. In 1994, he heard someone yell "watch out!" and, looking up from his work, saw a 100-pound box of meat falling towards him. He reached out and caught it with one arm, but the force of the box caused him to fall backwards hitting his back on a metal table. The company doctor told him it was a pulled muscle, but after months of excruciating pain he got a second opinion and found out he had two herniated discs. A month after surgery, Vasquez

was back doing heavy labor in the plant. Taking on an extra shift, one night he was ordered to clean the gigantic blood tanks with liquid chlorine. Because no protection was given to him, he ended up in the hospital with severe chemical burns to his lungs. He still returned to work. Subsequent accidents included a shattered ankle and a broken leg, the reason for his being in a wheelchair and restricted to "light duty" work.

McCulloch could not believe the litany of horrors that had befallen Vasquez. But what the man said next chilled McCulloch even more:

> John, you should get out as soon as you can. You really don't want to know what goes on in the plant. Your supervisors are loyal only to the company, because they know they'd never get a job managing others anywhere else. They sell drugs to the workers so that they can work faster and longer. They harass and abuse female employees in exchange for easier work. They let tainted meat go out for sale. Trust me, the less you know the better.

A few days later, Vasquez was back on the line, cutting meat.

THE MEAT RECALL
AND THE LOADING DOCK

Around two months after McCulloch had begun working at UBP, head office sent a task force to the Blue River plant. UBP had gotten some bad press after several E. coli infections were traced back to some ground beef produced at Blue River. UBP upper management wanted to hold a press conference at the plant to announce a recall and show that they had nothing to hide. The company was recalling 250,000 pounds of ground beef, though by now, McCulloch knew that there was no way the company could be certain of how much meat had been infected. It mattered little; the USDA could only ask for a recall of tainted meat; it did not have the power to force the company to pull the meat from the shelves.

Greg Kramer was furious because this episode meant that the line had to be shut down for extensive cleaning. Shifts were added for the sanitation effort, and others were cancelled so the line did not look as frenetic when the reporters arrived. "We'll be running at 400 an hour for a month to make up for this," Kramer complained.

The task force assigned McCulloch the duty of inspecting the non-core areas of the plant, such as the offices and loading dock, for anything that would look out of the ordinary. Upon arrival at the loading dock, McCulloch saw several boxes of beef sitting on the dock with no truck to pick them up. The time stamp on the box was six hours old, and the meat was sitting in 30-degree Celsius temperatures. When he asked the dock foreman why this meat was there, the man looked at McCulloch quizzically. McCulloch repeated his question, and the foreman explained that this meat was "seconds," not of high quality, and would be sold under a brand name other than UBP's, so it was okay that it sat outside for a while until the truck came to get it.

around him, McCulloch wondered how much more he could take. He was in constant fear: of public exposure, of legal liability, of his wife and son's health and of the loss of his own sanity. He knew he had made a mistake coming to work for UBP, but there seemed to be little he could do about it now, short of uprooting his life and those of his family.

Looking through his in-box tray, McCulloch found a memo from Kramer (see Exhibit 4). It seemed that Vasquez suffered a heart attack the previous week and was in the hospital. The doctors said he would no longer be able to work in the plant, and his recovery would be long and expensive. Kramer was ordering McCulloch to fire Vasquez, as the company did not want to pay for his medical bills any longer. McCulloch sat down, put his head in his hands and wished he were someplace else.

BREAKING POINT

After three months of lost sleep, no appetite, depression and the stench of cattle constantly

NOTE

1. Based on information from *Fast Food Nation,* by Eric Schlosser. Published by the Houghton Mifflin Company, 2001.

Date: August 12, 2003

To: John McCulloch, Assistant General Manager

From: Greg Kramer, General Manager

Re: Bobby Vasquez

John:

If you haven't already heard from the floor supervisors, plant employee Bobby Vasquez is seriously incapacitated and unable to work at the plant for the next several months due to a heart attack.

Vasquez has never been that valuable an employee and is quite accident-prone. He was recently confined to a wheelchair because of a broken leg, and he has had problems with his back in the past as well. He has also displayed contempt for the company and is not considered loyal.

Head office and I agree that we would benefit from no longer having this individual on our payroll and enrolled in our benefits plan. Please ensure his employment is terminated as soon as possible. Do not wait until Vasquez contacts the plant; track him down and serve him with his termination papers. I understand he is recuperating at Blue River General Hospital, room 1115.

Greg

Exhibit 4   Memorandum

STEPHEN ZHANG'S OPPORTUNITY

*Prepared by Alan (Wenchu) Yang under the
supervision of Professor John Haywood-Farmer*

 Version: (A) 2002-12-11

Tell me yes or no next Monday. Tuesday or Wednesday? No way! It's Monday or No-day! Monday afternoon? Let me think about it. All right, Monday afternoon. That's it.

Stephen Zhang, project manager of Noble Consulting, put down the receiver and looked at his messy desk full of documents about the Salema project. It was early June, and Zhang had just received a phone call from Shen Rui, the former chief representative of Noble's Shanghai office, who had left the company six months earlier. Shen had just made Zhang a generous and attractive offer to join his start-up consulting firm. Although Zhang had been expecting such an opportunity and found the offer attractive, he was in the middle of the Salema project, Noble's most important recent assignment. If he left, the project would definitely not be completed on time. The consequences would be obvious: Noble would suffer significant losses of political influence, money and, probably, people.

Looking out of his office window high in a prominent Beijing tower, Zhang saw an earlier-than-normal traffic jam in the busy street below. A police officer was busy guiding the traffic with his body language. This view suddenly reminded Zhang that it was Friday afternoon. Zhang murmured to himself: "I wonder what I should do. Where should I go?"

COMPANY BACKGROUND

Noble Consulting was a consulting firm registered in Milan, Italy, that had been started by Frank Chan, a second-generation overseas Chinese. Following graduation with a business degree from a prestigious English university, Frank Chan had worked for a European consulting firm. Four years later, he became a manager. While on a trip to China in the 1980s with his father, who had been born in Beijing in the 1920s, Frank Chan was shocked to realize how isolated China was from the rest of the world after several years of the Cultural Revolution. He was also impressed by China's efforts to achieve the "Four Modernizations," namely, the modernization of industry, agriculture, defence, and science and technology.

With the idea that China was the last virgin market to be exploited, Frank Chan decided to act as a bridge to connect the Chinese market and Southern European manufacturers by setting up a consulting firm to provide European companies with various consulting services, from market research to project management. Frank Chan discussed the idea with his brother, Donald Chan, who had taken over a restaurant business from their father after graduating with a BSc degree. Donald Chan found the idea attractive and decided to invest in the company. The two became the founding partners of Noble Consulting.

DEVELOPMENT

Frank Chan had developed a large network in Southern European business circles. Soon, information about Noble's business became widely known, and Frank Chan gained considerable respect for his initiative. At that time, no international consulting firms operated in China; indeed, the term "consulting" was a novelty to many Chinese. When Noble registered its Beijing Representative Office, it became one of the first Western consulting firms to establish an office in China.

Noble's first client, a leading multibillion-dollar company in the soft packaging material and machinery business, thought that China, with a population of 1.3 billion, would be a promising market for packaged food and drinks.

Fully utilizing his cross-cultural background and communication skills in Mandarin, Italian and English, Frank Chan completed the project personally. The work went smoothly as Chinese organizations were very co-operative and willing to have more foreign companies introduce their new technologies and new products to China. An unforeseen result of the project was an RMB28-million[1] order for three sets of packaging machinery from a soft drink company. The client was shocked that this order seemed too good to be true. As a result, the company quickly signed an agreement with Frank Chan, making Noble its sole consultant and agent in China.

This success prompted other major companies to follow suit. Noble soon had over 10 leading European clients in manufacturing, telecommunications, automobile assembly and light industry.

Noble opened an office in England (its third) to diversify its clientele and expand its business into Western Europe. By this time, Toby Shawcross, a manager and former colleague of Frank Chan, had joined the company as a partner.

As China's post-Cultural Revolution reforms became more established, its economic scenario changed. Development and new business opportunities were especially pronounced in coastal areas. Particularly prominent was the coastal area flanking the Yangtze River delta—Shanghai, Jiangsu province (immediately north of Shanghai) and Zhejiang province (immediately south of Shanghai), which had a combined population of some 135 million and became increasingly important in the growth of China's gross domestic product. As more European companies began to have business activities there, Noble opened an office in Shanghai (its fourth).

The business climate in China was significantly affected by internal and external politics with consequential effects on the need for consulting services. For example, following the tumultuous events in Beijing's Tiananmen Square on June 4, 1989, the Chinese government became much less receptive to imported products. There was pressure to return to Mao Zedong's Cultural Revolution of the 1970s. The resulting tightened control over foreign currency reduced the availability of imported products. Foreign businesses quickly became very cautious about the Chinese market. Many companies shifted their activities from China to other nations in Southeast Asia, which were believed to have lower political risk. In 1990 and 1991, Noble lost virtually all its major revenue streams. However, in 1992, under Deng Xiaoping's leadership, China began to turn the situation around. The reformers regained power and put the market-economy-oriented reform back on track. From 1993, business began to recover for Noble and other foreign companies.

NOBLE'S BUSINESS AND REVENUE MODEL

Noble's revenue stream comprised three components: consulting fees, retention fees and agent fees. The company earned consulting fees from its work, and the associated research, on specific consulting projects. These fees were based on actual billable hours at fixed rates. New clients usually used this part of Noble's services. Once the first-stage consulting service was over, clients often found it necessary to keep an eye on the Chinese market, but were reluctant to be directly involved. In such cases, the client usually engaged a company such as Noble to act as its representative in the Chinese market to look for more business opportunities. For this service, clients usually paid a fixed retention fee. Although the fee varied greatly, depending on the size of the client's business and Noble's degree of commitment to it, the estimated time requirement for Noble usually served as a starting point for negotiation. The agent fee was similar to a commission. The agreements stipulated what portion of total contract value Noble would receive for transactions assisted by Noble.

In Noble's early years, the approximate revenue breakdown was: 40 per cent from consulting fees, 40 per cent from retention fees and 20 per cent from agent fees. However, more recently, many of Noble's long-term clients matured, set up their own operations in China and no longer needed Noble's services. Only two major companies and a few smaller ones remained. As a result, Noble lost 60 per cent to 70 per cent of its retention fee revenue.

Believing the trend to be permanent, Noble's partners concluded that the company had to rely more on consulting fees to sustain development. It began to focus on building up key competencies in market research and project consulting. However, beginning in the early 1990s, more professional consulting firms began to enter the Chinese market, bringing new levels of quality and efficiency. Noble tried to gain customer loyalty through its credibility and low cost.

NOBLE'S ORGANIZATION AND CULTURE

Structure

Noble's three partners, Frank Chan, Donald Chan and Toby Shawcross, each held the position of country managing partner for China, Italy and England, respectively. Frank Chan, who settled with his wife and two sons in Beijing, was also the chief representative of the Beijing representative office.

Below the managing partner were the division managers—roughly equivalent to the position of manager in other consulting firms. Noble had three division managers in Beijing, one in Shanghai, one in Italy and none in England. Division managers were supposed to be promoted to partnership in three to five years. Although there were no specific criteria for such advancement, loyalty and seniority were regarded as very important considerations. So far, none of the company's senior managers had been promoted to partnership. Even though there had been some informal lunch table discussions

about increasing the number of partners, the topic had recently been dropped, presumably because of the stagnant business conditions.

Project managers—the entry-level professionals—reported to division managers. It usually took a project manager three years to be promoted to division manager, depending on experience. The firm currently had 12 project managers in Beijing, two in Shanghai, two in Italy and one in England.

Corporate Culture

The company emphasized teamwork, and Frank Chan often used the phrase "one big family." Every day in the Beijing office, an *ahyi* (maid) treated the staff to free lunch in the office's dining hall—a separate room of 15 square metres with a large table and 12 chairs. The dining hall was well known in the office building, and Noble was viewed throughout as the "company with coherence." To cement the feeling of family, Frank Chan often invited staff to dinners and parties. Each staff member received a birthday cake on his or her birthday. And, in Frank Chan's office, there was a large Chinese painting of the Chinese character for family.[2]

On his desk Frank Chan kept a small yellow banner that read: "Rule #1: the boss is always correct; Rule #2: sometimes when the boss is wrong—refer to Rule #1." The marketing manager of a major client had originally given Frank Chan this banner as a gift. Frank Chan often described himself as a "family head" or put himself in the position of "father." It was well known that Frank was very sensitive to challenges to the authority of the "father."

THE BEIJING OFFICE

At least 70 per cent of Noble's recent revenue came from the Beijing office. Frank Chan explained: "Beijing is the capital of the nation and full of powerful organizations. It is usually the first stop for foreign companies getting into China. Besides, in Beijing, you always have the right person you need."

Apart from Frank Chan, 16 staff worked in the Beijing office. They were organized into three divisions: consulting services, project management and business development, each of which was headed by one of the division managers. The office manager, Luana Giampietri, an Italian, was in charge of general administration and staff scheduling.

The Consulting Services Division

The consulting service division, with six project managers, was the most important part of the Beijing office. Serving as the face of the company, the division accomplished the most difficult ice-breaking part of the job. After one of the partners secured a new client and defined the scope of the job, he or she passed the client and the project to the consulting service division. Working jointly with the office manager, the division manager formed a project team according to the projected work load and billable hours of the project, and the availability, experience, background and perceived "fit" of staff members. Although most projects were completed with a team purely from consulting services, some projects required a project manager from another division. Similarly, from time to time, other divisions or the Shanghai office required a consulting services project manager from Beijing.

The division manager, Chen Tong, in his early 30s, had an MBA from Sussex University in England and was regarded by the rest of the division as a "big brother." His easy-going personality made him approachable and easy to communicate with. Unlike other division managers, he was respected both for his knowledge and personality. Zhang commented: "You feel light-hearted when working with Chen. He listens to you carefully. Rather than giving orders, he gives suggestions and is willing to share his thoughts about an issue with you."

Chen's superior communication skills, knowledge and personality made him many friends among the clients. It was rumored within Noble that the Asia & Pacific managing director of a major client had once said: "We will leave Noble the day Chen Tong leaves."

STEPHEN ZHANG

Stephen Zhang graduated from Beijing's University of International Business and Economics, a school reputed to be one of China's best business schools, and began work at Noble. Recalling his experience with the company, he said:

What impressed me most was the corporate culture. The interviewer, Chen, was so different from the interviewers in other companies. I wanted to work with him. The most unexpected thing was the free lunch. I was invited to join them for lunch after the second round. Around the table, I saw a lot of young people. Everyone seemed happy. I decided to join them immediately.

However, after I joined Noble, I found that the company is not as perfect as I had thought. For one thing, it is a small firm and many decisions are made at the discretion of a partner. There is a very clear line between partners and the rest of the staff. People stay in their positions for too long and there is little prospect for promotion. When I asked Chen, "When are they going to promote you to partner?" he smiled with bitterness and replied, "Stephen, be patient. You'll get my position sooner or later." His answer made me a bit lost. Nobody seemed willing to touch the sensitive topic of promotion.

I find Frank's attitude unacceptable when it comes to disputes over business issues. Frank always dismisses the discussion with an impatient wave of his hand and says: "Cut it off. It's already decided. Just go ahead and do it." In my opinion, this attitude is by no means "professional"—a term Frank uses frequently.

I started my job doing back-office analysis and data crunching. I didn't really like it very much. I have an engaging personality and would feel more comfortable in a front-office field job. When I discussed the idea with Chen, he always said, "Step by step," or "You will have more chances." At the beginning of my second year, Chen arranged for me to do a field-intensive project in Shanghai for a large Belgian company. I did a good job there and both Chen and I were pretty satisfied with the result. But that was like a flash in the pan. Most of the time, I still run numbers.

COMPENSATION STRUCTURE

From the 1980s, any Chinese staff working for the local branch or liaison office of a foreign company had two employers: a real employer and a shadow employer. The local staff worked for and got most of their salary from their real employers. The shadow employer was the Foreign Enterprise Service Corporation (FESCO), an organization owned by the government of China and administered by the city of Beijing. Similar organizations existed in other Chinese cities. Any local staff working for a foreign company in Beijing had to have a work permit from FESCO, which co-ordinated the relationship between local staff and the foreign employer, and provided the benefits enjoyed by most employees of state-owned enterprises, such as life insurance, medical coverage, day-care subsidies, etc.

FESCO charged foreign employers a monthly administration fee for every local staff member they employed. The amount varied from person to person depending on the employee's seniority, position and qualifications; most fees ranged from RMB1,000 to RMB3,000 and were usually reviewed every two years. FESCO retained 90 per cent the monthly administration fee to finance its own operation and paid the remaining 10 per cent to the employee as salary.

Monthly salaries, ranging from several hundred to several thousand renminbi, were usually called an allowance. In addition to straight pay, most companies paid an extra month's pay at the end of the year, allowances for travel and overtime and year-end bonuses, as well as perks such as company cars, taxi subsidies, health club passes, etc. Such payments varied from company to company.

In Noble, entry level project managers usually received a monthly allowance of RMB800 to RMB1,000 from Noble, plus RMB250 to RMB300 from FESCO. Division managers usually received RMB2,000 to RMB3,000 from Noble and RMB400 to RMB500 from FESCO. Salaries were reviewed annually; annual increases averaged 10 per cent—about the same as the Chinese inflation rate at that time. The daily allowance for business travel was RMB50. A division manager could expect a week of travel per month; project managers' travel was much less frequent.

The annual bonus was tied to the general performance of Noble's Beijing office, with slight variations depending on individual performance. On average, one could expect an annual bonus amounting to one or two months' salary. Zhang recounted his situation:

> As a recent university graduate with little experience, I didn't leave much bargaining power, especially with Frank, who was not generous with salary. So everything was on the lower end. I got an RMB800 allowance from Noble, RMB200 from FESCO and a one-month bonus. I did not travel for the first year and there was no overtime allowance at all. I was single, and people usually thought it natural for a single person to leave the office late. I always had last-minute types of jobs. I think I did more than many others, but my salary was the lowest among the consultants. I needed money to get married. But, if you didn't get promoted or hunted by another company, your salary will remain low for years.

> Because of the subtle nature of the Chinese branches of foreign companies, staff are not regarded as employees in the real sense. So, there is no formal contract between a foreign employer and a local employee. Instead, there is a memo of understanding, the main clauses of which vary from company to company. They usually include details of compensation: working hours, holidays, annual review and performance measurement, termination of contract, etc. The memo is not legally binding.

> According to my memo from Noble, if either side wishes to terminate the contract, they should give the other side one month's notice. But Frank fired one guy on a week's notice and gave another one only three days. Frank gave them the full month salary plus severance equivalent to two to three months' of salary though. As far as I know, every one who has decided to leave Noble has given a month's notice to the company.

THE SHANGHAI OFFICE

Noble's Shanghai office had no managing partner. Shen Rui, head of the project management division in the Shanghai office, was the chief representative there. Two project managers reported to Shen. At the same time, he also personally took care of some consulting services. Sometimes, when he had a large project, he would ask the Beijing office to send someone to Shanghai to help him. Although the Shanghai office had had a good start, it had lost some of its momentum for a time but was now recovering.

Shen Rui

Shen graduated from the Beijing Foreign Studies University, majoring in Italian. Later, he worked as a secretary in the commercial section of the Chinese Embassy in Rome. His communication ability and good business sense allowed him to make many friends in Italy, where he became known as a "China expert." After four years, he returned to China and worked in the international co-operation division of the Ministry of Light Industry.

During Noble's first project, Frank Chan interacted intensely with Shen and was impressed with Shen's wide connections in the ministry and his ability to handle negotiations. Frank Chan subsequently recruited Shen, who joined Noble as chief representative and division manager in the Shanghai office.

Shen's experience in Italy brought Noble many new client leads. Although this contribution was important when the firm's clientele shrank following the Tiananmen Square events, Shen's biggest asset as far as Noble was concerned was his connection with ministry officials, who helped clients secure many orders, indirectly benefiting Noble.

Because of Shen's special contribution and position, he was widely regarded as the number two person in the organization. He was the only person in the organization whose opinion appeared to mean anything to Frank Chan.

The Waste Treatment Project

Zhang had recently spent two months in Shanghai working on a waste treatment project, which was supported by a loan from the Italian government. Zhang's responsibility was to research the client's technical and commercial requirements through analysing the production process and then to report his findings to the Italian water treatment manufacturer. The project team comprised Zhang and Shen, as well as two engineers from Italy and a project manger from Shanghai.

During the two-month project, Zhang developed mixed feelings about Shen. He found that Shen had a strong personality and was very performance-driven. Compared to Frank Chan, Shen was more like a businessman and was much more generous in rewarding good performance. He did not talk much about cultural matters and labelled Frank Chan as "hypocritical." Zhang was surprised to hear Shen say: "It's all about money. Mao Zedong was correct when he said 'There is no love without reason in this world.' Why should Frank love you?" Although he appreciated Shen's straightforward personality and good business sense, Zhang thought Shen was sometimes too cold-hearted. Nevertheless, he believed that, sooner or later, Shen would be "somebody."

A Showdown Between Two Tigers

The waste treatment project went smoothly, Noble was paid handsomely and add-on business was promised. When everyone was about to celebrate the achievement, Shen suddenly appeared in Noble's Beijing office to talk to Frank Chan. Zhang recalled the situation:

The conversation lasted all morning and then on into the afternoon; both men looked serious. At lunch, Shen asked the *ahyi* to buy him a hamburger from Uncle Sam's downstairs. At about 3 p.m., the two began to quarrel in Italian. Although no one could understand, it was obvious that both had lost their temper. At about 4:30 p.m., Shen came out and said loudly to the office: "OK, everyone, the game is over. I'm leaving. I wish you all good luck." Then he put on his coat and hurried away. Frank stayed on in his office, looking out of the window for long time. Nobody knew what exactly had happened. But it was rumored that, when he recruited Shen to join Noble, Frank had promised that Shen would be promoted to partner in less than three years. But he didn't live up to his promise and postponed it until "after a big project in Shanghai is pulled off." With the success of the Shanghai project, Shen raised the issue again and Frank was still beating about the bush. Shen couldn't tolerate it any more and blamed Frank for having bad faith. This led to a showdown.

In one mountain, there can't be two tigers. Both Frank and Shen are tigers in their animal year.[3] How could they get along?

During the two months following this incident, Noble's client cancelled its promised add-on business with the firm and another client had a big contract through the Ministry of Light Industry delayed. Everyone at Noble believed they knew why.

THE SALEMA PROJECT

While Frank Chan was still feeling the consequences of his dispute with Shen, Salema, a major Italian mass marketer of furniture, well known for its simple, modern, fashionable style, approached Noble for a report on the feasibility of entering the Chinese market. Salema's very strong design team believed that it could accurately forecast trends and match them with its furniture style. Salema had decided to investigate increasing its exposure to the region, including developing local suppliers and selling its products in China. Salema bundled the two ideas together in its request to Noble.

Salema sourced its products from around the world from a mixture of companies in which it had invested, along with some independent vendors. China played an important part in Salema's Asian strategy. Its size and rich resources, which included timber products and manufacturing infrastructure, gave China a great potential to become a major supplier. Salema also sold its products in many nations. The economic conditions in China and many other Asia-Pacific nations—particularly their rapidly expanding middle class—led Salema to believe that the area

would see rapid growth in the demand for Salema's furniture.

Chen described Salema's interest as being "too good to be true." After some initial discussions, Noble prepared a proposal and subsequently won the contract, which was signed in early April. The contract called for two major deliverables: a report on sourcing furniture components in China, and a report on marketing Salema's products in China. Although no one in the office except Frank Chan knew the exact value of the project to Noble, it was widely estimated that, in view of its scope, depth and time frame, it was worth at least RMB1.6 million.

The most critical part of the project was its demanding delivery schedule: the two final reports had to be delivered by the end of June, less than three months away. Because the project would involve a great deal of interaction with government authorities, administrative organizations, industrial experts and field research agencies, whose time was beyond control, managing the project's time line appeared to be particularly challenging. But, as Frank Chan said: "We couldn't afford to lose."

Because of the importance of the project and its time frame, Noble formed an "all-star" project team of five, headed by Chen and including Zhang. Work began almost immediately. Zhang recalled:

The prevailing feeling was that you couldn't stress the importance of the project enough. Frank was almost drained of cash flow. The project was just like a big shower after a long drought. Besides, since Noble was looking to rely more on consulting services to lead its development, Salema was a good reference-builder because of its wide popularity among global consumers. And, if the first phase was successful, the add-on business could double the revenue because of the relative complexity of the production processes for consumer products.

Chen elaborated on the importance of timing in the first session of the project:

One reason Salema chose us is our richer experience in China and our promise of faster delivery.

The delivery time is no longer than three months. If we can't provide a product that is up to standard by then, we will lose our last 20 per cent payment. As well, we'll not be able to have any add-ons and our reputation will be ruined. Should that happen, someone here might have to go.

On hearing this last sentence, Zhang concluded: "He probably means me."

The project team found it easier to work on the marketing portion of the project because Noble's many previous projects had given it considerable relevant expertise. In contrast, it had relatively little experience in supply-related problems. The project team thus decided to devote more resources to the sourcing report.

Stephen Zhang's Role in the Project

The project team had a very well-defined division of labor. Because of the team's human resource constraint, each team member had more than one task. Zhang's two major responsibilities were modelling and field research. Modelling included developing the necessary analytical tools and models, designing research processes, developing a questionnaire, analysing and synthesizing the data and findings, and adjusting the models. His field research was primarily devoted to the report on sourcing. He was supposed to travel to a number of provinces to check the availability of both raw materials and candidates for the manufacture of components and furniture. He was also responsible for communicating the findings to other group members and helping to integrate the whole report.

During April, the project's first month, Zhang focused on developing and testing models. He spent most of May travelling and investigating his part of the sourcing report. Zhang's planned focus for June was the synthesis and analysis of data and information from the rest of group, and preparing the major findings for the final reports. The whole team had reported promising results and significant progress during April and May. The project was on time. Everyone knew that June would be an exhausting and critical month.

A Call From Shen Rui

After fading from sight for six months, Shen called Zhang and told him that he had registered his own Italian consulting firm named Petri, which was very similar to Noble but with a more Italian focus. Shen told Zhang that Petri was doing business with Noble's waste treatment client and that the firm was carrying on with its Shanghai project. In addition, Petri was also working on two other projects, one on a mobile warehouse and one on hardwood flooring. Shen said:

> I badly need someone to help, Stephen. You are the only one I want from Noble. Why should you stay with Frank? When do you think you will become a partner? Join me before it's too late. The conditions are simple: a 50 per cent increase in your salary, 13 months salary per year, plus a year-end performance bonus equivalent to at least two months' salary. The position is division manager in our Beijing office. But I need you *next week*. Tell me yes or no next Monday. Tuesday or Wednesday? No Way! It's Monday or No-day! Monday afternoon? Let me think about it. All right, Monday afternoon. That's it.

"To Be or Not to Be"

Zhang never expected a chance like this could come so unexpectedly and catch him so unprepared. All this had happened in just a few minutes. Shen was probably right: partnership at Noble was still far away. But could he work for that tough man Shen? Noble was at least safe and warm. But the greater responsibility, the chance to manage more people, the higher position and the better package all sounded much more attractive than what Zhang had at Noble. It was clear to Zhang that if he left Noble at this critical stage, nobody in Noble could take over the Salema project smoothly. The best scenario would be a delay in completing the project. Zhang did not even dare to imagine the worst situation. And, he was expected to give one month's notice before leaving, although it was clear that Shen had not done so. All of a sudden, Zhang found himself in the same situation as Shakespeare's Hamlet. "To be or not to be? That is, indeed, the question," thought Zhang to himself.

NOTES

1. RMB stands for renminbi, the Chinese currency. During the 1980s, its relative value varied from about RMB1.5 = US$1 to about RMB4.5 = US$1 and trended downward. Between 1990 and 1994, the relative value deteriorated to about RMB8.5 = US$1. From 1995, the relative value was quite stable at about RMB8.3 = US$1.

2. This character consisted of 11 lines, symbolizing "people" (six lines) under a "roof" (five lines, complete with a chimney).

3. This statement refers to the fact that both men were born in the Year of the Tiger, which occurs every 12 years in the Chinese Zodiac. The most recent such year was 1998.

TANYA SILK

Prepared by Niels Billou under the supervision of Professor David J. Sharp

Copyright © 1998, Ivey Management Services   Version: (A) 1999-08-20

"Quick, buy me another 1,000 coffee contracts," said an excited Ted Jennings on the phone to his investment adviser, Tanya Silk, "and if I were you, I'd put some money into it myself—prices are going to go through the roof tomorrow!" It was early May 1994, and Tanya Silk, investment adviser at Peterman Futures Securities (PFS), in Mississauga, Ontario wondered whether to heed the words of her client. Jennings, a senior weather analyst at Environmex, a private weather forecasting service, explained to Tanya that he had, just a few minutes previously, received the latest downloaded weather satellite data for Brazil. It indicated unusually low temperatures, especially in the coffee-producing regions, with frost very likely in many areas. He said that the information would be made known to his clients later that day, and it would make national news, probably within a day or two. Silk thought to herself, "Jennings was spot-on with his last two buy orders; maybe it's time I put in some of my own capital, and had a quick word with some of my clients. But I wonder, is there anything fishy about this? Is it too good to be true? Am I doing anything illegal? Is Jennings?"

BACKGROUND

Tanya Silk was 35 years old, single, and had been in the securities industry for the last 10 years. She joined PFS five years ago after receiving her options trading certificate. PFS was a small independent brokerage firm that specialized in the trading of futures and options. Most of the firm's investment advisers were young, in their 20s and 30s and the firm generally attracted younger investors with fairly good investment knowledge.

Ted Jennings was 35 years old, single and had been a weather analyst at Environmex for the past six years. Jennings' current job was to interpret raw weather data that his company downloaded from weather satellites in order to prepare customized weather reports for private clients, such as major commodities buyers, farmers and television stations across North America. Although his area of responsibility was Canada, the data he received covered all of North and South America. He had opened an options and futures margin account with Silk in mid-1993, and listed his investment knowledge as good.

PREVIOUS TRADES

In January of 1994, Jennings had called Silk with a request to buy 200, 90-day Brazilian coffee contracts at US$72.50. At that time, he had mentioned to Silk that the latest weather satellite data for tropical South American countries indicated somewhat lower than normal temperatures.[1] Silk made the trade; however, she was skeptical of the accuracy of Jennings' forecast. By late March of 1994, with early forecasts of the 1994 harvest predicting lower than expected yields, the price of coffee contracts had risen to US$80.85. At that time, Silk, with Jennings' instructions, had sold the 200 contracts and bought 500 60-day contracts at US$82.90.

CURRENT SITUATION

It was now early May 1994, and the coffee contracts that Silk had bought on behalf of Jennings were trading at US$100. The lower temperatures had continued to restrict output during the usually warm months of January to May. Using the latest data, Jennings was able to forecast that the generally cooler months of June to October were going to be very cool indeed, with a high probability of frost in the coffee-producing highland regions. From her limited knowledge of coffee growing, Silk knew that frost would seriously damage the harvest, killing many of the frost-sensitive plants. If Jennings' forecast were accurate, the price of coffee would skyrocket.

Silk sensed there was the opportunity to make a substantial profit by putting in a buy order now. At the same time, however, she felt a little uneasy about using information that was not yet public. Silk thought to herself, "The time to get in is now—should I go for it or not?"

NOTE

1. Lower temperatures could adversely effect the world supply of coffee beans, 43 per cent of which were generated by Brazil and Colombia. With increasing worldwide demand for coffee and a reduced output, prices would increase.

About the Editor

David J. Sharp is the Donald Hunter Professor of International Business at the Richard Ivey School of Business, The University of Western Ontario, Canada, and Associate Professor in the managerial accounting and control area. Before joining Ivey in 1992, he taught at the Wallace E. Carroll School of Management at Boston College and The Gulf Polytechnic, Bahrain. He received his Ph.D. in International Business from MIT. He has written ethics cases and conducted research in the area of accounting ethics for more than a decade. His other research interests include the performance of international joint ventures and, most recently, the role of business in reducing health care costs.